Facts, Frameworks, and Forecasts

Facts, Frameworks, and Forecasts

Advances in Criminological Theory, Volume 3

Joan McCord
editor

Transaction Publishers
New Brunswick (U.S.A.) and London (U.K.)

First paperback printing 2011

Copyright © 1992 by Transaction Publishers, New Brunswick, New Jersey.

This book is printed on acid-free paper that meets the American National Standard for Permanence of Paper for Printed Library Materials.

Library of Congress Catalog Number: 2011026249
ISBN: 978-0-88738-363-2 (cloth); 978-1-4128-4256-3 (paper)
ISSN: 0894-2366
Printed in the United States of America

Library of Congress Cataloging-in-Publication Data

Facts, frameworks, and forecasts / Joan McCord, editor.
      p. cm. -- (Advances in criminological theory ; v. 3)
   ISBN 978-1-4128-4256-3
      1. Criminology. 2. Criminal behavior. 3. Criminal behavior, Prediction of. 4. Crime forecasting. I. McCord, Joan.

HV6025.F23 2011
364.01--dc23

                                                        2011026249

Contents

Introduction   vii
    Joan McCord

1. Biological Correlates of Criminal Behavior   1
    Guenther Knoblich & Roy King

2. Reconceiving Some Confounding Domains of
    Criminology: Issues of Terminology, Theory, and
    Practice   23
    Daniel Glaser

3. Opponent-Process Theory: Implications for Criminality   47
    Robert A. Rosellini & Robin L. Lashley

4. Family Management and Child Development: Insights
    from Social Disorganization Theory   63
    Robert J. Sampson

5. Taking Reasoning Seriously   95
    Ellen S. Cohn & Susan O. White

6. Understanding Motivations: Considering Altruism and
    Aggression   115
    Joan McCord

7. Childhood Aggression and Adult Criminality   137
    L. Rowell Huesmann & Leonard D. Eron

8. The Sociogenesis of Aggressive and Antisocial
    Behaviors   157
    Robert B. Cairns & Beverly D. Cairns

9. The Prediction of Delinquent Behavior from Childhood
   Behavior: Personality Theory Revisited   193
   Richard E. Tremblay

10. A Developmental Perspective on Drug Use and
    Delinquency   231
    Judith S. Brook & Patricia Cohen

11. Explaining the Beginning, Progress, and Ending of
    Antisocial Behavior from Birth to Adulthood   253
    David P. Farrington

12. Autonomic Activity/Reactivity, Behavior, and Crime in
    a Longitudinal Perspective   287
    David Magnusson, Britt af Klinteberg, & Håkan Stattin

Contributors   319
Subject Index   323
Names Index   325

Introduction

In a preface to the first volume of *Advances in Criminological Theory,* Marvin Wolfgang noted that criminological theory had stagnated. In that volume, I called for rethinking how theory should be developed. My hand was forced when Bill Laufer and Freda Adler put out the challenge: guest edit a volume. In accepting, my premise was that good theory begins with good data.

In the pages that follow, you will find an exciting smorgasbord of information. The volume begins with a chapter about biological conditions that have theoretical links with criminal behavior and ends with a chapter describing results of a study showing such links.

Early chapters discuss general issues related to crime. These are followed by expositions of theoretical orientations not typically found in criminological literature. The second half of the book describes seven longitudinal studies in four countries. Authors interpret their data to expose biological, social, and psychological factors they believe influence criminal behavior.

In the first chapter, Guenther Knoblich and Roy King discuss arousal systems, the gonadal axis, and serotonergic functioning. The presentation suggests several approaches to understanding how biological and social conditions may be linked to influence criminal behavior.

In the next chapter, Daniel Glaser takes an encompassing look at the variety in crimes. He sketches the contours of five "ideal types" before turning to consider crime prevention policies. In discussing primary, secondary, and tertiary crime prevention, Glaser integrates his broad experience of the criminal justice system with a review of theories about causes of crime.

Robert A. Rosellini and Robin Lashley describe Opponent-Process theory in terms that make sense of behaviors as diverse as opiate addiction and parachute jumping. They note differences in emphasis on attractive and aversive consequences as these shift through time and repetition. Their analyses suggest a developmental typology of criminal behavior.

Robert J. Sampson integrates community-level data with family differences and individual-level explanations of behavior. The integration includes developing the concept of social capital and linking it to differences in crime rates among communities. Sampson reminds us that families are affected by their communities even as individuals are affected by their families.

Susan O. White and Ellen S. Cohn describe an experimental study of legal socialization among college students. Their interpretation of the results leads them to focus on role-taking as a central means by which socialization occurs. They suggest that integration of beliefs and action is facilitated by taking the role of another.

After considering studies of altruism and aggression, I use data from the Cambridge-Somerville Youth Study to test the relationship between criminal behavior and motives to injure and to help. The results lead me to focus on beliefs as playing a central role in criminal behavior.

L. Rowell Huesmann and Leonard D. Eron provide a guided tour through territory in which biological and environmental data interweave. They argue that cognitive processes formed early in life account for the high degree of continuity in aggression discovered in so many studies. Their chapter describes an information processing theory in which scripts are learned, rehearsed, and retrieved in response to variations in cues.

In describing their study, Robert B. Cairns and Beverly D. Cairns illustrate methodological issues of longitudinal research. The article links results of animal studies with those of aggressive and non-aggressive boys and girls from two cohorts. The developmental approach that infuses this research provides information about changing peer relationships and comparisons between self-evaluations and those by others.

Richard E. Tremblay gives historical perspective to personality theories before turning to his own longitudinal study tracing children through elementary school. Using descriptions of children in kindergarten to check the predictive value of a three-dimensional personality theory, Tremblay discovers important differences in patterns of antisocial behavior coinciding with earlier personality configurations.

Judith S. Brook and Patricia Cohen discover similarities and differences in the routes to drug abuse and delinquency among children studied over a ten-year period. They examine family context, parental and sibling antisocial behavior, child rearing, school environment, and peer influences and then use net regression techniques to specify which of the differences are statistically reliable. Their work addresses the issues related to whether various manifestations of deviance should be considered in terms of a single underlying tendency.

Working with data collected in Great Britain over the last twenty-four years, David P. Farrington emphasizes continuities through time and across traditional classifications of behavior. He contrasts short-term with long-term influences and develops a model to differentiate among people and to explain changes in their rates of offending.

The final chapter, by David Magnussen, Britt af Klinteberg, and Håkan Stattin, shows the power of combining a biological and psychosocial perspective on development. The authors discover developmentally significant differences appearing at age thirteen that distinguished between transient and persistent criminals. The data lend themselves to proposing two types of adolescents who commit crimes: those whose criminal activities are driven primarily by environmental conditions and those whose criminal activities are more closely linked to biological dispositions (which, they note, may be created by socialization practices or a result of interactions between biological and social events).

The heart of empirical science, I believe, begins with Plato's observation that if we do not know what we are looking for, we will not recognize it. Yet if we could not discover what we do not expect, we would be unable to correct false beliefs. Progress, then, depends on playing back and forth between developing theory and interpreting data. The authors in this volume have shown you some of the "play." I hope you find the result both enlightening and enjoyable.

JOAN MCCORD

1

Biological Correlates of Criminal Behavior

Guenther Knoblich and Roy King

The origins of antisocial behavior have been studied from multiple vantage points including sociological, psychological, and biological perspectives, all of which have competed somewhat unnecessarily to be recognized as possessing the definitive model of criminal behavior. An accurate review would transcend overly reductive boundaries of academics to draw a more complete picture of the criminal. Therefore, although this review will focus on the biological concepts of violent behavior, it will be informed by current psychosocial models of criminality. With the recent development of strict criteria in the psychiatric literature for the diagnosis of antisocial personality disorder, it has been possible to start to delineate its etiology. Unfortunately, psychiatric literature has not fully considered the broader concept of psychopathy. That is, antisocial personality disorder emphasizes behavioral misconduct continuing from childhood to adulthood rather than interpersonal defects such as lack of empathy and egocentricity that are encompassed by the construct of psychopathy. This neglect of the idea of psychopathy is unfortunate because in attempting to uncover the etiology of enduring behavior, it is useful to look at more specific characteristics of individuals and how those contribute to the development of long-lasting conduct as seen in sociopathy. It is not a priori clear that biological differences would predict misconduct as well as it does interpersonal-affective problems; however, such differences are helpful in uncovering how affective disorders affect behavior, violent or otherwise. Hence, the biological paradigm of human behavior is most useful when looking at how such environmental influences as isolation, neglect, abuse, and other conditioning variables are imprinted into individuals to cause predictable, incorrigible behavioral disorders years later. So biological psychiatry does not contradict any of the conclusions of other fields as to the importance of contextual variables on personality and behavior; it simply addresses the possibility that these conditioning experiences are mediated into long-ranging behavior through known and newly discovered biological and neurobiological systems. Indeed, many of the animal models of behaviors hypothesized to be related to psychopathy, such as aggressiveness, fit a social interaction paradigm. Therefore, a useful scheme for integrating these viewpoints is to segment the complex construct of antisocial behavior to consider it a composite of more easily investigated factors such as arousal, dominance, and aggression. Each of these component factors has been studied in humans using a dimensional model of personality traits leading to interesting hypotheses about the relationship between psychosocial variables, neurobiological function, and personality. The structure of this paper will be to report on studies of impulsivity and related traits, such as sensation seeking and extroversion, as well as presenting important studies on human aggressiveness. Finally these two sets of findings will be integrated to organize a conceptual heuristic for exploration of models of sociopathy.

1. Arousal models of psychopathic behavior

The classic neurobiological explanation of criminal behavior suggests that individuals prone to engage in nonconforming, impulsive, or rule breaking behavior have low levels of baseline "arousal" in some central arousal system. Several measures of arousal have been investigated including peripheral autonomic activity, electroencephalographic (EEG) patterns, plasma/urinary catecholamine levels, and plasma/urinary cortisol levels. Thus certain studies show that psychopaths have lower skin conductance levels (Raine, Venables, and Williams 1990), others indicate that these subjects often have increased slowing of the EEG similar to a drowsy pattern (Howard 1984). Likewise, a study of conduct-disordered children showed them to have lower indices of cardiovascular arousal; namely, lower heart rate and blood pressure (Rogeness et al. 1990). On the neurochemical side, urinary adrenaline appears to be reduced in certain impulsive and psychopathic individuals (Lindberg et al. 1978). A problem with generalizing from these findings is that most evidence suggests that there are multiple arousal systems in the brain. For example, autonomic arousal and electrocortical arousal may not be tightly linked (Raine, Venables, and Williams 1990) and peripheral catecholamine levels often fluctuate independently of corticosteroid levels in a variety of experimental paradigms (Coover 1983). Thus, some of the failure to replicate this low arousal theory of psychopathy may be related to the individual response specificity of a particular person's arousal mechanisms as well as to the influence of situational factors on modifying arousal levels. Indeed, the conflicting reports on psychopathy and arousal may be due to protocols that have only looked at one arousal parameter. One way of circumventing this is assessing arousal across the variety of response systems and weighting these measures to optimally distinguish an overall arousal factor for the individual. Raine et al. attempted such an unique design in which psychophysiological measures of male adolescents were taken at age fifteen in order to relate low arousal in response modes to criminal behavior at age twenty-four. In particular, those with criminal records at twenty-four had lower skin conductance levels, low resting heart rate and slower EEG activity at age fifteen than their cohorts with no criminal status. In fact, this discriminate analysis showed promise in distinguishing criminal from noncriminal groups (Raine, Venables, and Williams 1990). This evidence within a single study implicates the interrelationship between both cortical and autonomic arousal and antisocial acts. However, such mathematical manipulations involving weighted scores are often difficult to replicate across studies and ignore the qualitative distinctions between the arousal systems themselves. Also, although we have thus far focused on conventional arousal system correlates and predictors of criminality, there exist less well studied systems of equal importance, such as neuroendocrine and biochemical arousal states. Several studies, using populations of criminals and individuals with criminal and criminal related behaviors, have looked at neuroendocrine levels of cortisol, a hormone implicated in many different forms of stress response. Virkunnen (1985) has shown that habitually violent sociopaths had lower levels of urinary cortisol that other less violent offenders. In addition, King et al. (1990) found that plasma cortisol was lower in a sample of patients with a diagnosis of substance abuse than controls. Furthermore, within the group of normals, impulsivity as measured by the Eysenck Personality Inventory correlated negatively with plasma cortisol. This result is interesting in light of Ballenger's findings that, within a group of normals, cortisol was negatively correlated with the mania scale of the MMPI (Ballenger, Post, and Goodwin 1983). Thus, the measures of activity of the hypothalamic-pituitary-adrenal axis seem to reflect a lower baseline arousal in impulsive, disinhibited, or violent individuals. This is consistent with measurements of other metabolic parameters showing a less excitable state. For instance, low glucose nadirs upon a glucose tolerance test (GTT) have been found in habitually violent sociopaths (Virkunnen 1982). This probably reflects a parasympathetic bias in these individuals causing a release of pancreatic enzymes from sympathetic inhibition. This is supported by findings of low GTT levels and increased insulin secretion in arsonists and individuals with intermittent explosive disorder (Virkunnen 1986).

Most frequently the arousal models of psychopathy predict that in psychopaths, anticipatory anxiety is reduced to an aversive stimuli. Thus, psychopaths may show deficient socialization, at least compared to individuals with normal or high levels of arousal. This assumes, of course, that much of socialization may involve the inhibition of impulsive or reward driven behavior. A second interpretation of the low arousal models is the idea that for every individual there is an optimal level of arousal, and that the relationship between arousal level and performance follow an inverted U-shaped curve. Psychopaths situated at the lower end of the arousal performance curve can increase performance and/or pleasure through manipulating the environment to increase their level of arousal. Such behavior is often termed sensation seeking behavior, and although it is classically associated with criminal acts such as violence or illicit drug use, such arousal-driven behavior is also purported to fall with a dimension of normal variations, embodied by activities such as rock climbing or skydiving. However, such models simplify the complex dynamics of interpersonal processes.

All of social behavior cannot be reduced to punishment; for instance, prosocial interactions can clearly, of themselves, be rewarding. Thus, low arousal per se may not lead to antisocial acts but could lead to heightened sociability under certain circumstances. It is possible that interpersonal defects such as those defined under the characteristic of psychopathy (or using a more recent personality disorder scheme, those who show narcissistic qualities) would be prone to manifest enduring antisocial acts. Thus, low arousal may be a necessary but not complete explanatory factor in the construct of criminality.

2. Testosterone and Aggression

Few neurobiological models have received such widespread societal attention as that of testosterone and its effects on aggression. Associations between this steroid hormone and violent and criminal behavior appear in popular media on a regular basis. However, the ideas surrounding this biological model within the scientific community are unclear at best. Numerous groups have studied the effects of testosterone on behavior dating back over forty years (Beeman 1947), but the mass of data produced in those four decades has failed to provide a cohesive, encompassing picture of its role in human behavior. It has, however, provided a base of findings that may prove helpful in the ensuing years in which new methodology and innovative techniques in the field of neurobiology may produce a clearer model of aggression and its biological source.

The many animal and human studies on the effects of testosterone on behavior break up into three main groupings. First, studies focusing on developmental effects have shown associations between higher levels of the androgen and later aggression, as is seen in the behavior of offspring when natural prenatal steroid exposure was extrapolated from intrauterine contiguity of male fetuses (Gandelman, vom Saal, and Reinisch 1977). The second related type of animal studies are those in which testosterone has been shown to have significant effects on later aggression when animals are exposed in the perinatal period (Bronson and Desjardins 1968; Edwards 1969), during which important neural connections are made and neural development occurs rapidly, and environmental stimuli or their absence can be predicted to have long lasting effects. This effect of androgen on the development of aggression has also been replicated in humans, linking umbilical levels of testosterone to aggression some eighteen months down the line. The findings of increased testosterone in more aggressive boys strongly points at a steroid-dependent neural development of antagonistic behavior, even at the human level (Jacklin, Maccoby, and Doering 1983). Both of these first two effects are clearly mediated by regulation of the genome at a molecular level, determining later factors such as neurotransmitter receptor number and other "hardwiring" of the neural system, and surely further research in this direction will produce a clearer understanding of violent behavior, the cause of its genetic linkage, and the role of testosterone at a molecular level.

There is a third area of study, however, that is much less clear in terms of biological modeling. This area is that of the effects of testosterone levels on the adult, in which environmental factors make the association between biological findings, such as testosterone, and overt behavior, such as aggression, much more complex. In order to organize the mass of observations it helps to define precisely which types of behavior we mean by aggression. Moyer (1976) has broken these up into six categories, two of which, intermale and irritable aggression, seem to be related to testosterone and which break up the different observations well.

Intermale aggression is, as the name indicates, aggression between two males, which in animal studies is characterized by attacks, grabbing, biting, and other dominance-related actions. Such aggression can be seen to be testosterone dependent through use of animal experiments. For instance, castrated mice will not display intermale aggression while their castrated cohorts with testosterone implants do (Albert, Dyson, and Walsh 1987; Albert, Dyson, Walsh, and Wong 1988). Such behavior is not only dependent on the steroid, however, as the environmental stimulus of provocation is also necessary to produce aggressive attacks, using such experimental paradigms as competition for food (Albert, Petrovic, and Walsh 1989). This fits the human data in which in a population of normal males, levels of testosterone were best correlated with aggression indices that included provocation (Olweus et al. 1980).

Such studies are interesting in that they indicate that there exists an aggression that is state dependent. That is, given similar development, a change in aggression can be seen in the adult by changes in testosterone levels. This observation is supported by clinical anecdotal reports that describe previously psychiatrically normal young men who begin to use anabolic steroids and suddenly commit suicide (Brower et al. 1989), homicide, and other violent, antisocial acts (Pope and Katz 1990). This change in behavioral state accompanying biological state changes also fits the present prevailing "biosocial theory of status" (Mazur 1985). That is, a change in a biological parameter effects a state change in an individual's temperament or behavior, and then this behavior feeds back on the level of the biological progenitor itself. Similar feedback systems have been implicated in other neurobiological systems associated with behaviors such as drug addiction (King et al. 1990). In the case of testosterone, this theory would indicate that the increase in intermale aggression seen with increases of testosterone would effect a rise in the individual's dominant status by augmentation of winning in social conflicts. This winning behavior would then regulate the testosterone levels themselves. Such a model is supported not only by the previously mentioned correlations of testosterone and aggressive attack, but by data showing that winning causes increases in testosterone in animal studies (Rose, Bernstein, and Gordon 1975) as well as in human studies of college tennis players (Booth et al. 1989) and wrestlers (Elias 1981). Additionally, the increase in testosterone is seen not only in individual wins but is sequentially elevated by each victory, increasing the chance of social dominance, presumably by increasing aggression, and setting up the type of cybernetic feedback that Mazur's theory implicates in enduring behavior.

The other type of aggression detailed by Moyer is irritable aggression. This subset of behaviors has less easily identifiable releasers and therefore corresponds to such behaviors as spontaneous, unprovoked violence. This paradox of an aggression system independent of stimuli seems to contradict theories that all biological response is environmentally bound, and seems to form a more deterministic picture of behavior. Indeed, an unsophisticated view of any of the correlational studies would imply that testosterone is a *causal* factor in violence. This is obviously not the case, as it is doubtful that any neurobiological system follows such simplistic cause-effect relationships. There exist several possible alternatives that may explain this concept of spontaneous irritable aggression as well as the contradicting evidence against testosterone affecting adult aggression. First, retrospective correlation studies of human aggression rely on baseline levels of androgen correlated to either self-reported feelings of aggression or history of antisocial acts. However, in primates, the relationship between testosterone and aggression is related to the social and developmental context in which one observes the behavior (Coe and Levine 1983; Coe, Smith, Mendoza, and Levine 1983). Furthermore, Sapolsky has found that although baseline levels of testosterone were unrelated to dominance behavior, the *response* of circulating testosterone to stress in individuals differs (Sapolsky 1982, 1986). Taking these facts together, it is plausible that irritable aggression may actually not be a trait-like behavior, but simply dependent on the social context one is in. The implications question in terms of criminality are significant in that if violent behavior really is a trait-like phenomenon, the possibility of rehabilitation would be as poor as for other trait-like problems. However, it may be that aggressive individuals simply have a greater propensity of impulsive, destructive acts at the specific times they are faced with stress, or their response at these times may be different from those in less aggressive individuals. Further studies into the activity of the hypothalamic-pituitary-gonadal system during both normal and violent states in humans will be needed to resolve this problem.

Even with such a cursory review, it is obvious that the biological basis of aggression, even just as related to testosterone, is a large mass of data which is difficult to interpret and even harder to draw generalizations from, as the debate includes such difficult concepts as states vs. traits, dominance, and even aggression itself. Most likely, the field of psychobiology will need to turn away from correlational studies using such gross biological sampling as plasma neuroendocrine levels used in most studies of testosterone. Studies using testosterone implants and lesions have recently been possible and have shown such interesting results as localization of a neural aggression system in the septum, a central structure in the greater emotional processing limbic system (Owen, Peters, and Bronson 1974; Slotnik and McMullen 1972). Such pinpointing of structures involved will be needed to proceed towards a true picture of the neuroendocrine basis of aggression and any role androgens may play.

3. Serotonin, Anxiety, Aggression, and Impulsive Violence

One of the most extensively studied biological correlates of criminal behavior is that of depressed central serotonergic (5HT) functioning and its effects on aggression and violent acts. Numerous studies have implicated reduced levels of serotonergic functioning in persons who have committed suicide (Agron 1986; Banki et al. 1984; Åsberg, Träskman, and Thorén 1976), impulsive violent offenders (Linnoila et al. 1983), alcoholics (Ballenger et al. 1979), as well as associations with such personality variables as hostility, anxiety (Rydin, Schalling, and Åsberg 1982), and aggression (Coccaro 1989; Brown et al. 1979). These disparate human findings are supported by a wealth of animal studies which use conflict and anxiety paradigms to implicate central serotonergic functioning in the same types of behaviors, but with a greater degree of resolution due to the ability to use more exacting behavioral and biochemical testing in experimental designs. This section will attempt to review some of the correlates of human criminal behavior through the lens of pertinent animal data.

Before any discussion can occur with regard to the role of serotonergic functioning in behavior, at least a cursory review of serotonin is needed. Serotonergic cell bodies originate in the midbrain raphe nuclei, and project to almost every brain area, including extensive innervation of the limbic system, (involved in emotional status), as well as all parts of the cortex. The cortex is involved in behavioral inhibition (Harvey, Schlosberg, and Yunger 1975) among all the other higher brain functions. The ubiquitous nature of this neurochemical adds to the difficulty in understanding its role in global brain functioning. Also adding to the experimental problems is that peripheral sampling of serotonin's major metabolite, 5-HIAA, is used in most human studies, even though its accuracy in predicting actual levels of central serotonin (5HT) functioning is disputable (Banki and Molnar 1981). Unfortunately, more exacting biochemical binding techniques employed in vivisection are not available in antemordem human studies.

As with most neurobiological systems, the major techniques used in elucidating neurochemical functions include those which directly change levels of the specific neurochemical system (i.e., receptor agonists, neural lesioning), and those which indirectly manipulate the levels of the transmitter (i.e., uptake inhibitors, degradative enzyme inhibitors). Such techniques using the class of minor tranquilizers, benzodiazepines, have been at the forefront of serotonin studies, and have been the core of the argument implicating serotonin as a mediator of anxiety. The prototypical experimental design in which these compounds are tested is called the "conflict test," in which a certain action, such as pressing a lever, is paired with a reward, such as food. When the same action-reward setup is paired with pain, an electric shock for instance, the action is inhibited. However, under the influence of benzodiazepines, the performance under the same conditions is augmented (Gray 1982). This effect has also been achieved using chemical lesioning of animals to produce reduced serotonergic functioning with the same decrease in punishment induced inhibition seen (Thiébot, Hamon, and Soubrié 1982; Tye, Iversen, and Green 1979; Tye, Everitt, and Iversen 1977). For this reason, benzodiazepines have been termed "anxiolytic" medications, able to reduce the anxiety assumed to cause inhibition of behavior. However, the ascribing of anxiety as the mediating emotion (or any emotion at all) may be a mistake of inference, and arguments to that effect have been mounted in the literature. For instance, emotionality in animal studies, as usually tracked by the behaviors such as defecation in the open field, has been observed even after reduction of serotonergic transmission, despite the expected increase in locomotion and increase in exploratory behavior that occurs in novel situations (Deakin, File, Hyde, and MacLeod 1979; Vorhees, Schaeffer, and Barrett 1975). This would indicate that something besides a reduction in anxiety underlies a low serotonergic state, the state violent, impulsive criminals would presumably be in. This mechanism would be key in interpreting their aforementioned differences in neurometabolite levels.

Recently, an alternative explanation has been proposed for this paradox. Soubrié (1986) makes a convincing argument, using the spectrum of animal and human data, that the underlying mechanism of central serotonergic neurons is essentially that they are "brought into play when active and passive responses are in competition, when temporal or spatial obstacles prevent the organism from immediately reaching the reward while it is present or highly probable, and when the organism is selecting passive versus active behaviors for an appropriate response to relatively unknown situations" (p. 331). This idea apparently explains a great deal of the opposing animal data as well as shedding an interesting light on human psychopathology. That is, Soubrié's idea of serotonergic functioning is that it is not necessarily connected to a subjective internal state or emotion, only that it facilitates action in situations where novel or unpleasant external cues may cause the animal to delay. Hence, the presence of high levels of serotonergic functioning would grossly appear as a tendency for anxious, freezing behavior, and low levels would appear as impulsivity, due to the organism's ability to act without punishment induced type inhibition.

Keeping this mechanism in mind, it is also interesting to look at the long history of correlations of reduced 5HT functioning and aggressive behavior in animal studies. Over thirty years ago, experiments demonstrated that isolated mice will develop aggressive behavior (Yen, Stangler, and Millman 1959) and later this "isolated mouse syndrome" was found to correspond with reduced serotonergic functioning (Valzelli 1966). Numerous studies followed in which aggression, including muricidal (mouse killing), filicidal (pup killing), and other antagonistic behavior, was observed in mice in which serotonergic functioning was depressed by a variety of methods, such as electrolytic and chemical lesions (Katz 1980; Waldbillig 1979) or a diet low in tryptophan, a precursor of serotonin (Kantak, Hegstrand, and Eichelman 1981). For years, this association was thought to implicate some direct causal effect of serotonin on aggressive acts. However, the implication of aggression as the underlying mediator of these spontaneous, violent acts could lead to the drawing of the same type of erroneous conclusions as those previously mentioned in regard to the role of serotonin in anxiety. It may be that the facilitation to act out, with an increased propensity for impulsive violence may be the underlying cause for isolated, serotonin depleted mice to show hostile, violent behavior. This is supported by such data showing one function of serotonin is that of inhibiting aggression (Valzelli 1984) and that low levels of serotonin have more to do with the disinhibition of aggressive behavior than being the neurogenic cause of such behavior. It is pertinent to note here that "no neurochemical exists in a vacuum," and that although the neurochemical disinhibition makes it more probable for organisms to act on impulsive drives, those drives could certainly be mediated by other biological factors such as the neuroendocrine systems, including cortisol and testosterone, which we have previously implicated in arousal and aggression (See sections 1 and 2). We will come back to this idea of integration of neurochemical systems later.

First let us get on with the question we have been leading up to: what do all these animal studies have to do with human behaviors such as impulsive violence or suicide? As mentioned before, low serotonin levels have been found in people with a greater frequency of suicide attempts. It is difficult to interpret all the possible related behaviors leading to suicide, but when viewed through this disinhibited, impulsive, acting out behavior in the face of aversive arousal, the greater propensity to commit a violent act such as suicide in individuals prone to suicide due to depression and other etiologies, paired with defects in serotonergic functioning, is hardly surprising. One alternative explanation for this observation in suicidality is the possibility that a serotonin depleted state is actually associated with the depression in such individuals, a position supported by the empirical observations that have led serotonin uptake blockers to be used widely as antidepressants. Studies have shown, however, that in those individuals with low 5-HIAA who have attempted suicide, the low levels of 5-HIAA are not correlated with severity of depression, but with the number of suicide attempts (Oreland et al. 1981). Again, the underlying mechanism may be in impulse control rather than some dysphoric effect of the serotonin depleted state.

Among the best human studies implicating 5HT specifically in impulse rather than global aggression is one done with a group of violent offenders in which 5-HIAA was able to differentiate impulsive from nonimpulsive violent offenders, with lower indices of serotonergic function found in criminals who had a history of acting with spontaneous violent actions compared to those who had premeditated their crimes (Linnoila et al. 1983). Neurochemical/ neuroendocrine indices may be able to differentiate different subsets of criminal types: one, the impulsive, spontaneous criminal exhibiting behavior characterized by serotonergically disinhibited impulses, while another type of violent criminal may be in low arousal state due to a defect in the stress response and cortisol metabolism (see section 1).

The idea of reduced serotonin disinhibiting impulsive behavior, or in other words facilitating action in active situations, may explain the finding in humans besides those in suicide. The impulsive "quick-to-act-out" aspect of low serotonin and the observation of the lack of punishment induced inhibition of behavior could clearly be deduced to play some role in such behaviors as drug abuse, with its disinhibited use of psychoactive substances despite strong negative punishment. Indeed, low 5-HIAA has been found in a study of a group of alcoholics (Ballenger, Goodwin, Major, and Brown 1979) and differentiating serotonergic activity was also found in other types of substance abusers (Fishbein, Lozovsky, and Jaffe 1989). As well, obsessive compulsives have been found to have low CSF 5-HIAA (Thorén et al. 1980) and have been found to respond to serotonin uptake inhibitors such as Prozac, observations pointing to some possible defect in impulse control, although both of these need further study.

Finally, one of the most interesting ideas surrounding this low serotonin state comes from the realm of childhood development. If low 5-HIAA is stable over the course of many years, the implications of the lack of punishment induced behavioral inhibition is significant to the developing child. Assuming that much of social learning stems from punishment of unacceptable violent or aggressive behavior, it would be expected that individuals with low serotonergic functioning would have behavioral problems. Indeed, Brown has found an inverse correlation of CSF 5-HIAA with self reported problems during childhood (Brown et al. 1985) and Stoff has found low tritiated imiprimine platelet binding (an indirect index of serotonergic function) in children with conduct disorder as compared to age-matched controls (Stoff et al. 1987). The implications of this idea in the realm of developmental psychology and criminology are left to the reader.

Conclusion

Three biological systems have been described that may prove of some importance in understanding antisocial behavior. Low arousal appears to be of broad relevance to many kinds of impulsive actions including sensation seeking, conduct disorder, and extraverted behavior. The reviewed models show heightened arousal to be associated with anticipatory anxiety. Hence, states of boredom or relaxation may be expressions of reduced baseline arousal, leading such individuals to seek stimulating, arousing activities.

The second section focused directly on the gonadal axis, specifically on the neuroendocrine hormone testosterone and its effects on aggressive behavior. Prenatal and perinatal androgen levels have significant effects on development with an increase in later aggressive behavior. Likewise, levels of testosterone in the adult appear to predict, in part, the propensity to act out under the influence of environmental provocation. More weakly, levels of testosterone appear to be associated with irritable aggression. In fact, one study of veterans found DSM III-R personality antisocial traits are associated with elevated plasma testosterone (Dabbs, Hopper, and Jurkovic, 1990). However, the state dependent nature of the linkage with irritable type of aggression makes results hard to interpret.

Finally, in the third section, data linking low levels of serotonin activity to a variety of disinhibited behaviors were presented. This link has strong support by animal and human data and has been well integrated in theoretical reviews. Most of the human studies of serotonin link it to impulsive, violent actions. However, the best model of reduced 5HT activity is behavioral disinhibition toward a variety of stimuli.

One important aspect of these models which will need to be addressed in future studies in the interaction among these systems in producing and elaborating antisocial behavior. It appears that in those people assessed for reactive hypoglycemia (an arousal measure) and low levels of serotonergic functioning, these two defects do not appear to statistically overlap (Virkunnen, DeJong, Bartko, Goodwin, and Linnoila 1989), indicating that there may exist subtypes of habitually violent offenders with differing disturbances of neurophysiological systems. Also, when plasma cortisol and testosterone were concurrently measured, both were associated with MMPI-Hypomania, but only testosterone was linked to Psychopathic Deviate scores (Dabbs, Hopper, Jurkovic 1990; Dabbs and Hopper 1990), suggesting that the angry, rebellious aspects of sociopathy are linked to androgen excess rather than a pure arousal defect. Another important note is that a reduction in serotonergic metabolism would affect other biological systems. For instance, the isolated aggressive syndrome created in experimental settings has been linked primarily to reductions in serotonergic activity. However, perinatal exposure to elevated levels of testosterone can reduce later development of the serotonergic system in rats, developmentally linking key neuroendocrine and neurochemical systems (Ladosky and Gaziri 1970; Gulian, Pohorecky and McEwen 1973).

A good reason to begin to study the interaction among these different systems is that one can then start to observe how external substances, cues, or behaviors affect the dynamic neuropharmacologic/behavioral system. To use an example, one could look at the effect of alcohol on these biological systems and related behaviors. First, alcohol has been found to cause ethanol-induced reactive hypoglycemia, (Nikkilä and Taskinen 1975; O'Keefe and Marks 1977), thereby possibly exacerbating the low arousal state described in section 1. Also, high levels of testosterone have been found to correlate with DSM III-R alcoholism diagnosis in a study of over 5,000 subjects (Dabbs, Hopper, and Jurkovic 1990), despite the fact that alcohol appears to decrease testosterone levels (Gordon et al. 1976; Gordon, Southren, and Lieber 1978). In addition, alcohol has been found, in primate studies, to increase aggression only when testosterone levels are abnormally high (Winslow, Ellingboe, and Miczek 1988). Chronic alcohol ingestion, then, would be expected to effect the entire steroid-dependent aggression system discussed in section 2. Finally, reduced 5HT levels have been found in individuals with chronic alcohol abuse (Banki 1978). Hence, alcohol use could decrease serotonergic functioning and lead to problems with impulsivity as discussed in section 3. Therefore, as many crimes are committed under the influence of alcohol, it is of paramount interest that neurophysiologic studies seem to point at its role in creating arousal defects paired with aggression and loss of impulse control.

Thus, in order to create a more global picture of the criminal and possible subtypes of criminal behavior, future research should be directed toward the simultaneous monitoring of neuroendocrine, psychophysiological, and neurochemical measures, as well as utilizing emerging imaging techniques to localize these systems to specific functional neuroanatomic regions.

References

Albert, D. J., E. M. Dyson, and M. L. Walsh, 1987. "Competitive Behavior in Male Rats: Aggression and Success Enhanced by Medial Hypothalmic Lesions as well as by Testosterone Implants." *Physiology and Behavior* 40, 695–701.

Albert, D. J., E. M. Dyson, M. L. Walsh, and R. Wong, 1988. "Defensive Aggression and Testosterone-Dependent Intermale Aggression are Elicited by Food Competition." *Physiology and Behavior* 43, 21–28.

Albert, D. J., D. M. Petrovic, and M. L. Walsh, 1989. "Competition Experience Activates Testosterone-Dependent Social Aggression Toward Unfamiliar Males." *Physiology and Behavior* 45, (4), 723–27.

Åsberg, M., L. Träskman, and P. Thorén, 1976. "5-HIAA in the Cerebrospinal Fluid: A Suicide Predictor?" *Archives of General Psychiatry* 33, 1193–97.

Agron, H. 1986. "Symptom Patterns in Unipolar and Bipolar Depression Correlates with Monoamine Metabolites in Cerebrospinal Fluid II: Suicide." *Psychiatry Research* 3, 225–36.

Ballenger, J. C., R. M. Post, and F. K. Goodwin, 1983. "Neurochemistry of Cerebrospinal Fluid in Normal Individuals." In *Neurobiology of the Cerebrospinal Fluid,* vol. 2, edited by J. Wood. Plenum Press, New York.

Ballenger, J. C., F. K. Goodwin, L. F. Major, and G. L. Brown, 1979. "Alcohol and Central Serotonin Metabolism in Man. *Archives of General Psychiatry* 36, 224–29.

Banki, C. M., and G. Molnar, 1981. Cerebrospinal Fluid 5-Hydroxyindoleacetic Acid as an Index of Central Serotonergic Processes." *Psychiatry Research* 5, 23–32.

Banki, C. M., M. Arato, Z. Papp, and M. Kurcz, 1984. "Biochemical Markers in Suicidal Patients: Investigations with Cerebrospinal Fluid Amine Metabolites and Neuroendocrine Tests." *Journal of Affective Disorders* 6, 341–50.

Banki, B. M. 1978. "5-Hydroxytryptamine Content of the Whole Blood in Psychiatric Illness and Alcoholism." *Acta Psychiatric Scandinavica* 57, 232.

Beeman, E. A. 1947. "The Effect of Male Hormone on Aggressive Behavior in Mice." *Physiological Zoology* 20, 373–405.

Booth, A., G. Shelley, A. Mazur, G. Tharp, and R. Kittok, 1989. "Testosterone, and Winning and Losing in Human Competition." *Hormones and Behavior* 23, 556–71.

Bronson, F. H., and C. Desjardins, 1968. "Aggression in Adult Mice:

Modification by Neonatal Injections of Gonadal Hormones.'' *Science* 161, 705–6.

Brower, K. J., F. C. Blow, T. P. Beresford, and C. Fuelling, 1989. ''Anabolic-Androgenic Steroid Dependence.'' *Journal of Clinical Psychiatry* 50, 31–33.

Brown, G. L., F. K. Goodwin, J. C. Ballenger, P. F. Goyer, and L. F. Major, 1979. ''Aggression in Humans Correlates with Cerebrospinal Fluid Amine Metabolites.'' *Psychiatry Research* 1, 131–39.

Brown, G. L., W. J. Klein, and P. F. Goyer, et al. 1985. ''Relationship of Childhood Characteristics of CSF 5-HIAA in Aggressive Adults.'' Presented at IVth World Congress of Biological Psychiatry (Abstract 216.3), Philadelphia, Pa.

Coccaro, E. F. 1989. ''Central Serotonin and Impulsive Aggression.'' *British Journal of Psychiatry* 155, (8), 52–62.

Coe, C. L., and S. Levine, 1983. ''Biology of Aggression.'' *Bulletin of the American Academy of Psychiatric Law* 11, 131–48.

Coe, C. L., E. R. Smith, S. P. Mendoza, and S. Levine, 1983. ''Varying influence of Social Status on Hormone Levels in Male Squirrel Monkeys.'' In *Hormones, Drugs, and Social Behavior in Primates,* edited by H. D. Steklis and A. S. Kling, 7–32. New York, Spectrum Publications.

Coover, G. D. 1983. ''Positive and Negative Expectancies: The Rat's Reward Environment and Pituitary-Adrenal Activity.'' In *Psychological Basis of Psychosomatic Disease,* edited by H. Ursin and R. Murison. Pergamon Press, New York.

Dabbs, J. M., C. H. Hopper, and G. J. Jurkovic, 1990. ''Testosterone and Personality Among College Students and Military Veterans.'' *Personality and Individual Differences* 11, (12), 1263–69.

Deakin, J. F. W., S. E. File, J. R. G. Hyde, and N. K. MacLeod, 1979. ''Ascending 5-HT Pathways and Behavioral Habituation.'' *Pharmacology, Biochemistry and Behavior* 10, 687–94.

Dabbs, J. M., and C. H. Hopper, 1990. ''Cortisol, Arousal, and Personality in Two Groups of Normal Men.'' *Personality and Individual Differences* 11, (9), 931–35.

Elias, M. 1981. ''Serum Cortisol, Testosterone, and Testosterone-Binding Globulin Responses to Competitive Fighting in Human Males.'' *Aggressive Behavior* 7, 215–24.

Edwards, D. A., 1969. ''Early Androgen Stimulation and Aggressive Behavior in Male and Female Mice.'' *Physiology and Behavior* 4, 333–38.

Fishbein, D. H., D. Lozovsky, and J. H. Jaffe, 1989. ''Impulsivity, Aggression, and Neuroendocrine Responses to Serotonergic Stimulation in Substance Abusers.'' *Biological Psychiatry* 25, 1049–66.

Gandelman, R., F. S. vom Saal, and J. M. Reinisch. 1977. "Contiguity to Male Foetuses Affects Morphology and Behavior of Female Mice." *Nature* 266, 722–24.

Gordon, G. G., K. Altman, A. L. Southren, E. Rubin, and C. S. Lieber, 1976. "Effect of Alcohol (ethanol) Administration on Sex-Hormone Metabolism in Normal Men." *New England Journal of Medicine* 295, 793–97.

Gordon, G. G., A. L. Southren, and C. S. Lieber, 1978. "The Effects of Alcoholic Liver Disease and Alcohol Ingestion on Sex Hormone Level." *Alcoholism: Clinical and Experimental Research* 2, (3), 259–63.

Gray, J. A. 1982. Précis of "The Neuropsychology of Anxiety: An Enquiry into the Functions of the Septo-Hippocampal System." *Behavioral and Brain Sciences* 5, 469–534.

Gulian, D., L. A. Pohorecky, and B. S. McEwen, 1973. "Effects of Gonadal Steroids upon Brain 5-Hydroxytryptamine Levels in the Neonatal Rat." *Endocrinology* 93, 1329–35.

Harvey, J. A., J. A. Schlosberg, and L. M. Yunger, 1975. "Behavioral Correlates of Serotonin Depletion." *Federation Proceedings* 36, 1796–1801.

Howard, R. C. 1984. "The Clinical EEG and Personality in Mentally Abnormal Offenders." *Psychological Medicine* 14, 569–80.

Jacklin, C. N., E. E. Maccoby, and C. H. Doering, 1983. "Neonatal Sex-Steroid Hormones and Timidity in 6–18 Month-Old Boys and Girls." *Developmental Psychobiology* 16, (3), 163–68.

Kantak, K. M., L. R. Hegstrand, and B. Eichelman, 1981a. "Facilitation of Shock-Induced Fighting Following Intraventricular 5,7-dehydroxy-tryptamine and 6-hydroxydopa." *Psychopharmacology*. 157–160.

Katz, R. J. 1980. "Role of Serotonergic Mechanisms in Animal Models of Predation." *Progress in Neuro-Psychopharmacology* 4, 219–231.

King, R. J., J. Jones, J. W. Scheuer, K. Curtis, and V. P. Zarcone, 1980. "Plasma Cortisol Correlates of Impulsivity and Substance Abuse." *Personality and Individual Differences* 11, (3), 287–91.

Ladosky, W., and L. C. J. Gaziri, 1970. "Brain Serotonin and Sexual Differentiation of the Nervous System." *Neuroendocrinology* 6, 168–74.

Lidberg, L., S. E. Levander, D. Schalling, and Y. Lidberg, 1978. "Urinary catecholamines stress, and psychopathy: A study of arrested men awaiting trial." *Psychosomatic Medicine* 40, 116–25.

Linnoila, M., M. Virkunnen, M. Scheinin, A. Nuttila, R. Rimon, and F. K. Goodwin, 1983. "Low Cerebrospinal Fluid 5-Hydroxyindoleacetic Acid Concentration Differentiates Impulsive from Nonimpulsive Violent Behavior." *Life Sciences* 33, 2609–14.

Mazur, A. 1985. "A Biosocial Model of Status in Face-to-Face Primate Groups." *Social Forces* 64, 377–402.

Moyer, K. E. 1976. *The Psychobiology of Aggression.* New York: Harper and Row.

Nikkilä, E. A., and M. R. Taskinen, 1975. "Ethanol-Induced Alterations of Glucose Tolerance, Postglucose Hypolycemia, and Insulin Secretion in Normal, Obese, and Diabetic Sujects." *Diabetes* 24, 933–943.

O'Keefe, S. J. D., and V. Marks, 1977. "Lunchtime Gin and Tonic a Cause of Reactive Hypoglycemia." *Lancet* ii, 1286–88.

Olweus, D., Å. Mattson, D. Schalling, and H. Löw, 1980. "Testosterone, Aggression, Physical, and Personality Dimensions in Normal Adolescent Males." *Psychosomatic Medicine* 42, (2).

Oreland, L., A. Wiberg, M. Åsberg, L. Träskman, L. Sjostrand, P. Thorén, L. Bertilsson, and G. Tybring, 1981. "Platelet MAO Activity and Monoamine Metabolites in Cerebrospinal Fluid in Depressed and Suicidal Patients and in Healthy Controls." *Psychiatry Research* 4, 21–29.

Owen, K., P. J. Peters, and F. H. Bronson, 1974. "Effects of Intracranial Implants of Testosterone Proprionate on Intermale Aggression in the Castrated Male Mouse." *Hormones and Behavior* 5, 83–92.

Pope, H. G., and D. L. Katz, 1990. "Homicide and Near-Homocide by Anabolic Steroid Abusers." *Journal of Clinical Psychiatry* 51, (1) 28–31.

Raine, A., P. H. Venables, and M. Williams, 1990. "Relationships Between Central and Autonomic Measures of Arousal at Age 15 Years and Criminality at Age 24 Years." *Archives of General Psychiatry* 47, 1003–7.

Rogeness, G. A., C. Cepeda, C. A. Macedo, C. Fischer, and W. R. Harris, 1990. "Differences in Heart Rate and Blood Pressure in Children with Conduct Disorder, Major Depression, and Separation Anxiety." *Psychiatry Research* 33, 199–206.

Rose, R. M., I. S. Bernstein, and T. P. Gordon, 1975. "Consequences of Social Conflict on Plasma Testosterone Levels in Rhesus Monkeys." *Psychosomatic Medicine* 37, (1), 50–61.

Rydin, E., D. Schalling, and M. Åsberg, 1982. "Rorschach Ratings in Depressed and Suicidal Patients With Low Levels of 5-Hydroxyindoleacetic Acid in Cerebrospinal Fluid." *Psychiatric Research* 7, 229–43.

Sapolsky, R. M., 1982. "The Endocrine Stress-Response and Social Status in the Wild Baboon." *Hormones and Behavior* 16, 279–292.

Sapolsky, R. M., 1986. "Stress-Induced Elevation of Testosterone Concentrations in High-Ranking Baboons: Role of Catecholamines." *Endocrinology* 118, 1630–35.

Slotnick, B. M., and M. F. McMullen, 1972. "Intraspecific Fighting in

Albino Mice with Septal Forebrain Lesions." *Physiology and Behavior* 8, 333–37.

Soubrié, P., 1986. "Reconciling the Role of Central Serotonin Neurons in Humans and Animal Behavior." *The Behavioral and Brain Sciences* 9, 319–64.

Stoff, D. M., L. Pollack, B. Vetiello, D. Behar, and W. H. Bridger, 1987. "Reduction of [^{3}H]-Imipramine Binding Sites on Platelets of Conduct-Disordered Children." *Neuropsychopharmacology* 1, 55–62.

Thiébot, M. H., M. Hamon and P. Soubrié, 1982. "Attenuation of Induced Anxiety in Rats by Chlordiazepoxide: Role of Raphe Dorsalis Benzodiazepine Binding Sites and Serotonergic Neurons." *Neuroscience* 7, 2287–94.

Thorén, P., M. Åsberg, L. Bertilsson, B. Mellstrom, F. Sjoquist and L. Träskman, 1980. "Clomipramin Treatment of Obsessive-Compulsive Disorder. 2. Biochemical Aspects." *Archives of General Psychiatry* 37, 1289–94.

Tye, N. C., B. J. Everitt, and S. D. Iversen, 1977. "5-Hydroxytryptamine and Punishment." *Nature* (London) 268, 741–43.

Tye, N. C., S. D. Iversen, and A. R. Green, 1979. "The Effect of Benzodiazepines and Serotonergic Manipulations on Punished Responding." *Neuropharmacology* 18, 689–95.

Valzelli, L., 1966. CINP 5th International Congress. Washington, D.C. March, 1966.

Valzelli, L., 1984. "Reflections on Experimental and Human Pathology of Aggression." *Progress in Neuro-Psychopharmacology and Biological Psychiatry* 8, 311–26.

Virkkunen, M., 1982. "Reactive Hypoglycemia Tendency Among Habitually Violent Offenders." *Neuropsychobiology* 8, 35–40.

Virkkunen, M., 1985. "Urinary Free Cortisol Secretion in Habitually Violent Offenders." *Acta Psychiatrica Scandinavica* 72, 40–44.

Virkkunen, M., 1986. "Insulin Secretion During the Glucose Tolerance Test Among Habitually Violent and Impulsive Offenders." *Aggressive Behavior* 12, 303–10.

Virkkunen, M., J. DeJong, J. Bartko, F. K. Goodwin, and M. Linnoila, 1989. "Relationship of Psychobiological Variables to Recidivism in Violent Offenders and Impulsive Fire Setters." *Archives of General Psychiatry* 46, 600–03.

Vorhees, C. V., G. J. Schaeffer, and R. J. Barrett, 1975. "P-chloroamphetamine: Behavioral Effects of Reduced Cerebral Serotonin in Rats." *Pharmacology, Biochemistry and Behavior* 3, 279–84.

Waldbillig, R. J., 1979. "The Role of the Dorsal and Median Raphe in the Inhibition of Muricide." *Brain Research* 160, 341–46.

Winslow, J. T., J. Ellingboe, and K. A. Miczek, 1988. "Effects of Alcohol on Aggressive Behavior in Squirrel Monkeys: Influence of Testosterone and Social Context." *Psychopharmacology* 95, 356–63.

Yen, C. Y., R. L. Stangler, and N. Millman, 1959. "Ataractic Suppression of Isolation-Induced Aggressive Behavior." *Archives of International Pharmacodynamics* 123, 179–85.

2

Reconceiving Some Confounding Domains of Criminology: Issues of Terminology, Theory, and Practice

Daniel Glaser

Before phenomena can be explained scientifically, they must be represented by words or other symbols. In theory, the symbols employed largely determine what is explained, how it is explained, and what is ignored; in planning and directing research, symbols greatly influence what is looked for and what is overlooked.

In common speech people often argue about "correct terminology" and the "real" definition of a word, implying that definitions can be shown empirically to be true or false. What they are usually arguing about, however, is whether the word is being used or defined in accordance with common custom, or with an accepted dictionary's definition. In science it is important to remember that definitions are only nominal; they are not testable for truth or falsity, but for their utility in achieving particular purposes, such as the description or explanation of something. Definitions in science and other fields, of course, are not arbitrary; they may improve or impair communication, depending on their clarity, precision, reliability, or other qualities, including their consistency with common usage.

Most terms for distinguishing types or aspects of lawbreaking were developed mainly for purposes of justice administration. This sometimes confounds causal explanation of the behavior that the terms denote. For the ultimate purpose of redirecting both criminological research and criminal justice administration to achieve more effective crime prevention, some alternative conceptual distinctions, terminology, and definitions will be suggested.

Criminology's Domain

Crime will be defined broadly here, as any behavior lawfully punishable by a government. Therefore, offenses are extremely diverse, and vary somewhat with history and geography. Some changes in customary distinctions among certain crimes will be proposed here to facilitate more useful explanations, and more effective prevention policies.

The term *delinquency* was developed and applied primarily in judicial administration, for special concerns when dealing with young offenders. It refers to any crime committed by a person of a legally specified juvenile age, usually under eighteen, plus a variety of other conduct by these persons, such as their truancy from home or school, that legislators and judges deem conducive to crime. Eighteen is the median age of arrest for the Index crimes, and these offenses are the predominant concern of both criminologists and the public. Therefore, theorists who refer only to "delinquency" handicap themselves by trying to explain the Index offenses of only the youngest half of the presumed perpetrators of these crimes, with no reason to believe that the relevance of their explanation ceases when the persons to whom they refer reach the legal age limit for this designation. Indeed, the concept of "delinquency," as distinct from "crime," is largely useless in the causal theory of criminology.

Criminality will be defined here as an attitude favorable to committing crimes, identified confidently only by a person's criminal behavior, although also inferred from other indications of willingness to engage in offenses when safe opportunities to do so are perceived. It varies in intensity, stability, and other features, as well as in its correlates. A typology of criminality patterns is set forth here that includes some reclassifications of offenses, and it is followed by presentation of a trichotomy of crime orientations. Their implications for theory and practice are discussed.

Patterns of Criminality

Five broad patterns of criminology will be differentiated here on the basis of the role contexts in which they occur, and the offenders' inferred motives. It is believed that almost all crimes express one or more of these five patterns. The patterns are ideal types in the sense that, although often not found in pure form, identifying any in a particular offense helps to explain that offense. It should also be noted that several of these patterns can be differentiated into more specialized subpatterns, some of which will be indicated.

Adolescence-transition criminality is indicated by offenses that seem to be motivated by the perpetrators' desires to express an adult-like independence, and to rebel against authorities who cast them in the roles of children, even when they are at or near physical maturity. As the name implies, this type of criminality is most frequent among teenagers, but it also exists among preteens, and it persists or recurs in many persons long after their teen years. It typically involves engaging in crime in order to impress oneself and others with one's manliness or femininity, as well as with one's adult-like autonomy.

Because money and some types of property greatly facilitate display of one's autonomy, while stealing and getting away with it is one of the most readily available methods of expressing independence from conventional authority, adolescence-transition offenses are disproportionately property crimes, such as shoplifting. Nevertheless, because these are predominantly impulsive, opportunistic, and expressive acts, the perpetrators are generally not highly specialized in their types of offenses.

Hirschi and Gottfredson (1983; 1990, ch. 6) contend that the invariance over history and geography in the peaking of crime rates during the teen years is so great that the age-crime relationship cannot be well-explained by its correlates. Others (notably Blumstein et el. 1988) argue that there is sufficient variance in this relationship to infer that some of its correlates are causally important. Without digressing into their debate on the relative efficiency of cross-sectional versus longitudinal research (on this issue, see Menard and Elliott 1990), one may point out that findings from each of these investigative strategies suggest the influence of adolescence-transition criminality in the correlates of teenage crime rates, and in the small historical variations of the relationships between crime rates and age.

For example, the ages of self-reported crimes and of arrests of juveniles are highly correlated with indicators of the frequency or intensity of their conflict with parents or teachers. These indicators include truancy from home or school, statements expressing dislike for school or teachers, and claims to rights of independence from parent or teacher authority (Stinchcome 1964; Hirschi 1969; Rutter and Giller 1984). Also pertinent, in postwar Britain each of the one-year increases, several years apart, in the age limit of compulsory schooling, was followed by an increase in the peak age of arrest rates (McKissack 1967). In Japanese private secondary schools, self-reported crime rates are more closely related to grade in school (entry year, middle year, final year) than to chronological age, peaking in the middle year (Tanioka and Glaser, in press). In the United States, the peak, median and mean ages of arrest declined from 1940 to 1960, and again from 1960 to 1980 (Steffensmeier et al. 1989).

These American trends may well be due to the continually increased duration of adolescence, and segregation of adolescents. The duration of adolescence is growing partly from the reported decrease during this century of the age of physical maturation of children, as objectively indicated by the age of initial menstruation in girls; it is growing mostly, however, from the longer duration of schooling and years of residence at home for most children (Heer et al. 1985). Segregation of adolescents from adults is growing due to the larger proportions of families with only one parent in the household, or with two but both employed, plus the increased size of schools and larger number of different students dealt with per day by most teachers (HEW 1978; Gottfredson and Gottfredson 1985).

Studies on changes in crime rates of individual youths in the year after they drop out of school have had somewhat inconsistent findings, some investigators concluding that most commit fewer offenses when they cease to be students, and others finding the reverse. After reviewing all studies of this type that they could find in Britain and in the United States, Farrington and associates (1986) concluded that crime rates of boys generally go down if they are employed after leaving school, or if they marry nondelinquent girls;

if they are unemployed or marry a girl who is delinquent, their crimes increase, although this increase is almost exclusively in property offenses. These authors infer that the post-dropout declines are due to the change in associates from school peers to others. By our definition of adolescence as the period of transition from childhood to adult roles, jobs and stable marriages terminate adolescence, hence the pattern of criminality associated with it; they also create a stake in conformity that an arrest would jeopardize.

Few persons go from childhood to adulthood without committing any crimes, but lawbreaking in this period varies greatly in intensity, stability, and duration from one individual to the next. Adolescence-transition criminality seems to be the wellspring of most lifetime crime. Although offenses usually diminish greatly or cease completely when people establish themselves in adult roles, many gradually develop a different criminality pattern during and after adolescence, or their lawbreaking lapses only temporarily and reemerges at a later age as a different pattern.

Vice-propelled criminality is manifested as either (1) the practice of a vice that is in itself a crime, because it is lawfully punishable by the government; (2) illegal acts to facilitate pursuit of the vice; (3) offenses committed to pay for a vice; or (4) criminal behavior that results from the psychophysiological effects of the vice.

"Vice" will be defined here as behavior pursued so compulsively as to endanger one's capacity to meet one's role responsibilities. This conception is consistent with common usage, but it does not imply the morality or immorality of vices, and they need not fit the description by Skolnick as "conduct that can be enjoyed and deplored at the same time, sometimes by the same people" (1978, 8). Most vices are extreme forms of behavior considered normal if done moderately. Thus, everyone eats, most adults drink alcoholic beverages occasionally, many smoke, most do some gambling, and nearly everyone at times tries to gratify sexual desires; but almost all regard as vices persistent overeating despite obesity, habitual drunkenness, chain smoking, gambling much on hunch alone, and pursuing sexual gratification avidly without concern about pregnancy, disease, feelings of the partner, or disgrace.

Of course, overeating is not a crime, since it is in itself not formally punishable by governments (although some might interpret upper weight limits for government employment as punishing over-eaters!). Drunken driving is a crime partly identified by blood-alcohol content or other evidence of the body's physiological condition when the offender was driving. Smoking is only a crime in specified places, such as in a commercial airplane. In many places the criminality of some forms of gambling has ceased in recent decades, as has that of homosexual behavior between consenting adults in private. Currently of great concern to the public is the criminal use of psychoactive drugs.

These variations highlight a bifurcation of all offenses into two types, predatory and nonpredatory, that contrast markedly in their legal history, and in their amenability to counting and control. Acts traditionally viewed as crimes and not vices, such as burglary or robbery and the other FBI Index Offenses, are *predatory* or *victimizing*. Unlike the vices, these are acts in which the offender directly injures others, usually regarded as the victims, by physically or psychologically hurting them, or by taking away their property or their rights. Because for most of these offenses the victims are likely to report the crime to the police, official statistics on such lawbreaking have long been regularly maintained by many governments, and despite notable deficiencies, have been very useful for both criminological research and criminal justice administration.

Historically, the number of types of behaviors that are punishable as predatory crimes have been cumulative, especially in modern times, because laws that define as criminal types of conduct that clearly victimize others are seldom repealed (although they are sometimes reformulated or recodified), and because new technologies regularly create new ways of victimizing others. Usually the victims can at first only sue in the civil courts for compensation from those who injure them, but when they and their sympathizers are dissatisfied with this remedy and have sufficient influence, they get laws enacted imposing government penalties for such conduct. This was true even in the early history of laws against theft in the English-speaking world (see Hall 1952). More recently, pollution of air, land, and soil have been made subject to government penalties, hence crimes.

Vices, contrastingly, are *nonpredatory* or *victimless* crimes. They are usually voluntary activities of all the participants, none of whom regard themselves as victimized by the others. Therefore, few of these offenders—such as illegal gamblers, prostitutes and their customers, or illegal drug sellers, buyers or users—initiate the reporting of these crimes to the police. Furthermore, the kinds of nonpredatory acts lawfully punishable by the government do not increase cumulatively, but instead, tend to have a somewhat standardized life-history cycle in the criminal law.

A vice becomes a crime only after a sufficiently influential group of persons finds it morally or otherwise offensive and can get the government to prohibit it. Usually the prohibition law is absolute, banning all quantities of the behavior rather than only extreme amounts of it, and also penalizing acts deemed conducive to it (e.g., punishing possession or transfer of substances used for vices). In the United States, there was not even temporarily a successful national movement for alcohol and narcotics prohibition laws until the twentieth century, and most other vices were prohibited only by state or local laws.

Because voluntary participants in pursuing or facilitating prohibited vices rarely report such activities to the police, official statistics on the number of vice-propelled crimes known to the police are so deficient as to be almost worthless, especially if the vice consists of behavior that is readily hidden. Also, enforcement activities are relatively unsuccessful in any even moderately long run, despite great claims after each crackdown.

But proponents of a vice prohibition law, especially those seeking careers in agencies to enforce it, respond to complaints about their failure to markedly reduce the vice by calling for more extreme penalties and more enforcement resources. However, these rarely reduce for long the prevalence of illegal vices. Meanwhile, if many people pursue the vice and it costs money (e.g., to pay for alcohol, drugs, gambling, or prostitutes), organized crime develops to sell these goods or services. Also, many persons with the vice commit predatory crimes to procure the means of paying for them. This evokes increasingly frenzied enforcement efforts.

After much recurrent failure to reduce society's costs from a vice, government efforts seem eventually to change from trying to prohibit it to instead mainly regulating its location and visibility, and to combat it more by treatment and education than by the criminal law. During the 1930s we reached this last stage in combatting alcohol consumption, when even teetotallers agreed that costs seemed to exceed benefits from the Prohibition Amendment. More recently we have widely entered this last stage in combatting homosexuality and gambling. Most of Western Europe focuses much more than we do on education and treatment, rather than punishment, in dealing with prostitution, as do Britain and the Netherlands also in coping with drugs. Movements to follow these models seem to be gaining strength also in the United States.

Since adolescents are attracted to vices, especially drinking and drug abuse, as ways of expressing adulthood and independence from authority, vice-propelled and adolescence-transition criminality often occur together. However, vices are so widespread that the crimes which they propel frequently accompany all the patterns of criminality discussed here.

Professional criminality, as the phrase will be used here, refers to a well-established commitment to crime as a lifetime vocation at which one works carefully, cautiously, and with pride in one's expertise. This contrasts with the use of "career criminal" in the past decade or two for programs funded by the U.S. Department of Justice, in which the primary focus has been on intensive adolescence-transition criminality, identified by unspecialized and high-rate law breaking from an early age on. The persons labeled "versatile predators" or "dangerous offenders" in reports and comments on Rand Corporation research (Chaiken and Chaiken 1982; Moore et al. 1984), and "career criminals" in prosecution programs, usually have only a "short happy life" in crime, for they take high risks in unspecialized but often violent offenses. Consequently, they are repeatedly caught and incarcerated, for increasingly long terms, so that they do not have long years of lawbreaking in the community.

What is designated here as "professional criminality" is more often manifested by predatory behavior that is relatively safe and quite consistently lucrative for the offenders, who are seldom caught. Such patterns of criminality are described in many criminological case studies, for example: Sutherland's *Professional Thief* (1937); the accounts of "fences" by Klockars (1974), Steffensmeier (1986) and Walsh (1977); Lemert's (1967, ch. 8) "systematic check forgers"; Maurer's (1940) confidence men; the enormous literature on relatively stable organized crime groups, such as "the Mafia" and its successors (Abadinsky 1977; Ianni 1974; Nelli 1976). Organized crime, of course, derives much of its income from supplying goods and services to persons with illegal vices, so that the criminality it involves is vice-propelled. However, some professionally oriented organized crime groups also engage in a diversity of predominantly successful predatory offenses, including extortion under the guise of "protection," counterfeiting, and wholesale— often international—transfer of stolen automobiles or other valuable goods.

Most professional crime patterns do not fit Gottfredson and Hirschi's (1990) identification of criminality with low self control. Like people in legitimate professions, those who fit the conception of professional criminality defined here are proud of their knowledge and skills, and are highly selective in whom they allow to be partners in their illegal enterprises. They take a variety of precautions to avoid risk in their crimes, rather than committing offenses impulsively. Many develop their criminal expertise through an apprenticeship or other training experience with more established career offenders, acquire a subculture of lore on what techniques are most successful, and blend into conventional noncriminal society. Some retire or enter legitimate businesses from a criminally achieved "nest egg" to become accepted as part of "respectable" social circles in their communities.

Legitimate-occupation criminality is oriented to committing offenses that are only feasible because the perpetrators have conventional types of employment. It has three broad subpatterns, related to the legitimate roles of the offenders. Crimes against employers range from pilfering of company supplies, padding of expense accounts, and unreported absences from the job for which the employee draws pay, to embezzlement of six- or seven-digit sums of money from funds to which the employee's work provides access. Indeed, "embezzlement" is a legal term for criminal violation of trust that is logically applicable to all of these offenses, but in practice is only applied to those involving the largest amounts of money.

Crimes against employees that have become especially prominent in recent decades consist mainly of dangerous working conditions. They include not only workplaces and task requirements that are accident prone, but especially, those that have insidious dangers of gradual and long-term exposure to lead or other poisons, or to asbestos or other carcinogens. While traditionally such victimization could only be combatted by civil suits against the employers, laws have been enacted at an accelerating rate that establish government inspection programs and subject violators to fines or other punitive measures. These make such employers criminals, by our broad definition of crime.

Crimes against the public that are feasible only because of the perpetrators' legitimate occupations, are extremely diverse. They include sale of dangerous products and misrepresentation in sales, securities and exchange rule violations, pollution of the environment in extracting minerals or manufacturing, and bribery or influence peddling in the administration and policymaking activities of both government and business organizations, as well as what Chambliss (1989) calls "state-organized" crime. All such activities have in recent decades increasingly become subject to lawful punishment by governments, hence crimes by our definition.

Legitimate-occupation criminality overlaps Sutherland's concept of "white-collar crime," but it is certainly a much more precise and objective conceptualization than the denotation by apparel that he introduced, or than any of its replacements, such as "corporate" or "organizational" crime. This field is badly in need of theoretical analysis because it is not only more costly to society than the other patterns of criminality, but it seems to result from causal factors and processes somewhat different from those underlying the other patterns, yet not entirely different. Such theoretical analysis may be facilitated by the reconceptualization proposed here.

Passion-driven criminality is primarily the expression of intense emotions by criminal activity. The passions most prominent are rage and sexual lust, but panic sometimes also underlies criminal acts. Of course, all criminality expresses emotions, especially that of adolescence transition, but our concern here is with criminal acts in which sheer emotion, rather than procuring economic gain or displaying adulthood, motivate physically assaultive or sexual aggression. Homicide and rape are the most prominent of passion-driven crimes, but they include the much more frequent offenses of spouse battering, child molestation, incest, and nonlethal, anger-motivated assaults. Robbery is unlikely to be primarily passion driven; it seems usually to be a fairly deliberate effort to gain wealth by force or threat of force, and to express adolescence-transition, vice-propelled or professional criminality.

Human emotions integrate physiological reactions with learned ways of expressing one's feelings. We share with other animals an autonomic nervous system that makes us respond without thinking to unusually strong and sudden stimuli, such as loud noises or sharp physical pain, as well as to pleasant gradual stimulation of sense organs, particularly in the erogenous zones. Each of these types of autonomic stimulation prompt the release of hormones that mobilize the body to physical action. Yet the arousal can be conditioned to a variety of cues with which it becomes linked (such as the appearances and sounds that cultures define as sexually attractive). Furthermore, emotional arousal and its expression may be considerably modified by the central nervous system, in ways that are socially learned and reflect cultural influences (Kemper 1987; Hochschild 1983).

In at least half the arrests for assaults in our country, including large proportions of those that have lethal consequences and are prosecuted as homicides, the offender had been drinking at the time of the violent behavior. Alcohol especially, and other drugs as well (and also, sheer fatigue) can impair the ability of the central nervous system to control the arousal of emotional states in the autonomic nervous system, and their expression as overt behavior. Some psychoactive drugs, particularly cocaine, are alleged to stimulate sexual arousal. Thus, much passion-driven criminality may also be vice-propelled. In addition, the insanity defense is especially likely to be invoked in passion-driven offenses, which when successful makes them not lawfully punishable by the government.

The differences indicated among the five broad patterns of criminality that have been roughly defined here suggest that any explanation for all of them by a single causal theory, such as those now prominent in criminology, can be no more than a first step towards guidance of practical policies.

For the objective of crime prevention, a trichotomy of types of prevention will be proposed here, and will be discussed in relation to leading criminality causation theories. *Primary prevention* stops offenses from occurring by eliminating the causes of criminality. *Secondary prevention* tries to reform offenders by reducing or eliminating their criminality. *Tertiary prevention* tries to stop crimes physically, by incarcerating or otherwise restraining persons presumed to be of high criminality, and by guarding the potential targets of their predations.

Primary Crime Prevention

Preventing crime by reducing the causes of criminality is especially pertinent to adolescence, the period of transition from childhood to adult roles in which lawbreaking is not only most frequent, but may either persist long in its early impulsive and unspecialized forms, or evolve into the vice-propelled, professional or legitimate occupation patterns.

Policies for achieving primary prevention are implied by all theories of criminality causation. *Control theory* (Hirschi 1969) implies prevention of adolescence-transition criminality by promoting, especially for juveniles, attachment to conventional persons, involvement in conventional activities, commitment to conventional pursuits, and anti-criminal beliefs. *Differential association* theory (Sutherland and Cressey 1978) has similar implications: the promotion of early, intimate, intense, and frequent interaction of youths with anti-criminal persons; but it also implies discouraging their interaction with pro-criminal persons. For the practical purpose of primary prevention of adolescence-transition criminality, it would appear to complement rather than contradict control theory; as previously suggested (Glaser 1979, 213), the two theories could readily be combined as a "differential control" theory.

Differential association theory also complements the "delinquent subculture" theories of Shaw and McKay (1969), and the two are not identical, although both are grouped by Hirschi (1969) as "cultural deviance" theories. Shaw and McKay emphasized the extent to which residents of high-crime rate neighborhoods have early, intimate, intense, and frequent interaction with pro-criminal persons. Sutherland, by considering both bonds to conventional society and bonds to offenders, answered the complaint of the Gluecks (1950) that Shaw and McKay failed to account for the presence of some "good boys" in high delinquency neighborhoods, and some offenders in low-crime rate areas. Indeed, anti-criminal and pro-criminal siblings can develop even in the same household due to differential association patterns there (see Glaser et al. 1971).

It is interesting that control theorists from Hirschi on, like the Gluecks before them, have been challenged by the finding that where either self-reported or official delinquency is the dependent variable, the independent variable with which it has the highest statistical relationship is usually a measure of the extent to which the friends of the delinquents are also delinquent. Theorists in the Shaw and McKay tradition pointed to such data as evidence of the causal impact of delinquent subcultures, but Hirschi and others repeated the rebuttal by the Gluecks that this only shows that "birds of a feather flock together," that such groupings of delinquent peers are consequences rather than causes of delinquency.

Hirschi's distinctive and important addition to the issue was his 1969 evidence that nondelinquents have closer bonds with their peers than do delinquents; good peers seem to influence juvenile conduct more than do bad peers. Nevertheless, numerous statistical studies show that most delinquency is committed by small groups of juveniles, and that this group feature occurs at increasing rates as the youths increase the seriousness of their offenses (see, for example, Hindelang 1971; Liska 1973). Also, in ethnographic studies and in the memories of most of us who were involved in some delinquency as juveniles, it is clear that youths take risks collectively that they would not take alone. Even if birds of a feather flock together, and delinquents respect their peers less than nondelinquents do, group support certainly reinforces much delinquent behavior, as does the need of adolescents to avoid losing "face" before their peers whenever any of them proposes risky conduct to display their courage.

Anomie (or "strain" or "opportunity") *theory* (Merton 1957) implies that primary crime prevention is achievable for all patterns of criminality by reduction of inequalities of opportunity for legitimate success in a society. If the criteria for success are economic, the crime prevention focus implied by anomie theory is to increase noncriminal economic opportunities for those who are relatively deprived of them. However, criteria for success vary somewhat from one culture to another, are always multiple, and may include some goals that are sought largely as a means of obtaining other goals.

Anomie theory, in Merton's first formulation, implied that deviant behavior, including that which is lawfully punishable by the government (crime), occurs when individuals perceive that they have readier access to deviant than to socially conforming means of achieving success. In reply to his critics, however, Merton (1964) distinguished between "anomia," as an individual's sense of relative deprivation, and "anomie" as a collective condition that a group of anomic individuals socially reinforce by interaction with each other. Anomie, thus conceived, is a socially shared sense of relative deprivation and consequent normlessness that is communicated among the members of a group of people, who may collectively be called "anomic." This is about how Durkheim (1893, 1897) originally used these two terms. The implication of anomie theory, therefore, is that for primary crime prevention one should prevent the social separation of relatively deprived individuals from the rest of society. Anomie theory, thus conceived, complements rather than contradicts control and differential association theory, and the three could readily be combined as a "differential anticipation" or "differential expectation" theory (see Glaser et al. 1971; Glaser 1978).

All three of these sociologically derived theories are what Cornish and Clarke (1986) call "rational choice perspectives on offending," for they conceive of criminality as the logical pursuit of what offenders perceive as the most probably available and effective way of meeting their needs. Control and differential association theories focus specially upon interpersonal bonding, beliefs, and commitments as sources of these perceptions, while anomie theory is concerned with the impact on such perceptions of the offender's social, cultural, economic, and political circumstances.

Although these three sociological types of explanatory theory are discussed above only with reference to the primary prevention of adolescence-transition criminality, they also apply to preventing other criminality patterns. Because illegal vices are socially learned and subculturally supported ways of life, "differential expectancy" theory implies that primary prevention of vice-propelled crime requires early and continuous differential associations for the social promotion of alternatives to the vices: physical fitness instead of alcohol or drug addiction, rational investment instead of gambling, and so on. Primary prevention of professional criminality would be achieved mainly by prevention of adolescence-transition and vice-propelled criminality, which are its usual sources.

Legitimate-occupation criminality requires a prior successful achievement of a noncriminal occupation, hence the predominant influence of bonds with conventional rather than pro-criminal associates, and prior perceptions of more achievable success in legitimate than in criminal pursuits. However, studies show that one of its three forms, crimes of employees against employers, occurs most often among employees with some prior criminal experience and with low expectations of advancement in their employment, as well as with the social support of other employees who develop workplace-specific subcultural norms of tolerance for cheating the company (see Ditton 1977; Hollinger and Clark 1983).

Crimes by employers against employees may not be associated with adolescence-transition or other criminality in the life histories of the employers. They may instead reflect subcultural norms in particular industries, differ from one industry to another, and even vary with different working conditions within an industry. Hence, their prevention requires diverse rules and penalties for diverse industries, as our complex volumes of Occupational Safety and Health Administration (OSHA) regulations attest.

Braithwaite (1985) contends from experience in Australia and elsewhere that the most effective prevention requires rules specific to particular plants within industries, as they are so variable. In what he calls "enforced self-regulation," the government appoints a local committee of representatives of management, labor, and the public interest which is assigned to draw up a set of regulations, in accordance with government guidelines and aided by government consultants. The committee then checks on compliance, reports noncompliance, and is in turn checked by the government.

Criminality directed against the general public by persons in legitimate occupations is even more diverse, ranging from illegal stock market manipulation to criminal pollution of the environment, and much more. Although this diversity implies that the most useful primary preventatives will be offense-specific, deviant subcultures within industries and companies that support criminality are found in most of these offenses. Therefore, effective primary prevention requires organized and well-tested efforts to promote anti-criminality norms.

Efforts at primary prevention of criminality that are guided by control, differential association, and anomie theories (collectively labelled "differential expectation" here) strive to achieve a utopian society. These efforts include education of parents for warm and "authoritative"—rather than authoritarian or overly permissive— relationships with their children (Dornbusch et al. 1987). Also included are remedial education, as well as "Headstart" and its followup programs in schools; Job Corps, on-the-job training, child-care, and other endeavors to help people, especially youth, achieve gratification in legitimate employment; elimination of extremes of economic deprivation, insecurity, and inequality of opportunity in society. Overall, primary prevention per these sociological theories seeks what Braithwaite (1989) calls "communitarianism," or "ag-gregative interdependency," whereby each person has a concern with the welfare of everyone else, and a sense of obligation to try to help others. Utopia is, by definition, an unachievable perfection, but the theories discussed thus far imply that its pursuit is what maximizes primary prevention of criminality.

Some crime-causation theories that are grounded in more purely individual psychology, and less clearly conceive the offender as rational, also merit our attention.

Physiological psychology has demonstrated statistical correla-tions between criminality and a variety of abnormal conditions of the nervous and/or hormonal systems. Some of these conditions evidently are transmitted genetically, and some develop from pre-natal, infantile, or subsequent infections, toxins, traumas, or nutri-tional deficiencies (see Mednick et al. 1987). These theorists con-ceive of such physiological deviance as fostering crime by one or two alternative processes. One process is by impairing a person's ability to learn conventional ways of attaining success, as occurs if the mental condition is low intelligence, but they especially stress sluggishness of response in the autonomic nervous system, which seems to impair the ability to learn from reward or punishment. The second process is by physiological impediments to inhibition of impulses, such as those manifested temporarily when a person is intoxicated, but also apparently an enduring or recurrent condition even without intoxicants in some people expressed as ostensibly uncontrollable emotions in passion-driven offenses.

Primary prevention of physiological handicaps that are not ge-netic, such as mental deficiencies due to alcohol or drug use by the pregnant mother, or to poor nutrition or lead poisoning of children, requires programs directed at these problems. Obvious examples include guaranteed prenatal care, public education on nutrition, and elimination of toxins in the environment. Little prevention can now be done for genetically transmitted deficiencies, but there are beginnings of gene substitution surgery. However, it is noteworthy that not all persons who have genetic or other physiological handicaps manifest criminality. More research is needed on how such handicaps to achieving a noncriminal career are overcome. One suspects that it is through anti-criminality features of the social and cultural environment strong enough to foster bonds with conventional society and achievement of success in noncriminal occupations despite handicaps.

Thus, physiological theories that emphasize either central or autonomic nervous system learning disabilities are quite compatible with control, differential association, and anomie theories. Such learning disabilities increase the odds of a person being relatively unsuccessful in school and other legitimate pursuits, developing weak bonds with conventional society, and thus welcoming the attention gained by delinquency, including acceptance by delinquent associates. This implies that primary prevention of adolescence-transition criminality in these cases requires exceptional effort to promote strong bonds with conventional parents, peers, teachers, and others, to provide remedial education and training, and to separate the handicapped individual from pro-criminal persons. Physiological theories that ascribe passion-driven criminality to uncontrollable emotions, if a court can be convinced of their validity in particular cases, provide primary prevention through the defense of insanity, for this makes violence by persons with these conditions now lawfully punishable by the government, hence not officially crime.

Psychoanalytic theories are set forth by psychiatrists, psychoanalysts, and other psychological clinicians who are called upon primarily to account for cases of apparent criminality that are not readily explained as rational. They infer that offenses result from the offender's subconscious perceptions, reasoning, and motivations in which what seems to other observers to be one thing may actually be only a symbolic expression of something else. These are disproportionately offenses that might be defended legally as expressing insanity, but in any case, their primary prevention according to psychoanalytic theory requires more optimum child rearing in the family. This is a preventive strategy also urged by control and differential association theorists, but with some difference in emphases from those of psychoanalysts. However, psychoanalysts are usually not called upon to advise on how to prevent crime before it occurs, but to explain puzzling types of offenses, such as ostensibly motiveless crimes (for example, persistent petty theft by a wealthy person) or bizarre sex offenses. This concern with what to do about criminality after it has been manifested in lawbreaking is not primary prevention, but our next concern.

Secondary and Tertiary Prevention

Secondary prevention copes with the failures of primary prevention by trying to reduce the criminality of known offenders, to prevent their recidivism. *Tertiary prevention* copes with the failures of both primary and secondary prevention by physically restraining offenders presumed to be unreformed, thereby making them incapable of committing further crimes. Often these strategies are combined, by physically incarcerating offenders or restricting their activities in the free community for tertiary prevention, while simultaneously endeavoring to reform them. Also included as tertiary prevention here are target-hardening strategies, such as teaching potential victims to avoid behavior that increases their vulnerability to predations, as well as increased guarding and lighting of crime targets.

Just as each of the theories of criminality already discussed implies a method of primary prevention to eliminate the causes of crime, each also implies a similar approach to secondary prevention. Control theory directs one to try to increase offenders' bonds with conventional society, differential association reminds one also to try to alienate them from other criminals, and anomie theory inspires an effort to expand their prospects of success in legitimate pursuits. Nevertheless, there are some theories that focus on ways of reacting to known criminals, rather than on the primary prevention of crime among presumed nonoffenders.

Labeling theory, as applied to crime, is usually (but not exclusively) concerned with preventing recidivism, when criminality has become manifest. As pioneered by Lemert (1967 ch. 3), it is a theory of "secondary deviation" which implies that when someone is labeled an offender because of an alleged or actual initial offense, the labeling itself is often a cause of further criminality. The mechanisms by which this is effected, Lemert indicates, include stigmatization, as when a youngster who is labeled a "bad boy" because of a delinquent act is kept by neighborhood parents from associating with "good boys," and is therefore more differentially associated with other delinquents. Lemert also ascribes secondary deviance to the sense of injustice that is evoked by what the offender perceives as the inconsistency of penalties, or what anomie theorists called a sense of "relative deprivation." But he especially ascribes recidivism to the more concentrated exposure to criminality-supportive subcultures that results from incarceration with other offenders.

When persons are erroneously labeled criminals, then the social consequences of the label indicated above may foster initial criminality, rather than recidivism. Thus, labeling theory can be applied to the primary prevention of crime as well as to reforming criminals. Its implication in either case is that those who are presumed to have broken the law should not be rejected by conventional society and be given little hope of acceptance. Consistent with differential association theory, it implies trying to involve both alleged and adjudicated offenders in collaborative and gratifying activities with conventional persons, and separating them if possible from other lawbreakers, especially those in close-knit groups. It also implies that great care should be taken to avoid unjust or exaggerated designation of persons as criminals. Pertinent here is a theory of crime-preventive punishment.

Deterrence theory asserts that fear of punishment keeps people from committing crimes, and that this deterrent effect varies with the severity, speed, and certainty of the penalty. The theory has two forms: as "general deterrence" it is a theory of primary prevention, for it claims that noncriminals refrain from committing crimes because of their fear of the penalties imposed on offenders; as "special deterrence" it is a theory of secondary prevention, for it contends that the punishment of known criminals makes them refrain from recidivating by instilling fear of further punishment.

Labeling and deterrence theory have contradictory implications for secondary prevention. Labeling theory seems to imply that most official penalties, especially incarceration, are unavoidably criminalizing, whether or not the subject is a criminal when labeled as one. Deterrence theory asserts that failure to punish a crime adequately reinforces the offender's criminality. It is probably because both theories have some validity, but each is strongest with particular types of subjects and circumstances, that studies to test each separately have had inconsistent results.

If a person who has a strong stake in conformity nevertheless commits an offense, the shame of the crime, and possibly aid by conventional kin or friends, are likely to be reformative if the penalty is probation or a suspended sentence, while long incarceration with more advanced offenders would be criminalizing. Conversely, an already highly criminalized offender without strong bonds to conventional persons is unlikely to be reformed by probation, and would not have so great an increment of criminalization from incarceration; yet even some of these individuals are reached by reformative training and social contacts with outsiders during confinement, and by intensively supervised release programs that increase their post-release ties with conventional persons and their successful experience in legitimate jobs.

During the last two decades sentencing in the United States has increasingly abandoned the goal of reforming offenders in favor of imposing "just desert" for the offense. This is irrational as a secondary crime preventative, because (1) the best predictors of recidivism are attributes of the offender, especially prior criminal and correctional record, and alcohol or drug addiction, rather than the type of offense for which a sentence is imposed; (2) the most active adolescence-transition and vice-propelled offenders are usually the least specialized in their crimes and are arrested in less than 10 percent of them, so chance alone largely determines which of the many types of crimes that they commit is the basis of their sentence.

Just deserts is also irrational for primary prevention by general deterrance to keep nonoffenders from committing crimes, since nonoffenders have such a stake in conformity that they are deterred by much less severe penalties than are likely to be given to offenders for special deterrence. Just deserts is rational as a sentencing principle only in determining lower and upper limits for an offense's penalties, the lower when necessary to assure the public that a crime is not regarded as trivial, and the upper to avoid the injustice of penalties more severe than just deserts would warrant.

Tertiary prevention by imprisoning highly criminalized offenders, thus incapacitating them from committing crimes, may contribute to secondary prevention not only through the deterrent effects of this punishment but also because only during years of confinement is there much prospect of such persons gaining remedial education, vocational training, or even strengthening of bonds with noncriminals (e.g., Alcoholics Anonymous groups in prisons are regularly visited by members of outside A.A. groups). Unfortunately, however, most prison management in the United States seems much more oriented to the pacification of prisoners than to their reformation.

Reform in confinement is especially related to extensive and practical academic and vocational education there, as well as to bonds that some prisoners develop with anti-criminal persons despite incarceration, and maintain after their release (Glaser 1964, ch. 4; McKee 1985; Shover 1985). Incapacitation in the community by intensive supervision, even with electronic monitoring, also seems more effective than traditional probation or parole in the reformation of moderately advanced offenders, perhaps in large part because it limits their leisure time in criminalizing places, and increases their experience at regular employment and/or schooling (Ball et al. 1988; Morris and Tonry 1990).

This chapter is based in part on an unpublished book manuscript tentatively entitled "Realistic Crime Control."

References

Abadinsky, H. 1977. *Organized Crime*. New York: Allyn & Bacon.

Ball, Richard A., C. Ronald Huff, and J. Robert Lilly. 1988. *House Arrest and Correctional Policy*. Newbury Park, Cal.: Sage.

Blumstein, A., J. Cohen, and D. P. Farrington. 1988. "Criminal Career Research." *Criminology* 26:1–35.

Braithwaite, J. 1985. *To Punish or Persuade*. Albany, N.Y.: State University of New York Press.

———. 1989. *Crime, Shame, and Reintegration*. Cambridge: Cambridge University Press.

Chaiken, J. M., and M. R. Chaiken. 1982. *Variations of Criminal Behavior*. Santa Monica, Cal.: Rand Corp.

Chambliss, W. J. 1989. "State-Organized Crime." *Criminology* 27:183–208.

Cornish, D. V., and R. B. Clarke, eds. 1986. *The Reasoning Criminal*. New York: Springer-Verlag.

Ditton, J. 1977. *Part-Time Crime*. London: Macmillan.

Dornbusch, S. M., P. L. Ritter, P. H. Leiderman, D. F. Roberts, and M. J. Freleigh. 1987. "The Relation of Parenting Style to Adolescent School Performance." *Child Development* 58:1244–57.

Durkheim, E. 1893. *The Division of Labor in Society*. Transl. by W. D. Halls, New York: Free Press, 1984.

———. 1897. *Suicide*. Transl. by J. A. Spaulding & G. Simpson. New York: Free Press, 1951.

Farrington, David P., Bernard Gallagher, Lynda Morley, Raymond J. St. Ledger, and Donald J. West. 1986. "Unemployment, School Leaving, and Crime." *British Journal of Criminology* 26:335–56.

Glaser, Daniel. 1964. *The Effectiveness of a Prison and Parole System*. Indianapolis, Ind.: Bobbs-Merrill (Revised and Abridged Edition, 1969).

———. 1978. *Crime in Our Changing Society*. New York: Holt, Rinehart & Winston.

———. 1979. "A Review of Crime-Causation Theory and its Application." In *Crime and Justice*, vol. 1, edited by N. Morris and M. Tonry. Chicago: University of Chicago Press.

Glaser, D., B. Lander, and W. Abbott. 1971. "Opiate Addicted and Non-Addicted Siblings in a Slum Area." *Social Problems* 18:510–21.

Glueck, S. and E. T. Glueck. 1950. *Unraveling Juvenile Delinquency*. New York: Commonwealth Fund.

Gottfredson, Gary D., and Denise C. Gottfredson. 1985. *Victimization in Schools*. New York: Plenum Press.

Gottfredson, M. R., and T. Hirschi. 1990. *A General Theory of Crime*. Stanford, Cal.: Stanford University Press.

Hall, Jerome. 1952. *Theft, Law and Society*. Indianapolis, Ind.: Bobbs-Merrill.

Heer, David M., Marcus Felson, and Robert W. Hodge. 1985. "The Cluttered Heart: Evidence That Young Adults are More Likely to Live at Home Now Than in the Recent Past." *Sociology and Social Research*. 70:436–41.

HEW (U.S. Department of Health, Education and Welfare). 1978. *Violent Schools—Safe Schools: The Safe School Study Report to the Congress*. Washington, D.C.: U.S. Government Printing Office.

Hindelang, M. J. 1971. "The Social v. Solitary Nature of Delinquent Involvements." *British Journal of Criminology* 11:167–75.

Hirschi, T. 1969. *Causes of Delinquency*. Berkeley: University of California Press.

Hirschi, T., and M. Gottfredson. 1983. "Age and the Explanation of Crime." *American Journal of Sociology* 89:552–84.

Hochschild, Arlie. 1983. *The Managed Heart*. Berkeley: University of California Press.

Hollinger, R. C., and J. P. Clark. 1983. *Theft by Employees*. Lexington, Mass.: Heath.

Ianni, F. A. J. 1974. *Black Mafia: Ethnic Succession in Organized Crime*. New York: Simon & Schuster.

Kemper, T. D. 1987. "How Many Emotions Are There?" *American Journal of Sociology*. 93:263–89.

Klockars, C. B. 1974. *The Professional Fence*. New York: Free Press.

Lemert, E. M. 1967. *Human Deviance, Social Problems, & Social Control*. Englewood Cliffs, N.J.: Prentice-Hall.

Liska, A. E. 1973. "Causal Structures Underlying the Relationship Between Delinquency Involvement and Delinquent Peers." *Sociology and Social Research* 58:23–36.

Maurer, D. W. 1940. *The Big Con*. Indianapolis: Bobbs-Merrill.

McKee, Gilbert J., Jr. 1985. "Cost-benefits Analysis of Vocational Training." In *Correctional Institutions*, 3rd ed., edited by Robert M. Carter, Daniel Glaser, and Lester T. Wilkins. New York: Harper and Row.

McKissack, I. J. 1967. "The peak age of property crimes." *British Journal of Criminology* 7:184–94.

Mednick, S. A., T. E. Moffitt, and S. A. Stack. 1987. *The Causes of Crime*. Cambridge: Cambridge University Press.

Menard, Scott, and Delbert S. Elliott. 1990. "Longitudinal and Cross-Sectional Data Collection and Analysis in the Study of Delinquency." *Justice Quarterly* 7:11–55.

Merton, R. K. 1957. *Social Theory and Social Structure*, rev. ed. New York: Free Press.

———. 1964. "Anomie, Anomia, and Social Interaction." In *Anomie and Deviant Behavior*, edited by M. B. Clinard. New York: Free Press.

Moore, M. H., S. B. Estrich, D. McGillis, and W. Spelman. 1984. *Dangerous Offenders*. Cambridge, Mass.: Harvard University Press.

Morris, Norval and Michael Tonry. 1990. *Between Prison and Probation*. New York: Oxford University Press.

Nelli, H. S. 1976. *The Business of Crime*. New York: Oxford University Press.

Rutter, M., and H. Giller. 1984. *Juvenile Delinquency*. New York: Guilford.

Shaw, C. R., and H. D. McKay. 1969. *Juvenile Delinquency and Urban Areas*. Revised ed. Chicago: University of Chicago Press.

Shover, Neal. 1985. *Aging Criminals*. Newbury Park, Cal.: Sage.

Skolnick, Jerome H. 1978. *House of Cards*. Boston: Little Brown.

Steffensmeier, D. J. 1986. *The Fence*. Totawa, N.J.: Rowman and Little-field.

Steffensmeier, D. J., E. A. Allan, M. D. Harer, and C. Streifel. 1989. "Age and the Distribution of Crime." *American Journal of Sociology* 94:803–31.

Stinchcombe, A. L. 1964. *Rebellion in a High School*. Chicago: Quadrangle Books.

Sutherland, E. H. 1937. *The Professional Thief*. Chicago: University of Chicago Press.

Sutherland, E. H., and D. R. Cressey. 1978. *Criminology*. Philadelphia: Lippincott.

Tanioka, I., and D. Glaser. (accepted for 1991 publication) "School Uniforms, Routine Activities, and the Social Control of Delinquency in Japan." *Youth and Society*.

Walsh, M. E. 1977. *The Fence*. Westport, Conn.: Greenwood.

3

Opponent-Process Theory: Implications for Criminality

Robert A. Rosellini and Robin L. Lashley

Crime, with its attendant costs to victims and to society at large, has long been the focus of study by social scientists from a wide range of disciplines, such as criminology, sociology, and psychology. In this chapter, we propose a potentially fruitful avenue of exploration of criminality based on a psychological theory of acquired motivation proposed by Solomon and Corbit (1974). This *opponent-process theory* has already been shown to be applicable to a wide range of empirical observations of both animal and human behavior (cf. Solomon 1977, 1980). The theory encompasses phenomena as diverse as the social attachment process in ducklings (Hoffman and Solomon 1974; Starr 1978), fear conditioning and adjunctive behavior in rats (Maier et al. 1976; Overmier et al. 1979; Rosellini 1985; Rosellini and Lashley 1982), test anxiety in college students (Craig and Seigel 1980), job satisfaction (Landy 1978), addiction to jogging (Solomon 1980), parachute jumping (Epstein 1967), and addiction to opiate drugs (Solomon 1977). In short, the theory has demonstrated applicability to a wide range of repetitive behaviors. The scope of opponent-process theory rests in its assumption of a common motivational mechanism that operates in all instances in which there is repeated exposure to an affect-arousing stimulus. Similar underlying processes are postulated for all addiction cycles, regardless of whether or not the stimulus has intuitively obvious addicting properties.

We will outline the application of opponent-process theory to criminal behavior. Guided by the theory, we will propose that at least certain aspects of criminal behavior may be understood as stemming from, and being supported by, an addiction cycle. In order to provide the reader with at least an intuitive application of the theory to criminal behavior, we will first provide several anecdotal examples of the general type of human motivation that the theory can explain. This will be followed by a formal presentation of opponent-process theory. In the final sections, we will use this theory to suggest a new topology of criminality and explore the major expectations of our proposal for an understanding of several aspects of criminal behavior.

Examples of Hedonic Experiences Encompassed by Opponent-Process Theory

Addiction to Opiate Drugs

As originally detailed by Solomon (1977), the affective dynamics of opiate use follow a particularly interesting time course. The first few experiences with an opiate such as heroin induce a potent pleasure (i.e., the "rush") that is followed by a less intense feeling of euphoria while the drug is still active. When the drug effect wanes, the individual experiences a state of mild discomfort—an aversive hedonic state, typically called "craving," which will dissipate with time. It is during this state that the individual, given the opportunity, may readminister the drug. If the individual does repeatedly reinject heroin, several affective changes will occur. The first is that the "rush" and the euphoria will be greatly dampened. Once the drug is metabolized, however, the original craving will be replaced by a much more intense aversive state which is typically referred to as the withdrawal syndrome.

Thrill-Seeking Behavior

The second example is taken from the category of thrill-seeking behavior—parachuting. The general description (Epstein 1967) of the affective dynamics of this sport closely parallels the experience of the heroin user, although at a somewhat reduced intensity.

During the initial jump, there is a considerable fear reaction. After a successful landing, there is typically a feeling of relief. Once the individual has executed à number of jumps, however, the hedonic reactions change markedly. The original experience of intense fear during the jump is reduced and may be replaced with slight tension or perhaps even eagerness. The after-effects of the experience also change dramatically. The original feeling of relief is replaced by a feeling of exhilaration that can last for several hours before a sense of normalcy returns.

These two examples highlight the commonality in affective dynamics induced by two very different mood-altering experiences. In each case, we observe that the initial affective reaction induced by the stimulus event is reduced by repeated experience with the event. The "rush" of heroin or the intense fear of jumping from an airplane is diminished in the experienced individual. Furthermore, repeated experience greatly amplifies the after-effects of the event—the heroin user experiences withdrawal and the parachute jumper feels exhilaration. It is these changes in affective dynamics that are captured by opponent-process theory. It is also these changes, particularly the intensification of the hedonic after-effects of a repeated event, that are proposed by the theory to be the basis for addictions, not only to chemical agents that may have physiological addicting properties, but to psychological "thrills" as well. The superficial similarity of at least the "thrill-seeking" component of the parachute jumping example to certain forms of criminal behavior may already be obvious to the reader.

We now turn to a formal exposition of opponent-process theory that will later allow us to make a more direct and rigorous application of the theory to criminal behavior. It should be noted that in our anecdotal examples we have emphasized the commonality of the pattern of hedonic experience induced by positive and negative events. After formal consideration of opponent-process theory as well as its relationship to well established Pavlovian and operant conditioning principles, we will be in a position to consider differences in the consequences of repeated exposure to initially positive versus initially negative hedonic events.

The Explanatory Model

Opponent-process theory assumes that the nervous systems of mammals are organized to oppose and suppress many types of emotional arousal, thereby seeking to maintain hedonic homeostasis. This is held to be the case whether the arousal-inducing event is pleasurable or aversive. That is, the experience of an affect-inducing event will engage an underlying primary process, called the "a-process," that will track the presence of the event. This a-process matches the inducing stimulus in hedonic quality, intensity, and duration. For example, a high dose of heroin should induce a larger a-process, and therefore a more intense and longer-lasting high, than would a small dose. Shortly after the a-process is set in motion, a secondary, opposing process, called the "b-process," is assumed to be aroused. The b-process is an automatic, slave reaction by the nervous system to any deviation from the baseline level of arousal. Because the b-process has an hedonic quality that is opposite in sign to that of the a-process, it serves to moderate the resultant impact of the inducing stimulus. Figure 3.1 schematically shows the postulated basic processing of hedonic events. For simplicity, we assume that the inducing cognitive-perceptual stimulus is one with instantaneous onset and offset (i.e., square-wave input). Onset of the stimulus engages an underlying hedonic process (the a-process) that is assumed to have a relatively short rise time to its asymptotic level. This a-process will remain at asymptotic level for the duration of the inducing stimulus and will return rapidly to baseline after stimulus offset. This primary a-process will in turn elicit a b-process that will oppose the affective disturbance induced by the eliciting event. Compared to the a-process, the b-process (1) has a slower onset; (2) requires more time to reach asymptote; and (3) is slower to decay, thereby requiring more time to return to baseline (for further elaboration and a review of the supportive evidence see Solomon 1977, 1980).

The temporal summation of these two postulated underlying processes determines the temporal dynamics of an affective reaction. The hedonic state of the organism at any point in time will be a function of the algebraic summation of the a- and b-processes. If the a-process is larger than the b-process, the organism is in state A, an affective state reflective of the hedonic value of the inducing event. If the b-process is larger than the a-process, the organism is in state B, an affective state whose hedonic value is opposite to that of the inducing event. The algebraic summation of the a- and b-processes will generate the standard temporal pattern of affective

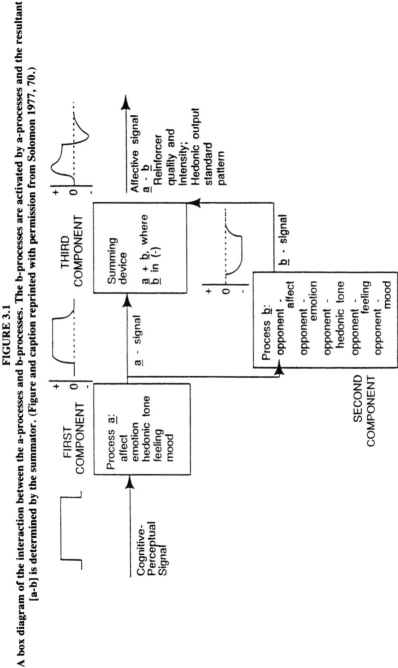

FIGURE 3.1

A box diagram of the interaction between the a-processes and b-processes. The b-processes are activated by a-processes and the resultant [a-b] is determined by the summator. (Figure and caption reprinted with permission from Solomon 1977, 70.)

dynamics shown in figure 3.2: a peak reaction at stimulus onset; a period of adaptation producing a lower steady state level that remains as long as the stimulus is present; a peak after-reaction at stimulus offset; and, finally, the slow decay of the after-reaction back to baseline.

Why do these affective reactions change so dramatically with repeated exposure to the inducing stimulus? Opponent-process theory can account for such changes with a single parsimonious assumption: the b-process strengthens with use, and weakens with disuse. That is, the b-process is assumed to increase in intensity and decrease in activation latency with each elicitation that occurs within some critical temporal duration since its last activation (for details of the assumption of Critical Decay Duration see Solomon 1977). Furthermore, although each exposure to the stimulus within some critical time period since the last exposure results in the growth of the b-process, the a-process is assumed to be unaffected. Since the unchanging a-process will be opposed by an ever-stronger b-process, the resulting state A will become progressively less intense with each repetition, while state B will become progressively more intense. Thus, the theory deduces the changes in affective reaction to an inducing stimulus as a function of repeated experience with that stimulus.

These changes in affect with experience are shown graphically in figure 3.3. Panel A of this figure shows the manifest affective reaction (top row), which replicates the basic patterns described in figure 3.2, as well as the underlying processes that produce this pattern detailed in figure 3.1.

To return to our anecdotal example of heroin use, this pattern describes the reported "rush" (peak of state A), the subsequent diminished positive affective state of euphoria while the heroin is still active in the system (the steady state level of state A), and the ultimate affective state of mild craving (state B) when the underlying a-process has returned to baseline, but the corresponding b-process is still active. Panel B of figure 3.3 shows the changes in the underlying b-process and the consequent changes in the manifest affective states produced by the same inducing stimulus after repeated experiences with that stimulus. As can be seen, the a-process is unchanged. The b-process, on the other hand, has grown considerably—it now has a faster onset latency, a higher asymp-

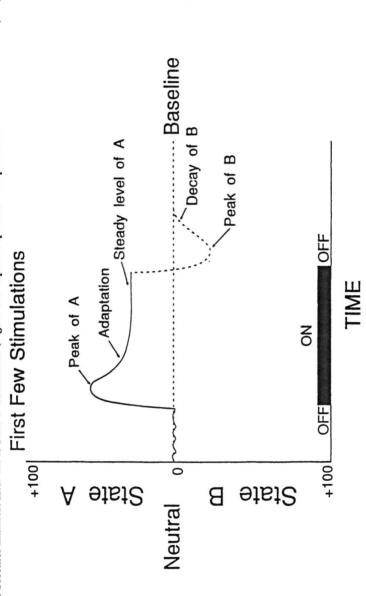

FIGURE 3.2

The standard pattern of affective dynamics, showing the five distinctive features of affect resulting from a typical square-wave input. The B-State becomes manifest after the A-State is terminated. (Figure and caption reprinted with permission from Solomon 1977, 71.)

FIGURE 3.3

The consequences of subtracting the b-process from the a-process when the b-process is weak and when it is strengthened by repeated use. The resultant A-State is small after the b-process is strengthened, but the B-State is more intense and longer lasting. (Figure and caption reprinted with permission from Solomon 1977, 75.)

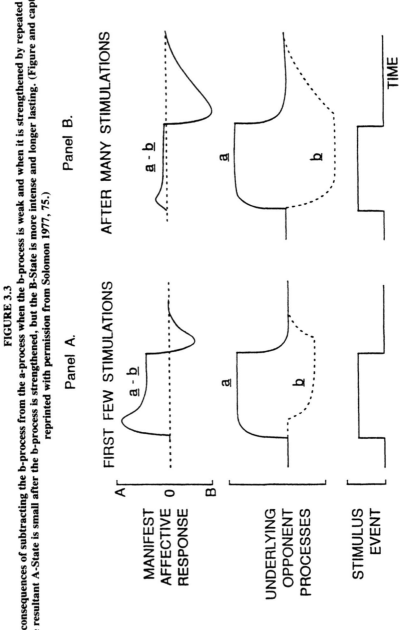

totic level, and a consequent slower return to baseline. The affective consequences of these changes in the b-process are clear. Even during the presence of the inducing stimulus, there is a minimal affective response. This is due to the increase in the b-process, opposing an unchanged a-process. Here, for example, the injection of heroin will no longer induce the originally-experienced rush or euphoria. Once the drug action has dissipated, however, the individual will experience an intense opponent affective state—withdrawal. This affective state will motivate the experienced user to seek more heroin and reinject. In short, this is the point at which the individual has become addicted to the drug and will continue to use it. It is interesting to note that from this theoretical position, the major reason that the addict injects heroin is to avoid the aversive hedonic consequences of the absence of the drug. As we will emphasize below, however, the theory does not deny that other factors may also play a role in the maintenance of the behavior.

Pavlovian Conditioning of States A and B

The aforementioned changes in the strength of the b-process, and therefore in the intensity of the manifest affective states A and B, are nonassociative in nature. That is, these changes are not dependent on associative learning; instead, they are assumed to come about simply as a function of repeated exposure to an affect-inducing stimulus.

The applicability of opponent-process theory can be broadened significantly by the additional assumption that both states A and B can be conditioned to (i.e., associated with) previously neutral stimuli as a function of experience. Throughout our discussion, we have described stimulus events (such as heroin injection and parachute jumping) that are intrinsically affect-arousing. In Pavlov's classical conditioning terminology, such events are referred to as Unconditional Stimuli (UCSs). The initial affective reaction to such a stimulus, which we have called state A, is a Pavlovian Unconditional Response (UCR). Thus, any previously neutral stimulus that is paired consistently with the affect-arousing stimulus (and, therefore, with the onset of state A) should become a Pavlovian conditional stimulus (CS_a—termed CS+ in the Pavlovian conditioning literature). This CS_a will acquire the ability to elicit an affective reaction similar to, although not as intense as, that induced by the unconditional stimulus (cf., Pavlov 1927; Mackintosh 1983). For instance, for the heroin user, a filled hypodermic syringe or other novel environmental stimuli will be consistently paired with state A—heroin's hedonically positive effects. Over time, these stimuli should become CS_as, capable on their own of eliciting a mild conditioned euphoric reaction (or, for the established addict, a temporary reduction in craving for the drug). Furthermore, if such CS_as are withdrawn, a mild state B should appear. This occurs because the b-process is a "slave" to the a-process; anything that elicits an a-process (for example, a filled syringe) will also elicit an opposing b-process when the stimulus is withdrawn. Thus, a heroin addict should temporarily be comforted by the presence of a filled syringe. But, should that syringe be removed (without being injected), the craving will be intensified, because a conditioned craving is superimposed on an already existing unconditioned craving.

What if a previously neutral stimulus is paired with the offset of the affect-inducing event (and thus with the onset of state B)? It, too, should become a conditional stimulus (in this case, a CS_b— termed a CS − in the Pavlovian conditioning literature), capable on its own of producing a conditioned state B. Thus, for the heroin addict, any stimuli that have been uniquely associated with the hedonically negative after-effects of drug injection should acquire the ability to induce a conditioned state B. For example, for a heroin addict having no money with which to buy heroin may be an event that will consistently be paired with the absence of a "fix" and consequent craving and withdrawal. Therefore, a lack of money will come to elicit a conditioned craving that will add to the unconditioned craving and intensify the addict's agony. Note that the affective reaction to a CS_a is biphasic—CS_a first elicits a conditioned state A, followed automatically by state B (since the b-process is a slave to the a-process). In contrast, the affective reaction to CS_b is monophasic—the b-process is aroused directly, after which it fades out.

Instrumental Conditioning and States A and B

In the previous section, we identified intrinsically affect-arousing stimuli as Pavlovian UCSs that could be used to condition States A and B to previously neutral stimuli. In this section, we focus on another property of these intrinsically-arousing stimuli—their power to serve as reinforcers. In the case of a naturally pleasant hedonic event, state A will be positively reinforcing and state B will be negatively reinforcing. For example, injection of heroin is positively reinforced by the initial "high" (especially during early experiences with the drug) and negatively reinforced by reduction of the craving generated by the preceding dose (especially once an addiction is established).

In the case of an aversive hedonic event, such as parachute jumping, state A is aversive (especially at first) and therefore negatively reinforcing, while state B is pleasant and therefore positively reinforcing. In the initial experiences with an aversive stimulus, the aversive state A is intense and the pleasant state B is weak. Since such an aversive state A should motivate avoidance of the affect-inducing stimulus, we must assume some fairly potent outside motivational force (perhaps social pressure?) sufficient to energize the early instrumental responses (e.g., the first few parachute jumps). After many repetitions, however, the aversiveness of state A (fear during the jumps) will be greatly reduced and the pleasantness of state B (exhilaration after the jumps) will be greatly enhanced, perhaps sufficiently to maintain the response at a high frequency even in the absence of extrinsic motivation. Thus, many seemingly counterproductive or even masochistic behaviors may be motivated by the learned expectation that extremely pleasant affective states will follow the termination of the stimulus event.

Opponent-process theory, when considered in combination with these Pavlovian and instrumental conditioning processes, has some interesting implications for the successful interruption of an addictive cycle. The breaking of an addiction is likely to be extremely difficult when a pleasant hedonic stimulus (like heroin) is involved. Our discussion of CS_as and CS_bs implies that the addict would do well to avoid both classes of stimuli. CS_as (stimuli that have been associated with the availability of the addictive substance) produce craving upon their removal; CS_bs (stimuli that have been associated with the nonavailability of the addictive substance) produce craving upon their presentation. A total change of physical and social environment might effectively eliminate both kinds of cues. But, recall that the b-process weakens with disuse. As the b-process weakens, state A regains its initial intensity and thus its power to positively reinforce new instrumental responses. If a relapse does occur at this point, the user will reexperience the intensely pleasurable state A. Of course, this will by necessity result in the growth of the B process. As a consequence of these two factors, the user may quickly become "hooked" again.

When the initial reaction to an hedonic stimulus is aversive (as in the case of parachute jumping), the addictive cycle should be easier to break. In the absence of outside motivation, such behavior should not be initiated or repeated in the first place. Early on, when the aversive initial reaction is more intense than the pleasant afterreaction, it should be relatively simple to interrupt the cycle. Even after a masochistic addiction is well established, "cold turkey" cessation should still be successful if it lasts long enough for the b-process to weaken, thereby making state A extremely aversive once again.

Application of Opponent-Process Theory to Criminal Behavior

A Proposed Criminal Typology

The most salient, and unique, feature of opponent-process theory is its ability to predict and explain changes in the affective response to an hedonic stimulus as a function of repeated exposure to that stimulus. Given the tremendous range of stimuli subsumed by the concept of "crime," and the equally heterogeneous group of people labelled as "criminals," it is difficult to even speculate what the precise nature of states A and B might be in specific cases. We claim, however, that these states should have opposite hedonic qualities—If state A is pleasant, then state B should be aversive, and vice versa. Furthermore, when we consider opponent-process theory in combination with the Pavlovian and instrumental conditioning processes outlined above, we can derive a typology of criminality and make predictions concerning several aspects of criminal behavior.

At the risk of adding yet another unsubstantiated criminal typology to the literature, let us suppose that there are two basic types of criminals. One type ("A-pleasant") feels little or no fear when confronted with a dangerous situation and, indeed, enjoys such an experience. Such an individual thus experiences a pleasant state A (enjoyment) during early criminal offenses, with a mildly aversive state B (a weak craving for more) afterward. With repeated offenses, the enjoyment should lessen, but the craving should intensify, creating a "crime addict" analogous in many respects to the heroin addict previously discussed. This type may also correspond, at least partially, to the sensation-seeking criminal described by Quay (1965).

The other type of criminal ("A-aversive") *does* feel intense fear (state A) during early offenses, with a feeling of relief (state B) after the event is over. These individuals do not enjoy their criminal acts and, at least initially, would not commit them without some relatively potent extrinsic motivation (e.g., peer influences; see Matsueda and Heimer 1987) or in the absence of some dispositional factors. Assuming that the initial terror is not overwhelmingly aversive, and that extrinsic motivation is still present, the crime may be repeated. If so, the affective states should gradually change. With repetition, the feelings of fear should gradually subside, while the after-reaction should intensify from mere relief to feelings of exhilaration and euphoria at "having gotten away with it." Now, even in the absence of outside motivation, an individual may be willing to put him/herself in a mildly fear-arousing situation in order to experience the "thrill" that follows. This type of criminal would be analogous to the parachute jumper of our previous example.

Assuming that the two types of criminals exist, several differences between them would be anticipated on the basis of opponent-process theory. First, "A-pleasants" should be motivated to intensify their offenses in an effort to restore the enjoyment they experienced during their initial crimes, analogous to the heroin addict who seeks to restore the initial "high" by increasing the doses of the drug. "A-aversives" should exhibit a lesser tendency to commit increasingly serious crimes, since the aversive state A should keep diminishing and the pleasant state B should keep intensifying, even if the seriousness of the crime (i.e., the intensity of the inducing stimulus) is held constant.

It might also be expected that the two types of criminals would differ in the probability that they would permanently desist from crime. According to opponent-process theory, long interoffense intervals that surpass the critical delay duration should preclude the strengthening of the b-process with repetition. Therefore, desistance (whether self-motivated or externally imposed) should allow the b-process to weaken back to its precrime intensity. In individuals for whom state A is aversive, this would restore their initial fearfulness to its full intensity, making further crimes less likely unless strong extrinsic motivation is present. In individuals who experience pleasant A states, however, long crimefree periods should restore their initial enjoyment of crime to its former intensity. Should such an individual commit another crime at this point, it would once again be strongly positively reinforced by an intensely pleasurable state A. Thus, we might predict greater recidivism and/or less desistance among "A-pleasants" than among "A-aversives." Of course, as is known to be the case for some heroin addicts, other factors such as "burn-out" may also play a role in desistance from crime.

In this application of opponent-process theory, we have painted in broad strokes a general outline of how such a theory of acquired motivation can point out a number of interesting and potentially important components of criminal behavior that appear to us to have been largely overlooked in the extant and current discussions of this topic. Our application is admittedly speculative because the type of data necessary for an adequate test of the assumptions of opponent-process theory in this specific domain do not appear to be available presently. However, the application is at least of considerable heuristic value since the theory does make specific predictions concerning the affective changes which should be experienced by the novice and experienced criminal and are eminently suited to empirical test. Future research aimed at testing the applicability of this theoretical framework to criminal behavior should specifically focus on the affective changes reported by individuals in their early and late criminal careers as well as focusing on the cyclical and repetitive nature of criminal activity vis-à-vis these hypothesized affective changes. In closing, we must introduce a caveat. Although opponent-process theory certainly emphasizes the role of affective dynamics as a causal factor in a potential addiction to criminal activity, it does not deny that other dispositional, environmental, societal, and economic factors are important for a complete understanding of the initiation and maintenance of criminal activity.

We wish to thank Dr. Scott Lillienfeld and Professors Richard L. Solomon and Joan McCord for their cogent comments on the views expressed in this chapter.

References

Craig, R. L. and P. S. Seigel. 1980. "Does Negative Affect Beget Positive Affect? A Test of the Opponent-Process Theory." *Bulletin of the Psychonomic Society* 14: 404–06.

Epstein, S. M. 1967. "Toward a Unified Theory of Anxiety." In *Progress in Experimental Personality Research,* vol. 4, edited by B. A. Maher. New York: Academic Press.

Hoffman, H. S. and R. L. Solomon. 1974. "An Opponent-Process Theory of Motivation: III. Some Affective Dynamics in Imprinting." *Learning and Motivation* 5: 149–64.

Landy, F. J. 1978. "An Opponent-Process Theory of Job Satisfaction." *Journal of Applied Psychology* 5: 533–47.

Maier, S. F., P. Rapaport, and K. L. Wheatley. 1976. "Conditioned Inhibition and the UCS-CS Interval." *Animal Learning and Behavior* 4: 217–20.

Mackintosh, N. J. 1983. *Conditioning and Associative Learning.* New York: Oxford University Press.

Matsueda, R. L. and K. Heimer. 1987. "Race, Family Structure, and Delinquency: A Test of Differential Association and Social Control Theories." *American Sociological Review* 52: 826–40.

Overmier, J. B., R. L. Paine, R. M. Brackbill, B. Linder, and J. A. Lawry. 1979. "On the Mechanism of the Post-Asymptotic Decrement Phenomenon." *Acta Neurobiologiae Experimentalis* 39: 603–20.

Pavlov, I. P. 1927. *Conditioned Reflexes.* Oxford: Oxford University Press.

Quay, H. C. 1965. "Psychopathic Personality as Pathological Stimulation Seeking." *American Journal of Psychiatry* 122: 180–83.

Rosellini, R. A. 1985. "An Application of Opponent-Process Theory to Adjunctive Behavior." In *Affect, Conditioning, and Cognition: Essays on the Determinants of Behavior,* edited by F. R. Brush & J. B. Overmier, 263–80. New York: Lawrence Erlbaum.

Rosellini, R. A. and R. L. Lashley. 1982. "The Opponent Process Theory of Motivation: VIII. Quantitative and Qualitative Manipulations of Food both Modulate Adjunctive Behavior." *Learning & Motivation* 13: 222–39.

Solomon, R. L. 1977. "An Opponent-Process Theory of Acquired Motivation: The Affective Dynamics of Addiction." In *Psychopathology:*

Experimental Models, edited by J. D. Maser and M. E. P. Seligman, 66–103. San Francisco: W. H. Freeman.

Solomon, R. L. 1980. "The Opponent-Process Theory of Acquired Motivation: The Cost of Pleasure and the Benefits of Pain." *American Psychologist* 35: 691–712.

Solomon, R. L. and J. D. Corbit. 1974. "An Opponent-Process Theory of Motivation: I. Temporal Dynamics of Affect." *Psychological Review* 81: 119–45.

Starr, M. D. 1978. "An Opponent-Process Theory of Motivation: Time and Intensity Variables in the Development of Separation Induced Distress Calling in Ducklings." *Journal of Experimental Psychology: Animal Behavior Processes* 4: 338–55.

4

Family Management and Child Development: Insights from Social Disorganization Theory

Robert J. Sampson

One of the most central and durable facts produced by the classic research of Shaw and McKay earlier in this century was that communities characterized by high rates of crime and delinquency are also plagued by high rates of infant mortality, low birthweight, tuberculosis, child abuse, and other detrimental aspects of child development. Indeed, Shaw and McKay argued that delinquency "is not an isolated phenomenon" (1969, 106) and went on to document the close association of delinquency rates with social problems that directly influence children. This empirical finding has remained remarkably stable over time. As but one recent example, Wallace and Wallace (1990) document that rates of violent death across communities in New York City are virtually coterminous with rates of low birthweight and infant mortality.

In this chapter, I consider some of the implications of this often ignored fact of crime for criminological theory. Specifically, I advance a community-level theory of social disorganization that places primary emphasis on families and child development. Previous research on communities and crime has focused largely on structural factors thought to affect later adolescent and adult motivation to crime (e.g., economic opportunities, relative deprivation, subcultures of violence). By contrast, I draw on social disorganization theory linked with the concept of social capital (Coleman 1990) to focus on the embeddedness of families and children in the social networks of local communities. In a nutshell, I argue that community structure is important mainly for its role in facilitating or inhibiting the creation of social capital among families and children. In this regard, I examine how factors such as prenatal care, child abuse, the monitoring and supervision of youth, and other family management practices are intertwined with community networks of social organization. By advancing a community-level theory of social disorganization I hope to provide new insights into a fundamental yet unresolved issue in criminology.

Communities and the Study of Crime

Unlike the dominant tradition in criminology which seeks to distinguish offenders from nonoffenders, the macrosocial or community-level of explanation asks what it is about community structures and cultures that produce differential areas of crime (Short 1985; Byrne and Sampson 1986; Bursik 1988). As such, the goal of macrolevel research is not to explain individual involvement in criminal behavior but to isolate characteristics of communities, cities, or even societies that lead to high rates of criminality (Short 1985; Byrne and Sampson 1986). From this viewpoint the "ecological fallacy"—inferring individual-level relations based on aggregate data—is not at issue because the unit of explanation and analysis is the community itself. However, another aspect of community research is contextual analysis, where the aim is to study individual-level variations in social behavior as a function of both individual *and* community-level factors (Sampson 1988).

In this paper I apply a dual community/contextual framework with a focus on neighborhoods or other local community areas in urban areas. Cities and metropolitan areas are large, highly aggregated, and heterogeneous units with politically-defined and hence artificial ecological boundaries. Although intra-urban units of analysis (e.g., census tracts, wards, block-groups) are imperfect proxies for the concept of local community, they generally possess more ecological integrity (e.g., natural boundaries, social homogeneity) than cities or SMSAs and are more closely linked to the causal processes assumed to underlie the etiology of crime (see also Bursik 1988).

The Shaw and McKay Model

The research of Shaw and McKay forms the infrastructure for modern American studies of the ecology of crime. In their classic work *Juvenile Delinquency and Urban Areas,* Shaw and McKay (1942, 1969) argued that three structural factors—low economic status, ethnic heterogeneity, and residential mobility—led to the disruption of local community social organization, which in turn accounted for variations in crime and delinquency rates (for more details see Kornhauser 1978). Shaw and McKay also demonstrated that high rates of delinquency persisted in certain areas over many years, regardless of population turnover. More than any other, this finding led them to reject individualistic explanations of delinquency and focus instead on the processes by which delinquent and criminal patterns of behavior were transmitted across generations in areas of social disorganization and weak social controls (1942; 1969, 320).

After a hiatus in the 1950s and 1960s, recent years have witnessed an increased concern with the role of communities in fostering crime (see Reiss 1986a; Byrne and Sampson 1986; Bursik 1988). This body of research has generally supported the basic Shaw and McKay model in terms of the correlates of poverty, mobility, and heterogeneity. In addition, recent research has established that crime rates are positively linked to community-level variations in population density, housing density, family disruption (e.g., percent single-parent households, divorce rates), and rates of community change and population turnover (for detailed reviews see Byrne and Sampson 1986; Bursik 1988; Sampson and Lauritsen 1991).

Perhaps more important, recent research has started to explicate in more detail the social processes that mediate the effect of structural characteristics on crime. This is a crucial issue, for the mere correlation of crime rates with ecological factors is consistent with many different theoretical perspectives, not to mention individual-level theories that emphasize self-selection and compositional effects (Sampson and Lauritsen 1991). For example, although many community-level studies show that proportions who are black, or living in poverty, and rates of family disruption, or mobility predict delinquency rates, this strategy does not really go beyond the steps taken by Shaw and McKay over forty years ago.

As Kornhauser (1978, 82) argues, most criminological theories take as their point of departure the same independent variables (e.g., socioeconomic status). The variables that intervene between community structure and crime are at issue, and consequently one must establish the relationship to crime of the interpretive variables a theory implies. I therefore turn to a brief overview of the theory of social disorganization. My goal is to highlight the major conceptualization underlying community social disorganization, and then extend the model to consider the idea of social capital and its role in linking communities, families, and children.

Community Social Disorganization

The theory of social disorganization refers to the inability of a community structure to realize the common values of its residents and maintain effective social controls (Kornhauser 1978, 120; Bursik 1988; Sampson and Groves 1989). The structural dimensions of community social disorganization can be conceptualized in terms of the prevalence and interdependence of social networks in a community—both informal (e.g., the density of acquaintanceship, intergenerational kinship ties) and formal (e.g., organizational participation)—and in the span of collective supervision that the community directs toward local problems (Sampson and Groves 1989; Kornhauser 1978). This approach is grounded in what Kasarda and Janowitz (1974, 329) term the "systemic" model, where the local community is viewed as a complex system of friendship and kinship networks, and formal and informal associational ties rooted in family life and ongoing socialization processes (see also Bott 1957; Sampson 1988, 1991). Social organization and social disorganization are thus seen as different ends of the same continuum with respect to systemic networks of community social control. As Bursik (1988) notes, when formulated in this way social disorganization is clearly separable not only from the processes that may lead to it (e.g., poverty, mobility), but from the degree of criminal behavior that may be a result. This conceptualization also goes beyond the traditional account of community as a strictly geographical or spatial phenomenon by focusing on the social and organizational networks of local residents (see especially Leighton 1988).

Sampson and Groves (1989) highlighted three dimensions of

community social organization relevant to adolescence and the control of delinquency. The first is the ability of a community to supervise and control teenage peer groups—especially gangs. Delinquency is primarily a group phenomenon (Thrasher 1963; Shaw and McKay 1942; Reiss 1986b), and hence, the capacity of the community to control group-level dynamics is a key theoretical mechanism linking community characteristics with crime. Indeed, a central finding underlying Thrasher's research was that the majority of gangs developed from the unsupervised, spontaneous play group (1963, 25). Shaw and McKay (1969) in turn argued that residents of cohesive communities were better able to control the teenage behaviors that set the context for group-related crime (see also Short 1963, xxiv). Examples of such controls include supervision of leisure-time youth activities, intervention in street-corner congregation (Thrasher 1963, 339; Maccoby et al. 1958; Shaw and McKay 1969, 176–85), and challenging youth "who seem to be up to no good" (Skogan 1986, 217; Taylor et al. 1984, 326). Socially disorganized communities with extensive street-corner peer groups are also expected to have higher rates of adult violence, especially among younger adults who still have ties to youth gangs (Thrasher 1963).

A second dimension of community social organization is local friendship and acquaintanceship networks. Systemic theory holds that locality-based social networks represent a core element in the social fabric of ecological communities (Sampson 1988, 1991). When residents form local social ties their capacity for community social control is increased because they are better able to recognize strangers, and are more apt to engage in guardianship behavior against victimization (Taylor et al. 1984, 307; Skogan 1986, 216). Also, the greater the density and multiplexity of interpersonal networks in a community, the greater the constraint on deviant behavior within the network.

A third component of social organization is the rate of local participation in formal and voluntary organizations. Community organizations reflect the structural embodiment of local community solidarity, leading Kornhauser (1978, 79) to argue that the instability and isolation of community institutions are key structural dimensions of social disorganization. That is, when links between community institutions are weak the capacity of a community to defend its local interests is weakened. Shaw and McKay (1969, 184–85), and more recently Taylor et al. (1984) and Simcha-Fagan and Schwartz (1986, 688), have also argued that a weak community organizational base serves to attenuate local social control functions regarding youth.

It is difficult to study social disorganization directly but at least two recent studies provide empirical support for the theory in terms of these three structural dimensions. First, Taylor et al. (1984) examined variations in violent crime (mugging, assault, murder, rape, shooting, and yoking) across sixty-three street blocks in Baltimore in 1978. Based on interviews with 687 household respondents, Taylor et al. (1984, 316) constructed block-level measures of what they termed "social ties" and "near home responsibilities." The former measured the proportion of respondents who belonged to an organization to which co-residents also belonged, whereas the latter measure tapped the extent to which respondents felt responsible for what happened in the area surrounding their home. Both of these dimensions of informal social control were significantly related to community-level variations in crime: organizational ties and near-home social control had standardized effects on violence rates of $-.20$ and $-.24$, respectively (1984, 320). Additionally, Taylor et al. (1984, 317) showed that blocks with higher levels of neighborhood identification as indicated by the proportion of residents who were able to provide a name for their neighborhood, had significantly lower rates of violence. These results support the social-disorganization hypothesis that levels of organizational participation and informal social control—especially of local activities by neighborhood youth—inhibit community-level rates of violence (see also Taylor et al. 1984, 326).

Second, Sampson and Groves (1989) analyzed the British Crime Survey (BCS), a nationwide survey of England and Wales conducted in 1982 and 1984. In the 1982 BCS, sampling procedures resulted in the proportionate selection of sixty addresses within each of 238 ecological areas in Great Britain. The sample drawn from each geographical unit was representative of a relatively small, homogeneous locality which reasonably approximated the concept of "local community." Survey-generated responses were aggregated within each of the areas and structural variables constructed (e.g., means, percentages).

Sampson and Groves (1989, 789) show that the prevalence of unsupervised peer groups in a community (e.g., teenagers hanging out making a nuisance) has the largest effect on rates of robbery and stranger-violence victimization in 1982 (betas of .35 and .19, respectively). The density of local friendship networks—measured by the proportion of residents with half or more of their friends living in the neighborhood—had a significant negative effect

$$(\text{beta} = -.19)$$

on robbery rates. The level of organizational participation by residents also had significant inverse effects on both robbery and stranger violence (1989, 789). The largest effect on personal violence *offending* rates in 1982 was unsupervised peer groups (1989, 793). These general findings were replicated in the 1984 BCS, as the level of unsupervised teenage peer groups had a large and substantial positive effect on rates of robbery and assault across 300 communities, while local friendship networks again had significant inverse effect (1989, 798). Overall, these results suggest that communities characterized by sparse friendship networks, unsupervised teenage peer groups, and low organizational participation had disproportionately high crime rates.

Moreover, for both survey years variations in structural dimensions of community social disorganization mediated in large part the effects of community socioeconomic status, residential mobility, ethnic heterogeneity, and family disruption in a manner consistent with social disorganization theory. For example, mobility had significant inverse effects on friendship networks, family disruption was the largest predictor of unsupervised peer groups, and socioeconomic status had the largest inverse effects on organizational participation in 1982. When combined with the results of research on gang delinquency that point to the salience of informal and formal community structures in controlling the formation of gangs (Thrasher 1963; Short and Strodtbeck 1965; Sullivan 1989), the empirical data thus suggest that the structural elements of social disorganization have relevance for explaining macrolevel variations in crime.

Community Cultures and Ethnography

Social disorganization theory also focuses on how the ecological segregation of communities gives rise to what Kornhauser (1978, 75) terms *cultural* disorganization—the attenuation of societal cultural values. Poverty, mobility, heterogeneity, and other structural features of urban communities are hypothesized to impede communication and obstruct the quest for common values, thereby fostering cultural diversity with respect to nondelinquent values. Accordingly, a second component of Shaw and McKay's theory was that disorganized communities spawned delinquent gangs with their own subcultures and norms perpetuated through cultural transmission.

Despite their relative infrequency, ethnographic studies generally support the notion that structurally disorganized communities are conducive to the emergence of cultural value systems and attitudes that seem to legitimate, or least provide a basis of tolerance, for crime and deviance. For example, Suttles' (1968) account of the social order of a Chicago neighborhood characterized by poverty and heterogeneity supports Thrasher's (1963) emphasis on age, sex, ethnicity, and territory as markers for the ordered segmentation of slum culture. Suttles found that single-sex, age-graded primary groups of the same ethnicity and territory emerged in response to threats of conflict and community-wide disorder and mistrust. Although the community subcultures Suttles (1968) discovered were provincial, tentative, and incomplete (Kornhauser 1978, 18), they nonetheless undermined societal values against delinquency and violence. Similarly, Anderson's (1978) ethnography of a bar in Chicago's South-side black ghetto shows how primary values co-existed alongside residual values associated with deviant subcultures (e.g., hoodlums) such as "toughness," "getting big money," "going for bad," and "having fun" (1978, 129–30; 152–58). In Anderson's analysis, lower-class residents do not so much "stretch" mainstream values as "create their own particular standards of social conduct along variant lines open to them" (1978, 210). In this context the use of violence is not valued as a primary goal, but is nonetheless expected and tolerated as a fact of life (1978, 134). Much like Rainwater (1970), Suttles (1968), and Horowitz (1987), Anderson's ethnographic research suggests that in certain community contexts the wider cultural values are simply not relevant—they become "unviable."

Whether or not community subcultures are authentic or merely "shadow cultures" (Liebow 1967) cannot be resolved here (see also Kornhauser 1978). But that seems less important than acknowledging that community contexts seem to shape what can be termed *cognitive landscapes* or ecologically structured norms (e.g., normative ecologies) regarding appropriate standards and expectations of conduct. That is, in structurally disorganized slum communities it appears that a system of values emerges in which crime, disorder, and drug use is less than fervently condemned and hence expected as part of everyday life. These ecologically structured social perceptions and tolerances in turn appear to influence the probability of criminal outcomes and harmful deviant behavior (e.g., drug use by pregnant women).[1] In this regard, I believe Kornhauser's attack on subcultural theories misses the point. By attempting to assess whether subcultural values are authentic in some deep, quasi-religious sense (1978, 1–20), she loses sight of the processes by which cognitive landscapes rooted in normative ecologies may influence behavior. Indeed, the idea that dominant values become existentially irrelevant in certain community contexts is a powerful one, albeit one that has not had the research exploitation it deserves.[2]

The foregoing review suggests that intervening dimensions of community disorganization—both structural and cultural—have potentially important effects on crime and delinquency. Having outlined the basic features of social disorganization, I turn now to a theoretical extension of the model that focuses more directly on children. My conceptualization rests on two fundamental aspects of child development: health and family management.

Child Development, Health Care, and Community

As noted at the outset of this paper, there is an empirical connection between the health-related problems of children and rates of crime and delinquency. Although not appreciated fully in the criminological literature, this fact is no accident from the viewpoint of social disorganization theory. Rather, community structure and the mediating processes of community social organization appear to be important determinants of variations in the accessibility and quality of prenatal care, child health services, and general child care. This section explores contextual influences on these and other developmental pathways to adolescence, and their repercussions for crime.

One of the most visible indicators of child health problems is the dramatic variations among communities in rates of infant mortality and low birthweight babies. Within New York City, rates of infant mortality range from a low of 6.6 per 1,000 live births in some health districts to as high as 43.5 in others (Lash et al. 1980, 176, 200). Wallace and Wallace (1990) document similar variations across both communities and time. Research on the causes of this variation is obviously complex and cannot be reviewed in full detail herein. However, one fact does seem to stand out—regardless of individual-level correlates of health care utilization (e.g., education), one of the primary sources of infant mortality and low birthweight is the availability and quality of prenatal care. For example, Lash et al. (1980) indicate that a substantial part of the variance in infant mortality and child health care is explained by the availability of services (see also Bronfenbrenner et al. 1984, 296). As predicted by social disorganization theory, it is also well documented that physician rates and the quality of health care vary significantly by community (Lash et al. 1980, 179, 210), with the poorest services found in lower-income, minority and/or heterogeneous, and often transient areas (Bronfenbrenner et al. 1984, 299).

Additional evidence consistent with social disorganization theory is found in a series of studies by Wallace and colleagues of community-level variations in low birthweight babies and infant mortality (Wallace and Wallace 1990; Wallace 1990a,b; Struening, Wallace, and Moore 1990). These authors document the strong upsurge in infant mortality and low birthweight in the late 1970s in New York City, especially in devastated areas of the Bronx. In particular, they found that poverty, overcrowded housing, and rapid population change were the main predictors of increased rates of low birthweight starting in 1974 (Struening et al. 1990; Wallace 1990a,b). Community instability was especially salient—population loss was strongly associated with increases in infant mortality, above and beyond what was expected based on migration patterns alone (Wallace and Wallace 1990; Wallace 1990a). Even in the most extreme poverty areas where minorities were concentrated, rates of low birthweight were directly proportional to the loss of housing and community devastation associated with forced migration and the general population collapse of the South Bronx in the mid- to late 1970s (e.g., from reduction in municipal services, arson, and housing project construction). These results strongly imply that understanding rates of low birthweight "cannot be divorced from an understanding of the processes affecting the communities in which women of childbearing age are embedded" (Struening et al. 1990, 476–77).

In brief, what appears to be especially devastating for the health of children in low income communities is rapid population loss coupled with inadequate health care services. The provision of city municipal services in terms of public health—based on political decisions presumably made with little if any thought to crime—thus appears to be implicated in the social disintegration of poor communities. As Wallace and Wallace (1990) concluded after their detailed analysis of the "planned shrinkage" of New York City services in recent decades: "The consequences of withdrawing municipal services from poor neighborhoods, the resulting outbreaks of contagious urban decay and forced migration which shred essential social networks and cause social disintegration, have become a highly significant contributor to decline in public health among the poor" (1990, 427). They go on to describe how the loss of social integration and networks from planned shrinkage increases behavioral patterns of violence which themselves become "convoluted with processes of urban decay likely to further disrupt social networks and cause further social disintegration" (1990, 427). This pattern of destabilizing feedback underscores the role of governmental policies toward local communities in fostering the downward spiral of high crime areas.

On the positive side, a recent evaluation by the National Academy of Sciences (1981) suggests that infant mortality rates can be reduced significantly with community interventions. This same study also found that community programs "significantly reduce the incidence of premature, repeated teenage pregnancy, the number who conceive after 35, and the number of families with more than four children" (National Academy of Science 1981, 58). The significant reductions in infant mortality and low birthweight associated with community interventions to increase the accessibility and quality of health services tends to undermine the notion that health care utilization is explained only by individual-level motivation (see also Olds 1980). Similarly, Wallace and Wallace (1990, 417–18) provide evidence that governmental community intervention helped to reduce the infant mortality rate in New York from 1966 to 1973. Child health, it seems, is related to the failure of institutional structures needed to link pregnant mothers with support systems.

A related dimension of community pertains to the informal protective factors that stable communities and intact social networks appear to provide to mothers coping with young children. Wallace (1990a,b) identifies at least three: (1) knowledge of or linkage to prenatal clinics, and encouragement to follow clinic recommendations, (2) general social support known to be positively related to personal health, and (3) social support to limit such high risk maternal behavior as smoking, drinking, or other substance use during pregnancy. This last point is related to the literature noted earlier on variation in community tolerance of deviant behavior. Although hard evidence is sparse, it seems reasonable to argue that community value systems are salient influences on mothers' drug use during pregnancy. In this sense, community culture may be seen as playing a role in promoting or inhibiting behavioral tendencies crucial to healthy and successful childbearing. I believe this may be one the most important but overlooked aspects of recent increases in drug use among pregnant inner-city young women.

In a similar vein Osofsky (1990) reports that informal social supports play a crucial role in understanding early childbearing among lower-income girls. Comparing pregnant and nonpregnant girls matched on key individual-level factors, she found "striking differences" in the degree of stability and support in their lives. The pregnant teenagers compared with the nonpregnant teens experienced considerable residential instability, and the nonpregnant teenagers reported a greater network of support in the area of providing advice, positive feedback, physical assistance, and social participation (1990, 2). Again, this notion integrates well with the idea stemming from social disorganization theory that the impact of communities is found primarily in the factors that facilitate or inhibit networks of social support. As Bronfenbrenner et al. (1984,

320) argue based on an exhaustive review of the literature on community effects: "A key factor determining [health care] accessibility is the existence of social networks that connect families and individuals with the main sources of material and social assistance."

A final link between community structure and child development comes in the form of child maltreatment. More specifically, child abuse is a major stress in childhood development, and its etiology can be traced in part to variations in community structure. Probably the best known work in this area stems from a body of research conducted by Garbarino on the connections between community ecology and parent-child interactions underlying child maltreatment. In an early study Garbarino (1976) established strong correlations at the county level relating socioeconomic and demographic sources of maternal stress to rates of child abuse. In a second study of twenty subareas and ninety-three census tracts *within* a city, Garbarino and Crouter (1978) found that poverty, residential mobility, and single-parent households accounted for over 50 percent of the variation in rates of child abuse.

Drawing on these insights, Garbarino and Sherman (1980) conducted a more fine-grained study of two neighborhoods matched on socioeconomic level and demographic composition but that varied dramatically in rates of child maltreatment. Going beyond census data, interviews were conducted with key informants (e.g., school teachers, mail carriers) and detailed neighborhood profiles were constructed. Samples of families were then drawn from each area, and interviews conducted to examine sources of stress, informal social networks, family support, and neighborhood support systems. Their findings validate a concept of neighborhood risk factors for abuse, regardless of socioeconomic position and other individual-level compositional factors. Namely, even though high-risk families may drift toward high-risk neighborhoods (a compositional effect), neighborhood characteristics directly influence family functioning (Garbarino and Sherman 1980, 196). In the context of child abuse, families in high-risk areas were exposed to what was termed "social impoverishment" and weak systems of social support (1980, 180). In other words, regardless of their predispositions, mothers in high-risk areas characterized by social isolation, sparse networks, and weak social supports are more apt to abuse their children than mothers in low-risk areas.

Individual motivations notwithstanding, the overall evidence points to a substantial link between community structure and the health of young children. As Bronfenbrenner et al. argue, "Health care is the sine qua non of adult and child development, and yet access to the health care system, even health itself, is contingent on the community in which one lives" (1984, 299). The relevance of this fact for criminology is potentially profound when one considers the impact of prenatal care, maltreatment, and general child health on cognitive development, social skills, peer and familial attachment, and later achievements in the school system and occupational sector (see also Garbarino 1977). In this sense, the adoption of a developmental perspective allows us to move beyond the simplistic notion often advanced by sociological theories that the causes of juvenile delinquency—whether poor scholastic achievement, social disability, or low self control—are somehow "exogenous" factors. Indeed, it has long been known that low birthweight and other indicators of impaired child development are predictive of the later developmental problems among youth and adults that are then used as explanations of crime (Wallace and Wallace 1990; Tonry, Ohlin, and Farrington 1990). Moreover, extant data suggest that child neglect and abuse are strong risk factors for long-term patterns of violence among adults (Widom 1989). What seems less appreciated is the linkage between these health-related aspects of child development and community context. When considered jointly and integrated as above, the literatures on child development and social disorganization suggest that the nexus of child abuse, infant mortality, low birthweight, and other child health problems is engendered by structural and cultural community disorganization, which in turn constitutes a major risk factor for later crime and delinquency.

Families, Social Capital, and Community

Having explicated the role of health-related aspects of child development, I now turn to another dimension of community risk that focuses more directly on the social processes of family management. The importance of family management practices in the understanding of crime and delinquency has been well established. Based on a recent meta-analysis of existing research, Loeber and Stouthamer-Loeber (1986, 29) found that socialization variables, such as lack of parental supervision, parental rejection, and parent-child involvement, were among the most powerful predictors of delinquency. Similarly, Hirschi (1983) and Patterson (1982) describe a set of parenting skills that revolve around the monitoring and supervision of youth behavior, consistent punishment, and the formation of close social bonds among parents and children. These three dimensions of family management—discipline, supervision/monitoring, and attachment—appear to be consistently related to delinquency according to existing research (see also McCord 1979; Laub and Sampson 1988; Gottfredson and Hirschi 1990).

However, when considering the role of families and crime, criminologists generally proceed like developmental theorists in viewing childrearing as a dyadic or mostly interpersonal activity that takes place within individual families or "under the roof" (Glueck and Glueck 1950). Although this viewpoint is certainly not wrong, it is incomplete and ignores the fact that parenting styles are an adaptation to considerations outside the household, especially the social organization of the community (Furstenberg 1990, 2). Exactly how parents perceive and manage their children's involvement in the world outside the household is a fascinating topic that has not received much research attention. This is unfortunate, for as Furstenberg notes, family management strategies tied to the community may be no less consequential for children's development than the more direct, proximate controls observed inside the home (1990, 3). Therefore, in this section I shall try to highlight what a community perspective has to offer criminology in regard to what is usually treated as a purely individualistic fact—childrearing.

I begin by introducing the concept of *social capital*. As Coleman (1990, 302) argues, the distinguishing feature of social capital lies in the structure of relations between persons and among persons. Social capital is created when the relations among persons change in ways that facilitate action. In other words, "social capital is productive, making possible the achievements of certain ends that in its absence would not be possible" (Coleman 1988, 98). By contrast, physical capital is wholly tangible, being embodied in observable material form (1990, 304), and human capital is embodied in the skills and knowledge acquired by an individual. Social capital is even less tangible, for it is embodied in the relations among persons (1990, 304). The core idea, then, is that independent of the forms of physical and human capital available to families (e.g., income), social capital is a central factor in facilitating effective family management.

Coleman's notion of social capital can be linked with social disorganization theory in a straightforward manner—lack of social capital is one of the primary features of socially disorganized communities as defined earlier (see also Coleman, 1990, 307). The theoretical task is to identify the characteristics of communities that facilitate social capital available to families and children. One of the most important factors according to Coleman (1990, 318–20) is the closure (i.e., connectedness) of social networks among families and children in a community. In a system involving parents and children, communities characterized by an extensive set of obligations, expectations, and social networks connecting the adults are better able to facilitate the control and supervision of children. This notion helps to understand parent-child relations that are not just "under-the-roof." For example, when closure is present through the relationship of a child to two adults whose relationship transcends the household (e.g., friendship, work-related acquaintanceship, etc.), the adults have the potential to "observe the child's actions in different circumstances, talk to each other about the child, compare notes, and establish norms" (593). This form of relation can also provide reinforcement for disciplining the child, as found when parents in communities with dense social networks and high stability assume responsibility for the supervision of youth that are not their own (Coleman 1990, 320; Sampson and Groves 1989).

The point here is that the closure of the network can provide the child with norms and sanctions that could not be brought about by a single adult alone, or even married-couple families in isolation. Moreover, the mere presence of a relationship among adults is not sufficient to produce social capital, and hence the idea of social capital goes beyond the notion of density of acquaintanceship (Sampson and Groves 1989; Sampson 1988, 1991). According to the theory, intergenerational closure—that is, cross-generational links among parents and children that are themselves tied to the parents or guardians of childhood friends in a community—proves most effective in the case of norms and supervision imposed on children. A simple example is where the parents' friends are the parents of their children's friends. By contrast, a parent who has many friends—even within the community—is constrained in the amount of social capital that can be drawn upon if the friends do not include parents or relatives of his/her own children's friends. One can extend this model to closure among networks involving parents and teachers, local religious and recreational leaders, businesses that serve youth, the police, and so on. Using mathematical models and computer simulation, Coleman (1990, 318–19) calculates the relative advantages and disadvantages faced by parents in communities with and without intergenerational closure among networks. By assuming that all obligations are balanced and all interests are equal, parents in communities without closure are shown to have less power relative to their children than parents in the community with closure. As predicted by the theory, the deficiency is due to lack of relation among parents (Coleman 1990, 319).

The ideas developed at this juncture suggest that the quantity of social capital available to families depends in large part on the stability of local communities and the closure of social networks connecting adults and children. It should be apparent that this conceptualization is congruent with the emphasis in social disorganization theory on the structural characteristics—for example, residential instability, heterogeneity, density of friendship networks—that facilitate or inhibit community social organization. Perhaps more important, the theory is consistent with the empirical data available. As noted earlier, poverty and ethnic heterogeneity have been shown to predict mediating dimensions of social organization such as social participation and supervision of teenage peer groups, which in turn predict variations in crime and delinquency (Taylor et al. 1984; Sampson and Groves 1989). Moreover, research has established that community residential stability is the primary determinant of the density of friend/acquaintanceship networks, which accounts for both increased levels of community social cohesion and reduced levels of crime and delinquency (Sampson 1988; Sampson and Groves 1989; Sampson 1991).

Family Disruption

Coleman's theoretical framework combined with social disorganization theory also helps to bring into sharper focus the effects of community family structure on crime. It is fairly well established in individual-level research that broken homes per se do not have much influence on delinquency (Gottfredson and Hirschi 1990). However, the structure of family relationships in a community may have important contextual influences. For example, elsewhere I have hypothesized that, all else equal, high levels of family "disruption" (e.g., divorce rates; single-parent families with children) facilitate crime by decreasing community networks of informal social control. Examples of informal social control include neighbors taking note of and/or questioning strangers, watching over each others' property, assuming responsibility for supervision of youth activities, and intervening in local disturbances (Sampson and Groves 1989; Taylor et al. 1984). This conceptualization is similar to Coleman's idea of social capital (i.e., facilitation of action such as supervision) and does *not* necessarily assume that it is the children of divorced or separated parents that are engaging in crime. Rather, I suggest that youth in stable family areas, regardless of their own family situation, have more controls placed on their leisure-time activities, particularly with peer groups (see also Sullivan 1989, 178; Anderson 1990, 91). A well-documented finding is that delinquency is a group phenomenon, and hence neighborhood family disruption is likely to be important in determining the extent to which neighborhood youth are provided the opportunities to form a peer-control system free of the supervision or knowledge of adults (Reiss 1986a). The ratio of married adults to children in a community is another indicator of the extent to which parents have the power to exert control over children and youth (Coleman 1990, 596).

The empirical support for this theoretical idea is not extensive but it does seem to be fairly consistent. As reviewed by Sampson and Lauritsen (1991), several recent studies report a large and positive relationship between family disruption (usually percent female-headed families or divorce rate) and rates of crime. What is especially striking is the strength of family disruption in predicting crime in multivariate models. For example, Sampson (1985) found that rates of victimization were two to three times higher among residents of neighborhoods with high levels of family disruption compared to low levels, regardless of alternative predictors of victimization such as percent black and poverty. In fact, the percentage of families with female heads helped to explain in large part the relationship between percent black and crime. Namely, percent black and percent female-headed families are positively and significantly related; however, when percent female-headed families is controlled, percent black is not significantly related to violent victimization (1985, 27). Similarly, Smith and Jarjoura (1988) report that family structure, especially percent single-parent families, helps account for the association between race and violent crime at the community level: racial composition was not significantly related to violent crime in multivariate models once percent single-parent families was included.

Furthermore, Sampson (1987) examined racially disaggregated rates of homicide and robbery by juveniles and adults in over 150 U.S. cities in 1980. Despite a tremendous difference in mean levels of family disruption among black and white communities, the percentage of female-headed families had a large positive effect on juvenile violence for both races. In fact, the predictors of white robbery were shown to be in large part identical in sign and magnitude to those for blacks. The effect of family disruption on crime thus appears to be independent of commonly cited sociodemographic explanations (e.g., race, poverty, region, urbanization, age), and cannot be attributed to unique cultural factors within the black community. The finding that family disruption had stronger effects on juvenile violence than on adult violence, in conjunction with the inconsistent findings of previous research on individual-level delinquency and broken homes, tends to further support the idea that the consequences of family structure are related to macro-level patterns of social control and guardianship, especially regarding youth and their peers. This idea is given added support by the finding noted earlier that unsupervised peer groups mediate the effect of community-level variation in family disruption on crime (Sampson and Groves 1989).

Family Management and Social Capital

Further evidence supporting an integration of social disorganization theory with a focus on families and social capital is provided in a recent study by Furstenberg (1990) of family management practices in inner-city neighborhoods of Philadelphia. The comparative ethnographic research process used by Furstenberg can be described as one of "focused fieldwork" (1990, 4): extended open-ended interviews with parents and teenagers residing in distinct communities that, although all poor, varied in levels of social organization. Space limitations preclude detailed description, but his findings serve to illustrate and extend the major contentions of this paper.

One of the communities studied by Furstenberg was a black housing project area in North Philadelphia. Besides structural characteristics such as poverty, transiency, and a high rate of single-parent households, a key feature of this community was that parents generally did not know one another and/or others' children. There was a high level of mistrust among neighbors, and consequently parents had to resort to a highly individualistic style of parental management where enormous personal time was devoted to monitoring, supervising, and controlling youth behavior (1990, 9). That is, precisely because of the anonymity and lack of intergenerational social networks to draw upon, parents were forced to fall back on strictly personal resources to manage family life in a dangerous environment. But social isolation is costly, for as Furstenberg argues, parents seemed unable to band together to solve common problems. Mistrust and separation were so bad that a favorite strategy for controlling children was negative comparisons—pointing out the improper behavior of their neighbors as a means of reinforcing family values. The daughter of one of the mothers interviewed was so convinced of her dissimilarity from her neighbors that she did not tell her closest friends at school where she lived and refused to bring friends home to the projects (1990, 10). Other mothers complained of their inability to distinguish neighborhood youth from strangers, and they bemoaned the alienated sense in which local parents ignored the open misbehavior of youth in the community.

Although preliminary and as yet not replicated in other settings, Furstenberg's research clearly supports the idea that the lack of social capital among adults and children is an important component of ineffective child rearing and problematic child development. Whether highly skilled as a parent or not, residents of the North

Philadelphia neighborhood were inclined to adopt an individualistic style of parental management. Families for the most part isolated themselves and their children from the surrounding community, and were not part of neighborhood institutions. They distrusted the local schools, regarded local services suspiciously, and, to the extent they used supportive services at all, they took their business outside the community (Furstenberg 1990, 11). The family system was thus largely disconnected from the community, and parents were left to "manage on their own" (1990, 14). The result was not only that children suffered greater risks associated with attenuated supervision and monitoring, but they also missed out on positive opportunities to be connected to the wider society through job, school, and friendship ties. This concept of individualistic strategies is similar to Wilson's (1987) notion of the social isolation prevalent in areas of concentrated urban poverty and racial segregation.

In contrast to the projects was a white, poor neighborhood in South Philadelphia labeled "Garrison Heights." There Furstenberg found the same range of parenting skills as in the projects. What differed was the form of social networks *among* families—even those with poor parenting skills. As such, despite similar individual-level backgrounds (e.g., poverty, family structure), the white youth in South Philadelphia faced quite different structural constraints than the black youth of the North Philadelphia projects. Consider Furstenberg's observational findings.

Heighter parents participated in a system that promotes shared parental responsibility through delegation of control and sponsorship to both formal agencies and informal networks. The availability of resources, the relatively high degree of normative consensus, and strong social bonds forged by kinship and friendship all contribute to a close connection between local institutions and the family. . . .Youth cannot easily escape the scrutiny of neighborhood, schools, and families when these agencies are so connected. The high degree of observability keeps youth in check. The task of parents inside the home is reinforced by the support rendered by other parents outside the home. It is for this reason that parenting in Garrison Heights must be viewed as a *collective* activity, a style that contrasts to the individualistic mode of family management forced upon parents in more anomic neighborhoods. (Furstenberg, 1990: 20, emphasis added)

The well-developed institutional resources and the extensive social networks in Garrison Heights created a supply of adults who assumed responsibility for the supervision of youth in the community. As one field worker described it, "The street life here, the unbelievable density of people on the streets in the evenings is strikingly reminiscent of a time gone by" (1990, 17).[3] Quantities of social capital available to families and children thus appear to be directly related to differential levels of community social organization.

The density and intergenerational closure of social networks in Garrison Heights made it possible for children in the community to be socialized not just by parents, but friends, relatives, and neighbors as well. This fact was essential for families with problems in the daily management and supervision of their children. For example, the detailed description of "Meg" and her family is quite telling, as we find that despite her "marginal" and probably even poor skills as a parent (Furstenberg 1990, 18), Meg was enmeshed in a wider network of friends, kin, and neighbors that spanned across generations. In fact, all of the families observed in the Garrison Heights section had at least one grandparent living within walking distance, and all had other siblings nearby (1990, 15). Family reputations were established and well known even to those with no apparent connection to the family in question. Meg, who not only was inconsistent as a mother in her discipline and supervision, had a son with behavioral and academic problems. Yet when her son committed a minor act of vandalism, Meg quickly heard about it through her priest who had in turn been contacted by the principal of the school for advice on the best way to handle the situation.

The foregoing is a striking example of the extent to which even marginal families are held afloat in areas of dense social networks and available social capital. Consequently, even children without the benefit of skilled and knowledgeable parents (i.e., human capital) and material resources (i.e., physical capital) may have other sources of community support—especially social capital—to draw upon so as not to fall through the cracks as was common in the North Philadelphia neighborhood that lacked all dimensions of capital. Parenting therefore appears to be more than the individualistic process that contemporary society makes it out to be, where we give all the credit to parents with good children, and we locate the full blame on parents whose children falter.

Summary and Conclusion

At the risk of oversimplification, I believe it is accurate to say that theories of communities and crime ignore child development, and that theories of child development ignore community ecology. For example, the dominant perspectives on community emphasize structural characteristics thought to influence motivation to crime (e.g., economic deprivation, inequality, subculture) and the control of juvenile gangs (see Byrne and Sampson 1986). Aspects of child development such as prenatal care, low birthweight babies, child abuse, and the daily monitoring and supervision of children are usually ignored. On the other hand, those who study child development usually neglect community context and focus instead on individual families "under the roof." In this paper I have attempted to counteract these limitations by linking a theory of social disorganization and social capital with theoretical concerns of family management and child development. The motivation was the empirical fact noted at the outset of this paper: the close connection, even in poverty areas, between indicators of child health and rates of crime.

The fact turns out to be perfectly predictable from the vantage point of social disorganization theory. As implied by Shaw and McKay's discovery many years ago, the essence of social disorganization theory is the inability of a community structure to realize the common values of its residents and maintain effective social controls (Kornhauser 1978, 120; Bursik 1988; Sampson and Groves 1989). More specifically, the theory focuses on the community-level structural determinants of the inability of communities to achieve social organization, especially residential mobility and population turnover, family disruption, housing/population density, poverty/ resource deprivation, inadequate health care resources, and the ecological concentration of the urban underclass (see also Sampson and Lauritsen 1991).

The mediating dimensions of social disorganization can in turn be conceptualized in both structural and cultural terms. In this paper I have emphasized mainly the structural components relating to social networks and social capital, but the cultural dimensions (e.g., neighborhood norms, community tolerance of drug use by pregnant women) are potentially just as powerful. In any case, the extension of social disorganization theory I propose helps to explain how mediating constructs—such as institutional-family connectedness; the observability, monitoring, and supervision of youth; intergenerational closure among adult-child networks; control of street-corner peer groups; local organizational participation; mutual social support and extensiveness of social networks; perceived normative consensus on parenting, social trust—directly and indirectly influence the care of children, and ultimately rates of delinquency and crime. In this integrated theory child rearing is treated as a complex phenomenon that has not only individual components but contextual ones as well. Indeed, the main component I have highlighted is the *social capital* generated in areas of social organization. Here not only the health-related aspects of early child development become important (e.g., low birthweight, child abuse, prenatal care, adequate day care) but the viability and effectiveness of family management practices in general—regardless of personal characteristics. Hence the embeddedness of families and children in community context is a central feature of the theory.

Before concluding a caveat is in order. My purpose in this paper was to provide new theoretical insights and suggestions for further development and empirical testing of social disorganization theory. As such, the review of the literature was highly focused and I did not address the problems associated with research on community effects. There is no doubt that numerous problems plague criminological research on the causal status of community characteristics. Among other limitations, the use of varying and sometimes highly aggregated units of analysis, potentially biased sources of information on crime, widely varying analytical techniques, high correlations among independent variables, potential selection (e.g., compositional) effects, and reciprocal effects from crime itself, all undermine our ability to make definitive statements about the role of communities in understanding crime (for a recent overview see Sampson and Lauritsen 1991). Moreover, the literature on child development is vast and complex, and my presentation was biased toward those studies that incorporated a community-level perspective.

Nevertheless, it is important to bear in mind that these research limitations are no worse than those found in individual-level research. The difference, I would argue, is that individual-research is usually accepted more at face value. Consider the issue of self-selection and compositional effects (or cross-level misspecification). Often ignored is the "individualistic fallacy"—the often-invoked assumption that individual-level casual relations necessarily generate individual-level correlations. The fact of the matter is that research conducted at the individual-level rarely questions whether obtained results might be spurious and confounded with community-level processes. A good example might be seen in the case of race, one of the most important individual-level correlates of violence (Sampson and Lauritsen 1991). It is commonplace to search for individual-level explanations for the race-violence linkage (including the ubiquitous reference to social class differences). But the thesis outlined earlier suggests possible *contextual* sources of the race-violence link among individuals. Although approximately 70 percent of all poor whites lived in nonpoverty areas in the five largest U.S. central cities in 1980, only 15 percent of poor blacks did. Moreover, whereas only 7 percent of poor whites lived in extreme poverty areas, almost 40 percent of poor blacks lived in such areas (Wilson 1987, 58). And potentially even more important, the majority of poor blacks live in communities characterized by high rates of family disruption; by contrast, poor whites—even those from "broken homes"—live in areas of relative family stability (Sampson 1987; Sullivan 1989, 230).

The consequences of these differential ecological distributions by race raise the substantively plausible hypothesis that individual-level correlations by race (and also class) may be systematically confounded with important differences in community contexts. As Wilson argues,

simple comparisons between poor whites and poor blacks would be confounded with the fact that poor whites reside in areas which are ecologically and economically very different from poor blacks. Any observed relationships involving race would reflect, to some unknown degree, the relatively superior ecological niche many poor whites occupy with respect to jobs, marriage opportunities, and exposure to conventional role models. (1987, 58–60)

Regardless of a black's individual-level, family, or economic situation, the average community of residence differs dramatically from that of a similarly situated white (Sampson 1987; Anderson 1990). Therefore, the relationship between race and crime may be largely accounted for by community context (e.g., segregation, concentration of family disruption, and joblessness; social isolation; sparse social networks; normative ecologies of violence). Or, in the theoretical language expressed in this paper, black families, regardless of individual and familial background, have less social capital than white families in terms of child development and family management. This certainly appeared to be the case for the two families studied by Furstenberg (1990)—one a white single-parent family in a socially organized community and the other a black single-parent family in a socially disorganized community.

Race and family structure are but two of the many areas where it may pay to rethink individual-level correlates of crime from the lens of a community-level conceptualization. In particular, it would seem that social disorganization theory holds great promise as a generator of ideas in the advancement of criminological theory.

I would like to thank the editor, Joan McCord, for very helpful comments on an earlier draft.

Notes

1. See also the arguments of Wilson and Kelling (1982) and Skogan (1986) regarding how neighborhood "incivilities" and signs of disorder (e.g., broken windows, prostitution, rowdy youth, public drinking, graffiti, etc.) lead to perceptions of social disorder, thereby encouraging a downward spiral of further crime and disorder. In particular, potential offenders may recognize signs of disorder and "assume that residents are so indifferent to what goes on in their neighborhood that they will not be motivated to confront strangers, intervene in a crime, or call the police" (Greenberg et al. 1985, 82).
2. To be sure, criminology has prominent cultural explanations of crime, especially regarding lower-class culture and the subculture of violence.

The most influential continues to be the subculture of violence theory (Wolfgang and Ferracuti 1967). The basic tenent of subcultural theory is that the overt use of violence "is generally viewed as a reflection of basic values that stand apart from the dominant, central, or parent culture" (1967, 385). However, neither the theory of lower-class culture nor subculture of violence refer explicitly to community-level processes of the sort explicated herein.

3. In this regard it is interesting to note that while we continue to hear from scholars that local communities are unimportant in mass society (for a discussion see Sampson 1988), communities continue to appear salient among residents themselves—even in major urban environments.

References

Anderson, E. 1978. *A Place on the Corner*. Chicago: University of Chicago Press.

———. 1990. *Streetwise: Race, Class, and Change in an Urban Community*. Chicago: University of Chicago Press.

Bott, E. 1957. *Family and Social Network: Roles, Norms, and External Relationships in Ordinary Urban Families*. London: Tavistock.

Bronfenbrenner, U., P. Moen, and J. Garbarino. 1984. "Child, Family, and Community." In *Review of Child Development Research, Volume 7: The Family*, edited by R. Parke, 283–328. Chicago: University of Chicago Press.

Bursik, R. J. Jr. 1988. Social Disorganization and Theories of Crime and Delinquency: Problems and Prospects." *Criminology* 26:519–52.

Byrne, J. and R. J. Sampson. 1986. "Key Issues in the Social Ecology of Crime." In *The Social Ecology of Crime*, edited by J. Byrne and R. J. Sampson, 1–22. New York: Springer-Verlag, Inc.

Coleman, J. S. 1988. "Social Capital in the Creation of Human Capital." *American Journal of Sociology* 94: S95–S120.

———. 1990. *Foundations of Social Theory*. Cambridge: Harvard Univ. Press.

Furstenberg, F. 1990. "How Families Manage Risk and Opportunity in Dangerous Neighborhoods." Paper presented at the 84th annual meeting of the American Sociological Association, Washington, D.C., August.

Garbarino, J. 1976. "A preliminary Study of Some Ecological Correlates of Child Abuse: The Impact of Socioeconomic Stress on Mothers." *Child Development* 47: 178–85.

———. 1977. "The Human Ecology of Child Maltreatment: A Conceptual

Model for Research." *Journal of Marriage and the Family* November: 721–35.

———. and A. Crouter. 1978. "Defining the Community Context for Parent-Child Relations: The Correlates of Child Maltreatment." *Child Development* 49: 604–16.

———. and D. Sherman. 1980. "High-Risk Neighborhoods and High-Risk Families: The Human Ecology of Child Maltreatment." *Child Development* 51: 188–98.

Glueck, S. and E. Glueck. 1950. *Unraveling Juvenile Delinquency.* New York: Commonwealth Fund.

Greenberg, Stephanie, William Rohe, and Jay Williams. 1985. *Informal Citizen Action and Crime Prevention at the Neighborhood Level: Synthesis and Assessment of the Research.* Washington, D.C.: Government Printing Office.

Gottfredson, M. and T. Hirschi. 1990. *A General Theory of Crime.* Stanford, CA: Stanford University Press.

Hirschi, T. 1983. "Crime and the Family." In *Crime and Public Policy,* edited by J. Q. Wilson. San Francisco: Institute for Contemporary Studies.

Horowitz, R. 1987. "Community Tolerance of Gang Violence." *Social Problems* 34: 437–50.

Kasarda, J. and M. Janowitz. 1974. "Community Attachment in Mass Society." *American Sociological Review* 39: 328–39.

Kornhauser, R. 1978. *Social Sources of Delinquency.* Chicago: University of Chicago Press.

Lash, T., H. Sigal, and D. Dudzinski. 1980. *State of the Child: New York City, II.* New York: Foundation for Child Development.

Laub, J. and R. Sampson. 1988. "Unraveling Families and Delinquency: A Reanalysis of the Gluecks' Data." *Criminology* 26: 355–80.

Leighton, B. 1988. "The Community Concept in Criminology: Toward a Social Network Approach. *Journal of Research in Crime and Delinquency* 25: 351–74.

Liebow, E. 1967. *Tally's Corner.* Boston: Little, Brown.

Loeber, R. and M. Stouthamer-Loeber. 1986. "Family Factors as Correlates and Predictors of Juvenile Conduct Problems and Delinquency." In *Crime and Justice: An Annual Review of Research* (vol. 7), edited by M. Tonry and N. Morris. Chicago: University of Chicago Press.

Maccoby, E., J. Johnson, and R. Church. 1958. "Community Integration and the Social Control of Juvenile Delinquency." *Journal of Social Issues* 14:38–51.

McCord, J. 1979. "Some Child-Rearing Antecedents of Criminal Behavior in Adult Men." *Journal of Personality and Social Psychology* 9: 1477–86.

National Academy of Sciences. 1981. *Toward a National Policy for Children and Families*. Washington, D.C.: Government Printing Office.

Olds, D. 1980. "Improving Formal Services for Mothers and Children." In *Protecting Children from Abuse and Neglect*, edited by J. Garbarino and S. Stocking. San Francisco: Jossey-Bass.

Osofsky, J. 1990. "Gender Issues in the Development of Deviant Behavior: The Case for Teenage Pregnancy." Paper presented at the "Workshop on Gender Issues in the Development of Deviant Behavior." Program on Human Development and Criminal Behavior, Radcliffe College, June 1990.

Patterson, G. 1982. *Coercive Family Process*. Eugene, Oregon: Castalia.

Rainwater, L. 1970. *Behind Ghetto Walls: Black Families in a Federal Slum*. Chicago: Aldine.

Reiss, A. J., Jr. 1986a. "Why are Communities Important in Understanding Crime?" In *Communities and Crime*, edited by A. J. Reiss, Jr. and M. Tonry 1–33. Chicago: University of Chicago Press.

———. 1986b. "Co-Offender Influences on Criminal Careers." In *Criminal Careers and "Career Criminals,"* edited by A. Blumstein, J. Cohen, J. Roth, and C. Visher, 121–60. Washington, D.C.: National Academy Press.

Sampson, R. J. 1985. "Neighborhood and Crime: The Structural Determinants of Personal Victimization." *Journal of Research in Crime and Deliquency* 22:7–40.

———. 1987. "Urban Black Violence: The Effect of Male Joblessness and Family Disruption." *American Journal of Sociology* 93:348–82.

———. 1988. "Community Attachment in Mass Society: A Multilevel Systemic Model." *American Sociological Review* 53: 766–69.

———. 1991. "Linking the Micro and Macro Level Dimensions of Community Social Organization." *Social Forces*, forthcoming.

Sampson, R. J. and W. B. Groves. 1989. "Community Structure and Crime: Testing Social-Disorganization Theory." *American Journal of Sociology* 94: 774–802.

Sampson, R. J. and J. Lauritsen. 1991. "Violent Victimization and Offending: Individual, Situational, and Community-Level Risk Factors." In *The Understanding and Control of Violent Behavior*, edited by A. J. Reiss, Jr., D. Farrington, and J. Roth. Washington, D.C.: National Academy of Sciences Press, forthcoming.

Shaw, C. and H. McKay. 1942. *Juvenile Delinquency and Urban Areas*. Chicago: University of Chicago Press.

———. 1969. *Juvenile Delinquency and Urban Areas* (Revised Edition). Chicago: University of Chicago Press.

Short, J. F. Jr. 1963. Introduction to the abridged edition. In *The Gang: A*

Study of 1,313 Gangs in Chicago, edited by F. Thrasher, xv–liii. Chicago: University of Chicago Press.

————. 1985. "The Level of Explanation Problem in Criminology." In *Theoretical Methods in Criminology,* edited by R. F. Meier, 51–74. Beverly Hills, CA: Sage.

Short, J. F. and F. Strodtbeck. 1965. *Group Process and Gang Delinquency.* Chicago: University of Chicago Press.

Simcha-Fagan, O., and J. Schwartz, 1986. "Neighborhood and Delinquency: An Assessment of Contextual Effects." *Criminology* 24: 667–704.

Skogan, W. 1986. "Fear of Crime and Neighborhood Change." In *Communities and Crime,* edited by A. J. Reiss, Jr. and M. Tonry, 203–29. Chicago: University of Chicago Press.

Smith, D. R. and G. R. Jarjoura. 1988. "Social Structure and Criminal Victimization." *Journal of Research in Crime and Delinquency* 25: 27–52.

Struening, E., R. Wallace, and R. Moore. 1990. "Housing Conditions and the Quality of Children at Birth." *Bulletin of the New York Academy of Medicine* 66: 463–78.

Sullivan, M. 1989. *Getting Paid: Youth Crime and Work in the Inner City.* Ithaca, N.Y.: Cornell University Press.

Suttles, G. 1968. *The Social Order of the Slum.* Chicago: University of Chicago Press.

Taylor, R., S. Gottfredson, and S. Brower, 1984. "Block Crime and Fear: Defensible Space, Local Social Ties, and Territorial Functioning." *Journal of Research in Crime and Delinquency* 21: 303–31.

Thrasher, F. 1963. *The Gang: A Study of 1,313 Gangs in Chicago* (Revised Edition). Chicago: University of Chicago Press.

Tonry, M., L. E. Ohlin, and D. P. Farrington with K. Adams, F. Earls, D. C. Rowe, R. J. Sampson, and R. E. Tremblay. 1990. *Human Development and Criminal Behavior: New Ways of Advancing Knowledge.* New York: Springer-Verlag.

Wallace, R. and D. Wallace. 1990. "Origins of Public Health Collapse in New York City: The Dynamics of Planned Shrinkage, Contagious Urban Decay and Social Disintegration." *Bulletin of the New York Academy of Medicine* 66: 391–434.

Wallace, R. 1990a. "Urban Desertification, Public Health and Public Order: 'Planned Shrinkage,' Violent Death, Substance Abuse and AIDS in the Bronx," *Social Science and Medicine,* 31: 801–13.

————. 1990b. " 'Planned Shrinkage,' Contagious Urban Decay and Violent Death in the Bronx: The Implications of Synergism." *Journal of Quantitative Criminology,* submitted for publication.

Widom, C. 1989. "The Cycle of Violence." *Science* 244: 160–66.

Wilson, J. Q. and G. Kelling. 1982. "Broken Windows." *Atlantic* (March): 29–38.

Wilson, W. J. 1987. *The Truly Disadvantaged: The Inner City, the Underclass, and Public Policy*. Chicago: University of Chicago Press.

Wolfgang, M. and F. Ferracuti. 1967. *The Subculture of Violence*. London: Tavistock.

5

Taking Reasoning Seriously

Ellen S. Cohn and Susan O. White

In this chapter, we explore the long-standing theoretical debate over the relative validity of explanations based on environmental influences versus explanations based on factors internal to the individual. In a study of legal socialization, we tested competing hypotheses from social learning theory and legal development theory.[1] Our purpose was to predict changes in legal reasoning, attitudes toward rules and their enforcement, and rule-violating behaviors over time. By testing competing hypotheses we were able to determine which theory was the better predictor of these legal socialization effects (Cohn and White 1986, 1990).

A major finding that legal reasoning was a better predictor than environmental influence prompted us to investigate the relationship between reasoning and moral/legal action. By taking reasoning seriously in this context, we were led to explore the connection between reasoning and action through path analysis. How is reasoning related to action? Is it a motive, or a justification, or an excuse (Hamlin 1988; Hartung 1965; Sykes and Matza 1957)? Is the relationship direct or indirect? What role is played by norms of behavior and attitudes toward rule enforcement? Does cognitive developmentalism give an adequate account of the relationship between reasoning and action? Our empirical conclusions suggest a new theoretical perspective which takes account of the experiential framework through which actions are conceptualized and the moral/legal context in which such reasoning takes place.

Acquiring Legal Values and Norms: Two Paradigms

Legal socialization is the process by which individuals acquire a society's values and norms concerning rule-governed behavior and learn to respond to rules and rule enforcement (Cohn and White 1990). There are two major, and distinctly different, approaches to legal socialization in the literature. Each is based on a general theory of learning rather than a specific model of legal socialization. Social learning theory explains the acquisition of legal values and norms in terms of the influence of the social environment. By contrast, cognitive developmental theory explains legal learning in terms of developmental changes in cognitive structures. Each approach acknowledges the existence of the other and the significance of the other's central theoretical questions, but each then pursues its own set of questions.

Comparing social learning theory and cognitive developmental theory raises a fundamental question about human behavior: are we creatures of our environment or do we as individuals control our own actions? This is an empirical question with normative implications. It is particularly salient in the context of theories about legal socialization because the socialization process can be an instrument of social control—or the foundation for individual autonomy.

Social learning theory assumes that the influence of the social environment is primary.[2] This implies that a range of individual actions, from value choices to obeying or disobeying the law, are shaped by outside pressures. The conditions under which authority is exercised, and pressures from family, school, or peers, combine to control choices and create the individual actor, rather than the other way around. The cognitive developmental paradigm, on the other hand, posits a different relationship between person and environment. On this account, individuals adapt to their environment through a cognitive process. Social interaction plays an important part in the process by which cognitive structures appear and change, but the individual is an active participant. The implication is that individuals shape the environment to their use rather than being the products of environmental influence.

The purpose of these empirical theories is to explain human behavior, but the relative validity of explanations based on environmental influence versus explanations based on factors internal to the individual clearly has normative implications as well. For example, the validity of normative assumptions in democratic theory depends in part on whether or not the capacity for individual autonomy is empirically possible. In a context that includes norms and rules and the exercise of authority, is self-direction an illusion or an attainable objective? Do the forces of that social environment inevitably determine behavior or can individual choice prevail? A test of the relative importance of factors external and internal to the individual is a significant step for both explanatory and normative reasons. We chose, therefore, to conceptualize our study of legal socialization around a test of competing hypotheses drawn from the social learning paradigm and the cognitive developmental paradigm.

Comparing the Paradigms

Social learning theory has its conceptual roots in the radical behaviorism of Skinner (1938) and Hull (1943), who stressed the conditioning effects of the environment on human behavior. The original model, a simple S → R sequence, eventually gave way to a S → R → S sequence which is based on the powerful role of consequence in the feedback process and is more persuasively applicable to a social context. Control by consequences remains the most fundamental concept in social learning theory, but it is difficult to test in the complexity of a social environment. Akers' (1985) differential association-reinforcement theory postulates a feedback-based learning process that is controlled by external reinforcement contingencies, including group membership, normative definitions of complying and noncomplying behavior, social approval and disapproval, and punishment. The theory seems to imply that anyone can become a deviant, depending on whether one is exposed to a deviant social environment. Indeed, it might be called a theory of the "normality of deviance" (Cohn and White 1990). Although cognitive factors such as normative definitions are included, they function within a feedback process that renders them conceptually quite different from individual choice.

The cognitive developmental paradigm, by contrast, self-consciously asserts the possibility of autonomous individual choice. It has its conceptual roots in the work of Piaget (1926, 1932), who believed that human learning was a matter of conceptual development by stages that occurred in invariant sequence. Later theorists postulated three stages of moral or legal development which are defined in terms of the kinds of cognitive structures that dominate an individual's reasoning process at each stage. For example, preconventional reasoning is based on fear of punishment, conventional reasoning on maintaining "law and order," and postconventional reasoning on principles that transcend law (Levine and Tapp 1977; Tapp and Kohlberg 1977; Tapp and Levine 1974).[3]

Cognitive developmental theory postulates that humans learn by adaptation, molding themselves to their environment and shaping it to their use in an interactive relationship. The fundamental mechanism in the learning process is the cognitive structure which is a representation of the environment through which people receive and organize information. Incoming information is "assimilated" into an existing cognitive structure which in turn acts on the information in order to "accommodate" to changes signalled by the new information. The interaction between the individual and environmental stimuli is kept in balance by a process of "equilibration." In other words, cognitive structures are essential to any relationship between person and environment because they are the vehicle by which information about the environment becomes available to the individual as well as the instrument for adapting the individual to environmental change.

We now turn to the research design which allowed us to test competing hypotheses drawn from social learning theory and cognitive developmental theory in order to determine the relative weight of environmental influence and individual choice in the legal socialization process.

Testing Competing Hypotheses

In order to test competing hypotheses, we used a naturalistic setting with a clearly defined rule-governed environment that allowed us to measure attitudinal and behavioral responses to rule enforcement as well as legal development level over time (Cohn and White 1986, 1990). The setting was a university residential community. The research design included a quasi-experiment: two residence halls with contrasting styles of rule enforcement, and two control halls. Two populations were surveyed at the beginning of fall semester and near the end of spring semester: a random sample of entering freshmen across all (nonexperimental) residence halls, and a representative sample of all residents in the four experimental halls.

The variables measured in the survey were legal development type (types of legal reasoning), approval/disapproval of twenty-four rule-violating behaviors, approval/disapproval of enforcing rules against the same behaviors, and reported frequency of engaging in the behaviors. The behaviors, almost all of which violated state laws as well as university rules, ranged from cheating to vandalism and assault. We created the two experimental conditions by varying the level and consistency of rule enforcement in two residence halls that were similar in size and population. In one (the external authority condition), the hall staff and police strictly enforced all of the rules, including those prohibiting underage drinking, loud parties, drunkenness, and other "partying" behaviors. Violators were disciplined by university boards established by the dean of students. Some faced criminal charges. In the other hall (the peer authority condition), the rules were enforced solely by an internal conduct board composed of residents who were selected by the group for that purpose. Enforcement in the control halls was representative of the prevailing practice in the residential system, and consisted primarily of loose, discretionary application of rules mixed with occasional crackdowns.[4]

We used the quasi-experiment to test our competing hypotheses. We wanted to predict differences over time in legal socialization effects, specifically the attitudes (approval/disapproval) toward rule-violating behaviors and toward enforcing the rules against these behaviors, and the frequency of engaging in the behaviors. The question was: which is the better predictor of these legal socialization variables: social learning theory or cognitive developmental theory? Social learning theory predicts such differences depending on the socializing conditions, while cognitive developmental theory predicts differences depending on respondents' legal development type regardless of the socializing conditions. If the social learning hypothesis is correct, we would expect to find systematic differences in attitudes and behaviors over time based on whether the respondents lived in the external authority condition or the peer authority condition. If the cognitive developmental hypothesis is correct, we would expect to find these differences based only on respondents' legal development type. In order to test these competing hypotheses, we conducted multiple regression analyses in which we predicted the spring norms of behavior and rule enforcement (attitudes) and the frequency of spring rule-violating behaviors using fall legal development type (type of legal reasoning) and residence hall as predictor variables.

Our findings supported the cognitive developmental hypothesis.[5] Legal development type was the better predictor of attitudes toward rule-violating behaviors and toward enforcing the rules, although neither legal development type nor the social learning condition predicted the frequency of engaging in the behaviors. These findings indicate that legal reasoning is a significant factor in the process of socialization to rules. Since we are confident from other findings (Cohn and White 1990, ch. 4) that our experimental manipulation resulted in distinctly different and strong interventions, we can only conclude that legal reasoning can override the effects of the social environment. Given the overwhelming amount of attention paid to social conditions in the literature on deviant behavior, and the relatively little attention paid to reasoning in the same literature, this is a startling finding. It suggests that new thinking is needed in order to determine how cognitive development, and specifically the cognitive structures that underlie legal reasoning, fit into patterns of both deviant and compliant behavior.

Taking Reasoning Seriously

The fact that cognitive developmental theory predicted norms of behavior and rule enforcement, but not (directly) the rule-violating behaviors themselves, poses a critical question about the relevance of legal reasoning to deviant behavior. Further analysis of our data produced some interesting answers. Following a suggestion by Blasi (1980), who reviewed the literature on moral cognition and moral action, we set out to investigate how legal reasoning might be related to rule-governed behaviors. In his review, Blasi found some studies in which moral cognition was shown to be related to behaviors, but many studies could not demonstrate such a relationship. Surprised at the paucity of valid positive findings in the literature, Blasi concluded that the hypothesized relationship might exist only through the mediation of some other variable(s). He suggested that personality variables could play that mediating role.

Blasi's suggestion led us to consider the possibility of a mediating model in which the relationship between legal reasoning and rule-governed behaviors is mediated by the norms of behavior and rule enforcement that were predicted by our cognitive developmental variable. We thought it made more sense in the moral/legal context to hypothesize a mediating model based on situational norms than on personality variables.[6] We developed a measure of behavioral norms based on our respondents' approval/disapproval of twenty-four rule-violating behaviors, and a measure of norms of enforcement based on their approval/disapproval of enforcing rules against these same twenty-four behaviors. Using path analysis, we found that these norms did in fact mediate the relationship between legal reasoning and rule-governed behaviors.[7] There were some instances in which the data fit a direct model (i.e., a significant predictive path between reasoning and behavior directly), but most of the data fit a mediating model (i.e., where a significant predictive path between reasoning and behavior was found only when norms of behavior and enforcement were included).

Three sets of questions are generated by the success of the mediating model. First, given the fact that norms or attitudes are necessary to the model, what then is the nature of a cognitive structure and how is it related to particular situations? Can a cognitive structure be measured independently of an attitude, or is it simply a theoretical construct? Second, what is the direction of the causal path between reasoning (the cognitive structure) and the behaviors? Since cognitive developmentalism argues that cognitive structures are the source of the capacity for individual choice and autonomy, what is their causal relationship to behaviors? Third, if cognitive structures are related to behaviors, how are they different from intentions or motives for action?

First, a cognitive structure is a general, conceptual structure that allows one to categorize reality. It organizes information so that it is meaningful. It provides the conceptual framework for interpreting particular situations. In moral/legal reasoning, the cognitive structure may well be a principle or a set of criteria for evaluating right or wrong or the morality of an action. In other words, a cognitive structure leads one to interpret information about a social situation in a certain way, and in so doing it creates moral meaning. The standard measures of legal reasoning ask "what is a rule?," "what is a law?," "why should people follow rules?," "are there times when it might be right to break a rule?" By contrast, norms of behavior and rule enforcement are specific to situations. As measured in our study, they indicate approval or disapproval of specific rule-violating behaviors and of enforcing rules against these behaviors. The mediating model suggests that these norms provide the linkage between the general conceptual structure and the particular situation.

Second, it was necessary to establish the causal direction of the relationship between legal reasoning and action. To do this, we used the statistical tool of path analysis (Blalock 1964; Duncan 1985) and statistically tested two different models, the "cognitive model" and the "behavioral model." In the cognitive model, legal reasoning in the fall led to the two mediating variables (norms of behavior and rule enforcement) in the spring which led to the spring rule-violating behaviors. In the behavioral model, behaviors measured in the spring (although cumulative from fall to spring) led to the two mediating variables in the spring which led to spring legal reasoning. The behavioral model fit the data significantly more often than did the cognitive model. Although path analysis is a descriptive rather than a predictive technique, the direction of the path suggests something about the relationship that is being depicted. We were led to ask, therefore, what is the nature of a moral/legal judgment when reasoning follows behavior? In short, the dominance of the behavioral model raises questions about how we should understand the role of conceptualization in its relationship to action.

We would suggest that the direction of the causal path is a function of the equilibration process by which balance is maintained between the individual and the social environment. Cognitive theorists argue that most fundamental learning takes place during periods of disequilibrium, which are particularly common during adolescence. In a period of personal disequilibrium in a new social environment, the balance between the individual and the environment is disrupted. For example, Kohlberg argues that equilibration analyses focus upon "discrepancies between the child's action system or expectancies and the experienced events, and hypothesize some moderate or optimal degree of discrepancy as constituting the most effective experience for structural change in the organism" (Kohlberg 1969, 356).

Under circumstances of disequilibrium, therefore, it is likely that the process of creating moral meaning in a situation stems first from experiencing or observing new behaviors. Kohlberg describes an imbalance of reciprocity "between the action of the organism upon the (perceived) object (or situation) and the action of the (perceived) object upon the organism" (Kohlberg 1984, 8) during disequilibrium. It is likely that new situations and experiences generate attitudes of approval or disapproval, which in turn trigger new assimilations and accommodations in existing cognitive structures. In other words, in a period of disequilibrium, cognition is more vulnerable to experiential pressures and the influence of the social environment. Our analysis concludes that sometimes the cognitive structures determine the moral meaning of a behavior and sometimes disequilibration reverses the process, allowing the behavioral experience to define the cognitive structure. Linking norms can either help the cognitive structure to interpret the behavior or can facilitate the formation of new cognitive structures. Furthermore, the linkage occurs for all subjects regardless of whether they followed or violated a rule.

This leads to our third question: how do cognitive structures differ from intentions or motives for action? A comparison with criminological discussions of motive is instructive. The analysis of both "vocabularies of motive" (Hartung 1965) and "techniques of neutralization" (Sykes and Matza 1957) are based on statements made by juveniles about their delinquent acts. The work of Sykes and Matza implies that these statements are not invented on the spur of the moment to excuse or justify these acts, but are rather verbal expressions that preexisted the acts. Such expressions are instrumental and may function as motives ("I did it for my friends") as well as means of neutralizing illegal or immoral acts. Recently, Hamlin attacked this approach, arguing that "reliance on causal relationships and instrumental thinking leads to the assumption that people have reasons for what they do. It is just as likely that a great deal of human behavior is nonrational. We provide rationality to the act after it has occurred" (1988, 429). We agree that these learned verbalizations, while important in their neutralizing role, are not causal "reasons for" what people do. Their use is just as valid before or after the fact because they are not causal. They are learned excuses or justifications for illegal or immoral acts.

We do not agree that human action is nonrational, however. Such a view perpetuates a false dichotomy between rationality and instrumental reasoning. Sometimes the most focused and thorough reasoning process cannot tell a person what to do or not to do in a particular case (Kohlberg 1984). Or that same reasoning process may yield alternative actions. One may do one or the other because of an itch, a telephone call from a friend, or an automobile accident, none of which is very interesting as a cause of that act or as an explanation of human action. More important are the cognitive structures that do or do not lead people to define their actions in moral terms (Hamlin 1988, 436). The process of conceptualizing one's actions in moral terms creates moral meaning. The function of reasoning relative to behavior is not to neutralize immoral or illegal acts in the sense intended by Sykes and Matza (1957). Rather, the function of reasoning is to categorize a situation and provide rules for its interpretation. These rules do not dictate a particular action but provide the conceptual lenses through which situations are interpreted and moral meaning is created.

We have argued that the connection between reasoning and action cannot be understood in terms of direct causation. A clearer picture of the relationship between reasoning and action can be obtained by analyzing reasoning in the context of its experiential base. That analysis begins with the concept of taking the role of the other, to which we now turn.

Reasoning and Role-Taking

The relationship between reasoning and action is a matter of congruence between person and environment through a balancing process of reciprocal interaction. This process is generally termed role-taking, or taking the role of the other. Although the concept of taking the role of the other is an important part of cognitive developmental theory, it did not originate with cognitive developmentalism. Mead (1934)), among others, discussed the effects of role-taking and attributed some kind of developmental power to it in his theory of social interaction. Therefore, we use the concept in a more generic sense than its specific application in, for example, Kohlberg's (1969) theory of moral development. Its most directly relevant formulation was by legal development theory (Levine and Tapp 1977; Tapp and Kohlberg 1977; Tapp and Levine 1974). Specifically, the different types ("levels") of reasoning postulated by legal development theory encompass different authority relationships between the individual and the community: (1) a command relationship, in which role-taking is based on fear of punishment (preconventional); (2) a community-centered relationship, based largely on different degrees of conformity to the community's need for order and reciprocity (conventional); and (3) a morally principled relationship, which is based on degrees of individual autonomy (postconventional). This formulation of the context for role-taking experiences was used as the basis of our measures of legal reasoning.

Cognitive developmentalism (Piaget 1932; Kohlberg 1969), and in particular legal development theory (Tapp and Levine 1974; Levine and Tapp 1977), postulates that conceptual change in social development occurs primarily through experiences in taking the role of the other. A concise statement of this process suggests that the concrete and egocentric outlook of the young child gradually gives way to a capacity to see other points of view and to understand the thoughts and feelings that underlie them. This capacity allows the individual to take the role of the other and thereby to experience diverse perspectives. Our study extends this claim to another level of theory by producing evidence that role-taking experiences not only bring about conceptual development but also facilitate connections between reasoning and action. The importance of role-taking experiences to cognitive development has led others to recommend that role-taking opportunities should be a primary goal of the educational system (Levine and Tapp 1977). Our findings provide further empirical support and an extended theoretical rationale for such recommendations.

The original purpose for our experimental manipulation, which established contrasting conditions of enforcement, was to allow us to test hypotheses according to an experimental design. An unforeseen dividend was the opportunity to observe the effects of role-taking on the legal socialization process. In the peer authority condition, residents controlled rule enforcement because all cases had to be resolved by their residential conduct board. The cases that went to the conduct board provoked considerable discussion and activity among the residents around the question of fair enforcement of the rules, as well as extensive debate within the board itself. By contrast, the external authority condition allowed no role-taking opportunities. Enforcement was conducted by staff strictly according to rigid and predetermined standards, with final resolution referred to an external conduct board. This procedure provoked resentment and retaliation against the enforcers and extensive vandalism within the residence hall.

These two experimental conditions produced striking differences in the connection between reasoning and action for the two residential populations. As mentioned above, we used path analysis to establish the relationship between legal reasoning and rule-governed behaviors as mediated by norms of behavior and rule enforcement. We conducted separate path analyses for each of the experimental conditions to determine the frequency that the path models predicted this relationship with reasonable accuracy (i.e., with significant beta weights). We found that significant predictive path models were more frequent in the peer authority condition than in the external authority condition. This finding indicates that the experience of participant rule enforcement makes it more likely that reasoning will be linked to action. We also found that significant predictive path models occurred more frequently in the control condition (characterized by loose enforcement with occasional crackdowns) than in the external authority condition, suggesting that strict, nonparticipant rule enforcement has the effect of decreasing connections between reasoning and action.

To further sharpen our operationalization of the concept of role-taking, we compared the experience of living in different rule enforcement situations with other factors that are independent of the variation in enforcement conditions but might also have facilitated the connection between reasoning and action by investing situations with moral/legal meaning. For the purpose of this comparison, we examined two ways in which an individual might be in conflict with a rule and/or its enforcement. The first possibility for conflict was strictly attitudinal: did the individual disagree with the rule (indicating conflict) or agree with the rule (indicating no conflict)? The second possible conflict was behavioral: did the individual violate the rule (indicating conflict) or follow the rule (indicating no conflict)? We then asked, across all subjects and conditions, whether the connection between reasoning and action was more likely to occur when subjects agreed with the rule or when they disagreed with the rule. The answer is that neither agreement nor disagreement with the rule had any systematic effect on the likelihood of a connection between reasoning and action. The same was true of following or violating. A connection between reasoning and action was as likely to occur for rule-followers as for rule-violators. This is in direct contrast to the effects of the experimental conditions, where the linkage was significantly more likely to occur in the peer authority condition than in the external authority condition.

In other words, it was only the role-taking experience of living in a participant rule enforcement situation that produced a connection between reasoning and action with significant frequency. Neither a specifically attitudinal response nor a specifically behavioral response to a rule was sufficient to engage legal reasoning with rule-governed actions. By contrast, legal reasoning became embedded in the situation through experiences of diverse perspectives because such experiences make situational sense of the cognitive structures and provide the substantive basis to link reasoning and norms and actions. In this way, these three factors of the mediating model—reasoning, norms, and actions—are translated into a shared context. Even though the measures of legal reasoning are at a high level of abstraction (e.g., ''Why should people follow rules?,'' ''Are there times when it might be right to break a rule?''), the experiential process of role-taking is one in which individuals are conceptualizing their own actions in moral/legal terms. Taking the role of the other is particularly effective for legal socialization because the measures of legal reasoning have to do with different kinds of authority relationships. Each type of reasoning suggests different roles for the individual and for the community with respect to rules, and a different relationship between the individual and the community in the enforcement process.

In sum, experiences of diverse perspectives and conflicting claims, and the accompanying cognitive disequilibrium, are at the heart of the legal socialization process. Therefore, the connection between reasoning and action can best be seen as a process of change and development instead of a more static event. The process is interactive, continuously reaching toward reciprocity or balance with the social environment. We interpret our findings to mean that opportunities for role-taking increase the possibilities for reciprocal interaction and therefore not only enhance conceptual development but also the connection between reasoning and action. Likewise, the lack of opportunities for role-taking has the opposite effect. Since cognitive structures are "rules for processing information and for connecting experienced events" (Kohlberg 1969, 349), the experience of reciprocal interaction induces the individual to create moral meaning by conceptualizing the social environment in terms that lead to a pluralistic perspective, to judgments about fairness, and to criteria for defining one's actions as moral or immoral.

Conceptualizing Actions: Creating Moral Meaning

Role-taking describes how people learn to conceptualize their actions in moral/legal terms. Our current research[8] explores how people are able to use that experiential learning to confer moral meaning on actions and events in their lives. Students in the same residential community were shown video tapes of mock hearings in which fellow students faced charges of violating rules. Divided into small groups, the students were then asked to deliberate to a decision of guilt or innocence. Audio and video tapes of these deliberations are being analyzed in terms of a number of qualitative and quantitative dimensions. Our preliminary analyses suggest that abstract principles are brought to bear on actions through an interpretive process. As members of the deliberation group debate the testimony they have heard, they gradually weave their own account(s) of the events in question ("what happened"). Sometimes competing accounts are created when the group cannot agree on a single interpretation. In either case, the process is one of creating a plausible story by applying frames for assessing the moral/legal features of the characters and their situation that are generated from the juror's own experience.

These frames, we would argue, are moral/legal cognitive structures in situ. For example, each juror is able to extract from her experience appraisals of a rule as good or bad, based upon a more abstract concept of justice. In the same way, actions are appraised as right or wrong; rule enforcement is fair or unfair. These appraisal frames are created over time, as they change over time, through an accumulation of experiences in which abstract principles mingle with norms of behavior and rule enforcement in the process of being applied to events and actions. This process includes perceptions of the acts of others and decisions both governing and justifying one's own actions. Therefore, one's self is defined in part through these same appraisal frames. Our data from these group deliberations suggest, in fact, that the process through which the pieces of the mediating model come together is a very personal one.

In what way do appraisal frames affect the person? The process by which accounts (Scott and Lyman 1968) are constructed in a jury (Hastie, Penrod, and Pennington 1983) always involves some degree of personalization. Our analysis suggests that individual jurors engage in joint interpretation to a certain extent, and will even negotiate some meaning within the group. But it is clear from the intensity of their involvement that something important about the self is on the line in these discussions. We would argue that personal identity is closely bound up with moral/legal identity. These accounts are being constructed in a legal context of blaming. Part of this construction has to do with social identification, which is at first more a matter of definition than appraisal. As the deliberators get closer to the point of assigning blame, it is clear that social identification gives way to appraisal. And it is here that the moral position of the self, relative to the other who is being judged, is at stake. Regardless of whether their conclusion is to blame or not to blame the defendant, the jurors in our study strongly defend their own account of "what happened" against competing accounts, and struggle to maintain their own sense of a just solution.

We believe that this personalization of the process of constructing accounts represents the mediating model in action, creating moral meaning in particular situations. It reflects the experiential medium in which legal reasoning takes place. While the principles are abstract, applying them is not, whether one is contemplating one's own actions or judging the actions of others. In fact, legal reasoning creates a link between one's sense of self and group norms, between one's moral/legal identity and the social environment. The link may be positive, but it may also be negative. That is, one can see oneself as a free and willing participant in the process of creating an ordered community, or as an alienated and defiant victim of authority. In both cases the individual is asserting her self, her personal moral/legal identity. Legal reasoning leads to individual choice.

Conclusion

This paper began by confronting the relative validity of environmental versus individual explanations. We tested competing hypotheses to determine which was the better predictor of legal socialization effects, and we suggested that the answer to that question would have important normative implications. We now come full circle and address those normative implications directly. The philosopher John Rawls compared our two paradigmatic theories in discussing how individuals acquire a "sense of fairness." He argued that for social learning theory "the aim of moral training is to supply missing motives," while for cognitive developmentalism "moral learning is not so much a matter of supplying missing motives as one of the free development of our innate intellectual and emotional capacities according to their natural bent" (1971, 458–59). Our finding that legal reasoning is a better predictor than environmental influence, and that it is related to rule-governed behaviors through a mediating process, lends a new perspective to Rawls' formulation of the contrast between the theories and particularly to his characterization of cognitive theory. We conclude that individual autonomy, understood as the capacity for reasoning and moral choice, can play a significant role in legal socialization processes.

As an empirical matter, Rawls' formulation suggests that if we take individual autonomy seriously, we must take reasoning seriously as well. Taking reasoning seriously led us to consider how conceptualizing action in moral/legal terms creates moral meaning in a situation. We conclude that reasoning is not simply an abstract mental activity that is remote from human action or moral dilemmas. Rather, it is embedded in the experiential process by which individuals make sense of their relationship to their social environment. Consequently, the personalized construction of accounts is an important focus for future research. In addition, exploring the behavioral effects of different ways of conceptualizing the relationship between the individual and the community, and of the different social contexts in which such reasoning takes place, can open up new areas for thinking about how individuals learn to be responsible for their actions. In sum, taking reasoning seriously implies that a better understanding of legal socialization processes, and in particular the development of moral/legal reasoning, can increase society's capacity to provide a positive and effective foundation for individual autonomy and moral choice.

Notes

1. This research was supported by National Science Foundation Grant SES-8112020.
2. Recent literature in the social learning mode has included a greater role for cognitive factors, but only as a regulator in the feedback process (Bandura 1986; Mischel and Mischel 1976). Akers' (1985) treatment is similar.
3. Cognitive developmentalism has been attacked because its concept of stage development ignores cultural, class, and gender diversity in moral/legal reasoning. Kohlberg's stages (1969) in particular imply a normative hierarchy in the "levels" of reasoning that fits mostly upper-middle class white males in Western cultures; by this implication, members of traditional cultures, lower economic classes, and women in general are unlikely to engage in higher stage moral reasoning (Gilligan 1982; Snarey 1985; Cohn and White 1990). It is our view that neither the concept of cognitive structures nor the developmental dynamic requires a hierarchy of stages. (We therefore adopt the term "type" in place of the term "level" in this paper.) In our data, for example, legal development type (type of reasoning) did not distinguish between those who followed and those who violated the rules even though the path analyses demonstrated a connection between legal reasoning and behaviors. Cognitive developmentalism provides a point of departure but not a theoretical straitjacket for understanding the role of reasoning in legal socialization.
4. Additional information about our measures and other issues of operationalization, as well as the complete research design for the legal socialization study, can be found in Cohn and White (1990), chapter 3. The findings and analysis discussed in this paper can be found primarily

in chapters 5 (test of competing hypotheses), 7 (path analyses of the linkage between reasoning and action), and 9 (role-taking).

5. A possible measurement problem should be noted: residence hall is a factor that is the same in the fall and spring, which may inflate the reasoning correlation.

6. From a statistical perspective, it is important to note Baron and Kenny's (1986) distinction between mediators and moderators. A mediator is a third variable which is essential to establish a relation between two other variables; without the mediating variable there will be no relation between the two variables. In contrast, a moderator is a third variable which affects the strength of the relation between the two variables but is not essential to establish a relation; without the moderating variable, the two variables will still be related. We predicted that norms of behavior and rule enforcement were mediating variables in both the statistical and conceptual sense.

7. We conducted several path analyses. First, we tested the direct model by measuring the regression coefficients between legal development level (level of legal reasoning) and rule-governed behaviors controlling for both norms of behavior and of rule enforcement (situational norms). Second, we tested the indirect cognitive model by measuring the regression coefficients between legal development level and the two situational norms, and between the two situational norms and the rule-violating behaviors. Third, we tested the indirect behavioral model by measuring the regression coefficients between rule-governed behaviors and the two situational norms, and between the two situational norms and legal development level. Each model includes a time difference.

8. This research is supported by National Science Foundation Grant SES-8606622.

References

Akers, R. L. 1985. *Deviant Behavior: A Social Learning Approach.* Belmont, Cal.: Wadsworth Publishing Co.

Bandura, A. 1986. *Social Foundations of Thought and Action: A Social-Cognitive Theory.* Englewood Cliffs, N.J.: Prentice-Hall.

Baron, R. M., and D. A. Kenny. 1986. ''The Moderator-Mediator Variable Distinction in Social Psychological Research: Conceptual, Strategic, and Statistical Considerations.'' *Journal of Personality and Social Psychology* 51: 1173–82.

Blalock, H. M. 1964. *Causal Inferences in Non-Experimental Research.* Chapel Hill: University of North Carolina Press.

Blasi, A. 1980. "Bridging Moral Cognition and Moral Action: A Critical Review of the Literature." *Psychological Bulletin* 1–45.

Cohn, E. S., and S. O. White. 1986. "Cognitive Developmental Versus Social Learning Approaches to Studying Legal Socialization." *Basic and applied social psychology* 7 (3): 195–209.

Cohn, E. S., and S. O. White. 1990. *Legal Socialization: A Study of Norms and Rules*. New York: Springer-Verlag.

Duncan, D. D. 1985. "Path Analysis: Sociological Examples." In *Causal models in the social sciences*, edited by H. M. Blalock, 55–79. New York: Aldine.

Gilligan, C. 1982. *In a Different Voice: Psychological Theory and Women's Development*. Cambridge, Mass.: Harvard University Press.

Hamlin, J. E. 1988. "The Misplaced Role of Rational Choice in Neutralization Theory." *Criminology* 26 (3): 425–38.

Hartung, F. E. 1965. *Crime, Law and Society*. Detroit: The Wayne State University Press.

Hastie, R., S. D. Penrod and N. Pennington. 1983. *Inside the Jury*. Cambridge, Mass.: Harvard University Press.

Hull, C. L. 1943. *Principles of Behavior*. New York: Appleton-Century.

Kohlberg, L. 1969. "Stage and Sequence: The Cognitive-Developmental Approach to Socialization." In *Handbook of socialization theory*, edited by D. A. Goslin, 347–480. Chicago: Rand McNally.

Kohlberg, L. 1984. *The Psychology of Moral Development: The Nature and Validity of Moral Stages*. San Francisco: Harper and Row.

Levine, F. J., and J. L. Tapp. 1977. "The Dialectic of Legal Socialization in Community and School." In *Law, Justice and the Individual in Society: Psychological and Legal Issues*, edited by J. L. Tapp and F. J. Levine. New York: Holt, Rinehart and Winston.

Mischel, W., and H. N. Mischel. 1976. "A Cognitive Social-Learning Approach to Morality and Self-Regulation." In *Moral Development and Behavior*, edited by T. Lickona, 84–107. New York: Holt, Rinehart, and Winston.

Mead, G. H. 1934. *Mind, Self and Society*. Chicago: University of Chicago Press.

Piaget, J. 1926. *The Language and Thought of the Child*. London: Routledge & Kegan Paul.

Piaget, J. 1932. *The Moral Judgement of the Child*. London: Routledge and Kegan Paul.

Rawls, J. 1971. *A Theory of Justice*. Cambridge, Mass.: Harvard University Press.

Scott, M. B., and S. M. Lyman. 1968. "Accounts." *American Sociological Review* 33 (1): 46–62.

Skinner, B. F. 1938. *The Behavior of Organisms.* New York: Appleton-Century.

Snarey, J. 1985. "The Cross-Cultural Universality of Social-Moral Development: A Critical Review of Kohlbergian Research." *Psychological Bulletin* 97: 202–232.

Sykes, G. M., and D. Matza. 1957. "Techniques of Neutralization: A Theory of Delinquency." *American Sociological Review* 22 (Aug. 1957): 664–70.

Tapp, J. L., and L. Kohlberg. 1977. "Developing Senses of Law and Legal Justice." In *Law, Justice and the Individual in Society: Psychological and Legal Issues,* edited by J. L. Tapp and F. J. Levine. New York: Holt, Rinehart, Winston.

Tapp, J. L., and F. J. Levine. 1974. "Legal Socialization: Strategies for an Ethical Legality." *Stanford Law Review* 27: 1–72.

6

Understanding Motivations: Considering Altruism and Aggression

Joan McCord

The fact that criminal actions are performed intentionally distinguishes them from accidental actions and from those performed as a consequence of mental illness. Intentional actions require motives, so motivations should play a central role in an adequate theory of crime. This article addresses what appears to be a gap in theories of criminal behavior: a gap between external forces and intentional behavior.

Although several theories of crime rely upon assumptions about underlying motives, the motives implicated by these theories would not qualify as such in a criminal court. For example, Cohen (1955) considered delinquency a response to "a chronic fund of motivation, conscious or repressed, to elevate one's status position" (122). Sutherland and Cressey (1924/1974) argued that delinquency occurs through adopting from the social surroundings beliefs that justify criminal behavior as reasonable. Yet neither desire for increased status nor desire to act reasonably could be considered grounds for distinguishing criminal from irrational or unintended action.

Sykes and Matza (1957) suggested that delinquents prepare the way for delinquency by defining criminal actions as excusable, necessary, or permissible if rightly understood. The set of beliefs which they termed "techniques of neutralization" and which Bandura (1986, 1990) called "disengagement" can be seen as justifying antisocial behavior; but the theory does not explain why such techniques are invoked. Glaser (1978) proposed that expectations created by biological and social conditions influence perception of opportunities and anticipation of consequences for committing crimes. Lurking behind these and other theories of crime is an assumption that people are motivated to do what they believe will benefit themselves. In this vein, Hirschi (1969) argued that criminality requires no explanation; rather, conventional children are rule-abiding because they care what their parents will think and, presumably, want to please their parents because they will be rewarded (88). More recently, Gottfredson and Hirschi (1990) asserted that people are criminals because they lack self-control and their behavior reflects their short-term assessment of personal gain.

Egocentric motivations are assumed also, without critical evaluation, by what has come to be called "rational" theories of crime (Cornish and Clarke 1986). In this view, crime is caused by desire to maximize the ratio of personal gain to pain. Some evidence indicates that people avoid some types of crimes when they believe that committing them will result in painful consequences to themselves (Erickson, Gibbs, and Jensen 1977; Farrington 1979; Grasmick and Bryjak 1980; Nagin 1978), but there is also evidence to suggest that most criminals do not consider such consequences before they commit crimes (Carroll 1982; Erez 1987).

Freud (1930/1961) linked eogcentrism with aggression: "Civilization has to use its utmost efforts in order to set limits to man's aggressive instincts. . . . and hence too the ideal's commandment to love one's neighbor as oneself—a commandment which is really justified by the fact that nothing else runs so strongly counter to the original nature of man" (59).

Aggression has been postulated as a dominant force underlying antisocial behavior. The association has sometimes been so close that studies of criminality have been interpreted as shedding light on aggression (e.g., Bandura and Walters 1959), as validating measures of aggression (e.g., Lefkowitz et al. 1977), and as support for the thesis that frustration leads to aggression (Dollard et al. 1939).

Longitudinal research has confirmed relationships between childhood aggressiveness and subsequent criminal behavior among blacks (Ensminger et al. 1983) and Caucasians (McCord 1983) in the United States, and in Great Britain (Farrington 1991; Farrington and West 1981), Finland (Pulkkinen 1988), and Sweden (Magnusson and Bergman 1988). There are therefore empirical grounds for arguing that aggression could be a motive for criminal behavior.

Aggression implies that an actor has a desire to injure others, so there are conceptual grounds for reasoning that there might be a motivational continuum along which a desire to help others would be at the opposite end of aggressiveness. Nevertheless, aggressiveness has been related to such socialized behaviors as striving and prosociality (Pulkkinen 1984; Friedrich and Stein 1973). As Eisenberg and Mussen suggest, "Moderate levels of aggression probably reflect outgoingness, emotional responsiveness, and assertiveness, and such qualities may facilitate young children's tendencies to engage in positive, prosocial interactions with others" (1989, 63).

Although only a handful of studies have embraced both antisocial and prosocial behavior, results of the separate studies provide a fairly coherent picture of etiology. Research into the development of aggression shows with some consistency that children imitate aggressive models—including their parents. Family conflict seems to produce aggression; aggressive fathers tend to have aggressive sons; children tend to imitate television aggression; and abusing parents overrepresent formerly abused children (Bandura, Ross and Ross 1961; Berkowitz et al. 1978; Eron and Huesmann 1984, 1986; Farrington 1978; Friedrich and Stein 1973; Goldstein and Arms 1971; McCord 1983; Widom 1989; Wilkens, Scharff, and Schlottman 1974).

Research into the development of helpful behavior seems to show that children imitate helpful or generous models—including their parents. Altruistic people tend to have altruistic children; children tend to imitate prosocial behavior seen on television or in films; and altruistic children tend to have parents who use principles of moral action in their discipline practices (Bryan and London 1970; Eisenberg 1986; Eron and Huesmann 1986; Rosenhan and White 1967; Rushton 1979; Staub 1979; White 1972; Zahn-Waxler, Radke-Yarrow, and King 1979).

Research into the development of aggression also shows that closeness to parents is related to low levels of aggression. Parental neglect is a strong predictor of aggression, and parental warmth seems to decrease the probability for aggression (Eron and Huesmann 1984; Farrington, Gundry, and West 1975; Loeber and

Stouthamer-Loeber 1986; McCord 1977, 1984). Evidence is mixed regarding the impact of parental warmth on altruism, with some studies indicating that closeness to parents and empathic care result in high levels of prosocial behavior (London 1970; Staub 1986; Whiting and Whiting 1975; Zahn-Waxler, Radke-Yarrow, and King 1979) and others failing to do so (Eisenberg and Mussen 1989).

To summarize, research about the development of aggression and the development of helpful behavior suggests that imitation influences both. The evidence that parental interaction affects aggressiveness and prosociality may be interpreted in the light of how parents provide models for interaction with others. If a child is exposed to aggressive models, the child's aggression can be anticipated; if a child is exposed to prosocial models, helpful behavior can be anticipated. And if a child is exposed to both types of behavior, it seems reasonable to anticipate that both aggressive and prosocial behavior will result.

Research into situational influences on aggression and on prosocial behavior indicate that opportunities for choice of action influences both. Assuming that restrictions of choice are frustrating and that doing poorly in school reduces opportunities, frustration provides a plausible account of why children who do poorly in school are aggressive (Berkowitz 1962; Dollard et al. 1939; Feshbach and Price 1984). Forced choices also seem to reduce voluntary helping (Aderman and Berkowitz 1983; Berkowitz 1973; Fabes et al. 1989). In sum: perceived restrictions of freedom appear to reduce altruistic behavior and to increase aggression.

Studies of motivations show that when people are happy, they are more likely to be helpful and generous (Berkowitz 1987; Eisenberg and Mussen 1989; Isen and Levin 1972; Marcus 1986; Moore, Underwood, and Rosenhan 1973; Rosenhan, Underwood, and Moore 1974). Angered subjects tend to become aggressive (Berkowitz 1965; Donnerstein and Wilson 1976; Wilkens, Scharff, and Schlottman 1974; Zillman 1979). Although aggressive and prosocial behaviors have different motivational links, friendships seem to reinforce helping behavior—and friendships seem to reinforce aggression (Cairns et al. 1988; Maccoby 1986).

Two hypotheses about the relationship between altruism and aggression are plausible.

1. Altruism and aggressiveness are opposite ends of a continuum.

In this view, to the extent that one is aggressive, altruism must be weak. Conversely, to the extent that one is altruistic, little aggression can be expected. To account for failure to detect a negative relationship between altruism and aggression, those persuaded by this view argue that what appears to be aggressiveness or what appears to be altruism is incorrectly viewed to be such.

2. Altruism and aggressiveness are independent dimensions. From this second perspective, the occurrence of altruism even among extremely aggressive youths would be possible. Evidence of negative relationships are particular to circumstances of measurement, individuals, or to the techniques for measuring.

In a certain sense, of course, altruistic and aggressive behavior are incompatible. As Plato (*Republic,* 436b) remarked, one cannot at the same time "do or suffer opposites in the same respect in relation to the same thing." This does not preclude the possibility of being altruistic at one time and aggressive at another, nor of being altruistic toward one person and aggressive toward another.

There are prima facie grounds for believing that aggression and altruism coexist as potential responses and as dispositional characteristics of ordinary people. Studies such as those that have randomly assigned people to roles, as in the Stanford Prison experiment where students were assigned to be prison guards (Zimbardo et al. 1974) and the studies of obedience by Stanley Milgram (1963, 1974), where students were assigned to give painful shocks to fellow students, have demonstrated aggressive behavior among people who volunteered to be subjects in laboratory studies and did so, presumably, with prosocial intentions. At the opposite extreme, medical doctors in Nazi prison camps were known to be occasionally kind to inmates (Staub 1989) and the SS at Auschwitz occasionally showed compassion (Pawelczynska 1979).

Before continuing an examination of the relationship between altruism and aggression, let us examine the concepts. In the works briefly summarized above, both "aggression" and "altruism" are used sometimes to refer to behaviors, sometimes to motives, and sometimes to actions. For example, a measure of aggression that depends on behavior is involved when peers are asked: "Who gets in fights a lot?" A measure of aggression that depends on motives is involved when subjects are asked: "Do you often want to hurt someone?" A measure of aggression that depends on actions is involved when teachers are asked: "Which children try to destroy the work of others?" Cairns and Cairns (1984) found little agreement between self-ratings of aggression and public ratings by observers, teachers, and peers. As they (Cairns and Cairns 1986) and Hinde (1986) point out, the criteria for identifying aggression may be different across raters.

The links among behaviors, motives, and actions are not always obvious. A classic example comes from the Kwakiutl Indians who have great potlatches (Benedict 1934; Boas 1897). At these ceremonies, the Kwakiutl donate and destroy property competitively; they do so in order to demonstrate status. In these, as in other instances of conspicuous consumption, gifts are inextricably merged with an intention to injure.

Impulsiveness, linked conceptually and empirically with aggressive behavior in some studies, may be altruistic as well as aggressive (Pulkkinen 1984). Giving aid can be as self-interested as aggression. In viewing human behavior as fundamentally a competitive striving for status, Homans argued that a recipient of services gives up status: "The social approval he gives Other is at the same time an admission of his own inferiority" (1961, 61). Similarly, Gouldner (1960) was persuaded that strong and universal expectations for reciprocal benefits provided incentives for apparently altruistic actions. "Between the time of Ego's provision of a gratification and the time of Alter's repayment," he wrote, "falls the shadow of indebtedness" (174). As Blau (1964) noted, benefits from apparently altruistic behavior are broader than suggested by the norm of reciprocity, so that much that passes for altruistic may be mistakenly so conceived.

Some injuries are accidental, so not all injurious actions should be attributed to aggression. There are actions that injure, people who perform actions that injure, and people who intend to injure through their actions, though they may fail or find that another has done the work for them. For purposes of clarity, let me stipulate: *Aggression refers to injurious actions performed with the intention of injuring.*

In parallel, there are actions that help others; people who perform actions that help others; and people who intend to help others through their actions, though they may fail. For purposes of clarity, again let me stipulate: *Altruism refers to helpful actions that a person performs with the intention of helping someone else.*

Measures of aggression and of conduct disorder have confounded two types of motivation: actions intended to injure others and actions intended to benefit oneself. Some do so by defining a scale on which helpful behavior is at one end and misbehavior at the other (e.g., Klinteberg, Schalling, and Magnusson 1990). Others have incorporated general misconduct, conduct that disregards the welfare of others, as part of the meaning of aggressiveness (e.g., Kellam, Simon, and Ensminger 1983; Robins and McEvoy 1990; Tremblay, Desmarais-Gervais, Gagnon, and Charlebois 1987). A theory of crime that takes motivations as a starting point would expect differences in behavior related to these seemingly different motives.

Empirical Evidence

I used data from a longitudinal study (McCord 1983) to look at the relationships of aggression and altruism to criminal behavior. Designed to prevent delinquency and evaluate the intervention, the study included ratings by approximately 200 teachers of boys living in blighted areas of Cambridge and Somerville Massachusetts. In 1936 and 1937, the teachers had checked descriptive phrases on a "Trait Record Card." Initially, there were 506 males in the study. I used those who were less than age ten at the time data were collected and selected only one boy per family. This resulted in having 468 males for analyses. They ranged in age from four to nine, with a median and mode of eight years at the time of teachers' ratings.

Boys were considered to have been aggressive if their teachers checked "fights" as part of their description (N = 95). They were considered conduct disordered if their teachers checked more than three of the following eleven possibilities: frequent truancy; blames others for his difficulties; secretive, crafty, sly; rude, saucy, impudent; disobeys; refuses to cooperate; cruel; cheats; lies; steals; destroys property.

In 1948, police records were searched for evidence of criminal behavior. In 1978, when the average age of the subjects was fifty years, records were collected from the courts, mental hospitals, vital statistics, and clinics treating alcoholics. Criminal records were used to classify the men according to a scale of seriousness for their criminal histories. Each person was classified according to his most serious conviction. Records from juvenile courts were combined with those from adult courts. Misdemeanor crimes were considered less serious than felony crimes against property, which were considered less serious than felony crimes against persons. As table 6.1 indicates, boys who were aggressive in primary grades were more likely than other boys to be convicted for crimes against persons.

The subjects were retraced between 1975 and 1980. All but eighteen (4 percent) were located. Among those located, forty-eight (10 percent) had died. The remainder were asked to respond to a questionnaire and to consent to an interview. Requests for completing the questionnaire appealed to altruistic motives by using some version of the following: "You were once a member of the Cambridge-Somerville Youth Study, which makes your opinions important for helping other parents and children." No other incentives were used. For the interviews, we offered "$20 for your time." Men were counted as altruistic if they responded to the questionnaire. Some men failed to answer the questionnaires because of poor reading or because the questionnaires had been misplaced; therefore, men were also counted as altruistic if they were interviewed but refused to take the $20 offered to them.

A majority of the men (60.2 percent) were classified as altruistic. This proportion was composed of 66.4 percent of the noncriminals,

TABLE 6.1
Behavior of Young Child and Subsequent Criminal Behavior
(percent of group)

	Not Aggressive or Conduct Disorder (N = 340)	Aggressive (N = 62)	Conduct Disorder (N = 33)	Conduct Disorder & Aggressive (N = 33)
No crimes	30.6	16.1	30.3	12.1
Minor only	43.2	41.9	36.4	45.5
Property	12.1	17.7	24.2	24.2
Person	14.1	24.2	9.1	18.2
	100.0	99.9	100.0	100.0

$X^2_{(9)} = 18.114$, p = .034

and 64.4 percent of those convicted only for minor crimes, but only 49.1 percent of those convicted for crimes against property, and 45.6 percent of those convicted for crimes against persons ($X^2_{(3)} = 10.998$, $p = .012$).

As indicated in table 6.2, neither aggressiveness nor conduct disorder was reliably related to a lack of altruism.

Discussion

Other studies have shown continuity in aggressive behavior (e.g., Huesmann, Eron, Lefkowitz, and Walder 1984; Olweus 1979). The longitudinal evidence linking aggression to crimes of violence corroborates these studies. In addition, the evidence suggests that although egocentric behavior (represented by property crimes) is not conducive to altruism, altruism is not merely the inverse of aggression.

Immanual Kant (1785/1959) observed that "the principle of one's own happiness is the most objectionable of all . . . . for it puts the motives to virtue and those to vice in the same class, teaching us only to make a better calculation" (61). Many helpful actions are doubtless due to self-interest, so not all helpful actions can be attributed to altruism. Yet there is reason to believe that at least sometimes, some people perform altruistic actions.

Many of the theories used to account for altruism refer only to self-interest. These include Attribution Theory, which in one form considers altruism to be dependent upon attributing socially desirable characteristics to oneself (Berkowitz 1965; Grusec and Dix

TABLE 6.2
Behavior of Young Child and Subsequent Altruistic Behavior
(percent of group)

	Not Aggressive or Conduct Disorder (N = 294)	Aggressive (N = 50)	Conduct Disorder (N = 28)	Conduct Disorder & Aggressive (N = 30)
Altruistic	61.6	50.0	64.3	60.0
Not	38.4	50.0	35.7	40.0
	100.0	100.0	100.0	100.0

$X^2_{(3)} = 2.595$, $p = .458$

1986; Heider 1946) and Reactance Theory, which considers behavior a response to a quest for perceived freedom or control (Brehm and Brehm 1981). Reciprocity theories of a variety of types, including those that claim self-rewards motivate altruistic acts, make the assumption that giving depends on expectations for receiving (Baumann, Cialdini, and Kenrick 1981; Cialdini et al. 1987; Hatfield, Walster, and Piliavin 1978; Hinde 1979; Rosenhan 1978).

Hoffman (1963) found negative correlations between the use of power-oriented punishment and consideration of others. Attempting to develop an alternative to altruism as an explanation, Hoffman (1980) favored an empathy-based theory. At the time, Hoffman pointed to physiological arousal from others' pain and assumed that this gave rise to pain in the self which became guilt if the cause of pain was attributed to one's own actions.

Critics noted that Hoffman had provided an explanation involving concealed psychological egoism. If the pain of others gives pain, then relieving ones own pain motivates what appears to be altruistic behavior.

Cialdini and his co-workers (1987) claimed support for the egoistic view of altruism. In their study, they contrived to convince some subjects that a drug they had taken (which really was a placebo) had fixed the mood of the subjects. Only those students who, according to the experimenters, believed they had "labile" moods agreed to help a student described as needing help because of a recent automobile accident. The experimenters do not discuss alternatives to their own explanation, one of which is the possibility that student subjects resented giving the extra time it would take to wait out drug effects. But more importantly, they mistake the issue. It would be foolish to argue that *all* help-giving is altruistic; rather, the issue at stake is whether there can be *any* altruistic behavior.

In a seminal article, Hoffman (1981) asked "Is altruism part of human nature?" Countering critics, Hoffman pointed to the ad hoc nature of ecoistic interpretations. After an apparently altruistic act, psychological egoists "invent" plausible stories about the nature of benefits that might be attributed to the actor. Such postulated motivations ought not be mistaken as evidence. Furthermore, research indicates that giving help is reduced when others are present (Clark and Word 1972; Latané and Dabbs 1975; Latané and Darley 1968; Levy et al. 1972)—a finding that runs contrary to at least one basis for converting altruistic acts into covertly hedonistic ones. Had giving help increased, one could argue that desire for approval provided a motive. Hoffman concluded that giving help is "difficult to explain without assuming an independent altruistic motive system" (135).

Experiments designed to test some of the hedonistic accounts of altruistic behavior have been added to the arsenal against psychological hedonism. In one of these, Batson et al. (1988) manipulated subjects so that it looked as though, by giving correct answers, subjects could relieve a partner from the pain of being shocked. Their empathy and mood were measured. Then half were told of a change in plans; the partner would not receive shock. These subjects' help was unnecessary. Empathy and mood were again measured.

The experimenters reasoned that if helping actions provided self-rewarding relief, the subjects would be disappointed by loosing an opportunity to help. On the other hand, if altruism motivated help-giving, the relief should be as great whether or not it was the subject who acted to do the relieving. In fact, the evidence in this study and in others (including one with a Stroop task in which subjects named colors of neutral words and words relevant to altruism, punishment, and rewards) supported the conclusion: "More and more, it appears that the motivation to help evoked by feeling empathy is at least partly altruistic. If it is, then psychologists will have to make some fundamental changes in their conceptions of human motivation and, indeed, of human nature" (75–76).

Altruism appears to be as natural as aggression (Zahn-Waxler and Radke-Yarrow 1982; Zahn-Waxler, Radke-Yarrow, Wagner, and Pyle 1988). Rheingold and Emery (1986) found that by eighteen months, children show patterns of nurturance. By the time children are three to four years old, their friendship choices reflect prosocial behavior (Denham, Mckinley, Couchoud, and Holt 1990). Like curiosity, altruism apparently can be reduced through training. In studying children in primary school, Staub (1970) discovered that eleven-year olds were less likely than seven-year olds to attempt to help a child in the next room who had apparently fallen off a chair. Staub (1979) suggested that punishment probably reduced altruism by focusing the children's attention on themselves.

Connections between a focus on oneself and reduced altruism

have been confirmed through experiments in which randomly selected subjects are induced to focus on themselves, for example by
being told they would soon hear how well they have done on a test,
and then asked for help (Aderman and Berkowitz 1983). Those who
were waiting to hear test results gave less help than those who had
performed a similar task under a different description.

Self-awareness, under some circumstances, also increases helping (Berkowitz 1987; Duval, Duval, and Neely 1979; Gibbons and
Wicklund 1982; Wicklund 1975). The conditions under which these
favorable consequences occur seem to depend on absence of anxiety.

Awareness of how others feel is related to both aggression and
popularity among very young children (Denham, McKinley, Couchoud, and Holt 1990). Children may believe that injuring others is
permissable or that others do not feel a pain they themselves do
not feel. By training delinquents to understand one another, Chandler (1973) reduced their delinquency.

Childrearing techniques teach children what to expect from others and therefore influence estimates about the consequences of
their own actions. Parents who help others, including their children,
are teaching that benefitting others is a reasonable thing to do. Use
of rewards and punishments, on the other hand, provides demonstrations that instruct children to do things for their own benefit
(McCord 1991).

Continuity that has been attributed to character might well be
due to constancy in beliefs. We select (Festinger 1957, 1964), create
(Dodge 1986; Dodge and Somberg 1987; Eron and Huesmann 1986),
and recall (Eich, Rachman, and Lopatka 1990) experiences that
tend to confirm the beliefs we already have. As researchers, we've
spent far too little time considering how children interpret the
lessons we intend.

Criminal behavior ought to be studied with recognition that crime
is a consequence of motives to injure others or to benefit oneself
without a proper regard to the welfare of others. Practices that
foster these motives are likely to promote crime. Claims that all
behavior is egoistic, that crime requires no explanation, and that
beliefs are irrelevant to criminal action have been a disservice to
criminological theory.

References

Aderman, D. and L. Berkowitz. 1983. "Self-Concern and the Unwillingness to be Helpful." *Social Psychology Quarterly* 46, 4: 293–301.

Bandura, A. 1986. *Social Foundations of Thought and Action.* Englewood Cliffs, N.J.: Prentice-Hall.

Bandura, A. 1990. "Selective Activation and Disengagement of Moral Control." *Journal of Social Issues* 46, 1: 27–46.

Bandura, A., D. Ross, and S. A. Ross. 1961. "Transmission of Aggression Through Imitation of Aggressive Models." *Journal of Abnormal and Social Psychology* 63: 575–82.

Bandura, A., and R. H. Walters. 1959. *Adolescent Aggression.* New York: Ronald.

Batson, C. D., J. L. Dyck, J. R. Brandt, J. G. Batson, A. L. Powell, M. R. McMaster, and C. Griffitt. 1988. "Five Studies Testing Two New Egoistic Alternatives to the Empathy-Altruism Hypothesis." *Journal of Personality and Social Psychology* 55, 1: 52–77.

Baumann, D. J., R. B. Cialdini, and D. T. Kenrick, 1981. "Altruism as Hedonism: Helping and Self-Gratification as Equivalent Responses." *Journal of Personality and Social Psychology* 40, 6: 1039–46.

Benedict, R. 1934. *Patterns of Culture.* Boston: Houghton Mifflin Co.

Berkowitz, L. 1962. *Aggression: A Social Psychologist Analysis.* New York: McGraw-Hill.

Berkowitz, L. 1965. "The Concept of Aggressive Drive: Some Additional Considerations." In *Advances in Experimental Social Psychology Vol. 2,* edited by L. Berkowitz, 301–29. New York: Academic Press.

Berkowitz, L. 1973. "Reactance Theory and Helping." *Psychological Bulletin* 79, 5: 310–17.

Berkowitz, L. 1987. "Mood, Self-awareness, and Willingness to Help." *Journal of Personality and Social Psychology* 52, 4: 721–29.

Berkowitz, L., R. D. Parke, J. P. Leyens, S. West, and J. Sebastian. 1978. "Experiments on the Reactions of Juvenile Delinquents to Filmed Violence." In *Aggression and Anti-Social Behaviour in Childhood and Adolescence,* edited by L. A. Hersov and M. Berger, 59–71. Oxford: Pergamon Press.

Blau, P. M. 1964. *Exchange and Power in Social Life.* New York: Wiley.

Boas, F. 1897. "The Social Organization and the Secret Societies of the Kwakiutl Indians, Based on Personal Observations and on Notes Made by Mr. George Hunt." *Annual Report of the Board of Regents of the Smithsonian Institution for the Year ending June 30th 1895. Report of the United States National Museum, 1895,* 311–738, Washington, D.C.

Brehm, S. S. and J. W. Brehm. 1981. *Psychological Reactance: A theory of Freedom and Control*. New York: Academic Press.

Bryan, J. H. and P. London. 1970. "Altruistic behavior by children." *Psychological Bulletin* 73, 3: 200–11.

Cairns, R. B. and B. D. Cairns. 1984. "Predicting Aggressive Patterns in Girls and Boys: A Developmental Study." *Aggressive Behavior* 10(3): 227–42.

Cairns, R. B. and B. D. Cairns. 1986. "The Developmental-Interactional View of Social Behavior: Four Issues of Adolescent Aggression." In *Development of Antisocial and Prosocial Behavior*, edited by D. Olweus, J. Block, and M. R. Yarrow, 315–42. New York: Academic Press.

Cairns, R. B., B. D. Cairns, H. J. Neckerman, S. D. Gest, and J. Gariépy. 1988. "Social Networks and Aggressive Behavior: Peer Support or Peer Rejection?" *Developmental Psychology* 24, 6: 815–23.

Carroll, J. S. 1982. "The Decision to Commit the Crime." In *The Criminal Justice System*, edited by J. Konecni and E. B. Ebbesen, 49–67. San Francisco: W. H. Freeman.

Chandler, M. J. 1973. "Egocentrism and Antisocial Behavior: The Assessment and Training of Social Perspective-Taking Skill." *Developmental Psychology* 9: 326–32.

Cialdini, R. B., M. Schaller, D. Houlihan, K. Arps, J. Fultz, and A. Beaman. 1987. "Empathy-Based Helping: Is it Selflessly or Selfishly Motivated?" *Journal of Personality and Social Psychology* 52, 4: 749–58.

Clark, R. D., III and L. E. Word. 1972. "Why Don't Bystanders Help? Because of Ambiguity?" *Journal of Personality and Social Psychology* 24, 3: 392–400.

Cohen, A. K. 1955. *Delinquent boys*. Glencoe, Ill.: Free Press.

Cornish, D. and R. Clarke. 1986. "Introduction." In *The Reasoning Criminal: Rational Choice Perspectives on Offending*, edited by D. B. Cornish and R. V. Clarke, 1–16. New York: Springer-Verlag.

Denham, S. A., M. McKinley, E. A. Couchoud, and R. Holt. 1990. "Emotional and Behavioral Predictors of Preschool Peer Ratings." *Child Development* 61, 4: 1145–52.

Dodge, K. A. 1986. "Social Information-Processing Variables in the Development of Aggression and Altruism in Children." In *Altruism and Aggression: Biological and Social Origins*, edited by C. Zahn-Waxler, E. M. Cummings, and R. Iannotti, 280–302. Cambridge: Cambridge University Press.

Dodge, K. A. and D. R. Somberg. 1987. "Hostile Attributional Biases Among Aggressive Boys are Exacerbated Under Conditions of Threats to the Self." *Child Development* 58: 213–24.

Dollard, J., L. W. Doob, N. E. Miller, O. H. Mowrer, and R. R. Sears. 1939. *Frustration and Aggression.* New Haven: Yale University Press.

Donnerstein, E. and D. W. Wilson. 1976. "Effects of Noise and Perceived Control on Ongoing and Subsequent Aggressive Behavior." *Journal of Personality and Social Psychology* 34, 5: 774–81.

Duval, S., V. H. Duval, and R. Neely. 1979. "Self-Focus, Felt Responsibility, and Helping Behavior." *Journal of Personality and Social Psychology* 37, 10: 1769–78.

Eich, E., S. Rachman, and C. Lopatka. 1990. "Affect, Pain, and Autobiographical Memory." *Journal of Abnormal Psychology* 99, 2: 174–78.

Eisenberg, N. 1986. *Altruistic Emotion, Cognition, and Behavior.* Hillsdale, N.J.: Lawrence Erlbaum.

Eisenberg, N. and P. H. Mussen. 1989. *The Roots of Prosocial Behavior in Children.* Cambridge: Cambridge University Press.

Ensminger, M. E., S. G. Kellam, and B. R. Rubin. 1983. "School and Family Origins of Delinquency: Comparisons by Sex." In *Prospective Studies of Crime and Delinquency,* edited by K. T. Van Dusen and S. A. Mednick, 73–97. Boston: Kluwer-Nijhoff.

Erez, E. 1987. "Situational or Planned Crime and the Criminal Career." In *From Boy to Man, from Delinquency to Crime,* edited by M. E. Wolfgang, T. P. Thornberry, and R. M. Figlio, 122–33. Chicago: University of Chicago Press.

Erickson, M. L., J. P. Gibbs, and G. F. Jensen. 1977. "The Deterrence Doctrine and the Perceived Certainty of Legal Punishments." *American Sociological Review* 42 (Apr.): 305–17.

Eron, L. D. and L. R. Huesmann. 1984. "The Relation of Prosocial Behavior to the Development of Aggression and Psychopathology." *Aggressive Behavior* 10(3): 201–11.

Eron, L. D. and L. R. Huesmann. 1986. "The Role of Television in the Development of Prosocial and Antisocial Behavior." In *Development of Antisocial and Prosocial Behavior,* edited by D. Olweus, J. Block, and M. R. Yarrow, 285–314. New York: Academic Press.

Fabes, R. A., J. Fultz, N. Eisenberg, T. May-Plumlee, and F. S. Christopher. 1989. "Effects of Rewards on Children's Prosocial Motivation: A Socialization Study." *Developmental Psychology* 25, 4: 509–15.

Farrington, D. P. 1978. "The Family Backgrounds of Aggressive Youths." In *Aggression and Anti-Social Behaviour in Childhood and Adolescence,* edited by L. A. Hersov and M. Berger, 73–93. Oxford: Pergamon.

Farrington, D. P. 1979. "Experiments on Deviance with Special Reference to Dishonesty." In *Advances in Experimental Social Psychology, Vol. 12,* edited by L. Berkowitz, 207–52. New York: Academic Press.

Farrington, D. P. 1991. "Childhood Aggression and Adult Violence: Early Precursors and Later Life Outcomes." In *The Development and Treatment of Childhood Aggression,* edited by D. J. Pepler and K. H. Rubin, 5–29. Hillsdale, N.J.: Lawrence Erlbaum.

Farrington, D. P., G. Gundry, and D. J. West. 1975. "The Familial Transmission of Criminality." *Medical Science Law* 15, 3: 177–86.

Farrington, D. P. and D. J. West. 1981. "The Cambridge Study in Delinquent Development (United Kingdom)." In *Longitudinal Research: An Empirical Basis for Primary Prevention,* edited by S. A. Mednick and A. E. Baert, 137–45. Oxford: Oxford University Press.

Feshbach, S. and J. Price. 1984. "Cognitive Competencies and Aggressive Behavior: A Developmental Study." *Aggressive Behavior* 10(3): 185–200.

Festinger, L. 1957. *A Theory of Cognitive Dissonance.* Stanford, Cal.: Stanford University Press.

Festinger, L. 1964. *Conflict, Decision and Dissonance.* Stanford, Cal.: Stanford University Press.

Freud, S. 1930/1961. *Civilization and Its Discontents.* Translated by J. Strachey. New York: W. W. Norton.

Friedrich, L. K. and A. H. Stein. 1973. "Aggressive and Prosocial Television Programs and the Natural Behavior of Preschool Children." *Monographs of the Society for Research in Child Development* 38, 4 (Serial No. 151): 1–64.

Gibbons, F. X. and R. A. Wicklund. 1982. "Self-focused Attention and Helping Behavior." *Journal of Personality and Social Psychology* 37, 10: 1769–78.

Glaser, D. 1978. *Crime in Our Changing Society.* New York: Holt, Rinehart & Winston.

Goldstein, J. H. and R. L. Arms. 1971. "Effects of Observing Athletic Contests on Hostility." *Sociometry* 34, 1: 83–90.

Gottfredson, M. R. and T. Hirschi. 1990. *A General Theory of Crime.* Stanford, Cal.: Stanford University Press.

Gouldner, A. W. 1960. "The Norm of Reciprocity." *American Sociological Review* 25, 2: 161–78.

Grasmick, H. G. and G. J. Bryjak. 1980. "The Deterrent Effect of Perceived Severity of Punishment." *Social Forces* 59, 2, 471–91.

Grusec, J. E. and T. Dix. 1986. "The Socialization of Prosocial Behavior: Theory and Reality." In *Altruism and Aggression: Biological and Social Origins,* edited by C. Zahn-Waxler, E. M. Cummings, and R. Iannotti, 218–37. Cambridge: Cambridge University Press.

Hatfield, E., G. W. Walster, and J. A. Piliavin. 1978. "Equity Theory and Helping Relationships." In *Altruism, Sympathy, and Helping,* edited by L. Wispé, 115–39. New York: Academic Press.

Heider, F. 1946. "Attitudes and Cognitive Organization." *Journal of Psychology* 21, 107–12.

Hinde, R. A. 1979. *Towards Understanding Relationships*. London: Academic Press.

Hinde, R. A. 1986. "Some Implications of Evolutionary Theory and Comparative Data for the Study of Human Prosocial and Aggressive Behaviour." In *Development of Antisocial and Prosocial Behavior,* edited by D. Olweus, J. Block, and M. R. Yarrow, 13–32. New York: Academic Press.

Hirshi, T. 1969. *Causes of delinquency*. Berkeley: University of California Press.

Hoffman, M. L. 1963. "Parent Discipline and the Child's Consideration for Others." *Child Development* 34, 573–88.

Hoffman, M. L. 1980. "Moral Development in Adolescence." In *Handbook of Adolescent Psychology,* edited by J. Adelson, 295–343. New York: Wiley.

Hoffman, M. L. 1981. "Is Altruism Part of Human Nature?" *Journal of Personality and Social Psychology* 40, 1, 121–27.

Homans, G. C. 1961. *Social Behavior: Its Elementary Forms*. New York: Harcourt Brace.

Huesman, L. R., L. D. Eron, M. M. Lefkowitz, and L. O. Walder. 1984. "Stability of Aggression Over Time and Generations." *Developmental Psychology* 20, 1120–34.

Isen, A. M. and P. F. Levin. 1972. "Effect of Feeling Good on Helping: Cookies and Kindness." *Journal of Personality and Social Psychology* 21, 3, 384–88.

Kant, I. 1785/1959. *Foundations of the Metaphysics of Morals,* trans. L. W. Beck. Indianapolis: Bobbs-Merrill.

Kellam, S. G., M. B. Simon, and M. E. Ensminger. 1983. "Antecedents in First Grade of Teenage Substance Use and Psychological Well-Being: A Ten-Year Community-Wide Prospective Study." In *Origins of Psychopathology,* edited by D. F. Ricks and B. S. Dohrenwend, 17–42. Cambridge: Cambridge University Press.

Klinteberg af, B. D. Schalling, and D. Magnusson. 1990. "Childhood Behaviour and Adult Personality in Male and Female Subjects." *European Journal of Personality* 4, 57–71.

Latané, B. and J. M. Dabbs. 1975. "Sex, Group Size, and Helping in Three Cities." *Sociometry* 38, 2, 180–94.

Latané, B. and J. M. Darley. "Group Inhibition of Bystander Intervention in Emergencies." *Journal of Personality and Social Psychology* 10, 3, 215–21.

Lefkowitz, M. M., L. D. Eron, L. O. Walder, and L. R. Huesmann. 1977.

Growing Up to be Violent: A Longitudinal Study of Aggression. Elmsford, N.Y.: Pergamon.

Levy, P., D. Lundgren, M. Ansel, D. Fell, B. Fink, and J. E. McGrath. 1972. "Bystander Effect in a Demand-Without-Threat Situation." *Journal of Personality and Social Psychology* 24, 2 (Nov.), 166–71.

Loeber, R. and M. Stouthamer-Loeber. 1986. "Family Factors as Correlates and Predictors of Juvenile Conduct Problems and Delinquency." In *Crime and Justice,* vol. 7, edited by M. Tonry and N. Morris, 29–149. Chicago: University of Chicago Press.

London, P. 1970. "The Rescuers: Motivational Hypotheses about Christians who saved Jews from the Nazis." In *Altruism and Helping Behavior,* edited by J. Macaulay and L. Berkowitz, 241–50. New York: Academic Press.

Maccoby, E. E. 1986. "Social Groupings in Childhood: Their Relationship to Prosocial and Antisocial Behavior in Boys and Girls." In *Development of Antisocial and Prosocial Behavior,* edited by D. Olweus, J. Block, and M. R. Yarrow, 263–84. New York: Academic Press.

Magnusson, D. and L. R. Bergman. 1988. "Individual and Variable-Based Approaches to Longitudinal Research on Early Risk Factors." In *Studies of Psychosocial Risk: The Power of Longitudinal Data,* edited by M. Rutter, 45–61. Cambridge: Cambridge University Press.

Marcus, R. F. 1986. "Naturalistic Observation of Cooperation, Helping, and Sharing and their Associations with Empathy and Affect." In *Altruism and Aggression: Biological and Social Origins,* edited by C. Zahn-Waxler, E. M. Cummings, and R. Iannotti, 256–79. Cambridge: Cambridge University Press.

McCord, J. 1977. "A Comparative Study of Two Generations of Native Americans." In *Theory in Criminology: Contemporary Views,* edited by R. F. Meier, 83–92. Beverly Hills: Sage.

McCord, J. 1983. "A Longitudinal Study of Aggression and Antisocial Behavior." In *Prospective Studies of Crime and Delinquency,* edited by K. T. Van Dusen and S. A. Mednick, 269–75. Boston: Kluwer-Nijhoff.

McCord, J. 1983. "A Forty Year Perspective on Effects of Child Abuse and Neglect." *Child Abuse & Neglect* 7, 265–70.

McCord, J. 1984. "A Longitudinal Study of Personality Development." In *Handbook of Longitudinal Research, Vol. 2, Teenage and Adult Cohorts,* edited by S. A. Mednick, M. Harway, and K. M. Finello, 522–31. New York: Praeger.

McCord, J. 1991. "Questioning the Value of Punishment." *Social Problems* 38, 2, 167–179.

Milgram, S. 1963. "Behavioral Study of Obedience." *Journal of Abnormal and Social Psychology* 67, 371–78.

Milgram, S. 1974. *Obedience to Authority: An Experimental View*. New York: Harper.

Moore, B. S., B. Underwood, and D. L. Rosenhan, 1973. "Affect and Altruism." *Developmental Psychology* 8, 1, 99–104.

Nagin, D. 1978. "General Deterrence: A Review of the Empirical Evidence." In *Deterrence and Incapacitation: Estimating the Effects of Criminal Sanctions on Crime Rates*, edited by A. Blumstein, J. Cohen, and D. Nagin, 95–139. Washington, D.C.: National Academy of Sciences.

Olweus, D. 1979. "Stability of Aggressive Patterns in Males: A Review." *Psychological Bulletin* 86, 4, 852–75.

Pawelczynska, A. 1979. *Values and Violence in Auschwitz: A Sociological Analysis*, translated by C. S. Leach. Berkeley: University of California Press.

Plato. *The Republic*, translated by Paul Shorey.

Pulkkinen, L. 1984. "The Inhibition and Control of Aggression." *Aggressive Behavior* 10(3), 221–25.

Pulkkinen, L. 1988. "Delinquent Development: Theoretical and Empirical Considerations." In *The Power of Longitudinal Data: Studies of Risk and Protective Factors for Psychosocial Disorders*, edited by M. Rutter, 184–99. Cambridge: Cambridge University Press.

Rheingold, H. and G. N. Emery. 1986. "The Nurturant Acts of Very Young Children." In *Development of Antisocial and Prosocial Behavior*, edited by D. Olweus, J. Block, and M. R. Yarrow, 75–96. New York: Academic Press.

Robins, L. N. and L. McEvoy. "Conduct Problems as Predictors of Substance Abuse." In *Straight and Devious Pathways from Childhood to Adulthood*, edited by L. N. Robins and M. Rutter, 182–204. Cambridge: Cambridge University Press.

Rosenhan, D. L. 1978. "Toward Resolving the Altruism Paradox: Affect, Self-Reinforcement, and Cognition." In *Altruism, Sympathy, and Helping: Psychological and Sociological Principles*, edited by L. Wispé, 101–13. New York: Academic Press.

Rosenhan, D. L., B. Underwood, and B. Moore. 1974. "Affect Moderates Self-Gratification and Altruism." *Journal of Personality and Social Psychology* 30, 4, 546–52.

Rosenhan, D. and G. M. White. 1967. "Observation and Rehearsal as Determinants of Prosocial Behavior." *Journal of Personality and Social Psychology* 5, 424–31.

Rushton, J. P. 1979. "Effects of Prosocial Television and Film Material on the Behavior of Viewers." In *Advances in Experimental Social Psychology, Vol. 12*, edited by L. Berkowitz, 321–51. New York: Academic Press.

Staub, E. 1970. "A Child in Distress: The Influence of Age and Number of Witnesses on Children's Attempts to Help." *Journal of Personality and Social Psychology* 14, 2, 130–40.

Staub, E. 1979. *Positive Social Behavior and Morality: Socialization and Development*, vol. 2, New York: Academic Press.

Staub, E. 1986. "A Conception of the Determinants and Development of Altruism and Aggression: Motives, the Self, and the Environment." In *Altruism and Aggression: Biological and Social Origins*, edited by C. Zahn-Waxler, E. M. Cummings, and R. Iannotti, 135–64. Cambridge: Cambridge University Press.

Staub, E. 1989. *The Roots of Evil: The Origins of Genocide and Other Group Violence*. Cambridge: Cambridge University Press.

Sutherland, E. H. and D. R. Cressey. 1924/1974. *Criminology* (9th ed.). Philadelphia: Lippincott.

Sykes, G. and D. Matza. 1957. "Techniques of Neutralization: A Theory of Delinquency." *American Sociological Review* 22, 667–70.

Tremblay, R. E., L. Desmarais-Gervais, C. Gagnon, and P. Charlebois. 1987. "The Preschool Behaviour Questionnaire: Stability of its Factor Structure Between Cultures, Sexes, Ages and Socioeconomic Classes." *International Journal of Behavioral Development* 10(4), 467–84.

White, G. M. 1972. "Immediate and Deferred Effects of Model Observation and Guided and Unguided Rehearsal on Donating and Stealing." *Journal of Personality and Social Psychology* 21, 2, 139–48.

Whiting, B. B. and J. W. M. Whiting. 1975. *Children of Six Cultures: A Psycho-Cultural Analysis*. Cambridge: Harvard University Press.

Wicklund, R. A. 1975. "Objective Self-Awareness." In *Advances in Experimental Social Psychology, Vol. 8*, edited by L. Berkowitz, 233–75. New York: Academic Press.

Widom, C. S. 1989. "Child Abuse, Neglect, and Violent Criminal Behavior." *Criminology* 27, 2, 251–71.

Wilkens, J. L., W. H. Scharff, and R. S. Schlottman. 1974. "Personality Type, Reports of Violence and Aggressive Behavior." *Journal of Personality and Social Psychology* 30, 2, 243–47.

Zahn-Waxler, C. and M. Radke-Yarrow. 1982. "The Development of Altruism: Alternative Research Strategies." In *The Development of Prosocial Behavior*, edited by N. Eisenberg, 109–37. New York: Academic Press.

Zahn-Waxler, C., M. Radke-Yarrow, and R. A. King. 1979. "Child-Rearing and Children's Pro-Social Initiations Toward Victims of Distress." *Child Development* 50, 319–30.

Zahn-Waxler, C., M. Radke-Yarrow, E. Wagner, and C. Pyle. 1988. "The Early Development of Prosocial Behavior." Presented at the ICIS meetings, Washington, D.C., April.

Zillman, D. 1979. *Hostility and Aggression*. Hillsdale, N.J.: Lawrence Erlbaum.

Zimbardo, P. G., C. Haney, W. C. Banks, and D. Jaffe. 1974. "The Psychology of Imprisonment: Privation, Power, and Pathology." In *Doing Unto Others*, edited by Z. Rubin, 61–73. Englewood Cliffs, N.J.: Prentice Hall.

7

Childhood Aggression and Adult Criminality

L. Rowell Huesmann and Leonard D. Eron

The sociological/criminological literature for many years has emphasized the existence of an association between prevalence and/or incidence of criminal behavior and certain sociological variables. (e.g., Hirschi 1969). It is undeniable that there are positive correlations between criminal convictions and race (Hawkins 1985; Matsueda and Heine 1987), gender (Hindelang 1979; Jensen and Eve 1976), age (Farrington 1986; Hirschi and Gottfredson 1983), place of residence (Messner and Tardiff 1986; Reiss and Tonry 1986) family structure (McCord 1982; Kolvin, Miller, Fleeting, and Kolvin 1988), socio-economic status (Miethe, Stafford, and Long 1987; Cohen, Klugel, and Land 1981) and ethnic group (Hagedorn 1988; Rieder 1985). However, the correlations at best are in the moderate range, and the underlying causes of these correlations remain uncertain. A number of these researchers have gone beyond the simple correlations to show that the relations of social context with criminality are often a product of third variables or are indicative of complex interactions with other behaviors also related to social context (e.g., Farrington 1986; McCord 1982; Reiss and Tonry 1986).

But others have argued for the explanatory value of social context by itself (e.g., Hirschi 1969; Hirschi and Gottfredson 1983). Yet, not every African-American male in late adolescence, raised in a single parent family of low socio-economic status and living in a disorganized, high-crime neighborhood in the inner city engages in criminal behavior. Probably only a minority of them do. In order to understand why some youngsters in these circumstances develop criminal behavior and others do not, we must understand the processes by which this type of behavior develops. Why do youngsters growing up under these ecological/environmental conditions develop differing norms, expectations and attitudes about behaving and responding towards others? Why within each of the narrow segments of society defined by social conditions are there wide variations in propensities for antisocial and criminal behavior? The answers to these questions become clearer when one examines them within the context of a comprehensive model of the psychological processes that underlie the development of both normal social behavior and aberrant antisocial behavior.

Early Predictors of Adult Criminality

One of the clearest findings concerning adolescent and adult criminal behavior is that such behavior is predictable statistically from early antisocial, aggressive, and hyperactive behavior (Ensminger, Kellam, and Rubin 1983; Farrington 1982, 1991; Huesmann, Eron, Lefkowitz, and Walder 1984; Moffitt 1990; Loeber and Dishion 1983; Magnusson, Duner, and Zetterblom 1975; Olweus 1979; Robins and Ratcliff 1980; Spivack 1983). The more aggressive child is likely to become both the more aggressive adult and the more antisocial and criminal adult. No other factor measured in childhood, whether physiological, cognitive, environmental, or familial, has been shown to predict more of the variation in adult antisocial behavior than does early aggression. For example, in a study conducted in New York State, we and our colleagues found that peer-nominations of a child's aggression and antisocial behavior measured at age eight predicted a whole variety of aggressive and antisocial behaviors displayed twenty-two years later at age thirty including officially tallied criminal convictions (See table 7.1).

Does that mean, as some have suggested, that we believe that all criminal behavior is aggressive behavior? No, of course not. What it does suggest is that the developmental psychological processes underlying aggressive behavior also underlie other forms of antisocial and criminal behavior. Furthermore, aggression is a behavior

TABLE 7.1
Correlations of Peer-Nominated Aggression at Age 8 with Antisocial Behavior
at Age 30

| | Age 8 Peer-Nominated Aggression | | | |
| | Males | | Females | |
Age 30 Antisocial Behaviors	n	r	n	r
Scales F + 4 + 9 of MMPI	190	0.30****	209	0.20**
Abuse of Spouse	88	0.27***	74	ns
Harsh Physical Punishment of Own Child	63	0.24*	96	0.24**
Criminal Justice Convictions	335	0.24****	207	0.10 +
Seriousness of Arrests	332	0.21****	207	0.15**
Moving Traffic Violations	322	0.21****	201	ns
Driving While Intoxicated	322	0.24****	201	ns
Self-reported Violent Aggression	193	0.29****	209	ns

*$p. < .10$ **$p < .05$ ***$p < .01$ ****$p < .001$

that occurs frequently among even very young children and therefor is amenable to study as part of a developmental process.

What Is Aggressive Behavior?

An aggressive behavior is a behavior that is intended to injure or irritate another person. This commonly accepted definition includes both behavior motivated primarily by a desire for tangible rewards and behavior motivated primarily by hostility. However, it does not include many commonplace meanings of the word including assertive behaviors, for example, an aggressive salesperson. As with many definitions in psychology, there are numerous grey areas in which the classification of behaviors as aggressive or nonaggressive is problematic. For some of these areas, for example, contact sports and war, the key distinction may be whether the behavior is under specific discriminative stimulus control and sanctioned by society. In war, for example, one might argue that most individual acts of killing derive from prosocial rather than antisocial motives. Suffice it to say that the aggressive behavior of concern in children as a precursor of adult criminality is antisocial aggressive behavior.

Early Development of Aggressive Behavior

Individual differences in social behavior related to aggression (e.g., early temperament) have been detected before age two (Kagan 1988), and it has been shown that at least by age six, a number of children have adopted aggressive patterns of behavior in their interactions with others (Parke and Slaby 1983). The extent of aggressive behavior in children tends to increase into adolescence. However, by age eight, children are characteristically more or less aggressive over a variety of situations, and aggression becomes a stable characteristic of the individual youngster (Huesmann et al. 1984; Olweus 1979). Further, investigations have found long-term stability of aggression originally measured when the subjects were eight years of age. The more aggressive child becomes the more aggressive adult. In figure 7.1, for example, a structural model is displayed showing the stability of aggression over the twenty-two years from age eight to thirty for a sample of 409 New York State subjects (Huesmann et al. 1984).

FIGURE 7.1
A structural model showing the stability of an hypothesized latent trait of aggression within all subjects over 22 years.

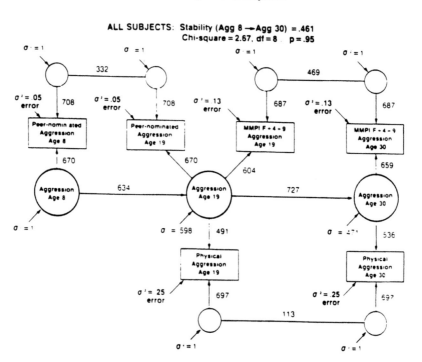

The implications of this stability and the relation between adult criminality and child aggression are notable for interventions aimed at preventing criminal behavior. As aggression is already apparent with wide individual differences by age six and becomes a stable characteristic of the individual by age eight, that leaves just a brief period of developmental years during which preventive action must begin by parents, teachers, and other socializing agents. How these persons respond to the first indications of aggression will probably be more important in determining subsequent development or inhibition of such behaviors than any organized efforts of the criminal justice establishment at later ages.

Causes of Early Aggression

The observed developmental trends for aggressive behavior are not inconsistent with aggression being a product of a number of interacting factors: genetic, perinatal, physiological, familial, and learning. In fact, it seems most likely that severe antisocial aggressive behavior occurs only when there is a convergence of many of these factors.

The evidence for a heritable predisposition to aggression has mounted in recent years with the advance of experimental behavior genetics. Adoption studies in Scandinavia, where subjects are easily tracked for years, show more concordance between adults' antisocial and aggressive behavior and their natural parents' behaviors than with their foster parents' behaviors (Cloninger and Gottesman 1987; Mednick, Gabrielli and Hutchings 1984). In fact, both twin and adoption studies now provide compelling evidence that many personality characteristics tied to social behavior are influenced by heredity (Bouchard 1984; Loehlin, Willerman, and Horn 1985; Rowe 1987; Rushton, Fulker, Neale, Nias, and Eysenck 1986). While the methodologies of many studies in these areas are necessarily complex and open to criticism, the evidence that there is a substantial heritable predisposition to aggression now seems compelling. However, that does not mean that situational and environmental variables are unimportant. On the basis of extrapolations from the animal literature, it seems quite probable that a heritable predisposition to aggression manifests itself in characteristic early social interactions. The animal literature also suggests that early interactions of an appropriate type can greatly mitigate the genetic predisposition to aggression. Lagerspetz and Lagerspetz (1971), for example, have shown that selective breeding for aggression can produce highly aggressive strains of mice in just a few generations. However, the extent to which even mice from the most aggressive strain (after thirty generations) will evidence aggression as adults depends on their early social interactions with other mice (Lagerspetz and Sandnabba 1982). Mice who are predisposed to be aggressive but who are raised in an environment in which "prosocial" behavior is rewarded do not evidence such strong aggressive tendencies. Genetic predispositions interact with an organism's early learning experiences.

It also seems likely that the effects of specific chronic neurophysiological deficits that promote aggression and the effects of neurotoxins (such as lead) interact with early environment to affect adult aggressive behavior. The evidence for the involvement of neurophysiological abnormalities in many cases of severe aggression is strong (Lewis, Moy, Jackson, Aaronson, Restifo, Serra, and Simos 1985; Moyer 1976; Nachson and Denno 1987; Pontius 1984). Less extreme individual differenes in aggression sometimes seem to be related to naturally occurring variations in hormones, for example, testosterone, estrogen, and progesterone (Dalton 1977; Olweus, Mattsson, Schalling, and Low 1980; Olweus 1988). Individual differences in characteristic heart rates have also been linked to individual differences in adolescent aggression (Raine and Jones 1987) and also to the differences in early childhood temperament that are related to aggression. Specifically, low heart-rate children are more at risk for aggression. What does seem clear is that the effects on social behavior of individual differences in neurophysiology are exacerbated and mitigated by both a child's early learning experiences and situational factors in the person's environment. For example, Olweus's (Olweus et al. 1980) data suggest that a high testosterone adolescent would only be prone to behave aggressively in situations in which he were strongly provoked. Similarly, in many cases of extreme aggressive reactions linked to neurophysiological deficits, the responses have been triggered by situational factors producing stress and/or early experiences that promoted aggression.

Our theme is that severe early aggression, which is clearly a predictor of adult antisocial and aggressive behavior, is multiply

determined. Seldom does a single factor explain why a child becomes aggressive; there must be a convergence of several factors.
While genetic and neurophysiological factors may predispose a
child toward aggression, children's early interactions with their
environment play a major role in the development of the children's
habitual styles of social behavior, whether aggressive or prosocial.
How the adolescent responds to provocations, environmental dep-
rivations, and frustrations is influenced by these early interactions.
Early learning experiences that promote affection and prosocial
behavior (e.g., McCord 1983) can block the slide from childhood
aggression to adult antisocial behavior. The goal of a developmental
theory for the explanation of adult aggression, antisocial behavior,
and criminal behavior should be to explain the mechanism through
which this occurs.

Cognitive Processes and Learning of Aggression

Because of the malleability of behavior in young children and the
relative intractability of aggressive and violent dispositions once
they have been developed, it is important that theories of criminality focus on aggression and antisocial behavior in preadolescent
children. As we have argued above, individual differences during
this period are influenced, of course, by factors with earlier loci of
affect, for example, genetics; but the major issue of interest is how
during early childhood individual differences in the propensity for
aggressive behavior develop as a consequence of the child's interaction with his or her environment. What are the dimensions and
parameters of the social learning processes that lead to these
enhanced individual differences? How do they interact with the
predisposing factors? In recent years a number of theories have
been offered which all implicate the child's cognitions in the learning and maintenance of aggressive habits during this period. Growing out of Bandura's formulation of social learning theory and
drawing on recent theorizing in cognitive psychology, these models
put the stress primarily on cognitive processes and the steps
through which a child must proceed to react appropriately, compe-
tently and nonaggressively to a social situation or stimulus. Among
the most influential of these have been the revised formulation of
Bandura (1986), the neo-associationist perspective of Berkowitz

(1984, 1988), the social-cognitive formulation of Dodge (1980), and the information processing theory put forth by Huesmann (1988; Huesmann and Eron 1984).

Recent Theoretical Formulations

According to Bandura's (1986) recent formulation, social behavior comes under the control of internal self-regulating processes. What is important is the cognitive evaluation of events taking place in the child's environment, how the child interprets these events and how competent he feels in responding in different ways. These cognitions provide a basis for stability of behavior tendencies across a variety of situations. Berkowitz, on the other hand, has emphasized the importance of enduring associations in explaining stable behavioral tendencies. Aggression is an aversively stimulated behavior. An aversive event produces negative affect which is associated in most people with "expressive-motor reactions, feelings, thoughts, and memories that are associated with both flight and fight tendencies" (Berkowitz 1988, 8). A variety of factors—genetic, learned, and situational—affects the strengths of the flight and fight tendencies. The stronger tendency wins out, and, if it is fight, the emotional experience is interpreted as anger. Attributions about the behavior may occur later as a "controlled" cognitive process, but the generation of the behavior and the associated anger is relatively "automatic."[1] Dodge (1980), on the other hand, emphasizes the importance of enduring attributional biases in affecting the stability of aggressive behavior across situations. Aggressive children are viewed as possessing defective cognitive processes for the interpretation of others' behaviors and the selection of their own behavior from a previously learned repertoire. Huesmann (1988; Huesmann and Eron 1984) has viewed the child as a processor of information who develops programs called "scripts" to guide social behavior. The aggressive child is one who has developed more aggressive scripts.

All of these approaches have the common theme that the child's cognitions play a key role in maintaining the stability of aggressive behavior over time and situation. The various predisposing and precipitating factors can influence behavior over time by affecting these cognitions. In turn, the direct effect of any predisposing factor may well be moderated by cognitions that the child has developed.

Script Theory and Prediction of Criminality

Of all these cognitive approaches, the information processing script theory developed by Huesmann (1988) is most directly intended to explain the stability of aggressive tendencies over time and the predictability of even "nonviolent" crime from early aggression. Huesmann's theory adopts the premise that social behavior is controlled to a great extent by programs for behavior that are established during a person's early development. These programs can be described as cognitive scripts (Abelson 1981) that are stored in a person's memory and are used as guides for behavior and social problem solving. A script suggests what events are to happen in the environment, how the person should behave in response to these events, and what the likely outcome of those behaviors would be. It is presumed that while scripts are first being established they influence the child's behavior through "controlled" mental processes (Schneider and Shriffrin 1977. See note 1), but that these processes become "automatic" as the child matures. Correspondingly scripts that persist in a child's repertoire, as they are rehearsed, enacted, and generate consequences, become increasingly more resistant to modification and change. According to Huesmann, the primary process through which scripts are formed is a learning process involving both observational and enactive components. However, the outcome of this process is heavily influenced by the child's environment and the predisposing factors discussed earlier. Furthermore, through a process of cognitive abstraction, subsets of learned scripts are converted into more general scripts that provide overall guiding principles for social behavior. Thus, the scripts that guide the child into "childish" aggressive behavior form the basis for a set of more general scripts guiding the adult into antisocial behavior.

Huesmann's full theory casts scripts as the central cognitive component of a complex psychological process that generates social behavior. However, a person's affective response to a situation and that person's concomitant cognitive interpretations also play a role in the process. It is assumed that a child enters any social interaction with a preexisting emotional state. The state consists of both a physiological arousal component and a cognitive component. This emotional state is determined to some extent by physiological predispositions that may be relatively stable, for example, neuroanatomy, or relatively transient such as dietary factors. The cognitive component of the emotional state will be influenced heavily by the child's past reinforcement history and the attributions the child has made about those reinforcements. For example, a child who is exposed repeatedly to frustrating situations and who attributes the goal blocking to the actions of other individuals may enter a social interaction in an aroused state with hostile feelings toward others. Recent environmental stimuli may also directly trigger conditioned emotional reactions and thus cue the retrieval from memory of cognitions that define the current emotional state. For example, to a child the sight of an "enemy" may provoke both instantaneous arousal and the recall of thoughts about the "enemy" that give meaning to the aroused state as anger.

Because emotional states may persist for some time beyond the exciting event, a child may enter a social interaction in an emotional state that is unrelated to the current situational cues. Nevertheless, that emotional state may influence both which cues the child attends to and how the child evaluates those cues. A highly aroused, angry child may focus on just a few highly salient cues and ignore others that convey equally important information about the social situation. Further, the angry child's evaluation of these cues may be biased toward perceiving hostility when none is present. In any case, as emotional states in children are transient and heavily situationally dependent, one outcome of the child's evaluation of the current cues would usually be a revised emotional state. This new emotional state, coupled with both the objective properties of the current stimulus situation and the evaluative cognitions cued by the stimulus situation, determine which scripts for behavior will be retrieved from memory.

Huesmann proposes, however, that not all scripts that occur to the child, that are retrieved, will be employed. Before acting out the script, the child reevaluates the appropriateness of the script in light of existing internalized social norms and examines the likely consequences. There may be great individual differences in the extent of this evaluation. Some children may not have the cognitive capacity to engage in a thorough evaluation. Even among children with similar capacities differing reinforcement histories and differing perceptions of social norms may lead to quite different evaluations. It is hypothesized that these evaluations of potential scripts for behavior are comprised of three related components.

First, the child needs to be able to predict the consequences of utilizing such a script. Children may differ in their capacities to think about the future and in their concern with the future. Generally, the more a child focuses on immediate consequences and the less the child is concerned with the future, the more palatable an aggressive solution to a social problem may seem. Children may also misperceive the likely consequences of an aggressive act because of a defective reinforcement history or because of biases in the sample of scenes of others behaving aggressively that they have observed. A second evaluative component is the extent to which a child judges him or herself capable of executing the script. A child with low perceived self-efficacy for prosocial behaviors may turn to aggressive scripts by default. But perhaps the most important component of a script's evaluation is the third component: the extent to which the script is perceived as congruent with the child's self-regulating internal standards. Scripts that violate the social norms that a child has internalized are unlikely to be utilized. On the other hand, a child with weak or nonexistent internalized prohibitions against aggression or who believes that everyone behaves aggressively is much more likely to adopt new aggressive scripts for behavior.

Encoding and Rehearsal of Scripts

So far we have examined how existing scripts may be accessed and used to guide behavior, and how certain individual and environmental factors could promote the use of aggressive scripts. Within this framework an habitually aggressive child is one who regularly retrieves and employs scripts (for social behavior) that emphasize aggressive responding. We have noted a number of factors that might promote the retrieval and utilization of aggressive scripts. It may be, for example, that the cues present in the environment trigger the recall only of aggressive scripts. However, the regular retrieval and use of aggressive scripts would suggest above all that a large number of aggressive scripts have been stored in memory. Thus, we must examine the process through which scripts are learned.

Learning is hypothesized to occur both as a result of one's own behaviors (enactive learning) and as a result of viewing others behave (observational learning). Scripts are initially stored in memory in much the same way as are programs and strategies for intellectual behavior—through a two-component process involving an initial "encoding" of observed behaviors followed by repeated rehearsals. By "encoding"[2] we mean the "formation of a representation of an external stimulus in the memory system" (Kintsch 1977, 485). A script may be closely associated with specific cues in the encoding context, or may be an abstraction unconnected to specific cues.[3] To encode an observed sequence of behaviors as a script, a child must first attend to the sequence. Thus, scripts with particularly salient cues for the child are more likely to be encoded. However, many observed sequences might never be encoded because the child perceives them as inappropriate. Here, again, the child's current emotional state and current memory contents may exert some influence. When highly aroused and angry, for example, children may view a physically active sequence of behaviors as more appropriate than they would otherwise. Similarly, a young boy who has watched peers solve their social problems aggressively all afternoon is more likely to encode a newly observed "aggressive script" into his own repertoire than is a boy who has watched his peers solve their problems in a prosocial manner.

To maintain a script in memory, a child would need to rehearse it from time to time.[4] The rehearsal may take several different forms from simple recall of the original scene, to fantasizing about it, to play acting. The more elaborative, ruminative type of rehearsal characteristic of children's fantasizing is likely to generate greater connectedness for the script, thereby increasing its accessibility in memory. Also, through such elaborative rehearsal the child may abstract higher-order scripts representing more general strategies for behavior than the ones initially stored. Of course, rehearsal also provides another opportunity for reevaluation of any script. It may be that some scripts initially accepted as appropriate (under specific emotional and memory states) may be judged as inappropriate during rehearsal.

In order for a script to influence future behavior, it must not only be encoded and maintained in memory, it must be retrieved and utilized when the child faces a social problem. A key element at this point is the extent to which specific cues are present in the current situation that mirror cues present when the script was encoded. A script would be much more likely to be utilized if the same specific cues were present in the environment at retrieval time as were present at encoding time. This is true even if the cues are irrelevant to the behaviors in question, for example, colors, sounds, smells, physical setting.

Enactive Learning

The transformation of a child's initial aggressive behavior into habitual aggressive behavior may depend as much on the responses of the child's environment to the child's aggression as on other causal factors. It is quite likely that for some young children aggressive behavior can be very rewarding. Their family and peer environment may both provide aggressive models and reward aggressive behavior. For these children, the encoding, retrieval, and utilization of aggressive scripts are heavily reinforced at a young age. Yet sooner or later these children emerge into environments (e.g., school, teams, clubs) where aggressive behavior has strong negative consequences. One of the puzzling aspects of habitual aggressive behavior is why it persists in the face of so many apparently negative consequences. The answer must rest in the failure of the child to unlearn encoded aggressive scripts through enactive learning. Several types of deficient information processing might contribute to this failure.

Children might misperceive the consequences of their actions either because they focus on the wrong dimension of feedback or because they do not look far enough ahead. For example, a boy who knocks another child down in order to grab a ball that he wants may focus on the immediate fact that he has obtained the ball and not attend to the longer term social ostracization that follows his act. By the time such ostracization becomes salient, the precipitating act may be removed so far in time that no connection can be made. However, even the child who perceives the immediate negative consequences of an aggressive act may fail to learn alternative scripts. Generally, prosocial solutions to social problems are less direct and more complex than aggressive solutions. If a child cannot think of any such solutions, as might be the case with a child of low intellectual competence, the child may have no alternative to a direct aggressive solution.

For the more intellectually able child, another possibility exists, however, in addition to learning a new script. Rather than change his aggressive behaviors, which perhaps provide immediate gratification in some dimensions, the child alters his internal self-regulatory standards to provide less negative feedback. One way to accomplish such a change is by incorporating some of the readily available aphorisms about aggression into one's regulatory schemata. The boy who is told he is bad because he pushed others out of the way may shrug his shoulders and think, "Nice guys finish last." The boy who shoves a child who bumped into him may think, "An eye for an eye." Internalized norms against aggression may also be reduced when many others are observed behaving aggressively, either in person or in the media.

Finally, a child may mitigate society's negative reinforcements for aggressive behavior by choosing environments in which aggression is more acceptable. Thus, the more aggressive boy may spend more time interacting with other aggressive children who accept his behaviors as a way of life. Not only do such social networks provide a child with an environment in which aggression is not discouraged, such social networks promote the internalization of social norms favoring aggression.

The Emergence of Criminal Behavior

Huesmann's theory suggests that childhood aggressive behavior develops early through the interaction of predisposing and precipitating individual and environmental factors with learning conditions that promote the formation of scripts for aggressive behavior. A child's initial observations of others behaving aggressively combine with learning conditions that reinforce aggression to establish aggressive scripts in the child's memory at a young age. Cognitive rehearsal of these scripts through fantasy, positive reinforcements for the aggressive behaviors suggested by these scripts, and behavioral strategies that allow the child to escape the negative consequences of aggression combine to cement these scripts in place. These cognitive scripts become increasingly unmalleable as the child grows up. Furthermore, the effect of the reinforcement may generalize to scripts that are abstractions of the specific script, promoting a generalized disinhibition of aggression. The boy who solves a social problem successfully by hitting will be more likely in the future not just to hit, but to kick, punch, or push.

As the child grows up, both the child's social goals and the situational constraints on the child's behavior change. It would be difficult to see how specific cue-behavior connections could promote stability of behavior across such boundaries. However, just as approaches to more adult intellectual problem solving grow out of abstractions of programs for earlier problem solving, so, Huesmann hypothesizes, would the programs for adult social problem solving be built on abstractions of the programs learned in childhood. Children who adopt scripts for childhood social behavior that violate societal rules and constraints would also be more likely to adopt specific scripts for adult behavior that violate societal rules. Thus, one would expect childhood aggressive behavior to be predictive of adult antisocial behavior whether such behavior is violent or nonviolent.

The Environment and Criminal Behavior

We opened this chapter by arguing that the theories that have attempted to explain criminal and antisocial behavior simply as a consequence of economic and social deprivation and stressful environments have missed the mark. Habitual criminal behavior requires a specific psychological orientation that develops only when a number of predisposing and precipitating factors converge with an environment that is conducive to the learning of aggression. Environment interacts with predisposing factors in the young child to promote the development of cognitions that guide social behavior not only in childhood but throughout life. Whether one views these cognitive structures as scripts, cue-behavior connections, self-regulating internal standards, or attributional biases, these structures seem remarkably resistant to change as the child moves into adolescence and young adulthood. The major conclusion one must draw about interventions aimed at reducing criminal behavior seems unambiguous. Interventions need to be directed at the young child. The adolescent's and young adult's environment may provide the precipitating factors that engender crime and reinforcing consequences for crime, but the psychological basis of the antisocial behavior was developed much earlier.

This research was supported in part by grant MH38383 from the USA National Institute of Mental Health. Portions of this chapter have appeared previously in Huesmann (1988).

Notes

1. The terms *controlled* and *automatic* are technical terms developed by cognitive psychologists to describe different modes of mental processing (Schneider and Shriffrin 1977). Automatic processes are mental processes that operate very rapidly with a person having little awareness of the mental operations involved, e.g., reading. Controlled processes operate much more slowly, and a person is much more aware that they are "controlling" the mental operations, e.g., mental arithmetic.
2. It is beyond the scope of this paper to elaborate the encoding processes in detail. A great deal of research in cognitive psychology has been devoted to understanding how humans encode and retrieve information from their memory system. The presumption is that the encoding and retrieval of scripts obey the same laws that regulate the encoding and retrieval of other information.
3. It is presumed that the processes identified by cognitive psychologists to explain how people form abstract cognitive concepts would apply to the derivation of more abstract scripts. A child who has utilized many different specific types of scripts with aggressive components to solve social problems would form a more abstract script connecting the general elements of social problems to the general characteristics of aggressive solutions, e.g., harm to others.
4. Again this presumption is based on a long line of research by cognitive psychologists (e.g., Kintsch 1977).

References

Abelson, R. P. 1981. "The Psychological Status of the Script Concept." *American Psychologist* 36, 715–29.

Bandura, A. 1986. *Social Foundations of Thought and Action: A Social Cognitive Theory*. Englewood Cliffs, N.J.: Prentice-Hall.

Berkowitz, L. 1984. "Some Effects of Thoughts on Anti- and Prosocial Influences of Media Events: A Cognitive-Neoassociation Analysis." *Psychological Bulletin* 95, 3, 410–27.

Berkowitz, L. 1988. "Frustrations, Appraisals, and Aversively Stimulated Aggression." *Aggressive Behavior* 14, 3–12.

Bouchard, T. J. 1984. "Twins Reared Together and Apart: What They Tell Us About Human Diversity." In *Individuality and Determinism: Chemical and Biological Basis,* edited by S. W. Fox, 147–84. New York: Plenum.

Cloninger, C. R. and A. Gottesman. 1987. "Genetic and Environmental Factors in antisocial behavior disorders." In *The Causes of Crime: New biological Approaches,* edited by S. A. Mednick, T. E. Moffitt, and S. A. Stack, 92–109. New York: Cambridge University Press.

Cohen, L., J. Klugel, and K. Land. 1981. "Social Inequality and Predatory Criminal Victimization." *American Sociological Review* 46, 505–24.

Dalton, K. 1977. *The Pre-menstrual Syndrome and Progesterone Therapy.* London: Heinemann.

Dodge, K. 1980. "Social Cognition and Children's Aggressive Behavior." *Child Development* 53, 620–35.

Ensminger, M. E., S. G. Kellam, and B. R. Rubin. 1983. "School and Family Origins of Delinquency." In *Prospective Studies of Crime and Delinquency,* edited by K. T. Van Dusen and S. A. Mednick, 73–97. Boston, Kluwer-Nijhoff.

Farrington, D. P. 1982. "Longitudinal Analyses of Criminal Violence." In *Criminal Violence,* edited by M. E. Wolfgang and N. A. Weiner, 171–200. Beverly Hills, Cal.: Sage.

Farrington, D. P. 1986. "Age and Crime." In *Crime and Justice* 7, edited by M. Tonry and N. Morris, 189–250. Chicago: University of Chicago Press.

Farrington, D. P. 1991. "Childhood Aggression and Adult Violence: Early Precursors and Later-Life Outcomes." In *The Development and Treatment of Childhood Aggression,* edited by D. J. Pepler and K. H. Rubin, 5–29. Hillsdale, N.J.: Erlbaum.

Hagedorn, J. 1988. *Gangs, Crime and the Underclass in a Rustbelt City.* Chicago: Lake View Press.

Hawkins, D. 1985. "Black Homicide: The Adequacy of Existing Research for Devising Prevention Strategies." *Crime and Delinquency* 31, 81–103.

Hindelang, M. J. 1979. "Sex Differences in Criminal Activity." *Social Problems* 27, 143–56.

Hirschi, T. 1969. *Causes of Delinquency.* Berkeley: University of California Press.

Hirschi, T. and M. R. Gottfredson. 1983. "Age and the Explanation of Crime." *American Journal of Sociology* 89, 521–84.

Huesmann, L. R. 1988. "An Information Processing Model for the Development of Aggression." *Aggressive Behavior* 14, 13–24.

Huesmann, L. R. and L. D. Eron. 1984. "Cognitive Processes and the Persistence of Aggressive Behavior." *Aggressive Behavior* 10, 243–51.

Huesmann, L. R., L. D. Eron, M. M. Lefkowitz, and L. O. Walder. 1984. "The Stability of Aggression over Time and Generations." *Developmental Psychology* 20, 1120–34.

Jensen, G. and R. Eve. 1976. "Sex Differences in Delinquency: An Examination of Popular Sociological Explanations." *Criminology* 13, 427–48.

Kagan, J. 1988. "Temperamental Contributions to Social Behavior." *American Psychologist* 44, 668–74.

Kintsch, W. 1977. *Memory and Cognition*. New York: Wiley.

Kolvin, I., F. J. W. Miller, M. Fleeting, and P. A. Kolvin. 1988. "Social and Parenting Factors Affecting Criminal Offense Rates." *British Journal of Psychiatry* 152, 80–89.

Lagerspetz, K. and K. M. J. Lagerspetz. 1971. "Changes in Aggressiveness of Mice Resulting from Selective Breeding, Learning and Social Isolation." *Scandinavian Journal of Psychology* 12, 241–78.

Lagerspetz, K. and K. Sandnabba. 1982. "The Decline of Aggression in Mice During Group Caging as Determined by Punishment Delivered by Cagemates." *Aggressive Behavior* 8, 319–34.

Lewis, D. O., E. Moy, L. D. Jackson, R. Aaronson, N. Restifo, S. Serra, and A. Simos. 1985. "Biopsychological Characteristics of Children who Later Murder: A Prospective Study." *American Journal of Psychiatry* 142, 1161–67.

Loehlin, J. C., L. Willerman, and J. M. Horn. 1985. "Personality Resemblances in Adoptive Families When the Children are Late-Adolescent or Adult." *Journal of Personality and Social Psychology* 48, 376–92.

Loeber, R. and T. Dishion. 1983. "Early Predictors of Male Delinquency: A Review." *Psychological Bulletin* 94, 68–99.

Magnusson, D., A. Duner, and G. Zetterblom. 1975. *Adjustment: A Longitudinal Study*. Stockholm: Almqvist & Wiksell.

Matsueda, R. and K. Heine. 1987. "Race, Family Structure and Delinquency: A Test of Differential Association and Social Control Theory." *American Sociological Review* 52, 826–40.

McCord, J. 1982. "A Longitudinal Study of the Link between Broken Homes and Criminality." In *Abnormal Offenders: Delinquency and the Criminal Justice System*, edited by J. Gunn and D. Farrington, 113–123. London: Wiley.

McCord, J. 1983. "A Longitudinal Study of Aggression and Antisocial Behavior." In *Prospective Studies of Crime and Delinquency,* edited by K. T. Van Dusen and S. A. Mednick, 269–75. Boston: Kluwer-Nijhoff.

Mednick, S. A., W. F. Gabrielli, and B. Hutchings. 1984. "Genetic Influences in Criminal Convictions: Evidence from an Adoption Cohort." *Science* 224, 891–94.

Messner, S. and K. Tardiff. 1986. "Economic Inequality and Levels of Homicide: An Analysis of Urban Neighborhoods." *Criminology* 24, 297–318.

Miethe, T., M. Stafford, and J. Long. 1987. "Social Differentiation in Criminal Victimization." *American Sociological Review* 52, 184–94.

Moffitt, T. E. 1990. "Juvenile Delinquency and Attention Deficit Disorder: Boys Developmental Trajectories from Age 3 to Age 15." *Child Development* 61, 893–910.

Moyer, K. E. 1976. *The Psychobiology of Aggression.* New York: Harper & Row.

Nachson, I. and D. Denno. 1987. "Violent Behavior and Cerebral Hemisphere Dysfunctions. In *The Causes of Crime: New Biological Approaches,* edited by S. A. Mednick, T. E. Moffitt, and S. A. Stack, 185–217. New York: Cambridge University Press.

Olweus, D. 1979. "The Stability of Aggressive Reaction Patterns in Human Males: A Review." *Psychological Bulletin* 85, 852–75.

Olweus, D., A. Mattsson, D. Schalling, and H. Löw. 1980. Testosterone, Aggression, Physical, and Personality Dimensions in Normal Adolescent Males." *Psychosomatic Medicine* 42, 253–69.

Olweus, D. 1988. "Circulating Testosterone Levels and Aggression in Adolescent Males: A Causal Analysis." *Psychosomatic Medicine* 50, 261–72.

Parke, R. D. and R. G. Slaby. 1983. "The Development of Aggression." In *Handbook of Child Psychology,* edited by P. Mussen, 547–642. New York: Wiley.

Pontius, A. A. 1984. "Specific Stimulus-Evoked Violent Action in Psychotic Trigger Reaction: A Seizure-Like Imbalance Between Frontal Lobe and Limbic System?" *Perceptual and Motor Skills* 59, 299–333.

Raine, A. and F. Jones. 1987. "Attention, Autonomic Arousal, and Personality in Behaviorally Disordered Children." *Journal of Abnormal Child Psychology* 15, 583–99.

Reiss, A. J. and M. Tonry, (Eds.) 1986. *Communities and Crime.* Chicago: University of Chicago Press.

Rieder, J. 1985. *Canarsie: The Jews and Italians of Brooklyn Against Liberalism.* Cambridge: Harvard University Press.

Robins, L. N. and K. S. Ratcliff. 1980. "Childhood Conduct Disorders and Later Arrest." In *The Social Consequences of Psychiatric Illness,* edited by L. N. Robins, P. J. Clayton, and J. K. Wing, 248–63. New York: Brunner/Mazel.

Rowe, D. C. 1987. "Resolving the Person-Situation Debate: Invitation to an Interdisciplinary Dialogue." *American Psychologist* 42, 218–27.

Rushton, J. P., D. W. Fulker, M. C. Neale, D. K. B. Nias, and H. J. Eysenck. 1986. "Altruism and Aggression: The Heritability of Individual Differences." *Journal of Personality and Social Psychology* 50, 1192–98.

Schneider, W. and R. Shriffrin. 1977. Controlled and Automatic Human Information Processing: Detection, Search and Attention." *Psychological Review* 84,(1) 1–66.

Spivack, G. 1983. *High Risk Early Behaviors Indicating Vulnerability to Delinquency in the Community and School.* Washington, D.C.: NIMH.

8

The Sociogenesis of Aggressive and Antisocial Behaviors

Robert B. Cairns and Beverley D. Cairns

Beliefs about the nature of personality development and social behavior have been prominent in the working assumptions of juvenile courts over the past century. There has been, however, considerable ambiguity about (a) what constitutes a developmental perspective and (b) what may be its distinctive contribution to understanding deviant behavior and antisocial behavior. In this chapter, we describe a longitudinal study and the fresh information that it provides on the development of aggressive and antisocial behavior. We then examine some implications for design and theory.

Why Longitudinal Investigation?

Ten years ago we initiated a prospective longitudinal study of social development, with a particular focus on the organization and emergence of antisocial patterns.[1] This project was the direct outgrowth of earlier investigations in which we had participated, beginning with a study of adolescent aggression (Bandura and Walters 1959). The prior studies, though diverse in method, were linked by a common focus upon aggressive behaviors and the processes by which they are regulated. These investigations were successful, for the most part, in achieving their limited goals. But taken together, they revealed a need for methodological and theoretical change.

One lesson concerned research design and measurement. Our earlier studies of aggressive phenomena had failed, with one exception, to capture the integrated nature of the individual's adaptations. For example, the correlated nature of the individual's actions and counteractions showed it was folly to divorce the individual's aggressive actions from the dynamic context in which they occurred. Yet virtually all experimental analyses and retrospective analyses, including our own, tended to disembody aggressive measurement from contexts and relationships. In addition, the separate measures of aggressive behaviors may be associated with each other in curious ways that shift over the course of development. Hence studies which rely upon a single assessment of aggressive behavior—whether self-reports, observations, public records, ratings, or projective tests—are handicapped at the outset.

The exception was instructive. It involved longitudinal investigations of animal aggressive behavior. We found that when genetic, experiential, maturational, and learning influences were considered simultaneously over the course of development, they provided a coherent picture of aggressive patterns in individual animals (Cairns, Gariépy, and Hood 1990). And when investigations of aggressive behavior development were combined with the study of neurobiological transmission, it was possible to identify a neurochemical basis for genetic differences in aggressive behavior (Lewis et al. in press). Interventions are now available for the prevention, regulation, or elimination of aggressive patterns in individual animals.[2] The developmental research strategy has proved to be key to much of the progress on this front.

A second general lesson was theoretical. In the course of completing the work with both human and nonhuman mammals, the overwhelming importance of development was repeatedly underscored for us by direct observations of change over time. Seemingly vague assertions about the dynamics of development and the fusion of influences in ontogeny took on fresh and concrete meaning. The addition of a time dimension turned out to be critical. Developmental considerations provided an avenue for making sense of the multidetermination of behavior. Since influences are fused during development, research must attend to the fusion process as it occurs over time (Cairns 1979, 1983).

We came to view longitudinal research designs to be necessary but not sufficient for understanding the determinants of aggressive patterns in humans. They were necessary because of the need to plot the synthesis of organismic and external influences in individual lives as well as social groups. They were not sufficient because of the need to employ measures that are sensitive to developmental processes and changes, along with microanalytic and experimental designs. Still, the obstacles to research upon developmental processes remain formidable because they are embedded in the discipline. In this regard, many of the measures, analyses, and concepts of contemporary psychology and sociology appear to be crafted to get rid of developmental changes and their effects (Cairns 1986).

A Longitudinal Investigation of Aggressive Behaviors

When the CLS project was envisioned, we felt that our work should replicate some of the features of prior investigations as well as explore new ground. Specifically, females have been virtually ignored in earlier studies of aggressive behavior, longitudinal and otherwise.[3] At the time, there seemed to be strong reasons— theoretical, practical, and temporal—to include girls in the longitudinal study. There was evidence for an accelerating incidence of antisocial aggressive behavior in females (Cairns 1979), a common genetic basis for heritable differences in the aggressive behavior of nonhuman males and females (Hood and Cairns 1988), the cross-generational transmission of aggressive behaviors by the activities of mothers (Eron and Huesmann 1984), and the multiple sequelae of childhood aggressive behavior in girls for problems of adaptation in women (Robins 1986). Hence it seemed important to plot the longitudinal development of aggressive behavior in girls as well as boys.

Another focus of our work was the extent to which aggressive and antisocial behaviors are embedded in social networks. Curiously, there have been virtually no attempts to track the development of social groups simultaneously with the development of individuals. For that matter, there is a large gap between studies of the group dynamics in adolescence and group dynamics in childhood. In the light of the prior work which demonstrates reciprocal effects in aggressive expression, it seemed important to place this information in the context of development.

A third concern involved the need to clarify the linkages between self-appraisals (i.e., self-concept, self-reports) and those measures outside the self (i.e., direct observations, peer ratings, teacher ratings, public records). One implication of a holistic developmental approach is the primacy of personal integration in development. The associations among domains of behavioral assessment—such as self-reports and direct observations—may shift as a function of age, context, and experience. Accordingly, it is important to employ multilevel measurement and to reassess the basis for the correspondence among measures across time. Given developmental changes in cognitive ability, behavioral expression, and social organization, the linkage between measures is not inflexible. As children grow older, they become more capable of taking the viewpoint of others, on the one hand, and they become more capable of rationalization and defense mechanisms, on the other. Accordingly, it is not sufficient to establish correspondence between measures at one age and to assume that a similar correspondence holds earlier or later. Nor is it safe to assume that the functions of social cognitions of other persons are the same as the functions of social cognitions about the self.

With these issues in mind, the aim of the CLS project was to plot the course of social development in a representative sample of boys and girls from childhood through early adulthood. We had a special focus upon the sociogenesis[4] of aggressive and antisocial behavior. The research design was longitudinal, multimethod, and multilevel. Two cohorts of subjects who differed in age at the onset of the investigation were studied simultaneously. By design, the two groups overlapped in coverage after three years because one group began annual assessments when they were in the fourth grade and the other group began assessments in the seventh grade. Within each cohort, subgroups of the most aggressive boys and girls were identified at the beginning of the study, along with control groups of individually matched, nonaggressive children (matched with respect to classroom attended, sex, race, physical size, age, and socioeconomic status/neighborhood).

In addition to the principal study, we conducted two collateral investigations. One was a preliminary, two-year investigation with the aim of (1) establishing the measurement properties of the procedures for the primary study, and (2) providing a dress rehearsal for the design and for our research team. A second collateral investigation was conducted to obtain information about extremely aggressive subjects to corroborate the results of the present investigation. Accordingly, 1300 extremely assaultive adolescent males and females were studied to determine the generality of the longitudinal ''at risk'' subgroups.

Subjects

We began collecting data for the CLS project in 1981. The subjects were initially located in the schools of four communities in the Atlantic Coast region of the United States. Two hundred and twenty children in the fourth grade (10.2 years) were selected from four different elementary schools, and 475 adolescents were selected from the seventh grade (13.4 years) of three middle schools. Overall, the sample was representative of their respective counties in race (75 percent white, 25 percent African-American) and socioeconomic status.

Within the larger sample, forty subjects—twenty girls and twenty boys—were judged by teachers, counselors, and principals to be highly aggressive (i.e., twenty highly aggressive subjects in each cohort). In order for an individual to be selected, he/she had to be nominated by two school personnel (teacher, counselor, or principal) who were closely acquainted with the subject. An additional group of forty nonaggressive control subjects were identified and matched individually on the basis of sex, race, and classroom attended, physical size, socioeconomic status, and chronological age. Pair-wise observations of each aggressive-control pair were conducted over a four-day period, with extensive observations daily over two contexts. These observations (not reported in this chapter) indicated that the aggressive subjects and nonaggressive controls differed in observed aggressive interchanges in the fourth and seventh grades.

Attrition: Lost and Found

All longitudinal studies are vulnerable to sample attrition, and our research was no exception. Loss of subjects could mean that the information one obtains will be biased toward the most stable and conventional members of the society. Reasons for sample attrition are multiple, but most subjects become "lost" because their parents or guardians move, or because the child's custody has been changed. Less often the adolescent may have run away from home, or may have been placed in residential custody. Other subjects are not lost at all; they simply no longer wish to participate.

In 1989–90, all living subjects from our original research sample were relocated and their school status was determined. Of that total, 98.8 percent (683/691) were individually interviewed and tested (table 8.1). A small proportion had died (0.6 percent, 4/695), and some declined to be interviewed (1.2 percent; 8/691). In mid-1990, the sample had become international in scope. The subjects lived throughout the United States, from Alaska to Florida, and California to Massachusetts, and beyond the U.S. in various countries of Western Europe and South America. Locating most of the subjects was routine; the task was not a major issue for seven out of ten subjects. The remainder were found with increasing difficulty (Cairns, Neckerman, Flinchum, and Cairns 1990).

On occasion, we found that some potential sources were not willing to cooperate. Certain subjects and/or their families actively avoided being found because of difficulties with creditors or the law, or fear of being identified in illegal activities. In addition, a small proportion of the parents and children were emotionally disturbed. Lack of cooperation also arose in cases of disputed guardianship between parents, or between foster parents and biological parents. The more difficult cases were those in which subjects were (a) "on the run" to avoid arrest for felonies or imprisonment for parole violations, (b) permanent runaways, (c) school dropouts who moved to other states and changed their names (because of their own marriages or parental remarriage), and/or (d) assigned to foster home placement or adoptions that involved several moves and one or more name changes. In our experience, some of the more serious problems and dramatic changes took place in the lives of individuals who would have been entirely lost from standard longitudinal tracking.

Measures and Observations

The heart of any longitudinal investigation lies in data quality; namely, the objectivity, replicability, and validity of the longitudi-

TABLE 8.1
Recovery Rate of CLS Project through 1990

	4th	5th	6th	7th	8th	9th	10th	11th	12th
Cohort I									
Grade	4th	5th	6th	7th	8th	9th	10th	11th	12th
Year	1981–82	1982–83	1983–84	1984–85	1985–86	1986–87	1987–88	1988–89	1989–90
N[a]	[220/220]	[200/220]	[194/220]	[191/220]	[198/220]	[209/219]	[214/219]	[217/219]	[217/219]
Recovery Rate	1.00	.91	.88	.87	.90	.95	.98	.99	.99
Cohort II									
Grade				7th	8th	9th	10th	11th	12th
Year				1982–83	1983–84	1984–85	1985–86	1986–87	1987–88
N				[475/475]	[456/474]	[446/474]	[446/472]	[461/472]	[466/472]
Recovery Rate				1.00	.96	.94	.94	.98	.99

[a]Embedded in each cohort are subsets of males and females who were judged to be extremely aggressive on the basis of school nominations by two or more principals/counselors/teachers. Non-nominated subjects were individually matched on the basis of sex, race, classroom attended, and physical size.

nal measures that it employs. The public transduction of empirical phenomena into theoretical constructs distinguishes this enterprise from commonsense and clinical intuition. We spent two years in preliminary study to ensure that the procedures were sensitive to the phenomena that we wanted to focus upon. In the light of the fallibility of single information sources, we employed multiple measures of each variable or characteristic. We also thought it essential to understand the source of variance that each measure captured before we attempted to combine the components. The procedures employed extend from information from teachers, peers, parents, social networks, the courts and probation departments, school records, school yearbooks and newspapers, and interviews with the individuals themselves. The measures included:

Social Network Assessments. The social networks in which the subjects are involved—or excluded from—have been assessed yearly. A quantitative, yet flexible and readily applied method for the identification of peer social networks has been developed in this project (Cairns, Gariépy, and Kinderman 1991). It is a social cognitive measure of extant networks, and the subject's role in them. Adolescent subjects tend to provide reliable and definable clusters of peers in response to the interview inquiry. "Are there people who hang around together a lot at school? Who are they?" Follow-up probes were designed to elicit specific information about the makeup of the clusters, accounts of the subject's own cluster if it had not been initially volunteered, persons who were isolated from the social system, including the subject if relevant, and peer groups outside the school. High levels of intersubject agreement are obtained in the identification of clusters and of isolates [i.e., 94 percent agreement index—agree/(agree + disagree)—for cluster assignments among independent subjects in the same classroom]. It has been shown that the social cognitive assessment of peer clusters corresponds closely with observed interaction patterns and such behaviors as school dropout, drug usage, and aggressive patterns.

Social Cognition Interview. The social cognition interviews were conducted individually and recorded with professional tape recorders, and verbatim transcripts were subsequently prepared. They have been given annually since the onset of the investigation. Standard modifications are made in the schedule to ensure that the probes are age and situation appropriate. Of special relevance for this chapter was a section of the interview in which social cognitive reports of specific aggressive conflicts and interchanges were obtained. A second section addressed peer social structures, and the subject's perception of his/her role in them. In a third section, information was obtained on the family structure, and the extent to which subjects perceived themselves and their associates to be monitored by their parents. Following verbatim transcription, the reports were coded by two independent raters. The median interjudge agreement was acceptable for the classification of response type, escalation, number of conflicts, identity of the other person, and self-responsibility (89 percent to 94 percent, with median 92 percent). Beyond providing social judgments and social attributions, the audiotaped interviews preserved a "living" record of the subject's behavior and affect over all years of the longitudinal study.

Behavior Interactions: Synchronized Observations. We made a substantial investment to obtain reliable and veridical behavioral information from the classroom. A two-tiered observational strategy was adopted that yielded focal and contextual data simultaneously. The behavioral observations involved two synchronized observers who simultaneously but independently observed interactions and social contexts in which the social interactions occurred. Four days of each week, one at-risk subject and his/her matched control was observed. Following this schedule, data collection over a three school year period was required to obtain observational information for forty highly aggressive subjects and forty matched controls (see Patterson 1979; Yarrow and Waxler 1979; Castellan 1979; Cairns and Green 1979).

Teacher Evaluations of Social Competence. Subjects were evaluated each year on the Interpersonal Competence Scale (ICS-T) by teachers or counselors who knew them well. The scale consists of items designed to assess four areas of interpersonal behavior (aggressive and coercive behavior, popularity, academic competence, and affiliative expression) and an overall measure of social competence. Extensive work was completed to determine its psychometric properties (reliability, validity) and convergence with other measures of the same characteristics. The LISREL measurement model indicated that, in all cohort samples, three major factors may be identified with high levels of communality (i.e., aggression, popularity, academic competence).

Self Evaluations of Social Competence. Self-appraisals were made yearly by all subjects on dimensions of social behavior and social competence. The device employed was the subject's form of the Interpersonal Competence Scale (ICS-S). The ICS-S consists of exactly the same items employed on the teacher's form of the scale, except for the inclusion of three filler items. Accordingly, the subject's self-appraisals could be directly compared to those offered by teachers, counselors, or principals well acquainted with the subject in the school setting, and with parental ratings. The procedure also yielded an overall scale score of interpersonal competence. The brief ICS-S scale was comparable in psychometric properties to other self rating scales (Harter 1983).

Peer Attributions and Nominations. In the course of the social cognitive interview, subjects identified persons with whom they have had recent conflicts, individuals who have recently given them assistance or help, persons who are their closest friends, and peers who belong to social clusters or who are isolated from the social groups or social system. By analyzing the patterns of nominations, corrected scores were given to all persons in that school grade.

Maturational Status. Yearly assessments of physical maturation, along with the several psychological measures, have been obtained. Three types of measures are used: age of menarche, ratings of physical maturation, and health records of height and weight (Tanner 1962; see also Friedrich-Cofer 1986; Magnusson 1988; and Simmons and Blyth 1987). In addition to the above measures, other sources of information have been obtained in the CLS project.[5] These measures and relevant findings are discussed in separate publications (e.g., Cairns and Cairns 1991).

Information from these multiple sources was obtained and updated annually. The tasks of collating, organizing, and retrieving the information occupied as much time and effort as getting it in the first place. Hence we had a primary concern with ensuring the accuracy and quality of each record. Some fourteen researchers were involved in primary data collection over the several years of this study. Each year, independent teachers were employed as raters. When appropriate, fresh investigators were introduced into the study to safeguard the objectivity of the measures and the coding. Interviewers were rotated to different subjects from year to year so that potential biases could be minimized. Appropriate safeguards were instituted to ensure that observers, interviewers, raters, and coders were blind with respect to the subject's standing on the relevant variables and information gathered from other sources.[6] Immediate access to information from several waves of data across two independent cohorts, in addition to separate companion longitudinal, cross-sectional, and methodological studies, has permitted cross-validation of the primary findings.

Social Networks, Growth, and the Self

Of special relevance to this chapter are the longitudinal findings on peer social networks and social group influence, on developmental trends in aggressive expression in males and females, and on the measurement and functions of self-evaluations relative to other measures.[7]

Aggression: An Outcome of Peer Rejection or Network Support?

One of the most extensively studied yet puzzling issues on social networks concerns aggressive expression and delinquency in adolescence (Parke and Slaby 1983). Is aggressive behavior the outcome of social support (such as gangs or coercive families, where "aggression begets aggression")? Or is it due to the inability of aggressive adolescents to form social attachments and/or their social skills inadequacies? The recent literature on these issues indicates that deviant group bonding is a primary determinant of delinquent behavior (Elliott, Huizinga, and Menard 1989). However, psychological studies of sociometric status have concluded that "rejected" and "isolated" children are at risk for a full range of behavior problems, including delinquent and antisocial behavior. Which interpretation is correct: do children and adolescents behave in a different fashion because they are removed from the social network, or do they behave badly because they are part of a distinctive social network?

Aggressive Homophily. The issue of peer group influence was a major concern of the CLS longitudinal program. Accordingly, social networks and aggressive behavior were identified in the first year of data collection in each grade-cohort (Cairns, Cairns, Neckerman, Gest, and Gariépy 1988). The measures of social networks (i.e., peer social cognitive maps, nominations for social isolation and rejection) yielded convergent findings. Highly aggressive subjects—both boys and girls—did not differ from matched control subjects in terms of social cluster membership or in being isolated or rejected within the social network. Peer cluster analysis and reciprocal "best friend" selections indicated a strong homophily, where aggressive subjects tended to affiliate with aggressive peers. The aggression-affiliation effect was found in both boys and girls, except the propensity was nonsignificant among fourth grade females. Even though highly aggressive children and adolescents were sometimes less popular than control subjects in the social network at large, they were equally often identified as being nuclear members of social clusters. Furthermore, aggressive subjects did not differ from matched-control subjects in the number of times they were named by peers as "best friend." Nor did the two groups differ in the probability of having friendship choices reciprocated by peers (Cairns et al. 1988).

We also observed that the lower levels of general popularity and likability of aggressive subjects may have obscured the social competencies that permitted these adolescents to survive in difficult conditions. As noted by Campbell (1980), being popular with the group as a whole may not be the only goal for these adolescents. Hence failure to achieve broad-based popularity in the "main stream" should not be taken as evidence of wholesale social rejection. Aggression and the life styles that they index appear to provide a highly salient basis for peer affiliations.

In discussing these results with respect to those of Giordano et al. (1986) and Coie and Dodge (1983), we concluded that aggressive children in both cohorts and in both sexes may be disliked by some classmates for legitimate reasons (bullying, ridiculing, victimizing). "Highly aggressive children and adolescents may have—on the average—a smaller circle of friends and admirers, but these relationships could be no less meaningful than those of less aggressive adolescents" (Cairns et al. 1988).

Another dark side to coercive cliques requires comment because of its relevance to how adolescents could themselves reject authority as much as vice-versa. In the course of development, coalitions of aggressive adolescents might be expected to come into conflict with adults as well as peers, and to threaten the existing order. Failures by the persons in charge of the school to abort the formation of such groups or to regulate them could be an abdication of responsibility. Hence coalitions among aggressive adolescents demand the attention of teachers and principals. Implicit and explicit rejection of aggressive adolescents by school personnel should guide and catalyze the attitudes of peers. Over time, members of coercive peer groups were more likely to drop out of school, or to be forced out through suspension and expulsion (Cairns, Cairns, and Neckerman 1989).

Attack Groups and Support Groups. Female clusters in adolescence can serve as "attack groups" as well as "support groups." To the extent that girls in early adolescence tend to employ indirect techniques of aggressive expression—including social exclusion, character defamation, and ostracism—as opposed to the direct confrontational techniques, social groups have an added dimension (see Feshbach and Sones 1971; Cairns, Cairns, Neckerman, Ferguson, and Gariépy 1989). In this form of social attack, the manipulation of the opinions and attitudes of one's peers can be essential, and necessary for self defense. It may be partly for this reason that the characteristics of "trust" and "honesty" figure importantly in the criteria for friendship in early adolescence (Bigelow 1977). On the nature of social networks and social conflicts in adolescence, we concluded that "the conflicts of adolescence provide a window into the raw politics of everyday life, and their complexity cannot be overestimated" (Cairns, Cairns, Neckerman, Ferguson, and Gariépy 1989). Nor can their subtlety.

A Theoretical Proposal. In the light of the empirical information now available, it cannot be gainsaid that both factors—personal attributes and reciprocal network properties—each make robust contributions to the behaviors and values of adolescents (Hartup 1983). The information from recent analyses is in line with the developmental models described by Cairns (1979), Jessor and Jessor (1977), Kandel (1978), Magnusson (1988), Strayer and Noel (1986), and Youniss (1986). The elements of this synthesized developmental-interactional framework may be summarized in the following five points (Cairns, Neckerman, and Cairns 1989):

1. There is a strong bias toward social synchrony at all developmental stages, in that actions and attitudes of other persons are readily enmeshed with the behavioral organization of the self. One by-product of this reciprocal integration is mutual similarity. Beginning in late childhood and early adolescence, there is a sharp developmental increase in the ability to reciprocate behaviors beyond the dyad in unstructured relationships with peers. The resultant peer clusters develop norms and behavioral similarities which can support—or compete with—those of other social units, including the family and the school.

2. Peer social clusters serve not only the prosocial functions of providing for intimacy and helping to define the personal identity of the members, they also serve to express individual aggression and control. The tools for aggressive expression include ostracism and character defamation, which are especially effective because they are "hidden" forms of attack and they conceal aggressors from possible counter-responses by victims. Because the peer clusters of early adolescence are in a state of unstable equilibrium—due in part to shifting alliances and jealousies from within and without—safeguards must be established for the maintenance of synchronized, reciprocal intragroup relations.

3. To promote intracluster synchrony, there are norms for initial acceptance into the cluster. Such "gate-keeping" criteria help to heighten the likelihood of initial similarity of cluster members with regard to key characteristics (i.e., "homophily"). Selection criteria and their inflexibility shift as a function of age and the goals and needs of the members. In childhood, gender membership is universally important and most childhood clusters are unisex. What is valued (or devalued) reflects local standards as well as the age-gender status of the individual. With the onset of adolescence, cluster boundaries become increasingly rigid, and the conditions for selection and entry become more clearly delineated in terms of behaviors, values, and personal characteristics.

4. Within the clusters of adolescence, strong reciprocal forces operate on all members toward conformity with respect to salient attitudes and behaviors. Hence the "socialization" with respect to various nonconventional behaviors (e.g., Jessor and Jessor 1977; Kandel 1978; Magnusson 1988; Rodgers, Billy, and Udry 1984). An extension of influence across persons within the cluster leads to the

establishment of generalized patterns of deviance, beyond the index behaviors that may have been required for initial group entry. But a common standard for deviance is only one of the outcomes of the reciprocal exchanges within groups. At a broader level, there is conformity with respect to a broad spectrum of behaviors and attitudes, including deviancy, areas of worry and concern, and "life style."

5. The informal clusters of adolescents are in a state of unstable equilibrium due to developmental changes in their members and to dynamic social forces within clusters. Among other things, suballiances shift among members and continuously challenge the integrity of the social organization itself. With the developmental breakdown of old clusters and the formation of new ones through renegotiated alliances, the cycle of differential selection and reciprocal similarity is repeated in a stepping-stone process across time. At every stage, individuals are changed by their associations, and they carry to the next set of relationships the behavioral residue of the recent past. These changes provide the basis for new alliances and a fresh network of supporting relationships. There is a dynamic exchange between enduring behaviors of the self and social relations with others, providing fresh meaning to Baldwin's (1902) assertion that personality is an "ever changing, never completed thing."

Development and Aggressive Behavior Patterns in Females and Males

A second general issue concerns developmental trends in the aggressive and deviant behaviors of females and males. Does aggression (a) increase, (b) decrease, or (c) remain the same in form and function from childhood through adolescence? Paradoxically, empirical support may be claimed for each of the three seemingly contradictory answers. On the possible increase, there is a sharp rise in mortality due to violence from twelve years of age through twenty years, followed by a gradual decrease to late maturity (Fingerhut and Kleinman 1990). These national statistics on violent deaths are mirrored by urban statistics violent injuries in the emergency departments of major trauma centers (Cairns, Nemhauser, and Nieman 1991). Using behavioral rather than health measures,

Eron and his colleagues (Eron, Huesmann, Brice, Fischer, and Mermelstein 1983; Huesmann, Lagerspetz, and Eron 1984) show a developmental increase in peer nominations for aggression from childhood through adolescence. Further, Ferguson and Rule (1980) have identified the rise of a brutality norm in adolescence (i.e., acceptability of physical aggression). With regard to a developmental decrease, Loeber (1982) has indicated that most longitudinal studies of children typically show decrements in ratings of aggressive behavior as they enter adolescence. Other reports, however, have found no significant age-related shifts in global ratings of aggressive behavior in children (e.g., Ledingham, Younger, Schwartzman, and Bergeron 1982).

Our findings relevant to this issue indicated that (a) the incidence of physical aggression diminished as a function of age, especially in boys, and (b) social aggression increased from childhood to adolescence, then remained at a high level in girls. However, male-male conflicts were three to six times more likely to involve physical aggression than social aggression. This ratio of physical aggression to social aggression diminished with age. On the other hand, female-female conflicts were two to four times more likely to involve indirect forms of social aggression than direct physical aggression. Taking the two cohorts together, there was remarkable overlap in the findings and the consistency of trends from childhood through late adolescence. The findings on large sex differences in social aggression extended the work of Kirsti Lagerspetz and her colleagues in Finland (Lagerspetz, Björkqvist, and Peltonen 1988).

Why should instances of social aggression increase over this age range while physical aggression decreases? With age, most males and females tend to adopt, in everyday conflicts, more sophisticated and less risky methods of expressing their anger. On this score, girls seem to be developmentally advanced compared to boys. The indirect aggression that characterizes the conflicts of females has several advantages for the aggressor. In social aggression, the immediate aggression-begets-aggression linkage is broken, along with an immediate escalation of the conflict. By employing the social network as a mediator for attack through rumor and ostracism, the identity of the aggressor is concealed. Even if aggressive intent is suspected, it may be difficult to prove and even more difficult to reciprocate since the victim becomes divorced from the social network resources required for counter-attacks. Within limits, the effects of social aggression can be more enduring and humiliating for the victim than those of physical aggression.

The decrease in the actual incidents of physical aggression was not mirrored by a decrease in the seriousness of the incidents that occurred. Arrests for assault increased sharply in adolescence, as did the severity of injury produced, including manslaughter and violence. Such outcomes are consistent with the assumption that the direct aggressive acts which do occur become more dangerous and pontentially harmful as the aggressor grows older. This increase in the stakes of direct confrontation—as individuals gain access to lethal weapons and become capable of inflicting serious injury—should also make more attractive the use of alternatives to direct confrontation, such as social aggression. The high prevalence of weapon availability is a special problem. In our sample, 85 percent of the adolescent males had direct access to firearms, and 49 percent of them own guns themselves (Sadowski, Cairns, and Earp 1989). More broadly, a developmental increase in the potential lethality of direct aggressive interchanges—whether they involve males or females—seems consistent both with (a) adoption of alternative, less risky expressions of anger, and (b) a decrease in their frequency.

Theoretical Implications. "Aggression" or "antisocial behavior" cannot be described by a single trajectory or psychometric function. Different curves are required because they depend on which measures are adopted, which relationships are depicted, and which aggressive strategies are described in each measure. The developmental curves also show different trajectories, depending on the sex of the subject and the sex of the victim (see also Barrett 1979). In male-male conflicts, there is support for the developmental persistence of the aggression-begets-aggression norm, with the outcome that Ferguson and Rule (1980) describe as a "brutality norm." Judging from the interview reports, there is a pervasive norm regarding the prohibition of physical assaults by boys toward girls, but not toward boys. The dual standard has methodological implications in that the disinclination of boys to name females as antagonists could directly influence peer nomination measures of aggression (e.g., Huesmann and Eron 1984).

Return now to apparent discrepancy between psychological measures and criminal (and epidemiological) assessments of the trajectory of developmental changes in aggressive behavior. A clue to the resolution of this difference is found in the subjects' reports of conflicts. Themes of physical brutality were more frequent for boys than for girls as they entered adolescence. Direct confrontation continued to be a strategy employed by adolescent boys in conflicts with other males. The stakes of confrontation became higher and the consequences of a single negative exchange became potentially severe as boys grew older. This outcome may have followed because of (a) an age-related increase in the ability to produce serious injury and (b) the persistence of direct confrontation as a strategy when male-male conflicts arise. In early adolescence, gender differences arise in the ability to produce serious injury. Beyond differences in physical strength and sexual dimorphism, there are gender differences in activities related to injury. For example, in this sample, firearm ownership was virtually nonoverlapping for adolescent boys and girls. The rate of serious injury in conflicts among males increases when impulsive weapon use becomes coupled with the strategy of direct confrontation. This relationship should hold even if weapon use in conflicts was rare and if the proportion of highly aggressive males actually diminished in adolescence—as the present data suggest is the case.

The construct of "aggression" itself becomes expanded in development. Evidence for the expansion was obtained from self-reports. Social ostracism—as involved in alienation, rumors, and social rejection—emerges as a major property of aggressive behavior in early adolescence, especially for girls (see also Feshbach and Sones 1971). Affiliation-romance-alienation themes recur in the conflicts reported by girls in early adolescence. The strategy adopted seemed to be consonant with the form of perceived injury: alienation of relationships leads to counter-alienation. Rather than report everyday offenses of peers to adults as they did in childhood, adolescent girls report to each other. In the early teenage years, boys persist in reliance upon direct confrontations and/or physical aggression if the conflict cannot be otherwise ignored or avoided. But it would be incorrect to conclude that girls did not retain the ability for direct aggressive confrontation. As the factor analyses in the seventh grade (and beyond) indicated, conflicts among girls can involve either direct confrontation or social manipulation. It is simply less frequent for girls than for boys.

The longitudinal data also illustrate why one must go beyond the correlational matrix in order to understand consistencies in social behavior. Specifically, "individual difference continuity"—relative standing of an individual with regard to the group over time— depends in part upon "factor structure continuity"—maintenance of the same structural relationship among variables at different ages (Cairns 1979, 379–90). Since there were developmental shifts in factor structure of aggression for girls, the measures of individual difference continuity for females were necessarily handicapped. Nor were males unaffected by developmental shifts. There was, for instance, a sharp drop across age among boys in the mean levels of ratings of "fighting." Continued developmental reduction in levels would lead to a floor effect, reduced variability, and a decrement in the utility of this dimension in individual difference analyses. Age-related changes in factor structure and measurement properties are critical for understanding behavioral continuity.

In sum, unraveling developmental trajectories of aggressive behavior requires simultaneous focus upon theory and assessment methods. A major hazard in this enterprise has been the propensity to reify the construct of aggression and to expect a single trajectory of growth, development, and decay. But aggressive behaviors cannot be divorced from the dynamic developmental contexts in which they occur. The properties of the construct of "aggression" change over development. At each developmental stage, the construct reflects the social judgments of society, the social attributions of researchers, and the constructions of the self. Different developmental trajectories may be described for the separate domains of aggression.

The Self, the Other, and the Real

A third issue of concern was the relationship between measures of aggressive behavior over time; specifically, agreement between measures of the self and measures obtained outside the self. Relative to the social consensus, are the self-perceptions of aggressive adolescents (a) lower and (b) more distorted than those of nonaggressive adolescents? This question addresses the issue of whether there are larger differences between self perceptions and the perceptions of others among aggressive adolescents than among non-aggressive adolescents.

Self-other congruence was initially assessed by differences in the mean levels of aggressive measures (table 8.2). Analysis of these means indicated a main effect of aggression and a sex-by-aggression interaction. Whereas the highly aggressive males and females did not differ, control group males obtained higher aggressive scores than the control group females. Were the control subjects more accurate in their self-assessments than were the risk subjects? Two difference measures were computed to determine mean levels of teacher-self discrepancy—(1) the algebraic teacher-self difference and (2) the absolute teacher-self difference. The direction of the algebraic difference {ICS-T minus ICS-S} means that a positive difference reflects self-enhancement (i.e., the self-assessments are less than the teacher assessments). The absolute difference {|ICS-T minus ICS-S|} reflects differences without regard to direction. The two differences are presented graphically for the two matched subsamples of aggressive and nonaggressive subjects, and for the sample-as-a whole (figure 8.1). The algebraic differences indicated that the male aggressive subjects tended to see themselves as being less aggressive than others saw them [$t(19) = 2.69$, p<.05]. The aggressive females also showed this self-enhancement bias [$t(19) = 2.53$, p<.05]. Interestingly, the general samples of females tended to see themselves as more aggressive than they had been rated by teachers.

TABLE 8.2
ICS-T and ICS-S Means and se$_m$ on ICS-T Aggression Factor:
Aggressive, Matched Control, and Whole Cohorts (I and II)

Gender	Group	N	ICS-T		ICS-S	
			Mean	se$_m$	Mean	se$_m$
Males	Aggressive Risk	20	4.37	.32	3.68	.23
	Matched-Control	20	3.60	.37	3.45	.21
	Cohort I	89	2.88	.15	3.20	.08
	Cohort II	224	3.36	.11	3.26	.06
Females	Aggressive Risk	20	4.67	.34	3.92	.19
	Matched-Control	20	3.02	.38	3.02	.25
	Cohort I	102	2.63	.15	3.03	.08
	Cohort II	246	2.60	.10	2.92	.05

FIGURE 8.1
Self-other differences in aggressive ratings as a function of subgroup (risk, control) and of cohort (I, II). The algebraic index of distortion (above) refers to the mean self-other difference in a self-enhancing direction (i.e., less aggressive than others see them), and the absolute index of distortion (below) refers to the combined mean self-other difference regardless of direction.

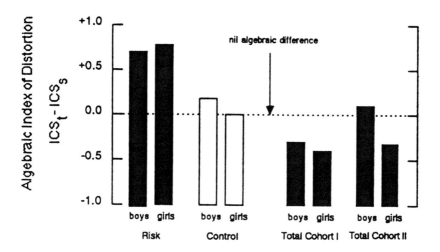

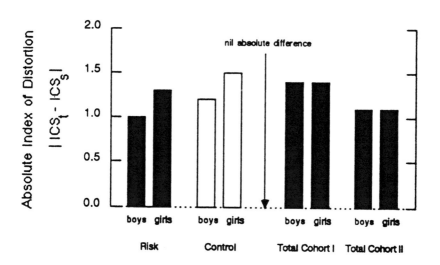

Conditions / Samples

To test differences in the absolute level of self-other discrepancy for aggressive and control subjects, a three-way analysis of variance was computed (i.e., Source-by-Sex-by-Aggression status). None of the main effects or their interactions was significant. As can be seen in figure 8.1, the absolute self-other discrepancy of the aggressive subjects was no different from that of a matched subgroup or of the entire sample.

Comparisons of mean levels were informative for two reasons. First, the algebraic discrepancies of the aggressive subjects were uniformly in the positive direction. If the analysis focuses only on the self-evaluations of the aggressive subjects relative to other subjects, it would appear that they had "low" self esteem. But the ratings of others indicated that the self-ratings of aggressive subjects were more self-enhancing (i.e., less aggressive) than the appraisals given to them by other persons. This self-enhancement was obtained in both cohorts of aggressive subjects. Second, the absolute difference scores indicated that the self-descriptions of control subjects and the general population were no more "accurate" (in terms of agreement with the social consensus) than were those of highly aggressive subjects. Parallel outcomes were obtained at both age-grade levels.

The level of agreement and accuracy may also be explored by correlational measures. In this regard, the congruence between the self and others for the entire sample was used to provide a baseline for agreement-disagreement. This outcome was compared to sub-

TABLE 8.3
Self-Other Congruence Correlations on Aggression Factor:
Aggressive, Matched Control, and Whole Cohorts (I and II)

Gender	Group	N	Congruence Correlation	p
Males	Aggressive Risk	20	.61	<.01
	Matched Control	20	.49	<.05
	Cohort I	89	.34	<.01
	Cohort II	224	.28	<.001
Females	Aggressive Risk	20	.48	<.05
	Matched Control	20	.18	>.10
	Cohort I	102	.23	<.05
	Cohort II	246	.35	<.001

samples of matched aggressive and nonaggressive subjects. There was modest self-other agreement on aggressive dimensions, regardless of the aggressive status of the individual (see table 8.3). When the extremely aggressive subjects were compared to nonaggressive controls subjects and to the overall sample in terms of self-other congruence correlations, there were few differences. Both male and female aggressive subjects showed marginally higher self-other agreement than either of the comparison groups on the aggressive dimension.

A Theoretical Proposal On Self-Esteem. At all ages, there are only modest relationships between how individuals describe themselves and how they are described by other persons. Children and adolescents normally see themselves as above average on virtually all domains of social, cognitive, and emotional adaptation. We may speculate that self-concepts of children and adolescents serve two masters: (a) to heighten internal integration and plans for living, and (b) to facilitate external adaptation to the social and objective environment. Any effort to understand discrepancies over time and between the self and others must take into account these multiple functions of the self systems. Specifically, we found that (1) at-risk children and adolescents provided somewhat lower levels of self-evaluation than nondeviant subjects, but (2) at-risk children had inflated views of their own capabilities, behaviors, and skills relative to the evaluations of others, and (3) at-risk, control, and normal groups showed similar absolute levels of self-other distortion. These outcomes may explain the failure of interventions that attempt to reduce antisocial behavior by raising the child's self-esteem. The problem may be that deviant children already think too highly of their skills and behavior (Cairns and Cairns 1988; Cairns 1990).

Why has it been so easy for society and science to accept the dual propositions (a) that problem children have low self-esteem and (b) that self-devaluation and social-cognitive deficits lie at the root of their behavior problems? A possible answer may be found in the propensity to attribute to antisocial children themselves those beliefs and attitudes that others have of them. We have proposed that *deviant children's self-esteem is not as low as the esteem in which they are held by others* (Cairns 1990). Hence the social consensus and beliefs about the unworthiness of antisocial children may be falsely attributed to the problem children themselves. Once projected, these beliefs are employed to explain their unacceptable behaviors.

On Longitudinal Designs

Beyond the specific findings, there are also some lessons to be gained from the CLS investigation on the nature of developmental study and some perils of longitudinal designs. Because of an explicit focus upon individual ontogeny—from conception to death—longitudinal research constituted the design of choice for the developmental perspective. No other reliable research strategy permitted us to plot individual trajectories and rates of growth and change over time. It also seemed necessary to identify the ways in which developmental mechanisms interact over time and thereby enhance individual adaptation.

But there are also pitfalls in longitudinal designs (see Kessen 1960; Magnusson and Bergman 1990; Loeber and LeBlanc 1990). Because of the large investment in individuals over time, data quality and retention of subjects emerge as primary concerns in the day-to-day conduct of the investigation. With each year, the margin of permissible error becomes smaller, and efficiency and accuracy gain in importance. This concern with data quality led us to reexamine the assumption that the least trained and least prepared researchers should be the ones who are in direct contact with subjects. In some cases, the priorities in the distribution of time and talent must be reversed to permit the most highly trained and sophisticated researchers to be in direct contact with the phenomena. In our research, we found it necessary to include the senior researchers, including ourselves, in data collection, but in ways that were consistent with the need to ensure objectivity in interpretation and integrity in the research activity.

Subject loss and lack of cooperation loom as a special problem in longitudinal studies of aggressive and antisocial behavior. Persons who are most likely to be lost are those who are at greatest risk for school dropout and other deviant outcomes (Farrington and West 1990; Cairns, Neckerman, Flinchum, and Cairns 1990). The maintenance of the sample also interacts with the issue of data quality, in that the instruments used should take into account the cost to subjects (both perceived and real) as well as the information that the procedures will yield. Quantity of information should not be equated with quality. Subjects may be overwhelmed by the number of questions and the level of their intrusiveness. Further, researchers may be tyrannized by the amount of data that are yielded. On this count, nothing can substitute for thoughtful, a priori analysis of instruments. Moreover, repeating exactly the same lengthy battery of inventories over multiple assessments may diminish, not enhance, the value of the study. If behavioral novelty and developmental changes are anticipated, the procedures should be age-appropriate and interest relevant. Ongoing analyses are important to ensure that the information obtained is relevant to the constructs that are assessed.

Statistics in Developmental Designs

It is a minor irony that many conceptual and statistical procedures introduced to study children of different ages have served to reduce or eliminate the impact of developmental change. For example, the statistic of choice for the study of continuity and change—the product-moment correlation—effectively eliminates real differences in performance associated with maturation. Similarly, statistical transformations that underlie the IQ ratio appear to have been introduced in order to get rid of age-related differences in cognitive functioning. Modern refinements of scaling have achieved the same outcome through standard scores, where same-age peers provide the reference group. These scaling techniques are not limited to the study of intelligence. They have become the strategies of choice for other domains of developmental assessment, including measures of aggressiveness, deviance, and unconventional behavior.

For any empirical investigation, the logic of the research task and the nature of the phenomenon should be the criteria against which to judge the adequacy of a given design or statistical analysis. Accordingly, it has seemed reasonable to assume that because deviant phenomena are multidetermined and complex, the procedures and statistical analyses employed to study them should be equally complex. Although this assumption may appear self-evident, it demands critical scrutiny. Exactly the opposite conclusion may be reached if the principal task for developmental research is to understand and clarify. Reliance upon complexity in analysis to disentangle the network of multiple causes and outcomes may reflect shortcomings in other phases of the research task. To clarify complex issues, it is often the case that the simpler the statistic, the better. Parsimony in analysis may be permitted because the major analytic problems have been solved earlier, namely, in the design created, in the methods adopted, and in the precision of the hypotheses. When the complexity within the phenomenon is permitted to breed complexity in the analysis and interpretation, it often means that there has been a failure in theory or a lack of creativity in design.

Developmental researchers are usually confronted with networks of relationships, not single antecedent-consequent linkages. This state of affairs has yielded a cornucopia of positive findings and interpretations. The abundance of "significant" antecedent-consequent linkages in contemporary developmental research has also had a negative side, in that it shifts responsibility for understanding phenomena away from the data themselves. The findings have often become projective tests for the field, where the burden for interpretation shifts from data to a priori beliefs.

Beyond the usual challenges that face investigators who are confronted with complex data sets, developmental researchers have special problems. The first and more general difficulty is that some of the questions posed by developmental investigators seem inconsistent with the dominant statistical models that are available. One question concerns novelty in development, and how new adaptations emerge and lead to the reorganization of existing behavior patterns and dispositions. Virtually all "life-course" and "developmental" hypotheses presuppose that fresh influences and new opportunities arise, from within the individual or in the social context. Most theoretical constructs of personality and statistical models assume, however, that there is nothing new under the sun.

The assumption that there are stable factors or dimensions of personality seems implicit in many applications of structural equation models to longitudinal data sets. Presumably the same latent variables are operative, despite changes in weights, configurations, and reliabilities of observed variables. The stable dimension assumption is also implicit in the use of a single construct—"intelligence" or "aggression" or "deviancy"—to describe dispositions from early childhood to late maturity. On this score, it seems hazardous to assume at the outset that these dispositions are not themselves emergent over time.

How might categories and dimensions that permit novelty be introduced, without presupposing that the same pattern of latent variables are expressed at all developmental stages or in all persons? The factor or dimensional stability question has been investigated in our research by employing concrete categories at the first level of data collection. Whenever feasible, the initial coding distinctions are qualitative rather than quantitative. We adopted measures which preserved the concrete characteristics, functions, and features of the behaviors of subjects. This technique of data recording was followed in direct behavioral observations, in interview reports, and in community reports. The use of qualitative categorical classifications permitted us to determine whether some concrete behaviors would rise and others would fall across time, and still others would emerge anew or disappear. In addition, the information has permitted the use of factor analysis and LISREL measurement models to determine whether new dimensions appeared over time. This strategy permitted us to conclude, for example, that a new dimension of "social aggression" appeared in girls in early adolescence that co-existed with confrontational "aggression" (Cairns et al. 1989).

A second issue concerns the appropriate unit or dimension of analysis. Magnusson and Bergman (1984) observe that most analyses of behavior are "variable-oriented" rather than "person-oriented." An alternative to multivariate analysis would be a multiperson analysis, where the task is to identify the patterns of problem behaviors that occur across individuals—the "packages" of deviance. The second step in this strategy would be to determine why delinquent characteristics covary in particular combinations. Such a "person-oriented" analytic strategy would support investigations which are addressed to the processes and dynamics of deviant behavior rather than to their dissection in populations. The proposal may be subsumed by the more radical proposition that certain developmental phenomena are sufficiently unique as to require analysis at the individual, configural level rather than at the sample, population level. Generalizations may then be reached on the basis of the lawfulness of processes within persons over time as opposed to the lawfulness of associations within populations (see Allport 1937). The unit of study becomes the individual, not populations. One enduring problem in behavioral study concerns the issue of how to translate ephemeral processes about individual adaptation—actions and interactions—into quantifiable patterns without a loss of essential information.

One strategy that we have adopted has been to identify configurations of boys and girls who have common behavioral and demographic profiles in childhood. Such a configural strategy is based on the assumption that developmental trajectories of aggressive behavior reflect the operation of both personal and social factors over time. Hence the simultaneous employment of internal and external characteristics should be key to isolating commonalities in developmental pathways. This analytic procedure has proved to be most effective in identifying the behavioral trajectories leading to educational failure and school dropout (Cairns, Cairns, and Neckerman 1989). The dropout rates in the eleventh grade, given membership in one of seven clusters identified four years earlier in the seventh grade, ranged from 0 percent to 82 percent in males, and from 0 percent to 49 percent in females.

The homogeneous groups also provided a means for identifying persons who did not conform to the trajectory of other members of their group. Analysis of the developmental experiences of the 2 percent of the male cluster who dropped out vs. the 98 percent who did not provides a clue on the nature of emergent risks. Conversely, comparison of the 51 percent of the girls in the deviant cluster who did not drop out vs. the 49 percent of the females who did drop out yielded information about protective factors. Such a strategy directs as much attention to the "failures" of prediction as to the "successes." The hazard with conventional models has been that developmental phenomena may themselves become distorted by the very operations designed to make them accessible to empirical analysis. The problem is magnified when standard multivariate analyses treat distinctive trajectories of individual development as error variance.

A Concluding Comment

At the beginning of this chapter we observed that interventions are now available for the prevention, regulation, or elimination of aggressive patterns in individual animals. This progress in animal behavior has been achieved by the combination of experimental, observational, neurobiological and genetic studies in a developmental framework. Our goal in employing animals was to determine whether aggressive phenomena would be clarified by integrated developmental study.

Is a systematic analysis of aggressive and antisocial behavior in humans also likely to pay off in our time? We think it will. To be sure, there are obstacles that remain in the analysis of antisocial aggressive behavior in humans. But the congruence of our longitudinal findings with the results of other longitudinal studies of antisocial and aggressive phenomena is impressive. Indeed, one of the more surprising outcomes of this research is how closely the findings on antisocial behavior mirror those which have been obtained in radically different circumstances and populations. Direct comparisons indicate that the similarities outweigh the dissimilarities when appropriate comparisons are made to the findings on lower-class London boys (Farrington 1986; Farrington and West 1990) and boys and girls in medium-sized cities in Sweden (Magnusson 1988; Olweus 1979) and Finland (Lagerspetz et al. 1988; Pulkkinen 1982), and samples of American youth (Elliott et al. 1989; Huesmann, Eron, and Lefkowitz 1984; McCord 1986).

But some fundamental issues remain to be resolved. The recent history of the field suggests that there are more basic obstacles to progress than the inaccessibility of children to significant, lifelong experimental manipulations. The study of aggressive patterns in human beings is presently burdened by concepts, methods, designs, and measures that diminish or eliminate the processes of developmental change. A systematic reexamination of traditional methods and concepts would seem to be a first priority for the discipline. A second priority is related to the first. Since the developmental perspective requires attention to time-regulated changes in both persons and social networks, procedures must be devised to make joint analyses possible and feasible. The available data suggest that these changes are not independent, and that they operate together to support—or inhibit—antisocial behaviors.

Notes

1. This research program was originally called the Carolina Longitudinal Study. Because of the expansion of the work to include subjects beyond

the region, its title was changed to the CLS project, and this designation will be employed throughout the chapter. R. B. Cairns and B. D. Cairns have served as co-directors of the CLS longitudinal research since its inception. This work has involved the joint efforts of a significant number of colleagues over the past decade. In particular, we thank our longterm co-investigators H. J. Neckerman and T. R. Flinchum for their contributions to this chapter and to the project.

2. The "therapeutic" or interventional strategies range from genetic, pharmacological, endocrinological, experiential manipulations to the experimental control over dyadic interchanges, rearing conditions, and social organization.

3. There are some notable exceptions, including the work of Eron and his colleagues (1973), Pulkkinen (1986), and Magnusson (1988).

4. By sociogenesis, we refer to the collaboration between ontogenesis (development of the individual) and phylogenesis (development of the species and society) in the establishment of social patterns. Sociogenesis implies that nature and nurture typically collaborate rather than compete in the genesis of social patterns (Cairns and Cairns 1988; Cairns 1979).

5. The additional measures included (1) individual interviews with the parents and grandparents, (2) measures of community adaptation (e.g., court records, Department of Motor Vehicle records, newspaper analyses), (3) firearm ownership, (4) school records and school activities (including failure, special placement, dropout, scholarships, extracurricular activities as documented in yearbooks and school newspapers, graduation), (5) marital status, (6) job history, and (7) ecological assessments of neighborhoods and communities.

6. Exceptions to this rule occurred under circumstances were the PIs themselves were involved in data collection. When this occurred, objectivity was protected by the inclusion of an observer who was blind with respect to the status of the subject or family.

7. Any brief summary can be misleading, and it cannot substitute for an examination of the evidence itself. This work has been described in technical publications cited in the references and below in the text.

References

Allport, G. W. 1937. *Personality: A Psychological Interpretation.* New York: Holt, Rinehart, & Winston.

Baldwin, J. M. 1902. *Social and Ethical Interpretations in Mental Development: A Study in Social Psychology.* 3rd ed. New York: Macmillan. (Originally published in 1897.)

Bandura, A. & Walters, R. H. 1959. *Adolescent Aggression.* New York: Ronald.

Barrett, D. E. 1979. "A Naturalistic Study of Sex Differences in Children's Aggression." *Merrill-Palmer Quarterly* 25, 193–207.

Bigelow, B. J. 1977. "Children's Friendship Expectations: A Cognitive-Developmental Study." *Child Development* 48, 246–53.

Cairns, B. D., H. J. Neckerman, T. R. Flinchum, and R. B. Cairns. 1990. "Lost and Found in Longitudinal Study: I. Recovery of Subjects." Unpublished manuscript, University of North Carolina at Chapel Hill.

Cairns, C. B., J. Nemhauser, and J. Nieman. 1991. "Trauma Admissions and Violent Injury Among Children and Young Adults." Paper presented at the Society for Academic Emergency Medicine, Washington, D.C.

Cairns, R. B. 1979. *Social development: The Origins and Plasticity of Interchanges.* San Francisco: Freeman.

Cairns, R. B. 1983. "The Emergence of Developmental Psychology." In P. H. Mussen (Gen. Ed.). and W. Kessen (Vol. Ed.), *Handbook of child psychology,* (pp. 41–102). Vol. 1 (4th ed.). New York: Wiley.

Cairns, R. B. 1986. "Phenomena Lost: Issues in the Study of Development." In *The Individual Subject and Scientific Psychology,* edited by J. Valsiner, 97–112. New York: Plenum Press.

Cairns, R. B. 1990. "Developmental Epistemology and Self Knowledge: Towards a Reinterpretation of Self-Esteem." In *Theories of the evolution of knowing: The T. C. Schneirla conference series,* edited by E. Tobach and G. Greenberg, 69–86. Vol. 4. Hillsdale, NJ: Lawrence Erlbaum Associates.

Cairns, R. B., and B. D. Cairns. 1981. "Self-Reflections: An Essay and Commentary on 'Social cognition and the acquisition of self.' " *Developmental Review* 1, 171–80.

Cairns, R. B., and B. D. Cairns. 1988. "The Sociogenesis of Self Concepts." In *Persons in Social Context: Developmental Processes,* edited by N. Bolger, A. Caspi, G. Downey, and M. Moorehouse, 181–202. New York: Cambridge University Press.

Cairns, R. B., and B. D. Cairns. 1991. *Adolescents in Our Time: Lifelines and Risks.* Unpublished manuscript, University of North Carolina at Chapel Hill.

Cairns, R. B., B. D. Cairns, and H. J. Neckerman. 1989. "Early School Dropout: Configurations and Determinants." *Child Development, 60,* 1437–1452.

Cairns, R. B., B. D. Cairns, H. J. Neckerman, L. L. Ferguson, & J-L Gariépy. 1989. "Growth and Aggression: I. Childhood to Early Adolescence." *Developmental Psychology* 25, 320–30.

Cairns, R. B., B. D. Cairns, H. J. Neckerman, S. Gest, & J-L Gariépy. 1988. "Social Networks and Aggressive Behavior: Peer Support or Peer Rejection?" *Developmental Psychology* 24, 815–23.

Cairns, R. B., J-L. Gariépy, and K. E. Hood. 1990. "Development, Microevolution, and Social Behavior. *Psychological Review* 97, 49–65.

Cairns, R. B., J-L Gariépy, and T. Kindermann. 1991. "Identifying social clusters in natural settings. "Unpublished manuscript, University of North Carolina at Chapel Hill.

Cairns, R. B., & J. A. Green. 1979. "How to Assess Personality and Social Patterns: Ratings or Observations?" In *The Analysis of Social Interaction: Methods, Issues, and Illustrations,* edited by R. B. Cairns, 209–26. Hillsdale, NJ: Erlbaum.

Cairns, R. B., H. J. Neckerman, and R. B. Cairns. 1989. "Social Networks and the Shadows of Synchrony." In *Advances in adolescent development,* edited by G. R. Adams, T. P. Gullota, and R. Montemayor, 275–305. Beverly Hill, CA: Sage.

Campbell, A. 1980. "Friendship as a Factor in Male and Female Delinquency." In *Friendship and Social Relations in Children,* edited by H. C. Foot, A. J. Chapman, and J. R. Smith, 365–90. Chichester: John Wiley.

Castellan, N. J., Jr. 1979. "The Analysis of Behavior Sequences." In *The Analysis of Social Interactions: Methods, Issues, and Illustrations,* edited by R. B. Cairns, 81–116. Hillsdale, N.J.: Erlbaum, 1979.

Coie, J. D., and K. A. Dodge. 1983. "Continuities and Changes in Children's Social Status: A Five-Year Longitudinal Study." *Merrill-Palmer Quarterly,* 29, 261–82.

Elliott, D. S., D. Huizinga, and S. Menard. 1989. *Multiple Problem Youth: Delinquency, Substance Use, and Mental Health Problems.* New York: Springer-Verlag.

Eron, L., and L. R. Huesmann. 1984. "The Control of Aggressive Behavior by Changes in Attitudes, Values, and the Conditions of Learning." In *Advances in the Study of Aggression, vol. 1,* edited by R. J. Blanchard and C. Blanchard, 138–70. New York: Academic Press.

Eron, L., L. R. Huesmann, P. Brice, P. Fischer, and R. Mermelstein. 1983. "Age Trends in the Development of Aggression, Sex Typing, and Related Television Habits." *Developmental Psychology, 19,* 71–77.

Farrington, D. P. 1986. "Stepping Stones to Adult Criminal Careers." In *Development of Antisocial and Prosocial Behavior: Research, Theories, and Issues,* edited by D. Olweus, J. Block, and M. Radke-Yarrow, 359–84. New York: Academic Press.

Farrington, D. P., and D. J. West. 1990. "The Cambridge Study in Delinquent Development: A Long-term Follow-up of 411 London

Males." In *Criminality: Personality, Behavior, and Life History*, edited by H.-J. Kerner and G. Kaiser. Berlin: Springer-Verlag.

Ferguson, T. J., and B. G. Rule. 1980. "Effects of Inferential Set, Outcome Severity, and Basis of Responsibility on Children's Evaluation of Aggressive Acts." *Developmental Psychology* 16, 141–46.

Feshbach, N. D., and G. Sones. 1971. "Sex Differences in Adolescent Reactions to Newcomers." *Developmental Psychology* 4, 381–86.

Fingerhut, L. A., and J. C. Kleinman. 1990. "International and Interstate Comparisons of Homicide among Young Males." *Journal of the American Medical Association* 263, 3292–95.

Friedrich-Cofer, L. 1986. "Body, Mind, and Morals in the Forming of Social Policy. In *Human Nature and Public policy: Scientific Views of Women, Children, and Families*, edited by L. Friedrich-Cofer, 97–174. New York: Praeger.

Giordano, P. C., S. A. Cernkovich, and M. D. Pugh. 1986. "Friendship and Delinquency." *American Journal of Sociology* 91, 1170–1201.

Hall, W. M., and R. B. Cairns. 1984. "Aggressive Behavior in Children: An Outcome of Modeling or Reciprocity?" *Developmental Psychology* 20, 739–45.

Harter, S. 1983. "Developmental perspectives on the self-system." In P. H. Mussen (Gen. Ed.) and M. Hetherington (Ed.), *Handbook of Child Psychology* (pp. 275–386), Vol. 4, 4th ed. New York: Wiley.

Hartup, W. W. (1983). Peer groups. In *Handbook of Child Psychology*, edited by P. H. Mussen and M. Hetherington, 103–196, Vol. 4, 4th ed. New York: Wiley.

Hood, K. E., and R. B. Cairns. 1988. "A Developmental-Genetic Analysis of Aggressive Behavior in Mice: II. Cross-Sex Inheritance." *Behavior Genetics* 18 (5), 605–19.

Huesmann, L. R., K. Lagerspetz, and L. D. Eron. 1984. "Intervening Variables in the TV Violence-Aggression Relation: Evidence from Two Countries." *Developmental Psychology* 20, 746–75.

Huesmann, L. R., L. D. Eron, and M. M. Lefkowitz. 1984. "Stability of Aggression Over Time and Generations." *Developmental Psychology* 20, 1120–34.

Jessor, R., and S. L. Jessor. 1977. *Problem Behavior and Psychosocial Development: A Longitudinal Study of Youth.* New York: Academic Press.

Kandel, D. B. 1978. Homophily, Selection, and Socialization in Adolescent Friendships. *American Journal of Sociology* 84, 427–36.

Kessen, W. 1960. "Research Design in the Study of Developmental Problems." *Handbook of Research Methods in Child Development*, edited by P. H. Mussen, 36–70. New York; Wiley.

Lagerspetz, K. M. J., K. Björkqvist, and T. Peltonen. 1988. "Is Indirect Aggression Typical of females? Gender differences in Aggressiveness in 11- to 12-Year-Old Children." *Aggressive Behavior* 14, 403–414.

Ledingham, J. E., A. Younger, A. Schwartzman, and G. Bergeron. 1982. "Agreement Among Teacher, Peer, and Self-Ratings of Children's Aggression, Withdrawal, and Likability." *Journal of Abnormal Child Psychology* 10, 363–72.

Lewis, M. H., L. L. Devaud, J-L. Gariépy, S. B. Southerland, R. B. Mailman, and R. B. Cairns. (in press). "Dopamine and Social Behavior in Mice Bred for High and Low Levels of Aggression." *Brain Research Bulletin*.

Loeber, R. 1982. "The Stability of Antisocial and Delinquent Child Behavior: A Review." *Child Development* 53, 1431–46.

Loeber, R., and M. Le Blanc (1990). "Toward a Developmental Criminology." In *Crime and Justice: A Review of Research*, vol. 12, edited by M. Tonry and N. Morris, 375–473. Chicago, IL: University of Chicago Press.

Magnusson, D. 1988. *Individual Development from an Interactional Perspective: A Longitudinal Study*, vol. 1. In *Paths through Life*, edited by D. Magnusson. Hillsdale, NJ: Erlbaum.

Magnusson, D., and L. R. Bergman. 1984. "On the Study of the Development of Adjustment Problems." In *Human Action and Personality: Essays in Honour of Martti Takala*, edited by L. Pulkkinen and P. Lyytinen, 163–71. Jyväskylä, Finland: University of Jyväskylä.

Magnusson, D. and L. R. Bergman. 1990. "A pattern Approach to the Study of Pathways from Childhood to Adulthood." In *Straight and Devious Pathways from Childhood to Adulthood*, edited by L. N. Robins and M. Rutter, 101–115. Cambridge: Cambridge University Press.

McCord, J. 1986. "Instigation and Insulation: How Families Affect Antisocial Aggression." In *Development of antisocial and prosocial behavior: Research, theories, and issues*, edited by D. Olweus, J. Block, and M. Radke-Yarrow, 343–58. New York: Academic.

Olweus, D. 1979. "Stability of Aggressive Reaction Patterns in Males: A Review." *Psychological Bulletin* 86, 852–75.,

Parke, R. D., and R. G. Slaby. 1983. "The Development of Aggression." In *Handbook of Child Psychology*, edited by P. H. Mussen and M. Hetherington, 547–642, vol. 4, 4th ed. New York: Wiley.

Patterson, G. R. 1979. "A Performance Theory for Coercive Family Interaction." In *The Analysis of Social Interactions: Methods, Issues, and Illustrations*, edited by R. B. Cairns, Hillsdale, NJ: Erlbaum.

Pulkkinen, L. 1982. "Self-Control and Continuity from Childhood to Late

Adolescence.'' In *Life-Span Development and Behavior*, edited by P. B. Baltes and O. G. Brim, Jr., 64–105, vol. 4. New York: Academic.

Robins, L. N. 1986. ''The Consequences of Conduct Disorder in Girls.'' In *Development of Antisocial and Prosocial Behavior: Research, Theories, and Issues*, edited by D. Olweus, J. Block, and M. Radke-Yarrow, 385–414. New York: Academic.

Rodgers, J. L., J. O. G. Billy, and J. R. Udry. 1984. ''A Model of Friendship Similarity in Mildly Deviant Behaviors.'' *Journal of Applied Social Psychology* 14, 413–25.

Sadowski, L. S., R. B. Cairns, and J. A. Earp. 1989. ''Firearm Ownership Among Nonurban Adolescents.'' *American Journal of Diseases of Children* 143, 1410–13.

Simmons, R. C., and D. A. Blyth. 1987. *Moving into Adolescence; The Impact of Pubertal Change and School Context*. New York: Aldine.

Strayer, F. F., and J. M. Noel. 1986. ''The Prosocial and Antisocial Functions of Preschool Aggression: An Ethological Study of Triadic Conflict Among Young Children.'' In *Altruism and Aggression: Biological and Social Origins*, edited by C. Zahn-Waxler, E. M. Cummings, and R. Iannotti, 107–31. Cambridge: Cambridge University Press.

Tanner, J. M. 1962. *Growth at Adolescence*. Oxford: Blackwell Scientific Publications.

Yarrow, M. R. and C. Z. Waxler. 1979. ''Observing Interaction: A Confrontation with Methodology.'' In *The analysis of social interactions: Methods, issues, and illustrations*, edited by R. B. Cairns, Hillsdale, NJ: Erlbaum.

Youniss, J. 1986. ''Development in Reciprocity through Friendship.'' In *Altruism and Aggression: Biological and Social Origins*, edited by C. Zahn-Waxler, E. M. Cummings, and R. Iannotti, 88–106. Cambridge: Cambridge University Press.

9

The Prediction of Delinquent Behavior from Childhood Behavior: Personality Theory Revisited

Richard E. Tremblay

*We were left to the operation of the struggle
for existence among ourselves; bullying
was the least of the ill practices current among
us. Almost the only cheerful reminiscence in
connection with the place which arises in my
mind is that of a battle I had with one of my
classmates, who had bullied me until I could
stand it no longer. I was a very slight lad, but
there was a wild-cat element in me which,
when roused, made up for lack of weight, and
I licked my adversary effectually. However,
one of my first experiences of the extremely
rough-and-ready nature of justice, as exhibited
by the course of things in general, arose out
of the fact that I—the victor—had a black eye,
while he—the vanquished—had none, so that
I got into disgrace and he did not. We made it
up, and thereafter I was unmolested. One of
the greatest shocks I ever received in my
life was to be told a dozen years afterwards by
the groom who brought me my horse in a
stable-yard in Sydney that he was my quon-
dam antagonist. He had a long story of family
misfortune to account for his position; but at
that time it was necessary to deal very cautiously with mysterious strangers in New South
Wales, and on inquiry I found that the unfortu-*

nate young man had not only been "sent
out", but had undergone more than one
colonial conviction.
—T. H. Huxley, *Life and Letters of*
Thomas Henry Huxley

During the last three decades longitudinal studies were conducted with the explicit aim of linking children's behavior problems with juvenile delinquency and adult criminal behavior. This enterprise has been largely successful. There is now clear evidence that children manifesting disruptive behavior maintain the highest risk of subsequently developing juvenile delinquency and adult criminality (Farrington, Loeber, Elliott et al. 1990). To a certain extent these findings confirmed popular beliefs. The saying "as the twig is bent so grows the tree" is but one of those popular maxims which have traditionally guided parental discipline practices.

If the conclusion from these studies is not surprising, the methodological advances which were made are far from trivial. Child specialists have been busy designing a variety of instruments to measure all forms of children's behavior. Scientists and practitioners currently employ well-calibrated rating scales for teachers, parents, and peers; observation coding systems for home, schools, and laboratory settings; interview schedules for adults and children; as well as specific laboratory testing procedures (Prinz 1986; Rutter, Tuma, and Lann 1988). Although there remains a large amount of work to be carried out in order to upgrade these instruments in terms of reliability and validity, investigators are now equiped with sophisticated means of recording children's daily behavior allowing for prediction of future behavior.

From Behavioral Categories to Prediction

Classification is of primary importance for any scientific enterprise. Prior to the beginning of the twentieth century there were few systematic studies of children's behavior which were useful for classification purposes. Crutcher (1943) noted that the German physiologist Tiedeman, in 1787, may have been the first to publish careful observations pertaining to child development. A few of these descriptions were published at the end of the nineteenth century by Taine (1876) and Darwin (1877), followed by more comprehensive studies by Preyer (1888) and Sully (1895). At the same time, Moreau (1888) published what appears to be the first book dealing exclusively with children's deviant behavior. It should be noted however, that the 1913 English edition of Kraepelin's classic classifications of psychiatric disorders did not include specific disorders of childhood. Major progress was achieved during the first half of the twentieth century, probably as a function of interest in children's welfare, stimulated by the child guidance clinics, the Commonwealth Fund and the Mental Hygiene Movement (Crutcher 1943; Kanner 1959). The first classifications of children's behavior problems using "modern" statistical techniques were published in the 1940s (Ackerson 1942; Hart, Jenkins, Axelrad, and Sperling 1943; Hewitt and Jenkins 1946; Jenkins and Hewitt 1944; Jenkins and Glickman 1946, 1947). A decade earlier Bridges (1931), Dawe (1934), and Murphy (1937) had published results from extensive observations of children's social behavior in nursery schools, and Ackerson (1931) had published a classification of children's behavior problems based on more than 3,000 case reports from the Institute for Juvenile Research in Chicago (see Dreger 1981, 1982).

Cairns (1983) noted that these early descriptions of behavior lacked a theoretical foundation. In fact, most of the work on the classification of children's behavior up to now has been based on two different inductive procedures. The first was developed by ethologists who insist on having a relatively complete description of the repertoire of behaviors before conducting experimental work with a given species. By observing the behavior of a sample from the species, the ethologists slowly create an ethogram, that is, a complete catalogue of all behavioral patterns for a given species (Heymer 1977). McGrew (1972) made such an attempt for children's social behavior. The behaviors observed by ethologists are usually categorized according to either or both their causes and their functions (Hinde 1970, 1974). Masters (1979) has suggested that social behavior can be classified along two dimensions, with three poles. One dimension depicts the approach-avoidance phenomenon. The other dimension depicts the affiliation-agonism phenomenon. Thus three types of behaviors are purported to describe social behavior: aggression, affiliation, and flight.[1] Masters further proposed that all vertebrates display these categories of behaviors and that they are sufficient to describe the complexity of social behavior, if attention is paid to their interactions.

The second inductive tradition for classifying children's behavior is based on factor analytic studies of deviant behaviors. Typically, a large pool of items is generated which describe inadequate behaviors; the pool is reexamined in order to discard poor items and then given to judges who rate a sample of children using the new pool of items. The latter ratings are then submitted to factor analytic procedures in order to identify empirically meaningful groupings of the items. The factor analytic procedures will, of course, yield as many or as few dimensions as one wishes.

There have been two distinct tendencies in the classification of child maladjustment based on factor analytic procedures: "splitters" and "lumpers." In the splitting tendency, the investigator aims at obtaining as many dimensions as possible. For example, the Children's Behavioral Classification Project (Dreger 1977) generated fifty dimensions of children's behavior and considered thirty to be the optimum solution. The lumping strategy aims at obtaining as few dimensions as possible. For example, Achenbach and Edelbrock (1978) as well as Quay (1979) have suggested that children's behavior problems could be reduced to externalizing (aggression, hyperactivity, opposition) and internalizing (anxiety, withdrawal, etc.) problems. Achenbach and Edelbrock (1983, 1986, 1987) created a frequently used instrument which generates from seven to nine first order factors and two second order factors (externalization, internalization). A number of such instruments have been devised for teacher or parent ratings (e.g., Behar and Stringfield 1974; Conners 1969; Kohn 1977; Quay and Peterson 1987; Stott 1974) and for peer or self ratings (e.g., Lefkowitz et al. 1977; Pekarick et al. 1976; Masten et al. 1985).

Systematic observations of children's behavior and rational efforts of classification are clearly a recent scientific endeavor. There are some (Blurton Jones 1972; Strayer and Gauthier 1985) who maintain that too little descriptive work has been done before attempting to test explanatory hypothesis. Present day classifications will most probably be modified by further observations of children's behavior. However, the available classifications have led to the construction of instruments and their use for the prediction of deviant behavior. The results of these predictive studies can be used to validate or invalidate the behavioral classifications.

Loeber and Stouthamer-Loeber (1987) reviewed predictive studies of delinquent behaviors. They concluded that there are clear associations between a number of childhood behavior dimensions and future delinquent behavior, especially for boys. The best predictors of adolescent and adult delinquency were found to be aggressive, daring, and troublesome childhood behavior. Hyperactivity has also been related to subsequent delinquent behavior. (Weiss and Hetchman 1986; Satterfield 1987). It is not clear however, to what extent hyperactivity is in itself a predictor of delinquency. There is some evidence that the hyperactive children who become delinquents were also aggressive children (Farrington, Loeber, and Van Kammen 1990; Loney, Kramer, and Milich 1981; McGee, Williams, and Silva 1984). However, a number of the measures of aggressive and troublesome behavior include hyperactivity items (Tremblay 1991). This confusion of dimensions is mostly the result of the use of factor analytic techniques which generate dimensions that are given labels with a loose relationship to the variety of items they represent.

Two other dimensions of children's behavior have been negatively associated to future delinquency. Children with high levels of anxiety (Blumstein, Farrington, and Moitra 1985; Graham and Rutter 1973; McCord 1987) and high levels of prosocial behavior (Eron and Huesmann 1984) have been observed to be at lower risk for future antisocial behavior. These studies suggest that anxiety and prosociality in childhood behaviors are protective factors. However, it could also be the case that the absence of anxiety and the absence of prosociality increase the risk of delinquent behavior. The work on adult psychopaths does indicate that primary psychopaths are low in anxiety. They are also reported to lack warmth in interpersonal relationships and to lack concern for others (Cleckley 1976; McCord and McCord 1964; Schalling 1978; Spielberger, Kling, and O'Hagan 1978).

From Observations to Theory

The review of predictive studies by Loeber and Stouthamer-Loeber (1987) does show that a number of longitudinal studies have found predictive links between categories of children's behavior and later criminal activity. The best predictor category appears to be a set of behaviors which include aggressive, daring, trouble-some, and hyperactive behaviors. In their third revised version of the *Diagnostic and Statistical Manual of Mental Disorders*, the American Psychiatric Association (1987) labelled these behaviors "disruptive disorders." This classification manual is the latest version from a tradition of classification in psychiatry which dates back to Kraepelin. The behaviors of deviant individuals are de-scribed and then classified according to their similarity. Theories are intentionally absent from this effort because the purpose of the classification is to provide a means of communication among professionals with different theoretical orientations (Cantwell 1988).

One would expect that results from the predictive studies of delinquency from childhood behaviors could be included in a theory of human behavior. The most parsimonious theory to explain the relationship between childhood disruptive disorders and later anti-social behavior would be one of behavioral stability (Olweus 1979; Rowe and Osgood 1990), that is, criminals were already deviant in childhood; their antisocial behavior in adolescence and adulthood is simply an expression of an underlying trait which was expressed in the form of disruptive behavior during childhood. Such a theory could rely on a genetic inheritance paradigm (Mednick and Gabrielli 1984; Rowe and Osgood 1990), on an acquired neurological deficit paradigm (Buikhuisen 1987), or on a social learning paradigm (Eron 1987; Patterson 1982) to explain the presence of disruptive behavior in childhood.

A number of investigators have focused their attention on the stability of aggressive behavior as the direct expression of the underlying trait. Olweus (1979) in his review concluded that aggres-sion is as stable as intelligence from age three onwards. Huesmann et al. (1984) showed intra-individual and intergenerational stability after a twenty-four-year follow-up study of a group of children who were first assessed at age eight. It is of interest to note that the peer assessment aggression scale which was used in the data collection of the latter study, for age eight, included only three items which were clearly physical aggression items (Eron, Walder, and Lefkow-itz 1971). The other items refer to a variety of behaviors which involved not obeying the teacher, getting others in trouble, bothering others, getting in trouble, saying mean things, taking other's things. Other instruments with aggression scales for children have similar content (Tremblay 1991). Whatever is assessed in these studies may be stable and a good predictor of future antisocial behavior, but aggressive behavior, at least physical aggression, is not the main thrust of those assessments. Externalizing, active, disruptive, deviant behavior, appears to be the behavior pattern which is assessed both as predictor and as outcome.

Investigators have also shown that there is important overlap between the hyperactivity-inattentiveness-impulsivity syndrome, and the conduct problem syndrome (Farrington et al. 1990; Loney and Milich 1982; McGee, Williams, and Silva 1984). Hyperactivity starts early in development and appears to precede conduct problems (Barkley 1981). Moffitt (1990a) has shown that the hyperactive children who become juvenile delinquents had relatively stable conduct problems during childhood. If hyperactivity is an important factor in the development of conduct problems (these children are harder to manage), it could be an important underlying factor in the observed relationship between childhood conduct problems, including aggression, and later antisocial behavior (Loeber 1990; Moffitt 1990b; White et al. 1990). This line of reasoning would simply replace a theory of the stability of aggressive behavior by a theory of the stability of hyperactive behavior. An important step would be taken however by focusing on hyperactivity rather than aggression. A genetic theory of the stability of aggression requires the identification of a mechanism for its genetic transmission. This mechanism is not likely to be found (Adams 1989; Cairns 1979). On the other hand, the stability of hyperactivity hypothesis could rely on theories of genetic transmission of (and/or theories of the development of) the neurological system. Frequent aggression, oppositional, or antisocial behavior would thus be more clearly an acquired response by a given type of individual in a given type of environment (Cairns 1979). From the classification perspective of Gangestad and Snyder (1985), hyperactivity would be a latent underlying entity, a genotype source of influence, for a phenotypic phenomenon which includes troublesome, daring, aggressive behavior (Gorenstein and Newman 1980).

Given the complexity of behavior it is, however, unlikely that one behavioral dimension would be sufficient to explain antisocial behavior. We have seen that two other behavioral dimensions have been associated with the prediction of criminal behavior: namely anxiety and prosociality. Anxious and prosocial children have been found to be at lower risk for antisocial behavior than not anxious and not prosocial children (Blumstein, Farrington, and Moitra 1985; Eron and Huesmann 1984; McCord 1987). One would thus expect that children with high hyperactivity, low anxiety, and low prosociality would be at the highest risk of antisocial behavior in adolescence and adulthood.

At this point we can ask ourselves, is there a theory of human behavior that would fit these observations? Royce and Powell (1983) attempted to integrate empirical and theoretical knowledge of individual differences. From this major synthesis they observed that investigators had studied seven interacting systems in attempts to conceptualize human behavior. These systems were postulated to form a four-level hierarchy based on complexity. The first level includes the sensory and motor systems. The second level includes the affective and cognitive systems. The style and value systems constitute the third level. Finally, the fourth level is the total psychological system, which they have named the integrative personality. Clearly, the categories of childhood behaviors which have been studied by investigators to predict delinquency can be found at the second level, with particular reference to the affective system.

From their analysis, Royce and Powell argue that the affective level is composed of three higher factors: emotional stability, emotional independence, and introversion-extroversion. The interaction among these three affective functions leads to an affective type. For their definition of the three higher order factors, Royce and Powell relied heavily on the work of Eysenck and his collaborators (1970, 1976). This is interesting since Eysenck's theory predicts that criminality will be associated with high neuroticism (emotional instability), high extroversion, and high psychoticism (emotional independence). In a recent review of studies which have tested these predictions, Eysenck and Gudjonsson (1989) concluded that psychoticism was clearly related to criminal behavior "in all age groups and under all conditions studied" (p. 88). They also concluded that the relationship of neuroticism and extroversion with criminal behavior changes with age. Extroversion is positively related to criminality in younger subjects, whilst neuroticism is positively related to criminality in older subjects. Eysenck and Eysenck (1976) described individuals low in psychoticism as being empathic, unselfish, altruistic, and warm. Individuals high on psychoticism were described as cold, egocentric, and impersonal. Clearly this dimension fits rather well the prosocial dimension to which we have referred earlier. Individuals rated low on the prosocial dimension would be labeled high on the psychotic dimension.

The neurotic and extroversion dimensions of Eysenck's personality system have been less systematically associated to antisocial behavior. As Eysenck and Gudjonsson (1989) report, there seems to be an important age effect on the relationship of antisocial behavior with neuroticism and extroversion. This could be due to the effect of the interaction between biological dispositions (temperament) and experience (age), which we usually label maturation. Part of the problem may also be due to the way these two dimensions (neuroticism and extroversion) have been conceived. Gray (1970) has suggested that the neurotic and extroverted dimensions be replaced by an anxiety and an impulsivity dimension. As can be seen in figure 9.1, Gray's anxiety dimension is at a 45° angle to Eysenck's neurotic dimension. Similarly, Gray's impulsivity dimension is at a 45° angle to Eysenck's introversion-extroversion dimension. Gray (1970) suggests that this 45° rotation of Eysenck's basic personality dimensions gives a more parsimonious explanation of the observation that drug therapies can reduce anxiety. These agents appear to have an effect on a specific brain function, the behavioral inhibition system, based on a well defined physiological locus, the septo-hippocampal system (Gray, 1982). To account for these observations from Eysenck's personality dimensions we need to postulate that this brain mechanism controls both the neurotic and the introversion-extroversion dimensions. To the extent that we are looking for personality dimensions which are close approximations to brain functioning, Gray's anxiety dimension is clearly a more parsimonious solution. It is particularly appealing for a personality theory of criminal behavior, since, as we have seen, both childhood predictors and adulthood correlates of antisocial behavior include the anxiety dimension.

The impulsivity dimension is less clearly related to a biological

FIGURE 9.1
Gray's rotation of Eysenck's two personality dimensions

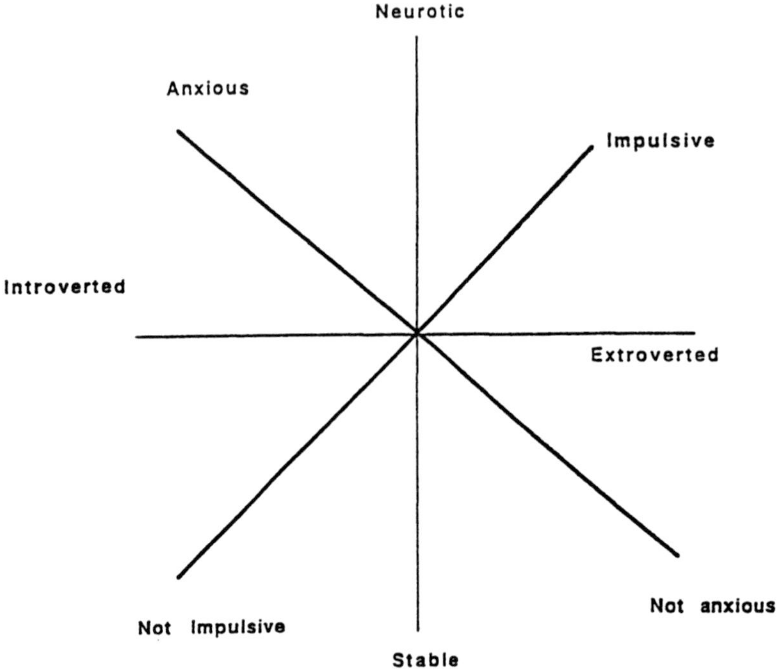

basis. It should, in some way, be related to a behavioral activation system. Gray (1983) has suggested that the brain processes which could explain the impulsivity dimensions are those that mediate responses associated with punishment or nonreward, responses associated with reward and nonpunishment, and aggressive responses following unconditioned punishment or nonreward. Newman (1987) has proposed a mechanism where, in a context of reward with negative feedback (punishment), impulsive subjects will allocate their attention to the original goal (the reward) rather than to the negative feedback; thus they will maintain their original goal behavior rather than adjusting their response to the context. They will also fail to learn from the negative experience because of the lack of reflective behavior.

There are two reasons why the impulsivity dimension appears to be particularly relevant for a personality theory of criminal behavior. First, a number of studies have shown that psychopaths show impulsive behavior (Hare and Schalling 1978; Zuckerman 1983);

Gray (1981) has in fact shown that impulsivity items in the Eysenck extroversion factor account for most of the correlation between extroversion and criminality. Second, impulsivity is clearly part of the hyperactive childhood syndrome (Barkley 1981; APA 1987). Weiss and Hechtman (1986) concluded that impulsivity was the most apparent adult problem of children who were hyperactive. Gorenstein and Newman (1980) suggested that childhood hyperactivity, hysteria, primary alcoholism, and psychopathy were all related to a common genetic diathesis. We can thus hypothesize that the observed relationship between childhood hyperactivity and future criminal behavior is related to Gray's impulsivity dimension.

It is of interest to note that Gray et al. (1983), in their discussion of different approaches to the concept of impulsivity addressed the issue of the link between impulsive and aggressive behaviors. They suggested that further research is needed to disentangle impulsive traits with and without aggressive behavior. It will be recalled that research on the childhood predictors of criminal behavior has identified hyperactive children with and without aggressive, or conduct problems (Farrington, Loeber, and Van Kammen 1990; Loney, Kramer, and Milich, 1983; McGee, Williams, and Silva 1984; Moffitt 1990a). Since Gray and his colleagues were referring mostly to studies with adults, it is possible that this reflects the same problem at two different periods of the life cycle, childhood and adulthood.

To recapitulate, we have thus far identified a tradition of personality theories which postulates that there are three main higher order dimensions to the affective subsystem. These dimensions vary somewhat according to authors, but there seems to be clear agreement that three orthogonal dimensions in a three dimensional space are necessary and sufficient to account for affective styles.[2]

Recently Cloninger (1986) has proposed a personality system which concurs with these principles. He employs Gray's anxiety and impulsivity dimensions while adding a third dimension which draws on Eysenck's psychotic dimension and Sjobring's (1973) stability dimension. According to Cloninger, this third dimension involves "a heritable neurobiological tendency to maintain behavior associated with reward and non-punishment." The high reward dependent individual will be sentimental, sympathetic, and warm. The low reward dependent individual will be tough-minded, detached, and emotionally cool. To a large extent this dimension fits the prosocial dimension which has been negatively associated with antisocial behavior. It should be noted here that there is an important difference between Cloninger's and Gray's attempts to account for reward dependent behavior. Gray (1982, 1983) associates reward dependant behavior with the impulsivity dimension. Cloninger (1986) differentiates the "incentive" and "maintenance" or "reinforcement" aspects of the behavioral activation system. He proposes that the incentive aspect is mediated by dopaminergic activity, while the maintenance or reinforcement aspect is mediated by noradrenergic activity. As we have seen, he has labeled "reward dependence" the maintenance or reinforcement aspect of the behavioral activation system which is dependent on noradenergic activity. He labels "novelty seeking" the incentive aspect of the behavioral activation system which is dependent on dopamine activity. This dimension was labelled "impulsivity" by Gray.

Cloninger's differentiation between the incentive and maintenance aspect of the behavioral activation system is similar to the differentiation between the BAS and the RAS discussed by Fowles (1980) (see note 2). It may be the answer to the problem of impulsivity with and without aggression discussed by Gray et al. (1983) referred to earlier. Subjects high on novelty seeking (high impulsivity) and high on reward dependence are unlikely to be aggressive, at least not in a proactive (offensive) mode, because of their susceptibility to positive and negative reinforcement. On the other hand, subjects high on novelty seeking and low on reward dependence would most likely be aggressive in a proactive mode, because of their low susceptibility to positive and negative reinforcement.

Cloninger has also labelled differently Gray's anxiety dimension. He uses the term "harm avoidance" to clearly describe the behavioral tendency. He suggests that the term anxiety used by Gray can lead to a confusion between chronic somatic anxiety, which is associated with high reward dependence, high novelty seeking and low harm avoidance, and chronic cognitive anxiety which is associated with low reward dependence, low novelty seeking and high harm avoidance.

Table 9.1 gives a summary of Cloninger's (1986, 1987) personality theory. *Harm avoidance* is influenced by the neuromodulator serotonine. It is related to the brain system identified by Gray as the behavioral inhibition system. Individuals high on harm avoidance will be cautious, apprehensive, and inhibited. Those who are low will be fearless, carefree, and uninhibited. *Novelty seeking* is influenced by dopamine and related to Gray's behavioral activation system. Impulsivity, exploratory behavior, and excitability are the behaviors which typify individuals high on this dimension. Individuals with low novelty seeking are best described by reflective, rigid, and stoic behavior. *Reward dependence* is influenced by (reflective) noradrenergic activity. It is related to a third brain system, the behavioral maintenance system. High reward dependent individuals are described as warm, sentimental, and persistent, while low reward-dependent individuals are described as tough-minded, detached, and emotionally cool.

It should be noted here that the names of the three personality dimensions and the typical behavior descriptors are relatively neutral compared to labels which have been used with children for the prediction of antisocial behavior (conduct disorder, aggression, disruptive, anxious, hyperactive, troublesome). A personality theory which is meant to predict deviant behavior should not include the deviant outcome behaviors in the predictors. Otherwise we can look only at the stability of deviant personalities.

TABLE 9.1
Cloninger's (1986) personality theory

Dimensions	Typical behavior	Neuromodulators
Harm avoidance		Serotonine
High	Cautious, apprehensive, inhibited	
Low	Fearless, carefree, uninhibited	
Novelty seeking		Dopamine
High	Impulsive, exploratory, excitable	
Low	Reflective, rigid, stoic	
Reward dependence		Norepinephrine
High	Warm, sentimental, persistent	
Low	Tough-minded, detached, emotionally cool	

An important characteristic of Cloninger's personality theory is the behavioral effect of the interaction among the three postulated dimensions. Each of these dimensions is postulated to be controlled by separate brain systems (behavioral activation, behavioral inhibition, behavioral maintenance) which interact in such a way that the response based on one system will vary depending on the response from the other systems. For example, high novelty seeking individuals will behave differently depending on whether they have low harm avoidance or not. Cloninger (1987) clearly indicates that the measurement of the underlying dimensions must not include behaviors which are already the product of interactions among the dimensions. This is an important caveat for the operationalization of this theory. Factor analytic procedures which have been the main tools to create instruments may not be the appropriate method, since factors may be the product of the interactions among the underlying dimensions. Likewise, tests of such theories may be more adequate with children than with adults, because children's behavior is less a product of the interaction between basic behavioral dimensions and environmental feedback. Finally, it should be noted that the idea of taking into account the interaction among three behavioral dimensions is similar to recent suggestions by Hinde and Dennis (1986) and Magnusson and Bergman (1990) to study profiles rather than associations among variables.

An Empirical Test of the Theory

Cloninger (1987) predicts from his biosocial theory that individuals most at risk of aggressive, antisocial behavior, will be those with high novelty seeking, low harm avoidance and low reward dependence ("antisocials" in figure 9.2). They are equated with the primary psychopath (Cleckley 1976; Hare and Schalling 1978). Other types of individuals are postulated to respond aggressively in certain situations. Those who are high on novelty seeking, high on reward dependence, and low on harm avoidance are predicted to be histrionics who exhibit angry outbursts accompanied by attention seeking and emotional dependence. Individuals who are high on novelty seeking, high on reward dependence, and high on harm avoidance ("passive-aggressives") are predicted to be verbally rather than physically aggressive. They will also be deferential and use indirect methods of manipulation. Finally subjects who are high on novelty seeking and harm avoidance, but low on reward dependence ("explosive schizoids") will manifest outbursts of rage and negative feelings towards others. Subjects who are low in novelty seeking, whether they are low or high on the other two dimensions would be less at risk of aggressive and antisocial behavior. Cloninger also postulates that the most adaptive blend of the three dimensions should be an average value. It is thus expected that the majority of individuals will have average values on each of the dimensions. It is hypothesized that only small groups of individuals will have extreme values on some or all of the dimensions.

There have been few tests of Cloninger's or Gray's models with young children. Cloninger, Sigvardsson, and Bohman (1988) used data from a longitudinal study of Swedish children to test the association among the three personality dimensions and alcohol abuse. Teacher ratings of children's novelty seeking, harm avoid-

FIGURE 9.2
Cloninger's three personality dimension model (From Cloninger, 1986)

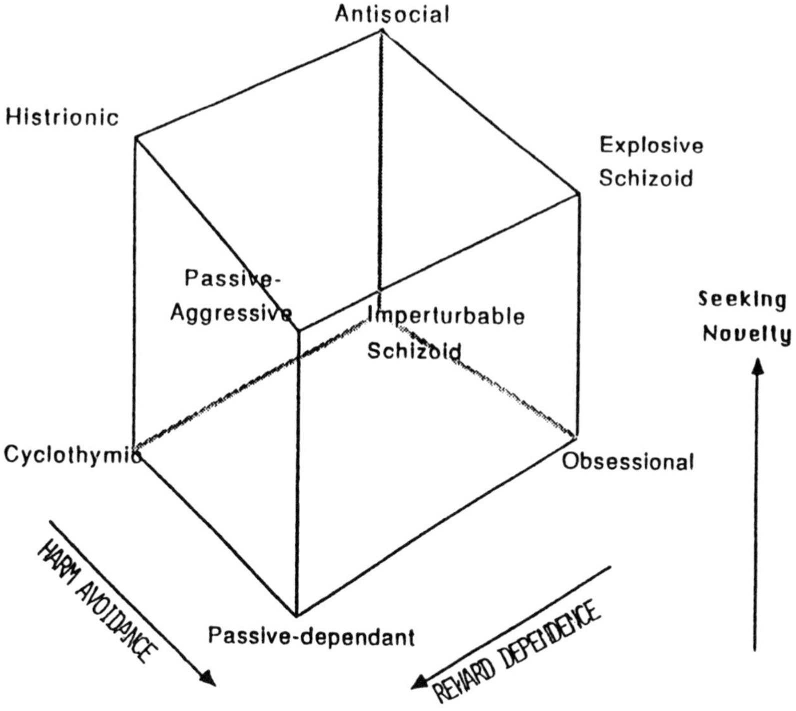

ance, and reward dependence at age eleven predicted early onset of alcohol abuse. Novelty seeking and harm avoidance were the best predictors. Two other studies used Gray's model to study clinic referred behavior problem boys. McBurnett et al. (in press) tested the hypothesis that the behavior of boys with anxiety disorders would be more strongly mediated by the behavioral inhibition system. They used salivary cortisol as a marker of the activation of this system. Results indicated that cortisol was related to anxiety disorders, but only when comparing boys who had conduct disorders to boys who had both conduct disorders and anxiety disorders. Boys with only anxiety disorders did not show higher salivary cortisol compared to boys without anxiety disorders, and conduct disorder. Walker et al. (in press) tested the hypothesis that anxiety as a manifestation of the behavioral inhibition system would be negatively related to antisocial behavior in clinic referred seven- to twelve-year old boys. Results showed that conduct disordered boys with anxiety disorders had lower levels of antisocial behavior than conduct disordered boys without anxiety disorders.

The findings from these three studies indicate that Gray's behavioral activation and inhibition model has some predictive validity for children's deviant behavior. The effect of a behavioral maintenance system was tested only in the Cloninger et al. (1988) study of early alcohol abuse. Results gave weak support for the effect of the maintenance system, but strong support for the effect of the activation and inhibition systems. Only further studies testing the effects of the postulated three dimensions will enable us to choose between a model with one, two, or three behavioral dimensions underlying antisocial behavior. In the course of a longitudinal study of a large sample of inner city boys, we have collected data which can serve that purpose. The following pages will describe the method used and the results which were obtained.

Subjects

In the spring of 1984, all teachers of kindergarten classrooms in schools of low socioeconomic areas of the French schoolboard of Montreal were asked to rate the behavior of each boy in their classroom. We obtained an 87 percent response rate from the kindergarten teachers. Questionnaires were received from fifty-three schools and 1161 boys were evaluated. The boys were six years old, on average, at the time of rating. To control for cultural effects, the boys were included in the study only if both their biological parents were born in Canada and the parents' mother tongue was French. These criteria created a homogeneous, white-francophone sample. After applying these criteria and eliminating families who refused to participate further in the study or could not be traced after this initial assessment, 1033 boys remained for the longitudinal aspect of the study.

The majority of the subjects lived with both of their parents (67 percent), but a large proportion (33 percent) were living in a non-intact family (24 percent alone with their mothers and 5 percent with their mothers and a man who was not the child's father). The mean age of the parents at the birth of the child was 25.4 (SD = 4.8) for mothers and 28.4 (SD = 5.6) for fathers. However this statistic varied from 15 to 45 for mothers and 16 to 56 for fathers. The mean number of school years completed by the parents was 10.5 (SD = 2.8) for the mothers and 10.7 (SD = 3.2) for the fathers. The mean score on the socioeconomic index (Blishen, Carroll, and Moore 1987) was 38.3 (SD = 12.0) for mothers and 39.5 (SD = 13.0) for fathers. The majority of the parents were unskilled workers.

Assessment of personality dimensions

The subjects' kindergarten behavior was rated by teachers with the Preschool Behavior Questionnaire (Behar and Stringfield 1974; Tremblay et al. 1987) and the Prosocial Behavior Questionnaire (Weir and Duveen 1981). From these ratings, items were selected to measure harm avoidance, novelty seeking, and reward dependence. For harm avoidance three items were retained: is worried, worries about many things; tends to be fearful or afraid of new things or new situations; cries easily. The alpha value for internal consistency was .72 and the test-retest reliability with a one-month interval on a similar sample was .63. For novelty seeking, two items were retained: restless, runs about or jumps up and down, doesn't keep still, squirmy, fidgety child. The alpha for internal consistency was .89 and test retest reliability for a one month interval on a similar sample was .69. For reward dependence ten items were retained: helps sick child, helps hurt child, praises others, helps child in a difficult task, helps clear up mess, shows sympathy, invites bystander, stops quarrels, helps pick up objects, comforts upset child. The alpha value for internal consistency was .91 and the test-retest reliability with a one month interval on a similar sample was .70. It should be noted that none of the items for the three dimensions could be seen as describing aggressive or antisocial behavior. They were the closest approximation available of Cloninger's basic personality dimensions in our data set. The items for harm avoidance appear to be a relatively good fit to Cloninger's dimension as well as Gray's behavioral inhibition system. The novelty seeking dimension items also fit well the positive extreme of the continuum (see Cloninger et al. 1988). This dimension may be more clearly an "activity" (or hyperactivity) dimension. This could in fact be a more adequate name for this dimension if, as suggested by Fowles (1980) (see note 2), it is related to a general arousal system, that is, the reticular activating system (RAS). Measurement of the reward dependence dimension fits quite well the altruistic-warm versus detached tough-mindedness components described by Cloninger. Note also that the items assessing each dimension were clearly oriented towards the upper end of the continuum. An inspection of the distribution of scores indicated that they were highly skewed for both the harm avoidance and novelty seeking dimensions. For both of these scales many subjects had zero scores (42.5 percent for harm avoidance, 40.6 percent for novelty seeking).

To select high harm avoidance and high novelty seeking subjects we used as cut-off point the sixtieth percentile of the entire sample. To select low harm avoidance and low novelty seeking subjects we used the zero score. The reward dependent scores were normally distributed. The sixtieth percentile of the entire sample was used as the cut-off point to identify the high reward dependent subjects. The fortieth percentile was used as the cut-off point to identify the low reward dependent subjects.

Table 9.2 presents the expected and observed distribution in the different personality types, for the 916 subjects (89 percent of the kindergarten sample) for whom we obtained complete follow-up data. The labels for the personality types are those used by Cloninger (1986, 1987). The first four types are those predicted to have the highest proportion of subjects who will be rated fighters and

TABLE 9.2
Distribution of Subjects in the Personality Profiles

Profiles	Dimensions			Expected		Observed	
	Novelty seeking	Harm Avoidance	Reward Dependence	N	%	N	%
1. Antisocial	High	Low	Low	62	6.7	53	5.8
2. Histrionic	High	Low	High	67	7.3	58	6.3
3. Passive Aggressive	High	High	High	74	8.1	70	7.6
4. Explosive Schizoid	High	High	Low	68	7.4	71	7.8
5. Schizoid	Low	Low	Low	58	6.4	59	6.4
6. Cyclothymic	Low	Low	High	63	6.9	91	9.9
7. Passive Dependent	Low	High	High	70	6.9	59	6.4
8. Obsessional	Low	High	Low	64	7.0	59	6.4
9. Others				389	42.5	396	43.2
Total				916	100	916	100

Likelihood ratio X^2 = 29.2, p = .08

delinquents. Among these four, the "antisocial" type should have the highest proportion of bullies and delinquents. The distribution of subjects in the categories was marginally similar to chance expectation. The largest deviations from expectation was for the cyclothymic group. Ten percent of the boys were classified as such, compared to the expected 7 percent.

Assessment of Outcomes

Teachers rated the boys' behavior at ages ten, eleven, and twelve. Three fighting items (bullies, kicks, bites, hits, fights), rated each year, were selected to create an index of stable high-fighting behavior. Those who were rated above the seventieth percentile each year were categorized stable high fighters. At age ten, eleven, and twelve the boys answered a twenty-seven item self-reported delinquency scale (LeBlanc and Fréchette 1989) which included a physical aggression subscale (seven items) and a stealing subscale (eleven items). Each item was answered on a four-point scale (never to very often). For each subscale and the total delinquency scale (twenty-seven items) the closest score to the ninetieth percentile was used as a cut-off point to discriminate highly deviant boys from the others.

Results

In table 9.3 the results of teacher-rated stable high fighting and self-reported high delinquency are reported. Based on Cloninger's (1986) personality theory it was anticipated that the four personality types with high novelty seeking (antisocial, histrionic, passive-aggressive, explosive) would have a high proportion of stable high fighters compared to the four personality types with low novelty seeking (obsessive, schizoid, cyclothymic, passive-dependent). We can see that this prediction was unequivocally confirmed. There were 16 percent of stable high fighters in the total sample. The proportion of these stable high fighters in the four low novelty seeking personality types was only 8 percent. In the four high novelty seeking personality types the proportion was 25 percent. However, the proportions varied among these four groups. As expected the passive-aggressive group had the lowest proportion of

TABLE 9.3
Percentages of Subjects above 90th Percentile on Teacher Rated Fighting and Self-Reported Delinquency (age 10 to 12)

Profiles	N	Teacher rated fighting	Self-reported physical aggression	Self-reported stealing	Self-reported total delinquency
1. NS+,HA-,RD- (Antisocial)	53	25	26	26	28
2. NS+,HA-,RD+ (Histrionic)	58	22	3	2	2
3. NS+,HA+,RD+ (Passive-Aggressive)	70	16	17	20	19
4. NS+,HA+,RD- (Explosive)	71	38	13	14	10
5. NS-,HA-,RD- (Schizoid)	59	14	12	10	9
6. NS-,HA-,RD+ (Cyclothymic)	91	7	7	3	4
7. NS-,HA+,RD+ (Passive-Dependent)	59	5	2	2	2
8. NS-,HA+,RD- (Obsessive)	59	7	7	5	6
9. Others	396	15	10	10	10
Total	916	16	10	10	10

NS = Novelty seeking
HA = Harm avoidance
RD = Reward Dependence
+ = High
− = Low

stable high fighters (16 percent); the explosive had the highest proportion of stable high fighters (38 percent), while the antisocial and histrionic groups had proportions of stable fighters higher than the whole sample's proportion (25 percent and 22 percent respectively).

The data from the ages ten to twelve self-reported delinquency questionnaire (table 9.3) also give general support to the predictions from Cloninger's personality theory. A larger proportion of boys with high novelty seeking behavior in kindergarten reported high physical aggression (15 percent), high stealing (15 percent), and high total delinquency (14 percent), than boys with low novelty seeking (7 percent for high physical aggression, 5 percent for high stealing, 5 percent for total delinquency). Within the high novelty seeking groups the antisocial group clearly had the highest proportion of self-reported high physical aggression (26 percent), stealing (26 percent) and total delinquency (28 percent). This is a confirmation that kindergarten boys who have an antisocial profile (high novelty seeking, low harm avoidance, and low reward dependence) are at highest risk for early onset of frequent delinquent behavior.

The histrionics were found to be the group of high novelty seekers least at risk of high delinquent behavior between the ages of ten and twelve. These results are different from those obtained for teacher ratings of stable high fighting behavior, where the histrionic group had almost as many stable high fighters as the antisocial group. The same phenomenon was observed with the explosive boys. Their percentage of self-reported high delinquents was one-third as great as the percentage of teacher rated stable high fighters. It appears from these results that a substantial proportion of elementary school histrionic and explosive boys engaged in frequent fighting with peers at school, but this was not an indicator of an antisocial orientation. On the other hand, there seemed to be a relatively good correspondence between the percentages of teacher rated high fighters and self-reported high delinquents for the antisocial and passive-aggressive groups. However, this correspondence does not guarantee that the same individuals were identified by the different criteria.

The question which can be asked is whether the teacher rated stable high fighters are the same individuals as the self-reported high delinquents. From most of the work on the association between aggression and antisocial behavior, one would expect relatively high comorbidity between stable high fighting and self-reported high delinquency. Table 9.4 presents the results of a cross-tabulation of teacher rated stable high fighting and self-reported high delinquency. We can see the comorbidity data for the whole sample, at the bottom of the table. There were 146 boys identified stable high fighters by teacher ratings and ninety-three boys who self-reported frequent physical aggression. Thirty-four boys were identified by both criteria. Thus 23 percent (34/146) of teacher rated stable high fighters also self-reported frequent physical aggression, and 37 percent (23/93) of self-reported frequent physical aggression boys were also rated stable high fighters by teachers. The antisocial and passive-aggressive boys had comorbidity rates similar to the whole sample for self-reported physical aggression. The histrionic and explosive boys had clearly lower comorbidity rates. It is of interest to note that the boys who were not classified in the eight extreme personality types ("others" in table 9.4), had a higher comorbidity rate than the rest of the sample (45 percent of self-reported physical aggressives were also teacher rated stable high fighters).

This latter result, and the differences in comorbidity between the antisocial/passive-aggressive and the histrionic/explosive, indicate that the association between teacher rated fighting and self-reported antisocial behavior varies with the personality profile. There is an indication that this association varies also with the type of antisocial outcome. This can be observed with the difference in comorbidity of the passive-aggressive group for self-reported physical aggression and self-reported stealing. Table 9.4 shows that only 7 percent of passive-aggressive self-reported frequent stealers had been rated stable high fighters by teachers. This is clearly the lowest comorbidity rate for this outcome, when we compare it to other groups with a substantial number of stealers. It is also a low comorbidity rate when compared to their comorbidity observed for self-reported physical aggression (33 percent). This is an indication that passive-aggressive boys who were frequent stealers were not physically aggressive. They would correspond to the covert antisocial group suggested by Loeber (1990), and confirm the prediction by Cloninger that the passive-aggressive would resort to indirect means to achieve their goals.

TABLE 9.4
Comorbidity of Teacher Rated Stable High Fighting (age 10 to 12) with Self-Reported High Delinquency (age 10 to 12)

	A. Teacher rated Stable high fighting	B. Self-reported physical aggression				C. Self-reported Stealing				D. Self-reported total delinquency			
	N	N	A+B[1]	%ofA[2]	%ofB[3]	N	A+C[1]	%ofA[2]	%ofC[3]	N	A+D[1]	%ofA[2]	%ofD[3]
1. NA+, HA−, RD[a] (Antisocial)	13	14	5	(39)	(36)	14	5	(39)	(36)	15	5	(39)	(33)
2. NS+, HA−, RD+ (Histrionic)	13	2	0	(0)	(0)	1	0	(0)	(0)	1	0	(0)	(0)
3. NS+, HA+, RD+ (Passive-Aggressive)	11	12	4	(36)	(33)	14	1	(9)	(7)	13	2	(18)	(15)
4. NS+, HA+, RD− (Explosive)	27	9	2	(7)	(22)	10	5	(19)	(50)	7	2	(7)	(29)
5. NS−, HA−, RD− (Schizoid)	8	7	3	(38)	(43)	6	2	(25)	(33)	3	2	(25)	(40)
6. NS−, HA−, RD+ (Cyclothymic)	6	6	1	(17)	(17)	3	0	(0)	(0)	5	2	(25)	(25)
7. NS−, HA+, RD+ (Passive-Dependent)	3	1	0	(0)	(0)	1	0	(0)	(0)	4	0	(0)	(0)
8. NS−, HA+, RD−	4	4	2	(50)	(50)	3	1	(25)	(33)	1	1	(25)	(33)
9. Others	61	38	17	(28)	(45)	41	21	(34)	(51)	40	19	(31)	(48)
9. Total	146	93	34	(23)	(37)	93	35	(24)	(38)	89	32	(22)	(36)

1. Number of subjects who were identified by both criteria (Comorbidity)
2. Percentage of teacher rated stable high fighters with comorbidity
3. Percentage of self-reported high delinquents with comorbidity
a. NS = Novelty seeking; HA = Harm avoidance; RD = Reward dependence; + = High; − = Low

The results presented above were based on assessments at ages ten to twelve. It could be argued that the teacher-rated stable aggressive boys at these ages would not be the same as those who were stable aggressive since kindergarten. Thus the results presented above would not generalize to results based on stable physical aggression since kindergarten. Table 9.5 presents the same analyses as those presented in table 9.4, except that teacher rated stable high fighting since kindergarten was used instead of ages ten to twelve teacher rated stable high fighting. Obviously the number of stable high fighters was smaller (N = 94 *vs.* N = 146), but the results were essentially the same as those presented above.

To test the rival hypotheses that there are one, two, or three systems which control behavior leading to antisocial behavior, we used logit analysis. For each of the dependent variables we tested models which included main effects and interactions among novelty seeking, reward dependence, and harm avoidance. In each case the best model was identified. Results (table 9.6) indicated that novelty seeking and reward dependence had clear main effects on each of the four dependent variables. Harm avoidance had clear effects for each self-reported delinquency outcome, but only through interactions with reward dependence and novelty seeking. It does appear from these results that the three behavioral dimensions underlying Cloninger's personality system are needed to explain antisocial behavior involvement in children.

Conclusion

In this chapter we have tried to identify a personality theory which would fit observations of the relationship between children's behaviors and later antisocial behavior. In the last three decades, four childhood behavioral dimensions have been associated with later antisocial behavior: aggression, hyperactivity, anxiety, and prosociality. We have argued that the aggressive dimension should be considered an antisocial outcome and should not be included amongst predictors of antisocial behavior, unless the stability or continuity of antisocial behavior is the aim of the study. The review of personality theories revealed that recent formulations included behavioral dimensions closely related to hyperactivity, anxiety, and prosociality. Gray's (1983) model clearly includes anxiety and

TABLE 9.5

Comorbidity of Teacher Rated Stable High Fighting (*age 6 to 12*) with Self-Reported High Delinquency (age 10 to 12)

	A. Teacher rated Stable high fighting	B. Self-reported physical aggression				C. Self-reported Stealing				D. Self-reported total delinquency			
	N	N	A+B[1]	%ofA[2]	%ofB[3]	N	A+C[1]	%ofA[2]	%ofC[3]	N	A+D[1]	%ofA[2]	%ofD[3]
1. NA+, HA−, RD− (Antisocial)	8	14	4	(50)	(29)	14	3	(38)	(21)	15	3	(38)	(20)
2. NS+, HA−, RD+ (Histrionic)	11	2	0	(0)	(0)	1	0	(0)	(0)	1	0	(0)	(0)
3. NS+, HA+, RD+ (Passive-Aggressive)	9	12	3	(33)	(25)	14	1	(11)	(7)	13	2	(22)	(15)
4. NS+, HA+, RD− (Explosive)	22	9	1	(5)	(11)	10	4	(18)	(40)	7	1	(5)	(14)
5. NS−, HA−, RD− (Schizoid)	3	7	2	(67)	(29)	6	1	(33)	(17)	3	1	(33)	(20)
6. NS−, HA−, RD+ (Cyclothymic)	3	6	1	(33)	(17)	3	0	(0)	(0)	5	1	(33)	(25)
7. NS−, HA+, RD+ (Passive-Dependent)	0	1	0	(0)	(0)	1	0	(0)	(0)	4	0	(0)	(0)
8. NS−, HA+, RD− (Obsessive)	1	4	1	(100)	(25)	3	1	(100)	(33)	1	1	(100)	(33)
9. Others	37	38	13	(35)	(34)	41	16	(43)	(39)	40	14	(38)	(35)
9. Total	94	93	25	(27)	(27)	93	26	(28)	(28)	89	23	(25)	(26)

1. Number of subjects who were identified by both criteria (Comorbidity)
2. Percentage of teacher rated stable high fighters with comorbidity
3. Percentage of self-reported high delinquents with comorbidity
a: NS= Novelty seeking; HA = Harm avoidance; RD = Reward dependence; + = high; − = Low

TABLE 9.6
Results from logit analyses (Odds ratio)

| | Age 10 to 12 | Age 10 to 12 self-reported delinquency | | |
	Teacher rated Stable high fighting	High fighting	High stealing	Total delinquency
Significant effects				
Novelty seeking (NS)	2.0**	1.5*	1.9**	1.6*
Harm avoidance (HA)	—	—	—	—
Reward dependence (RD)	1.4**	1.7**	1.6**	1.7*
HA by RD	—	—	1.7**	—
NS by HA by RD	—	1.5*	—	1.7*
Likelihood Ratio X² (p)	5.23 (.39)	0.0 (1.00)	5.99 (.11)	0.00 (1.00)
Entropy	.08	.08	.10	.12

*p<.05
**p<.01

hyperactivity (impulsivity). Cloninger's (1986) model adds a social reward (prosocial) dimension. Both models postulate that these behaviors are controlled by brain systems related to neuromodulators. Individual variations can be explained by genetic inheritance, injury to the neurological system, and learning.

We used data from a longitudinal study of boys between the ages of six and twelve to verify the extent to which the personality topology, generated from Cloninger's model, would enhance the prediction of early antisocial behavior. Results indicated that highly physically aggressive boys and highly delinquent boys were found mostly in the personality types predicted by the model. Kindergarten boys with high novelty seeking, low harm avoidance, and low reward dependence were found in the high delinquent behavior category from age ten to twelve, almost three times as often as the base rate. On the other hand, kindergarten boys with the same behavior profile, except for the prosocial dimension (high rather than low reward dependence) were found in the high delinquent behavior category one fifth as often as the base rate. This means a fourteen-fold risk rate difference, in high delinquent behavior from age ten to twelve, between these two groups of kindergarten boys, labelled "antisocial" and "histrionic" by Cloninger.

This difference in reported delinquent behavior is still more remarkable if we consider teacher reported stable high fighting. The "histrionic" boys (low risk delinquency) were found to be rated stable high fighters by teachers, from age ten to twelve, as often as the "antisocial" boys (high risk delinquency). These results either indicate that the "histrionic" boys are lying when answering the self-reported delinquency questionnaire or that there are important differences in the behavior patterns of the "histrionic" and "antisocial" groups. Assuming that there were no differences in lying between the two groups, we could explain the differences in self-reported delinquency by relating it to the reward dependence difference between the "histrionics" and "antisocial" boys. The "histrionic" are less at risk of delinquency because they are more reward dependent. However, if the "histrionic" boys were not engaging in frequent delinquent activities because of their high reward dependence, why were they engaging in high fighting behavior perceived by the teachers? Cloninger (1987) predicts that histrionics will have angry outbursts, but they will also be attention seekers who can be warm and charming. From this perspective, histrionic boys would attract the attention of teachers both by their charming and angry behavior. Teacher ratings of stable aggressive behavior would be explained by these angry outbursts. These boys however would not be frequently involved in the type of antisocial fighting which is assessed by the self-reported delinquency items (e.g., gang fights, fist fights, use of weapons in a fight).

The observed differences between the "antisocial" group and the other two high novelty seeking groups (passive-aggressive and explosive) are also interesting from a theoretical perspective. The "passive-aggressive" and the "explosive" are both high on harm avoidance (the "antisocial" are low on harm avoidance) but they are opposite on reward dependence. Results showed that these two groups had reversed results on teacher-rated stable high fighting and self reported total delinquency. Compared to the "passive-aggressive", the "explosive" group had more than twice as many teacher rated stable fighters and about half as many self-reported (total) delinquents. Because the "explosive" boys are high novelty seeking and low reward dependent, like the "antisocial" boys, one would expect that they would have a high proportion of self-reported delinquency. However, their rate was close to a third as large as the rate of the "antisocial" groups. On the other hand, their teacher-reported rate of stable fighting was one and a half times higher than the rate of the "antisocial" group. Clearly teacher rated stable fighting and self-reported delinquent behavior are not the same type of outcome.

Contrary to a belief that fighting in school is part of a general pattern of delinquency, the evidence here suggests that there may be two patterns of school fighters. In one, the fighters are also involved in high rate delinquency. In the other, the fighters are not involved in high rate delinquency. The interactions among Cloninger's three personality dimensions provide a means of differentiating these two groups of fighters. In fact the type of outcome interacts with the personality profiles. When teacher rated stable fighting was used as the outcome, *high* reward dependence was the protective factor for the "passive-aggressive" compared to the "explosive" boys. When self-reported delinquency was used as the outcome, the direction of the effects were completely reversed; *low* reward dependence was the protective factor for the "explosives" compared to the "passive aggressives," while *high* reward dependence was the protective factor for the "histrionics" compared to the "antisocial." Note also that when "histrionics" and "passive-aggressives" or "antisocials" and "explosives" were compared, it was harm avoidance which acted as a protective or a precipitating factor. High novelty seeking was, of course, a precipitating factor for each of these four groups when compared to the other four extreme groups (obsessive, schizoid, cyclothymic, passive-dependent).

The personality approach which we have taken in this chapter apparently helps to "organize" in a meaningful way the traditional childhood predictors of deviant behavior. It also helps elucidate the apparent discrepancies among outcomes which were thought to be similar. The clear, albeit complex, picture which resulted from our analyses could not have been obtained if aggressive behavior had been kept amongst the predictors. Aggressive behavior as measured by most rating scales is a mixture of prosocial, reactive, proactive, antisocial behavior which is relatively stable. Because of this stability, it gives relatively high predictive values, but because of its complexity it also hides many important interactions among other behavioral dimensions. It should be noted that an effort to disentangle aggressive behavior from personality dimensions of young children was made more than two decades ago by Pulkkinen (Pitkanen 1969; see also Pulkkinen 1986).

Results from our data analysis also clearly indicated that three behavioral dimensions were a better fit to the observations than one or two dimensions. If the measured behavioral dimensions were adequate assessments of brain systems, we could conclude that three, rather than two systems are needed to explain personality types related to antisocial behavior. We remain, however, far from having convincingly demonstrated that the observed behaviors are clearly related to separate brain systems. Gray (1983) concluded that there was good evidence for one brain system underlying the anxiety behavioral dimension but no clear evidence for the other brain systems. Cloninger (1986) argues for three brain systems. We will probably have to wait for the results of animal and drug experiments to reach more definitive conclusions. For the moment, a personality model with three behavioral dimensions explaining antisocial behavior appears to fit relatively well the work of an important tradition of personality theorists as well as predictive studies of antisocial behavior from childhood behaviors. One of the important keys to that fit is the use of aggressive behavior as an outcome of the interaction between basic behavioral dimensions (and of course environmental conditions) rather than as a basic dimension in itself.

This study was conducted with the financial assistance of Quebec's Social Research Council (CQRS), FCAR and the Social Sciences and Humanities Research Council of Canada. The self-reported delinquency data was collected under the direction of Marc LeBlanc. Pierre Charlebois, Claude Gagnon, and Serge Larivée collaborated in the planning and execution of the longitudinal study. Hélène Beauchesne and Lucille David coordinated the data collection. Hélène Boileau and Lyse Desmarais-Gervais created the data banks and analysed the data. Renée Beaumier and Minh T. Trinh provided the documentation. The manuscript was revised by Patricia Dobkin and typed by Chantal Bruneau. I especially wish to thank Lea Pulkkinen who provided the incentive to return to personality theories, and Joan McCord who provided the opportunity to report on this journey back to the future.

Notes

1. Note that these three behaviors are close approximations to the three emotions which were considered by Watson (1919) to belong "to the original and fundamental nature of man" (p. 199).

2. Although Gray (1982) has been mainly involved in describing the behavioral inhibition system (BIS), he clearly suggests that there are at least three systems (1983), the second being the behavioral activition system (BAS). He is less clear about the third system (Gray 1983), but Fowles (1980) suggests that the third system would be a general arousal system (the reticular activating system, RAS) which increases the vigor and intensity of activity. Fowles underlines the fact that the BIS increases arousal, thus the three systems would be arousal systems.

References

Achenbach, T. M. and C. Edelbrock. 1983. *Manual for the Child Behavior Checklist and Revised Behavior Profile.* Burlington, Vt.: University of Vermont Department of Psychiatry.

Achenbach, T. M. and C. Edelbrock. 1986. *Manual for the Teacher's Report Form and Teacher Version of the Child Behavior Profile.* Burlington, Vt.: University of Vermont Department of Psychiatry.

Achenbach, T. M. and C. Edelbrock. 1987. *Manual for the Youth Self-Report and Profile.* Burlington, Vt.: University of Vermont Department of Psychiatry.

Achenbach, T. M. and C. Edelbrock. 1978. "The Classification of Child Psychopathology: A Review and Analysis of Empirical Efforts." *Psychological Bulletin* 85, 1275–1301.

Ackerson, L. 1931. *Children's Behavior Problems* (V.1). Chicago: University of Chicago Press.

Ackerson, L. 1942. *Children's Behavior Problems: V.2 Relative Importance and Intercorrelations Among Traits.* Chicago: University of Chicago Press.

Adams, D. 1989. "The Seville Statement on Violence and Why it is Important." *Journal of Human Psychology* 29, 328–37.

American Psychiatric Association. 1987. *Diagnostic and Statistical Manual of Mental Disorders* (3rd edition revised). Washington, D.C.: Author.

Barkley, R. A. 1981. *Hyperactive Children: A Handbook for Diagnosis and Treatment.* New York: Guilford.

Behar, L. and S. Stringfield. 1974. "Behavior Rating Scale for the Preschool Child." *Developmental Psychology* 10, 601–10.

Blishen, B. R., W. K. Carroll, and C. Moore. 1987. "The 1981 Socioeconomic Index for Occupations in Canada." *Canadian Review of Sociology and Anthropology* 24, 465–88.

Blumstein, A., D. P. Farrington, and S. Moitra. 1985. "Delinquent Careers: Innocents, Desisters, and Persisters." In *Crime and Justice: An*

Annual Review, edited by M. Tonry and N. Morris, Vol. 6, 187–219. Chicago: University of Chicago Press.

Blurton Jones, N. 1972. "Characteristics of Ethological Studies of Human Behaviour." In *Ethological Studies of Child Behaviour,* edited by N. Blurton Jones, 3–33. New York: Cambridge University Press.

Bridges, K. M. B. 1931. *The Social and Emotional Development of the Pre-School Child.* London: Kegan Paul.

Buikhuisen, W. 1987. "Cerebral Dysfunctions and Persistent Juvenile Delinquency." In *The Causes of Crime: New Biological Approaches,* edited by S. A. Mednick, T. E. Moffitt and S. A. Stack, 168–89. New York: Cambridge University Press.

Cairns, R. B. 1979. *Social Development: The Origins and Plasticity of Interchanges.* San Francisco: W. H. Freeman.

Cairns, R. B. 1983. "The Emergence of Developmental Psychology." In *Handbook of Child Psychology,* edited by P. H. Mussen, 41–102. Toronto: John Wiley & Sons.

Cantwell, D. P. 1988. "DSM-III Studies." In *Assessment and Diagnosis in Child Psychopathology,* edited by M. Rutter, A. H. Tuma, and I. S. Lann, 3–365. New York: Guilford Press.

Cleckley, H. 1976. *The Mask of Sanity* (5th Ed.) St. Louis, Mo.: Mosby.

Cloninger, C. R. 1986. "A Unified Biosocial Theory of Personality and its Role in the Development of Anxiety States." *Psychiatric Developments* 3, 167–226.

Cloninger, C. R. 1987. "A Systematic Method for Clinical Description and Classification of Personality Variants: A Proposal." *Archives of General Psychiatry* 44, 573–88.

Cloninger, C. R., S. Sigvardsson, and M. Bohman. 1988. "Childhood Personality Predicts Alcohol Abuse in Young Adults." *Alcoholism: Clinical and Experimental Research* 12, 494–505.

Conners, C. K. 1969. A Teacher Rating Scale for use in Drug Studies with Children. *American Journal of Psychiatry* 126, 884–88.

Crutcher, R. 1943. "Child Psychiatry: A History of its Development." *Psychiatry* 6, 191–201.

Darwin, C. 1877. "A Biographical Sketch of an Infant." *Mind* 2, 285–94.

Dawe, H. C. 1934. "An Analysis of 200 Quarrels of Preschool Children." *Child Development* 5, 139–57.

Dreger, R. M. 1977. "The Children's Behavioral Classification Project: An Interim Report." *Journal of Abnormal Child Psychology* 5, 289–97.

Dreger, R. M. 1981. "The Classification of Children and their Emotional Problems." *Clinical Psychology Review* 1, 415–30.

Dreger, R. M. 1982. "The Classification of Children and their Emotional Problems. An Overview." *Clinical Psychology Review* 2, 349–85.

Eron, L. D. 1987. "The Development of Aggressive Behavior from the Perspective of a Developing Behaviorism." *American Psychologist* 42, 435–42.

Eron, L. D. and L. R. Huesmann. 1984. "The Relation of Prosocial Behavior to the Development of Aggression and Psychopathology." *Aggressive Behavior* 10, 201–11.

Eron, L. D., L. O. Walder, and M. M. Lefkowitz. 1971. *Learning of Aggression in Children*. Boston: Little, Brown & Company.

Eysenck, H. J. 1970. *The Structure of Human Personality*. (3rd ed.). London: Methuen.

Eysenck, H. J. and S. B. G. Eysenck. 1976. *Psychoticism as a Dimension of Personality*. London: Hodder & Stoughton.

Eysenck, H. J. and G. H. Gudjonsson. 1989. *The Causes and Cures of Criminality*. New York: Plenum.

Farrington, D. P., R. Loeber, and W. B. Van Kammen. 1990. "The Long Term Criminal Outcomes of Conduct Problem Boys With or Without Impulsive-Inattentive Behavior." In *Straight and Devious Pathways to Adulthood*, edited by L. N. Robins and M. R. Rutter, 62–81. New York: Cambridge University Press.

Farrington, D. P., R. Loeber, D. S. Elliott, J. D. Hawkins, D. B. Kandel, M. W. Klein, J. McCord, D. C. Rowe, and R. E. Tremblay. 1990. "Advancing Knowledge About the Onset of Delinquency and Crime." In *Advances in Clinical Child Psychology*, vol. 13, edited by B. B. Lahey and A. E. Kazdin, 283–342. New York: Plenum.

Fowles, D. C. 1980. "The Three-Arousal Model: Implications of Gray's Two-Factor Learning Theory for Heart Rate, Electrodermal Activity, and Psychopathy." *Journal of Psychophysiology* 17, 84–104.

Gangestad, S. and M. Snyder. 1985. "To Carve Nature at its Joints: On the Existence of Discrete Classes in Personality." *Psychological Review* 92, 317–49.

Gorenstein, E. E. and J. P. Newman. 1980. "Disinhibitory Psychopathology: A New Perspective and a Model for Research." *Psychological Review* 87, 301–15.

Graham, P. and M. Rutter. 1973. "Psychiatric Disorder in the Young Adolescent: A Follow-up Study." *Proceeding of the Royal Society of Medicine* 66, 1226–29.

Gray, J. A. 1970. "The Psychophysiological Basis of Introversion-Extraversion." *Behavioral Research and Therapy* 8, 249–66.

Gray, J. A. 1981. "A Critique of Eysenck's Theory of Personality." In *A Model for Personality*, edited by H. J. Eysenck, 246–76. New York: Springer.

Gray, J. A. 1982. *The Neuropsychology of Anxiety*. New York: Oxford University Press.

Gray, J. A. 1983. "Where Should We Search for Biologically Based Dimensions of Personality?" *Zeitschrift für Differentielle und Diagnostische Psychologie* 4, 163–74.

Gray, J. A., S. Owen, N. Davis, and E. Tsaltas. 1983. "Psychological and Physiological Relations Between Anxiety and Impulsivity." In *Biological bases of sensation seeking, impulsivity, and anxiety,* edited by M. Zuckerman, 189–218. Hillsdale, N.J.: Lawrence Erlbaum Associates.

Hare, R. D. and D. Schalling (Eds). 1978. *Psychopathic Behaviour: Approaches to Research.* New York: John Wiley & Sons.

Hart, H. H., R. L. Jenkins, S. Axelrad, and P. I. Sperling. 1943. "Multiple Factor Analysis of Traits of Delinquent Boys." *Journal of Social Psychology* 17, 191–201.

Hewitt, L. E. and R. L. Jenkins. 1946. *Fundamental Patterns of Maladjustment, the Dynamics of their Origin.* Springfield, Il.: State of Illinois.

Heymer, A. 1977. *Vocabulaire éthologique.* Paris: Presses Universitaires de France.

Hinde, R. A. 1970. *Animal Behaviour* (2nd Ed.). New York: McGraw Hill.

Hinde, R. A. 1974. *The Biological Basis of Human Social Behaviour.* New York: McGraw Hill.

Hinde, R. A. and A. Dennis. 1986. "Categorizing Individuals: An Alternative to Linear Analysis." *International Journal of Behavioral Development* 9, 105–19.

Huesmann, L. R., L. D. Eron, M. M. Lefkowitz, and L. O. Walder. 1984. "Stability of Aggression Overtime and Generations." *Developmental Psychology* 20, 1120–34.

Huxley, L. 1903. *Life and Letters of Thomas Henry Huxley,* vol. 1. New York: MacMillan & Co.

Jenkins, R. L. and S. Glickman. 1946. "Common Syndromes in Child Psychiatry." *American Journal of Orthopsychiatry* 16, 244–61.

Jenkins, R. L. and S. Glickman. 1947. "Patterns of Personality Organisation Among Delinquents." *The Nervous Child* 6, 329–39.

Jenkins, R. L. and L. Hewitt. 1944. "Types of Personality Structure Encountered in Child Guidance Clinics." *American Journal of Orthopsychiatry* 14, 84–94.

Kanner, L. 1959. "The Thirty-third Maudsley Lecture: Trends in Child-Psychiatry." *The Journal of Mental Science* 105, 581–93.

Kohn, M. 1977. "The Kohn Social Competence Scale and Kohn Symptom Checklist for the Preschool Child: A Follow-up Report." *Journal of Abnormal Child Psychology* 5, 249–63.

Kraepelin, E. 1913. *Lectures on Clinical Psychiatry.* New York: William Wood & Co.

LeBlanc, M. and M. Fréchette. 1989. *Male Criminal Activity from Childhood Through Youth.* New York: Springer-Verlag.

Lefkowitz, M. M., L. D. Eron, L. O. Walder, and L. R. Huesmann. 1977. "Growing Up to be Violent: A Longitudinal Study of Aggression." Elmsford, N.Y.: Pergamon.

Loeber, R. and M. Stouthamer-Loeber. 1987. "Prediction." In *Handbook of Juvenile Delinquency,* edited by H. C. Quay. New York: John Wiley & Sons.

Loeber, R. 1990. "Development and Risk Factors of Juvenile Antisocial Behavior and Delinquency." *Clinical Psychology Review* 10, 1–41.

Loney, J., J. Kramer, and R. Milich. 1981. "The Hyperactive Child Grown Up: Predictors of Symptoms, Delinquency, and Achievement at Follow-up." In *Psychosocial Aspects of Drug Treatment of Hyperactivity,* edited by K. D. Gadlow and J. Loney, 381–415. Boulder, Co.: Westview Press.

Loney, J. and R. Milich. 1982. "Hyperactivity, Inattention, and Aggression in Clinical Practice." In *Advances in Developmental and Behavioral Pediatrics,* vol. 2, edited by M. Wolraich and D. Routh, 113–47. Greenwich, Ct.: JAI Press.

Magnusson, D. and L. R. Bergman. 1990. "A Pattern Approach to the Study of Pathways from Childhood to Adulthood." In *Straight and Devious Pathways from Childhood to Adulthood,* edited by L. N. Robins and M. Rutter, 101–16. New York: Cambridge University Press.

Masten, A., P. Morison, and D. Pelligrini. 1985. "A Revised Class Play Method of Peer Assessment." *Developmental Psychology* 21, 523–33.

Masters, R. D. 1979. "Beyond Reductionism: Five Basic Concepts in Human Ethology." In *Human Ethology,* edited by M. Von Kranach, K. Loppa, W. Lepenies, and D. Ploog, 265–84. New York: Cambridge University Press.

McBurnett, K., B. B. Lahey, P. J. Frick, S. C. Risch, R. Loeber, E. L. Hart, M. A. G. Christ, and B. A. Hanson. (in press). "Anxiety, Inhibition, and Conduct Disorder in Children: II Relation to Salivary Cortisol." *Journal of the American Academy of Child and Adolescent Psychiatry.*

McCord, J. 1987. "Aggression and Shyness as Predictors of Problems: A Long-term View." Paper presented at the Biennial meeting of the Society for Research in Child Development, Baltimore (April).

McCord, W. and J. McCord. 1964. *The Psychopath: An Essay on the Criminal Mind.* Princeton, N.J.: Van Nostrand.

McGee, R., S. Williams, and P. A. Silva. 1984. "Behavioral and Developmental Characteristics of Aggressive, Hyperactive, and Aggressive-Hyperactive Boys." *Journal of the American Academy of Child Psychiatry* 23, 270–79.

McGrew, W. C. 1972. *An Ethological Study of Children's Behavior.* New York: Academic Press.

Mednick, S. A. and W. F. Gabrielli. 1984. "Genetic Influences in Criminal Convictions: Evidence from an Adoption Cohort." *Science* 224, 891–94.

Moffitt, T. E. 1990a. "Juvenile Delinquency and Attention Deficit Disorder: Developmental Trajectories from Age 3 to Age 15." *Child Development* 61, 893–910.

Moffitt, T. E. 1990b. "The Neuropsychology of Juvenile Delinquency: A Critical Review. In *Crime and Justice. A Review of Research,* v. 12, edited by N. Morris and M. Tonry, 99–169. Chicago: Chicago University Press.

Moreau, P. 1888. *La folie chez les enfants.* Paris: J. B. Baillières.

Murphy, L. B. 1937. *Social Behavior and Child Personality.* New York: Columbia University Press.

Newman, J. P. 1987. "Reaction to Punishment in Extraverts and Psychopaths: Implications for the Impulsive Behavior of Disinhibited Individuals." *Journal of Research in Personality* 21, 464–80.

Olweus, D. 1979. "Stability of Aggressive Reaction Patterns in Males: A review." *Psychological Bulletin* 86, 852–75.

Patterson, G. R. 1982. *Coercive Family Process.* Eugene, Ore.: Castalia Publishing Co.

Pekarik, E. G., R. J. Prinz, D. E. Liebert, S. Weintraub, and J. M. Neale. 1976. "The Pupil Evaluation Inventory. A Sociometric Technique for Assessing Children's Social Behavior." *Journal of Abnormal Child Psychology* 4, 83–97.

Pitkanen, L. 1969. "A Descriptive Model of Aggression and Nonaggression with Applications to Children's Behaviour." *Jyvaskyla Studies in Education, Psychology and Social Research,* (Whole No. 19). Jyvaskyla, Finland: University of Jyvaskyla.

Preyer, W. 1888. *The Mind of the Child.* New York: Appleton.

Prinz, R. J. 1986. *Advances in Behavioral Assessment of Children and Families,* vol. 2. Greenwich, Ct.: JAI Press.

Pulkkinen, L. 1986. "The Role of Impulse Control in the Development of Antisocial and Prosocial Behavior." In *Development of Antisocial and Prosocial Behavior: Research, Theories, and Issues,* edited by D. Olweus, J. Block and M. Radke-Yarrow, 149–75. New York: Academic Press.

Quay, H. C. 1979. "Classification." In *Psychopathological Disorders of Childhood,* 2nd ed., edited by H. C. Quay and J. S. Werry, 1–42. New York: Wiley.

Quay, H. C. and D. R. Peterson. 1987. *Manual for the Revised Behavior Problem Checklist.* Miami, Fl.: Department of Psychology, University of Miami.

Rowe, D. C., D. W. Osgood, and W. A. Nicewander. 1990. "A Latent Trait Approach to Unifying Criminal Careers." *Criminology* 28, 237–70.

Royce, J. R. and A. Powell. 1983. *Theory of Personality and Individual Differences: Factors, Systems, and Processes.* Englewood Cliffs, N.J.: Prentice Hall.

Rutter, M., A. H. Tuma, and I. S. Lann. (Eds) 1988. *Assessment and Diagnosis in Child Psychopathology.* New York: Guilford Press.

Satterfield, J. H. 1987. "Childhood diagnostic and neurophysiological predictors of teenage arrest rates: An eight-year prospective study." In *The Causes of Crime: New Biological Approaches,* edited by S. A. Mednick, T. E. Moffitt and S. A. Stack, 146–67. New York: Cambridge University Press.

Schalling, D. 1978. "Psychopathy-related personality variables and the psychophysiology of socialization." In *Psychopathic Behaviour: Approaches to Research,* edited by R. D. Hare and D. Schalling, 85–106. New York: John Wiley & Sons.

Sjobring, H. 1973. "Personality Structure and Development: A Model and its Application." *Acta Psychiatrica Scandinavia Supplement* (Whole No. 244).

Spielberger, C. D., J. K. Kling, and S. E. J. O'Hagan. 1978. "Dimensions of Psychopathic Personality: Antisocial Behaviour and Anxiety." In *Psychopathic Behaviour: Approaches to Research,* edited by R. D. Hare and D. Schalling, 23–46. New York: John Wiley & Sons.

Stott, D. H. 1974. *Manual for the Bristol Adjustment Guides.* San Diego: Educational and Industrial Testing.

Strayer, F. F. and R. Gauthier. 1985. Concepts et méthodes. In *Ethologie et développement de l'enfant,* edited by R. E. Tremblay, M. A. Provost, and F. F. Strayer. Paris: Stock.

Sully, J. 1895. *Studies of Childhood.* London: Longmans, Green and Co.

Taine, H. 1876. "Sur l'acquisition du language chez les enfants." *Revue Philosophiques* 1, 5–23.

Tremblay, R. E. 1991. "Aggression, prosocial behavior and gender: Three Magic Words but no Magic Wand." In *The Development and Treatment of Aggression,* edited by D. J. Pepler and K. H. Rubin. Hillsdale, N.J.: Lawrence Erlbaum.

Tremblay, R. E., L. Desmarais-Gervais, C. Gagnon, and P. Charlebois. 1987. "The Preschool Behaviour Questionnaire: Stability of its Factor Structure between Cultures, Sexes, Ages and Socioeconomic Classes." *International Journal of Behavioral Development* 10, 467–84.

Walker, J. L., B. B. Lahey, M. F. Russo, P. J. Frick, M. A. Christ, K. McBurnett, R. Loeber, M. Stouthamer-Loeber, and S. Green. (in press). "Anxiety, Inhibition, and Conduct Disorder in Children: I

Relations to social impairment and sensation seeking.'' *Journal of the American Academy of Child and Adolescent Psychiatry.*

Watson, J. B. 1919. *Psychology from the Standpoint of a Behaviorist.* Philadelphia: J. B. Lippincott.

Weir, K. and G. Duveen. 1981. ''Further Development and Validation of the Prosocial Behaviour Questionnaire for Use by Teacher.'' *Journal of Child Psychology and Psychiatry* 22, 357–74.

Weiss, G. and L. T. Hechtman. 1986. *Hyperactive Children Grown Up.* New York: Guilford Press.

White, J. L., T. E. Moffitt, F. Earls, L. Robins, and P. A. Silva. 1990. ''How Early Can We Tell? Predictors of Childhood Conduct Disorder and Adolescent Delinquency.'' *Criminology* 28, (4): 507–35.

Zuckerman, M. 1983. *Biological Bases of Sensation Seeking, Impulsivity, and Anxiety.* Hillsdale, N.J.: Lawrence Erlbaum Associates.

10

A Developmental Perspective on Drug Use and Delinquency

Judith S. Brook and Patricia Cohen

It is clear that drug use and delinquency tend to co-occur (Bachman, Johnston, and O'Malley 1981; Elliott and Huizinga 1984; Kaplan 1980; Clayton and Tuchfeld 1982; Brook, Lukoff, and Whiteman 1980). According to the common cause model, both drug use and delinquency may be the result of some common cause. It may be that some underlying factor, whether intrapersonal or interpersonal, leads some adolescents to use drugs and also become involved in delinquent acts. According to Robins and Wish (1977), drug use and delinquency may represent a syndrome that reflects an underlying conduct disorder. In a related vein, Jessor and Jessor (1977) refer to a deviant lifestyle, whereas Hawkins and Weis (1985) point to common social developmental processes as the underlying cause of drug use and delinquency.

The present report extends and uses as a model a previous study by our group that examined the common and uncommon pathways leading both to drug use and externalizing behavior. In the previous research, the findings supported a common pathway, in that some psychosocial factors posed a comparable risk for both drug use and external behavior. At the same time, the results indicated that certain risks related differentially to drug use and external behavior, the uncommon pathway. More specifically, we found that perinatal and early somatic problems appear to pose risks for both drug use and external behavior. Other risk factors, such as parental mental illness and parental sociopathy, posed a significantly greater risk for externalizing disorders than for drug use. The longitudinal research to be presented here, building on our previous analysis, is one of a very small number of studies that uses a prospective design and examines the factors associated with drug use and delinquency both broadly and specifically.

The compelling nature of the findings warrant extension on several accounts. First, because data on parenting style were limited in the early childhood data, we were unable to examine significant aspects of family interaction in depth. Subsequent data collections have enabled us to obtain a comprehensive assessment of parenting and parent/child relationships. One purpose of this paper, therefore, is to examine the independent contributions of components of family interactions to adolescent drug use and delinquency. We will attempt to differentiate risks that are common to these two forms of deviant behavior from those that are relatively specific to delinquency or to drug use.

A second extension concerns other aspects of the interpersonal environment, namely, peer relationships and the adolescent's commitment to school. The empirical literature on drug use and delinquency is surprisingly sparse in identifying studies that deal with shared or nonshared peer and school attributes as risks for drug use and delinquency. Features of both the peer environment and the adolescent's attachment to school are assumed to have an impact on drug use and delinquency. Thus, another aim of this study is to identify the common and uncommon or specific peer and school risks associated with drug use and delinquency.

In the following section, the evidence for the common and uncommon risk factors for delinquency and drug use will be presented. As previously noted, these two forms of deviant behavior have rarely been considered simultaneously in one study. A number of studies have looked at the family determinants of either drug use or delinquency. Family context variables such as low social class, large families, and dwelling in neighborhoods where there are models for criminality are implicated both in delinquency and drug use. Context variables are expected, based on previous experience, to be related equally to both drug use and delinquency. Family characteristics, such as drug use and criminal behavior, are also implicated both in delinquency and drug use. Several investigators have found that children whose parents or siblings engage in delinquency or crime are at increased risk for delinquency (Robins 1978; McCord 1979; Farrington 1986; Blumstein, Farrington, and Moitra 1985). Similarly, parental and sibling drug use are associated with the youngster's use of drugs (Brook, Whiteman, Gordon, and Brook 1990; Needle, Su, and Doherty 1990; Zucker 1979). Relying on the concept of observational learning or modeling, parental sociopathy is expected to be related to both delinquency and drug use in the adolescent. Parental discord has been found to be an important precursor of delinquency in many, but not all, studies. Parental discord has been assessed by examining variables including parental quarrelling, parental separation, divorce, and marital difficulty (Wilson and Herrnstein 1985). Most research on divorce and adolescent development has found that the negative effects of divorce do result in increased drug use (Needle et al. 1990; Brook, Whiteman, and Gordon 1985). Indeed, drug use may be one way that adolescents cope with the difficult circumstances resulting from parental divorce or difficulty in the parent-child mutual attachment (Fawzy, Coombs, and Gerber 1983). Nevertheless, the evidence for the relationship between adolescent drug use and family structure is not always consistent; for example, Robins and Przybeck (1987) reported that family structure had no appreciable predictive power for adolescent drug-using behavior. Similarly, while Needle had found that divorce had negative effects for boys, it had no impact on girls' drug use. A further qualification comes from Newcomb and Bentler (1988), who reported that family disruption is correlated with drug use only when the adolescents are disengaged from traditional values. Our assumption is that parental divorce and discord may be more highly related to delinquency than to drug use.

Another aspect of the family environment that is important in terms of both drug use and delinquency is the mutual attachment between parent and child. Mutual attachment refers to the affectional bond that the adolescent and the parent form with one another. A close mutual attachment is one in which the youngster identifies with an affectionate parent, there is intimate communication, and there is little conflict. A strong mutual attachment insulates the child from drug use and delinquency. According to social control theory, attachment to parents means caring about retaining the good opinion of the parents. In Hirschi's view (1969), individuals refrain from engaging in delinquent acts because they are under the control of certain social forces, and one of these social forces is the good opinion of the parent. These various components have been examined in a number of studies. For example, delinquency has been found to be related to lack of an affectionate identification with the parents (Patterson 1982), lack of parental affection (McCord and McCord 1959; West and Farrington 1973; Patterson 1986). In our own work, a close mutual attachment has been found to be associated with the development of drug resistant personality traits, which in turn insulate the adolescent from drug use.

A second dimension of parenting has to do with the kind of control techniques which the parents employ. Generally speaking, parental control, as assessed by structure, lack of permissiveness, and consistency in enforcing rules and regulations, is associated with less delinquency and drug use. Control variables may be related to both delinquency and drug use. Power assertion, a means by which parents control their children's behavior, has negative rather than positive effects on child outcome. This dimension is highly related to aggressive behavior in children. It is hypothesized that its relation with delinquency will be stronger than with drug use. Nevertheless, since childhood aggressiveness is predictive of later drug use, it is expected to relate to later drug use, perhaps less strongly than delinquency.

There are two views regarding the influence of peers on delinquency and drug use. One view is that delinquent and drug-using peer groups cause delinquency and drug use by altering the individual's values or changing the reward structure (Wilson and Herrnstein 1985). Another view is that young people are delinquent or use drugs, and then seek out peers who share their interest in drug use and delinquency. While our own findings indicate that both mechanisms are operative, the findings are more in accord with the second viewpoint. For example, when we hold constant a commitment to conventional values, the association between drug-using friends and drug use drops significantly (Brook, Whiteman, and Gordon 1983). Whatever the causal direction, associating with delinquent peers and with drug-using peers are the strongest correlates of both delinquency and drug use (Loeber and Dishion 1983; Brook et al. 1983; Kandel 1985), and are expected to be equally predictive of both forms of deviance.

Low school achievement and school failure have long been known to be predictors of persistent delinquency and drug use (Bachman et al. 1981; Farrington 1986; Hawkins and Lishner 1987; Loeber and Dishion 1983). Deviant adolescents are likely to be absent from school, to cut classes, to perform more poorly, and to report that they do not expect to attend college (Brook, Brook, Gordon, Whiteman, and Cohen, 1990a; Johnston, O'Malley, and Bachman 1986). Unable to do well in schoolwork that emphasizes verbal ability, these youngsters may rely on physical skills (including fighting) or use drugs to cope with a sense of failure. Attachment to school has long been recognized as a factor which inhibits the development of delinquency and drug use. Aspects of the school environment, such as the emphasis placed on positive learning, and the amount of conflict present, also appear to be related to deviance (Brook, Nomura, and Cohen 1989; Wilson and Herrnstein 1985). What is not clear from the existing research is when, developmentally, school factors become a stable predictor of delinquency and drug use, and to what extent school factors predict each of the forms of deviance.

The present study departs from previous research in a number of important ways. First, drug use and delinquency are studied simultaneously in an attempt to identify both common and uncommon risk factors. Second, this is a prospective study of delinquency and drug use within a nonclinical sample followed for more than fifteen years from early childhood to late adolescence.

Sample

These analyses are based on the Children in the Community Project's longitudinal cohort of children who have been assessed since early childhood. Families were originally sampled in 1975 when the children were ages one to ten and the families were living in one of two upstate New York counties (see Kogan, Smith, and Jenkins 1977 for a detailed description of the original sampling plan and study procedures). The families were recontacted for interview in 1983 and again in 1985–86. Eighty-five percent of the original 976 families were located and nearly 80 percent were reinterviewed in one or both of the follow-up interviews. However, families with the youngest children who were living in urban poverty areas were excessively lost to follow-up. In order to rebalance the cohort to better represent the population, an additional sample of fifty-four such families was drawn, using the same sampling procedures used in the original study. The age range was eleven to twenty-two with a mean of 16.3. Fifty-two percent were male. The resulting combined sample includes the full range of socioeconomic status, and is generally representative of families with children of these ages in the northeastern United States, although somewhat more rural, Catholic, and white because of the characteristics of the sampled counties (table 10.1).

Follow-up interviews were conducted with mothers and youth, separately but simultaneously, in their homes by pairs of trained lay interviewers. Families resided predominantly in the original

TABLE 10.1
Characteristics of the 1985–86 sample.

	N	%
Family income:		
Less than $10,000	63	9
$10,000 to $25,000	205	28
$25,000 to $50,000	232	46
$50,000 or more	121	17
Family on welfare	30	4
Family structure:		
Intact	497	67
Divorced or never married	115	16
Remarried	63	9
Other	59	8
Maternal education more than:		
12 years	287	39
Urbanicity:		
Urban	112	16
Suburban or small city	239	34
Small to medium towns	147	21
Rural or semi-rural	214	30
Catholic:	411	56

area, but also in twenty-seven other states. Interviews typically took about two hours each and covered a range of demographic, psychiatric, personality, health, environment, and quality of life issues. The current analyses are based on 748 children for whom the data on drug use and delinquency based on the T3 interview were complete.

Measures

In an earlier investigation based on this cohort (Cohen, Brook, Cohen, Velez, and Garcia 1990) we examined four domains of early childhood risk factors in relationship to drug use, externalizing, and internalizing behavior as assessed by maternal report on the Child Behavior Checklist (Achenbach and Edelbrock 1983). The domains included were the larger social context, family attributes, parent-child relationship, and biological risk. Risk factors were measured in the original interviews when the child was between one and ten years old and outcome variables were assessed at ages nine to eighteen, in the first follow-up.

In the current study risks were assessed primarily at the time of the first follow-up. Outcomes were assessed about 2½ years later, when the children were predominantly ages twelve to twenty. The outcome variables were a stage-frequency measure of drug use (Brook, Whiteman, Gordon, and Cohen 1989) and delinquent activities as assessed by the conduct disorder section of the Diagnostic Interview Schedule for Children (Costello, Edelbrock, Dulcan, Kalas, and Klaris 1984) administered to both parent and youth (alpha = .74). Delinquent activities covered included truancy, theft, robbery, burglary, serious and frequent fighting, fighting with weapon, cruelty to animals and to children, mugging, fire setting, and vandalism. Illicit drug use was not included, in order to keep the dependent variables as distinct as possible. The correlate between the drug use and delinquency measure was .54.

Context

The context of the family was assessed by six variables: (a) family socioeconomic status (pooling standardized measures of education of father and mother, family income, and occupational status of the father); (b) urban residence, measured on a seven point scale from rural to inner city; (c) mother-only family, in which the mother had never married or was divorced and not remarried; (d) stepfather family in which the mother was married to a man who was not the biological or adoptive father of the child; (e) no father figure, for those cases in which the youth indicated that there was no one in or out of the home who acted like a father; and (f) separate dwelling, in which the child was no longer living with the family. In the latter cases the residence included independent households, dormitories, or group quarters of some other kind.

Family Environment

This domain was represented by three variables: (a) parental conflict (Brook et al. 1990a); (b) parental sociopathy (the involvement of either or both parents in alcohol, drug, or police problems); and (c) sibling sociopathy (involvement in alcohol, drug, or police problems).

School Environment

This domain was represented by two scales based on Moos (1979) and Rutter, Maughan, Mortimore, and Ouston, (1979) that had been shown in earlier work to be related to the new onset of children's problems (Kasen, Johnson, and Cohen 1990). The scales reflect a high conflict environment (e.g., fighting, teachers spending their time trying to maintain discipline), and a learning-promoting environment (e.g., students interested in getting good grades, teachers motivated to make the material interesting).

Parent-Child Relationship and Child Rearing

This domain was based on a consolidation of a larger number of more specific scales, assessed by both parent and youth report. The summary measures used here include: (a) identification of the child with the mother (Brook et al. 1990a); (b) father-child bond (pooling affection and communication as reported by the child, Brook et al. 1990a); (c) child autonomy from mother and father (Brook et al. 1990a); (d) maternal inconsistency as reported by the child (Brook et al. 1990a); and (e) the use of punishment techniques as reported by child and parent (Brook et al. 1990a).

Peer Environment

This domain included a measure of the time spent with friends (see Brook et al. 1990a), peer deviant activities (see Brook et al. 1990a), and the achievement level of friends (Brook et al. 1983).

Each of the risk factors was assessed in the first follow-up. Prospective assessment minimizes the possible confusion of risk factors for child problems with effects of the child problems on the purported risk factor.

Method

The technique developed for our earlier comparison of the predictors of drug use, externalizing problems, and internalizing problems is called net regression. This procedure provides a statistical comparison of the partial or direct effects of risk factors on different outcome variables. Thus, the more common practice of noting that a risk is statistically significant for one outcome, but not for another, or that some estimate of magnitude of effect appears to be larger for one outcome than another, without assessment of the significance of these differences, can be avoided. In addition, net regression provides an overall test of the net differences in the partial regression coefficients, as well as a test of each risk factor. Thus, the overall test may be used to control Type II errors of inference.

In this procedure, an ordinary least-squares equation is produced for each of two standardized dependent variables, Y and Z, using all risk factors of interest. (In our case, we also included as covariates age, sex, and the age-by-sex interaction.) The two predicted or estimated dependent variables $\hat{Y}$ and $\hat{Z}$ are then produced. Their equations are, of course, the sum of the regression-weighted risk factors plus a constant. This sum for $\hat{Y}$ is then subtracted from Z, and this new variable, $Z = \hat{Y}$, is regressed on the original set of predictors (risk factors). The overall R for this equation and its associated F provides a test of the significance of the aggregate differences in risk factors, and each partial regression coefficient and its *t* indicates the magnitude and significance of the difference in risk for each variable. These analyses were accomplished readily by means of the SETCOR module of the SYSTAT statistical package for microcomputer (Cohen 1989; Wilkinson 1990).

Note that the tests provided by the net regression procedure are not the same as those that determine whether one dependent variable (such as delinquency) accounts for the association between risk factors and the other dependent variable (such as drug use). This different question is answered by partialling one dependent variable from the other, and regressing this partialled variable on the risk factors.

Findings

Table 10.2 presents the regression of drug use (DU) and delinquency (JD) on each of the independent variables, partialling linear and quadratic aspects of age, sex, and the age by sex interaction. Of the six variables in the context set, five were significantly related to one of the outcome variables; no variables were significantly related to both drug use and delinquency. All three variables in the family environment set were significantly related to JD, and parental sociopathy was related to DU as well. Of the variables in the parent-child set only autonomy was not related to DU nor to JD. We had included this variable because the development of autonomy is a major task of adolescence and may be reflective of positive adjustment. On the other hand, very high levels of independence may reflect a laissez-faire attitude and poor parental monitoring.

All variables in the school and peer environment were significantly related to both dependent variables.

Table 10.3 presents the effects of each of the five sets of dependent variables considered simultaneously. Variables in the context set that were significant in the bivariate analyses were also significant in these equations, with the exception of single parent families. Single parenthood effects have been shown in previous analyses to be attributable to the economic disadvantage experienced in many of these households (Cohen, Johnson, Lewis and Brook 1990).

In all of the analyses of sets two through five, the effects of family context as well as age and sex were partialled. In these analyses parental conflict did not show a significant effect on either

TABLE 10.2
Bivariate relationships of substance use and delinquency with risk factors.[1]

	Drug Use	Delinquency
1. Context		
Urbanicity	.04	.17*
Low SES	−.02	.14*
Single Parent	.01	.10*
Stepfather	.05	.06
No father figure	.05	.11*
Separate residence	.13*	.03
2. Family environment		
Parental conflict	.04	.11*
Parental sociopathy	.09*	.20*
Sibling sociopathy	.04	.12*
3. Parent-Child		
Identification with mother	−.24*	−.16*
Father affectional bond	−.21*	−.21*
Autonomy	.05	.05
Maternal inconsistency	.10*	.17*
Punishment	.12*	.21*
4. School		
School conflict	.14*	.18*
Positive learning	−.15*	−.10*
5. Peer		
Time spent with friends	.22*	.15*
Peer deviant activities	.30*	.27*
Peer achievement	−.26*	−.29*

[1]Betas net of child's age, sex, and age by sex.
*$p < .05$.

DU or JD net of these variables. However, parental sociopathy remained significant for both outcomes and sibling sociopathy for JD. It should be noted that data presented here are for the combined sexes. However, analyses not shown here indicate that the negative effects of no father and stepfather on drug use and delinquency are confined to boys. Other kinds of negative effects of these family structural variables are shown for girls, that is, depression.

Redundancy among the parent-child set variables, as well as the removal of the context effects, left only identification with mother and affectional bond with father significant prospective predictors of drug use and bond with father, maternal inconsistency, and punishment predictors of JD. Previous analyses have shown punishment to have effects on behavioral problems from early childhood (Cohen and Brook 1987).

TABLE 10.3
Partial relationships of substance use and delinquency with risk factors.

	Drug Use		Delinquency	
	Beta[1]	R	Beta[1]	R
1. Context		.15		.23
Urbanicity	.05		.14*	
Low SES	−.04		.09*	
Single Parent	.00		.06	
Stepfather	.04		.06	
No father figure	.05		.08*	
Separate residence	.13*		.02	
2. Family environment		.19		.29
Parental conflict	.03		.07	
Parental sociopathy	.09*		.13*	
Sibling sociopathy	.04		.08*	
3. Parent-Child		.32		.37
Identification with mother	−.18*		−.07	
Father affectional bond	−.12*		−.13*	
Autonomy	.06		.05	
Maternal inconsistency	.06		.13*	
Punishment	.05		.15*	
4. School		.23		.29
School conflict	.10*		.13*	
Positive learning	−.11*		−.09*	
5. Peer		.41		.38
Time spent with friends	.20*		.13*	
Peer deviant activities	.20*		.13*	
Peer achievement	−.17*		−.19*	

[1]Betas net of child's age, sex, and age by sex.
*$p < .05$.
Note: The context set has been partialled from all other sets.

All variables in the school and peer environment sets remained statistically significantly related to both JD and DU when considered simultaneously with control on the context set.

Multiple correlations for the context set and for each combination of context with another set are shown in table 10.3. In all of these equations the contribution to prediction of the age and sex covariate set is excluded from the multiple R. When all five sets of variables were examined simultaneously the multiple Rs for both DU and JD were .45.

Net Regression

Using net regression analysis, variables showing a significantly different relationship with DU and JD are shown in table 10.4. In

TABLE 10.4
Net regression analysis of significantly different partial relationships of substance use
and delinquency with risks.

	Delinquency/Drug Use Difference in Beta[1]
1. Context	
Urbanicity	.13*
Low SES	.08*
Single parent	.05
Stepfather	.06
No father figure	.09*
Separate residence	.04
2. Family environment	(NS)
Parental conflict	.04
Parental sociopathy	.03
Sibling sociopathy	.04
3. Parent-Child	
Identification with mother	−.10*
Father affectional bond	−.02
Autonomy	−.02
Maternal inconsistency	.08*
Punishment	.11*
4. School	(NS)
School conflict	.03
Positive learning	.01
5. Peer	(NS)
Time spent with friends	−.07
Peer deviant activities	−.05
Peer achievement	−.02

[1]A positive beta indicates a more positive or less negative relationship for delinquency than
for drug use.
*p < .05.

each case the variables in the equation were the same as those in
Table 10.3. Three of the context variables, urbanicity, low SES,
and the absence of any father figure for the child, were not only
predictors of JD but were also significantly greater predictors of JD
than of DU. Children who were living away from their families were
at excess risk of DU, but not significantly less so than for JD.

None of the variables in the family environment set (net of the
context set) was a significantly different predictor for DU as compared to JD. Thus, although sibling sociopathy was significant for
JD, but not for DU, we cannot assert that it is more important for
JD than for DU.

Three variables in the parent-child set were significantly different in their patterns of relationship with delinquency and drug use. Identification with mother was more predictive of subsequent drug use than of delinquency; maternal inconsistency and punishment were more predictive of delinquency than of drug use.

The school environment set was related approximately equally to the two outcome variables. None of the peer environment variables were significantly differently related to DU as compared to JD.

Discussion

This study attempted to assess the pathways common to both drug use and delinquency, as well as those unique and dissimilar pathways leading to either drug use or delinquency. It seems clear that the findings were consistent in part with a common causal model for both drug use and delinquency. A deviant family environment, peer environment, and school environment did not differentially predict drug use and delinquency. As regards the family environment, parental sociopathy predicts both drug use and delinquency. These findings confirm previous studies which indicate that children whose parents exhibit deviant behavior are at increased risk for both drug use and delinquency. (McCord 1979; Farrington 1986; Brook and Brook in press).

Peer risk factors were similar for both drug use and delinquency. Our findings point to the peer group as one of the major training grounds for drug use and delinquency, and are consistent with those of previous studies (Hirschi 1969; Huba and Bentler 1983). Several interpretations for the relation of peer factors and drug use and delinquency are possible. To begin with, peers probably supply the adolescent with opportunities to engage in specific delinquent acts. Peers may also supply the adolescent with values conducive to crime and drugs. Related to this, peers may be necessary to supply the adolescent with drugs. Then too, the adolescents may merely imitate the behavior of their friends. Finally, young persons who are delinquent and use drugs may seek out those peers who share their interest in delinquency and drugs, that is, "birds of a feather flock together." To our knowledge, a comparison of the modeling effects of delinquency and drug use has not been undertaken. Although the researchers differ in their account of how, and for what reason peers contribute to delinquency and drug use, it is apparent that the association between peer factors and drug use and delinquency is strong.

With respect to school factors, the present findings extend the growing body of research that shows the impact of schools on student achievement and on socioemotional development. The data are particularly significant in showing that both a learning-promoting environment with high academic standards, and a harmonious school setting with low school conflict reduce the risk for both drug use and delinquency. Although it is clear that there is an association between the school setting, drug use, and delinquency, the mechanism through which it operates is unclear. It may be that some schools frustrate the desires of certain adolescents to learn things that are relevant to their future prospects. Such frustration may be expressed either in drug use or delinquency. Then too, schools characterized by conflict may foster deviant subcultures, providing the youngster with models for drug use and delinquency. Based on these findings, one would assume interventions should focus not only on changing the individual and family environment, but the school environment as well.

In contrast to the findings regarding a deviant family environment, peer environment, and school environment, which were consistent with a common-cause model for both drug use and delinquency, the environmental context and parent-child domains were in accord with a dissimilar-cause model. Environmental context variables reflecting an urban setting, low SES, and no father figure were related to delinquency, but not to drug use. However, the magnitude of the relationship is not great. The empirical findings linking low SES and urban residence to delinquency are in keeping with trends in the literature (Wilson and Herrnstein 1985). We speculate that urban living affects delinquency because it creates conditions that threaten an individual's safety and that are met by reciprocal violence. Urban life and a low SES also provide multiple criminal opportunities and opportunities for the modeling of violence, as well as crowded, inadequate living conditions which impair the quality of life. Finally, boys who report no father figure are more likely to be delinquent. This finding may reflect the importance of a paternal role model with whom to identify to insulate against the development of delinquency.

In accord with the finding of dissimilar models, the parent-child domain did differentiate between drug use and delinquency. Although the magnitude of the effects of the parent-child relationship domain were not appreciably different in drug use and delinquency, the particular family mechanisms did differ. In drug use, mutual attachment, as assessed by material identification and the parental affectional bond, provides the youngster with a sense of inner security, which ultimately provides the child with a sense of inner control. This sense of inner control in turn insulates the youngster from drug use (Brook et al. 1990a; Wilson and Herrnstein 1985). In contrast, the parent-child risk factors for delinquency are more in line with a social-interactional perspective. The social-interactional perspective maintains that family members train the child to perform antisocial acts (Patterson 1982; Wahler and Dumas 1984). Parents are noncontingent in their use of reinforcers resulting in the reinforcing of coercive behavior in children (Snyder and Patterson 1986). The use of power-assertive discipline also teaches the child to control the behavior of others through the use of force. In an analysis of several different data sets, Patterson and his colleagues reported that disruptive parent practices, such as excessive parental discipline, were related to antisocial behavior in the child (Patterson 1986). Of course, the child may simply be imitating the behavior of others. Another possible interpretation, developmental in nature, rests on an examination of the major precursors of delinquency. One such precursor is aggression. Aggression first manifests itself at an earlier age than delinquency or drug use. When the child expresses aggression, parents may first respond by using reason. When this doesn't work, they may resort to the use of punishment. A reciprocal process then begins whereby the child's aggression leads to harsh parental discipline, which in turn leads to increased aggression in the child. This reciprocal feedback cycle is replicated many time and eventually manifests itself in delinquency. Since drug use is a later onset behavior than delinquency, the aforementioned developmental process is less likely to be implicated in drug use.

Overall, although there were a number of risk factors which were common to both drug use and delinquency, several of the risk factors showed substantial specificity. Thus, the findings are consistent with both shared and unshared environmental risks for these two adolescent outcomes.

In conclusion, successful prevention and treatment programs for both drug use and delinquency would probably include five components: context, family environment, parent-child relations, school, and peer factors. While the interventions would be similar for both drug users and delinquents, there would be some notable differences within the parent-child area. With drug users, it seems reasonable to enhance the mutual attachment between parent and child, whereas among delinquents, systematic parental training in effective management practices is called for.

The Children in the Community Project study from which these data are taken was supported by a grant from the W. T. Grant Foundation and by NIMH grant # MH36971, and by NIDA grant # DA03188 and Research Scientist Development Award DA00094 to Dr. Judith Brook.

The authors thank Dorothy Marion for her help with the compilation of this chapter.

References

Achenbach, T. M., and C. S. Edelbrock, 1983. *Manual for the Child Behavior Checklist and Revised Child Behavior Profile*. Burlington, VT: University of Vermont, Department of Psychiatry.

Bachman, J. G., L. D. Johnston, and P. M. O'Malley, 1981. "Smoking, Drinking, and Drug use Among American High School Students: Correlates and Trends, 1975–1979." *American Journal of Public Health* 71, 59–69.

Blumstein, A., D. P. Farrington, and S. Moitra, 1985. "Delinquency Careers: Innocents, Desisters, and Persisters." In *Careers and Justice,* vol. 6, edited by M. Tonry and N. Morris. Chicago: University of Chicago Press.

Brook, D. W., and J. S. Brook (in press). "Family Processes Associated with Alcohol and Drug Use and Abuse." In *Family Therapy of Drug and Alcohol Abuse: Ten Years Later,* edited by E. Kaufman and P. Kaufman. New York: Gardner Press.

Brook, J. S., D. W. Brook, A. S. Gordon, M. Whiteman, and P. Cohen. 1990a. "The Psychosocial Etiology of Adolescent Drug Use: A Family Interactional Approach." *Genetic, Social, and General Psychology Monographs,* 116(2).

Brook, J. S., I. F. Lukoff, and M. Whiteman, 1980. "Initiation into Adolescent Marijuana Use." *Journal of Genetic Psychology* 137, 133–42.

Brook, J. S., C. Nomura, and P. Cohen, 1989. "A Network of Influences on Adolescent Drug Involvement: Neighborhood, School, Peer & Family." *Genetic, Social, and General Psychology Monographs* 115(2), 221–41.

Brook, J. S., M. Whiteman, and A. S. Gordon, 1983. "Stages of Drug Use in Adolescence: Personality, Peer, and Family Correlates." *Developmental Psychology* 19, 269–77.

Brook, J. S., M. Whiteman, and A. S. Gordon, 1985. "Father Absence, Perceived Family Characteristics and Stage of Drug Use in Adolescence. *British Journal of Developmental Psychology* 2, 87–94.

Brook, J. S., M. Whiteman, A. S. Gordon, and D. W. Brook, 1990. "The Role of Older Brothers in Younger Brothers' Drug use Viewed in the Context of Parent and Peer Influences." *Journal of Genetic Psychology* 151(1), 59–75.

Brook, J. S., M. Whiteman, A. S. Gordon, and P. Cohen, 1989. "Changes in Drug Involvement: A Longitudinal Study of Childhood and Adolescent Determinants." *Psychological Reports* 65, 707–26.

Clayton, R. R., and B. S. Tuchfeld, 1982. "The Drug-Crime Debate: Obstacles to Understanding the Relationship." *Journal of Drug Issues* 12(2), 153–66.

Cohen, J. 1989. *SETCOR: A supplemental module for SYSTAT and SYGRAPH.* Evanston, IL: SYSTAT, Inc.

Cohen, P., and J. S. Brook, 1987. "Family Factors Related to the Persistence of Psychopathology in Childhood and Adolescence." *Psychiatry* 50, 332–45.

Cohen, P., J. S. Brook, J. Cohen, C. N. Velez, and M. Garcia, 1990. "Common and Uncommon Pathways to Adolescent Psychopathology and Problem Behavior." In *Straight and Devious Pathways from Childhood to Adulthood,* edited by L. N. Robins and M. Rutter. London: Cambridge University Press.

Cohen P., J. Johnson, S. Lewis, and J. S. Brook, 1990. "Single Parenthood and Employment: Double Jeopardy?" In *Stress Between Work and Family,* edited by J. Eckenrode and S. Gore, 117–32. New York: Plenum.

Costello, A., C. S. Edelbrock, M. K. Dulcan, R. Kalas, and S. H. Klaris, 1984. *Report of the NIMH Diagnostic Interview Schedule for Children (DISC).* Pittsburgh, PA: University of Pittsburgh, Department of Psychiatry.

Elliott, D. S., and D. Huizinga, 1984, April. *The Relationship Between Delinquent Behavior and ADM Problem Behaviors.* Paper prepared for the ADAMHA/OJJDP State of the Art Research Conference on Juvenile Offenders with Serious Drug/Alcohol and Mental Health Problems, Bethesda, MD.

Farrington, D. P. 1986. "Stepping Stones to Adult Criminal Careers." In *Development of Antisocial and Prosocial Behaviors,* edited by D. Olweus, J. Block, and M. Radke-Yarrow. Orlando, FL: Academic Press.

Fawzy, I., R. Coombs, and B. Gerber, 1983. "Generational Continuity in the Use of Substances: The Impact of Parental Substance Use on Adolescent Substance Use." *Addictive Behaviors* 8, 109–14.

Hawkins, J. D. and D. M. Lishner, 1987. "Schooling and Delinquency." In *Handbook on Crime and Delinquency Prevention,* edited by E. H. Johnson, 179–221. Westport, CT: Greenwood Press.

Hawkins, J. D., and J. G. Weis, 1985. "The Social Development Model: An Integrated Approach to Delinquency Prevention." *Journal of Primary Prevention* 6(2), 73–97.

Hirschi, T. 1969. *Causes of Delinquency.* Berkeley: University of California Press.

Huba, G. J., and P. M. Bentler, 1983. "Causal Models of the Development of Law Abidance and its Relationship to Psychosocial Factors and Drug Use." In *Personality Theory, Moral Development and Criminal Behavior,* edited by W. S. Laufer and J. M. Day, 165–215. Lexington, MA: Lexington Books.

Jessor, R., and S. L. Jessor, 1977. *Problem Behavior and Psychosocial Development.* New York: Academic Press.

Johnston, L. D., M. O. O'Malley, and J. G. Bachman, 1986. *Drug Use Among American High School Students, College Students, and Other Young Adults: National Trends Through 1985.* University of Michigan, Institute for Social Research.

Kandel, D. B. 1985. "On Processes of Peer Influence in Adolescent Drug Use: A Developmental Perspective." *Alcohol and Substance Abuse in Adolescence* 4(3–4), 139–63.

Kaplan, H. B. 1980. *Deviant Behavior in Defense of Self.* New York: Academic Press.

Kasen, S., J. Johnson, and P. Cohen, 1990. "The Impact of School Emotional Climate on Student Psychopathology." *Journal of Abnormal Child Psychology* 18, 165–77.

Kogan, L., J. Smith, and S. Jenkins, 1977. "Ecological Validity of Indicator Data as Predictors of Survey Findings." *Journal of Social Service Research* 1, 117–32.

Loeber, R., and T. Dishion, 1983. "Early Predictors of Male Delinquency: A Review." *Psychological Bulletin* 94, 68–99.

McCord, J. 1979. "Some Child-Rearing Antecedents of Criminal Behavior in Adult Men." *Journal of Personality and Social Psychology* 37, 1477–86.

McCord, W., and J. McCord, 1959. *Origins of Crime: A New Evaluation of the Cambridge-Somerville Study.* New York: Columbia University Press.

Moos, R. H. 1979. *Evaluating Education Environments.* San Francisco: Jossey-Bass.

Needle, R. H., S. Su, and W. J. Doherty, 1990. "Divorce, Remarriage, and Adolescent Substance Use: A Perspective Longitudinal Study." *Journal of Marriage and the Family* 54 (Feb.), 157–69

Newcomb, Michael D., and P. M. Bentler, 1988. "The Impact of Family Context, Deviant Attitudes, and Emotional Distress on Adolescent Drug Use: Longitudinal, Latent, Variable Analyses of Mothers And Their Children." *Journal of Research and Personality* 22, 154–76.

Patterson, G. R. 1982. *Coercive Family Process.* Eugene, OR: Castalia Publishing Co.

Patterson, G. R. 1986. "Performance Models for Antisocial Boys." *American Psychologist* 41, 432–44.

Robins, L. N. 1978. "Sturdy Childhood Predictors of Adult Anti-Social Behavior: Replications from Longitudinal Studies. *Psychological Medicine* 8, 611–22.

Robins, L. N., and T. R. Pryzbeck, 1987. Age of onset of drug use and other disorders." In *Etiology of Drug Abuse: Implications for Prevention,* edited by C. L. Jones and R. J. Battjes 178–192. National Institute on Drug Abuse Research Monograph, Series 56, Washington, D.C.: U.S. Government Printing Office.

Robins, L. N. and E. Wish, 1977. "Childhood Deviance as a Developmental Process: A Study of 233 Urban Black Men from Birth to 18." *Social Forces* 56, 448–73.

Rutter, M., B. Maughan, P. Mortimore, and J. Ouston, 1979. *Fifteen Thousand Hours: Secondary Schools and their Effects on Children.* New York: Cambridge University Press.

Snyder, J. J., and G. R. Patterson, 1986. "The Effects of Consequences on Patterns of Social Interaction: A Quasi-Experimental Approach to Reinforcement in Natural Interaction." *Child Development* 57, 1257–68.

Wahler, R. G., and J. E. Dumas, 1984. "Family Factors in Childhood Psychopathology: Toward a Coercion Neglect Model." In *Family Interaction and Psychopathology,* edited by T. Jacob. New York: Plenum Press.

West, D. J., and D. P. Farrington, 1973. *Who becomes Delinquent?* London, Heinemann Educational.

Wilkinson, L. 1990. *SYSTAT: The System for Statitics*. Evanston, IL: SYSTAT, Inc.

Wilson, J. Q., and R. J. Herrnstein, 1985. *Crime and Human Nature*. New York: Simon & Schuster.

Zucker, R. A. 1979. "Developmental Aspects of Drinking Through the Young Adult Years." In *Youth, Alcohol and Social Policy*, edited by H. T. Blane and M. E. Chafetz. New York: Plenum Press.

11

Explaining the Beginning, Progress, and Ending of Antisocial Behavior from Birth to Adulthood

David P. Farrington

Introduction

Shortcomings of Existing Theories

It is easier to document the inadequacies of existing theories of offending than to propose a new theory that overcomes these defects. However, there are three major clusters of inadequacies that this chapter will highlight and that my theory is designed to rectify. The first is the neglect of the continuity between offending and other types of antisocial behavior. The acts defined as offenses should be viewed as a subset of a wider category of antisocial or deviant acts. Hence, I will assume that offenses and other types of antisocial acts are behavioral manifestations of an underlying antisocial tendency. The second is the neglect of the continuity in antisocial behavior from childhood to adulthood, and the third is the exclusion of biological and psychological factors from most criminological theories.

Existing theories focus primarily on offending during the teenage years, which is the time when it is most prevalent (e.g., Farrington 1986). They concentrate on factors that correlate with the prevalence of official offending (arrests or convictions) or with the frequency or variety of self-reported offending. Hence, they emphasize theoretical constructs that might be particularly applicable to the teenage years, such as status frustration (e.g., Cohen 1955) or the strain between aspirations and what can be achieved by legitimate means (e.g., Cloward and Ohlin 1960). These kinds of theoretical constructs sometimes seem too far removed from key empirical variables like peer delinquency or reasons given by offenders for committing crimes such as boredom and excitement-seeking. These theories focus on what might be termed proximal influences on offending, as opposed to longer-term distal influences from the prenatal period or early childhood for example.

Existing criminological theories generally do not adopt a developmental approach. This is partly because of their focus on offending as opposed to antisocial behavior. Offenses such as burglary, robbery, or vehicle theft are rarely committed before the teenage years. Arrests and convictions rarely occur before the teenage years, and self-reports of offending are rarely collected before the teenage years. However, arguably analogous antisocial acts of stealing, aggression, and property damage are committed from early childhood onwards, and causal influences on these acts may be present before a child's birth. One of the aims of this chapter is to document and emphasize the continuity from childhood antisocial behavior to teenage offending, and from teenage offending to adult antisocial behavior such as child neglect, sexual promiscuity, and failure to pay debts.

Inevitably, criminological theories reflect criminological research traditions. Unfortunately, partly because of practical problems such as funding and the need for quick publications, most criminological research covers a very short time period, and is cross-sectional rather than longitudinal in nature. This design naturally draws theorists' attention to short-term rather than long-term influences, and limits their search for the causes of teenage offending to contemporaneous factors operating in the teenage years. In contrast, a longitudinal design forces attention to the development of offending and to long-term influences. The advantages of longitudinal over cross-sectional studies, for example in establishing causal order and in avoiding retrospective bias, have been argued many times (e.g., Blumstein, Cohen, and Farrington 1988; Farrington,

Ohlin, and Wilson 1986), but some theorists are not convinced (e.g., Gottfredson and Hirschi 1987, 1988).

The major criminological tradition that focuses on the development of offending is the criminal career approach (e.g., Blumstein and Cohen 1987; Blumstein, Cohen, Roth, and Visher 1986). This emphasizes the need to investigate such questions as why people start offending (onset), why they continue offending (persistence), why offending becomes more frequent or more serious (escalation), and why people stop offending (desistance). The factors influencing onset may differ from those influencing other criminal career features such as persistence, escalation, and desistance, if only because the different processes occur at different ages. Indeed, Farrington and Hawkins (1991) found that there was no relationship between factors influencing prevalence (official offenders versus nonoffenders), those influencing early versus later onset, and those influencing desistance.

In order to understand the causes of offending, it is important to study developmental processes such as onset, persistence, escalation, and desistance. However, it is also important not to restrict this study narrowly to offending, which is part of a much wider phenomenon of childhood and adult antisocial behavior. Theories should aim to explain more general antisocial behavior, not just offending. An underlying antisocial tendency may lead to offending in some circumstances and to other types of antisocial acts in other circumstances, forcing attention to interactive effects of influencing factors. In particular, there will be different antisocial manifestations at different ages from birth to adulthood. The variation in antisocial behavior with age is one of the key results that any theory needs to explain (see, e.g., Farrington 1986a).

Just as criminological theorists usually neglect the long-term development of antisocial behavior, they also usually neglect the possible influence of biological and psychological factors. This dislike of biology and psychology reflects the sociological training of most such theorists (see, e.g., Farrington 1987). Its roots lie to a considerable extent in the fierce criticism of biology and psychology by Sutherland, whose textbook in its various editions (e.g., Sutherland and Cressey 1974) dominated criminology for forty years. Most theories include only a narrow range of variables from a limited number of data sources, and could not in any sense be described as multidisciplinary. While the number of different variables that could be included is impractically large, it is nevertheless essential not to ignore important bodies of knowledge about antisocial behavior. This chapter aims to widen the range of variables and data sources that need to be taken account of and explained in criminological theories.

This review is restricted to research carried out in England, the United States, and similar Western democracies in the second half of the twentieth century. Within the scope of a single chapter, it is obviously impossible to review everything that is known about the development, causes, and correlates of offending and antisocial behavior. Inevitably, I will be very selective in focusing on some of the more important and replicable findings obtained in some of the more methodologically adequate studies. I will concentrate especially on results obtained in longitudinal projects, partly because I believe that such projects yield more convincing conclusions than cross-sectional studies, and partly because of my interest in explaining the development of antisocial behavior from birth to adulthood.

Fortunately or unfortunately, there is no shortage of factors that are significantly correlated with offending and antisocial behavior; indeed, literally thousands of variables differentiate significantly between official offenders and nonoffenders or correlate significantly with self-reported offending. The problem is to propose a simple theory that accounts for as much of the complex reality as possible. More is known about factors that facilitate antisocial behavior than about factors that inhibit it or that protect people against the influence of facilitating factors. (For a discussion of the meaning of protective factors, see Farrington et al. 1988a.)

Key Theoretical Issues

In trying to explain offending and antisocial behavior, there are many important choices that are often made implicitly rather than explicitly, and I will try to make some of them explicitly. In particular, most theories aim to explain variation between individuals rather than within individuals. For example, theories try to explain why unemployed people are more likely to commit offenses than employed people, as opposed to why people commit more offenses during their periods of unemployment than during their periods of employment. (For a within-individual study of unemployment, see Farrington et al. 1986b.)

It is important to document and explain both between-individual and within-individual variation. Both types of variation can be studied only in longitudinal research. In a cross-sectional study, all variation is between individuals. It is quite possible that different factors are needed to explain between-individual and within-individual variation. For example, long-term historical factors arising from family relationships in childhood (e.g., cold, harsh parenting) may explain between-individual differences in an underlying antisocial tendency; whereas more recent or immediate factors (e.g., alcohol use or unemployment) or biological changes (e.g., in testosterone levels or at puberty) may explain within-individual differences in when offenses are committed or when offending careers begin or end. In other words, it is important to explain not only between-individual differences in offending but also the development and time course of offending careers within individuals.

Factors such as sex and race can only vary between individuals, not within individuals. The causal influence of any variable on offending can be established most convincingly by studying within-individual variation, because of the superior control of extraneous influences (each person acting as his or her own control: see Farrington 1988). Also, within-individual changes are required if any implications are to be drawn about prevention or treatment. It is difficult to establish the causal influence of nonmanipulable factors such as sex and race with high internal validity. In view of the problems with these factors, I will not consider them as possible explanatory variables. In any case, their correlations with offending are usually explained by reference to manipulable factors such as parental child-rearing techniques (e.g., the argument that girls are more closely supervised than boys). It is important to treat sex and race as boundary conditions and to investigate whether the same theory might apply to males and females, or within different racial or ethnic groups. From now on, the male gender will be used in this chapter, because most of the research is based on males, and my theory applies particularly to males.

Restating the within-individual versus between-individual issue in slightly different terms, it is plausible to suggest that offending and antisocial behavior result from the interaction between a person (with a certain potentiality or propensity for such behavior) and the social and physical environment (which provides opportunities for such behavior, including victims). In this chapter, I am using the term "antisocial tendency" to refer to the underlying individual potentiality for antisocial behavior, which is a key theoretical construct. In any given environment, some people are more likely than others to commit antisocial acts, just as all people are more likely to commit antisocial acts in certain circumstances, situations, and environments than in others. It is important to explain both the development of antisocial persons and the occurrence of antisocial acts.

There is clearly continuity over time in antisocial tendency. In other words, the antisocial child tends to become the antisocial teenager and the antisocial adult, just as the antisocial adult then tends to produce another antisocial child. The relative ordering of any cohort of people on antisocial tendency is significantly consistent over time (see Farrington 1990a). However, the behavioral manifestations of this tendency change over time, and it is important to document and explain these changing manifestations. For example, the antisocial child may be troublesome and disruptive in school, the antisocial teenager may steal cars and burgle houses, and the antisocial adult male may beat up his wife and neglect his children. These changing manifestations reflect changes both within the individual (e.g., maturation) and in his environment.

The recognition that there are changing manifestations of theoretical constructs at different ages implies that different operational definitions are needed to measure them. Some measures are only applicable at certain ages; for example, truancy from school could not be measured at age thirty, just as absenteeism from work could not be measured at age ten. There is also the complication that manifestations of antisocial tendency may be different at different time periods, for example as fashionable drugs come and go (see, e.g., Farrington 1990a). A further complication is that the same indicator may reflect different underlying constructs at different ages. For example, having sexual intercourse at age thirteen is statistically deviant, but having sexual intercourse at age twenty-three is statistically normal. Only the developmental course or precocity of the behavior may be deviant or antisocial, not the behavior itself.

It is unfortunate that the static model of relationships between independent and dependent variables has dominated criminological research and theory. This model may have a veneer of plausibility in a cross-sectional study, at least if problems of causal order are neglected. However, it is not easily applied to longitudinal data, where all presumed explanatory constructs and all measures of antisocial behavior and offending are likely to change continuously within individuals over different ages. Relationships between an explanatory factor in age range X and a measure of antisocial behavior in age range Y may vary a great deal according to the values of X and Y, and this needs to be systematically investigated by researchers.

It may be better to focus on developmental sequences rather than relationships between independent and dependent variables. It is important to try to distinguish among three types of behavioral sequences (see Farrington et al. 1990a). First of all, different acts following each other may be different behavioral manifestations of the same underlying construct at different ages, as mentioned above. Second, different acts may be different behavioral manifestations of the same or similar underlying constructs at different ages and also part of a developmental sequence, where one act is a stepping stone to or facilitates another (e.g., where smoking cigarettes leads to marijuana use). Third, different acts may be indicators of different constructs and part of a causal sequence, where changes in an indicator of one construct cause changes in an indicator of a different construct (e.g., where school failure leads to truancy).

The first of these concepts can be distinguished empirically from the second and third. If acts in a sequence are all different behavioral manifestations of the same construct (like symptoms of an illness), then changing an early act in the sequence will not necessarily affect the probability of occurrence of later acts unless there is some change in the underlying construct. However, with developmental and causal sequences, changing an early act in the sequence will affect the probability of later acts. It is harder to distinguish the second and third ideas empirically, as the key distinction between them is conceptual.

Whether a factor is an indicator (symptom) or a possible cause of antisocial tendency is a very important theoretical issue. For example, do heavy drinking, truancy, unemployment, and divorce measure antisocial tendency, or do they cause (an increase in) it? It is important not to include a measure of the dependent variable as an independent variable in causal analyses, because this will lead to false conclusions and an overestimation of explanatory or predictive power (see e.g., Amdur 1989).

It is not unreasonable to argue that the above examples may be both indicative and causal. For example, variations between individuals in antisocial tendency may be mirrored by variations in alcohol consumption, just as variations within individuals in alcohol consumption may cause more antisocial behavior during the heavier drinking periods. The interpretation of other factors may be more clear-cut. For example, being exposed as a child to poor parental child-rearing techniques might cause antisocial tendency but would not be an indicator of it; and burgling a house might be an indicator of antisocial tendency but would be unlikely to cause it (although it might be argued that, when an antisocial act is successful in leading to positive reinforcement, this reinforcement causes an increase in antisocial tendency).

Cross-sectional studies make it impossible to distinguish between indicators and causes, since they can merely demonstrate correlations between high levels of one factor (e.g., unemployment) and high levels of another (e.g., offending). However, longitudinal studies can show that offending is greater (within individuals) during some periods (e.g., of unemployment) than during other periods (e.g., of employment). Because within-individual studies have greater control over extraneous influences than between-individual studies (as mentioned earlier), longitudinal studies can demonstrate that changes in unemployment within individuals cause offending with high internal validity in a quasi-experimental analysis. Longitudinal studies can also establish whether factors such as unemployment have the same or different effects on offending when they vary within or between individuals.

Indicators and Correlates

The Cambridge Study in Delinquent Development

The next two major sections of this chapter review knowledge about indicators and correlates of antisocial behavior. Since empirical results from my own research are discussed in both sections, I will briefly describe this first. The project, called the Cambridge Study in Delinquent Development, is a prospective longitudinal survey of 411 males. At the time they were first contacted in 1961–62, they were all living in a working-class area of London, England. The vast majority of the sample was chosen by taking all the boys who were then aged eight and on the registers of six state primary schools within a one-mile radius of a research office that had been established. The boys were overwhelmingly white, working class, and of British origin. The major results obtained in this survey have been reported in four books (West 1969, 1982; West and Farrington 1973, 1977) and in more than sixty papers listed by Farrington and West (1990).

The major aim in this survey was to measure as many factors as possible that were alleged to be causes or correlates of offending. The boys were interviewed and tested in their schools when they were aged about eight, ten, and fourteen, by male or female psychologists. They were interviewed in our research office at about sixteen, eighteen, and twenty-one, and in their homes at about twenty-five and thirty-two, by young male social science graduates. The tests in schools included measures of intelligence, attainment, personality, and psychomotor impulsivity, while information was collected in the interviews about such topics as living circumstances, employment histories, relationships with females, leisure activities, and offending behavior. On all occasions except at ages twenty-one and twenty-five, the aim was to interview the whole sample, and it was always possible to trace and interview a high proportion. For example, 389 of the 410 males still alive at age eighteen (94.9 percent) were interviewed, and 378 of the 403 still alive at age thirty-two (93.8 percent).

In addition to the interviews and tests with the boys, interviews with their parents were carried out by female social workers who visited their homes. These took place about once a year from when the boy was about eight until when he was aged fourteen to fifteen and was in his last year of compulsory education. The primary informant was the mother, although many fathers were also seen. The parents provided details about such matters as family income, family size, their employment histories, their child-rearing practices (including attitudes, discipline, and parental agreement), their degree of supervision of the boy, and his temporary or permanent separations from them.

The boys' teachers completed questionnaires when the boys were aged about eight, ten, twelve, and fourteen. These provided information about the boys' troublesome and aggressive school behavior, their attention deficit, their school attainments, and their truancy. Ratings were also obtained from the boys' peers when they were in their primary schools, about such topics as their daring, dishonesty, troublesomeness, and popularity.

Searches were also carried out in the national Criminal Record Office in London to try to locate findings of guilt of the boys, of their parents, of their brothers and sisters, and (in recent years) of their wives and cohabitees. Convictions were only counted if they were for offenses normally recorded in this Office, thereby excluding minor crimes such as common (simple) assault, traffic offenses, and drunkenness. The most frequent offenses included were thefts and burglaries. However, we did not rely on official records for our information about offending, because we also obtained self-reports of offending from the boys themselves at every age from fourteen onwards.

Summarizing, the Cambridge Study in Delinquent Development has a unique combination of features. Eight face-to-face interviews have been completed with the subjects over a period of twenty-four years, between ages eight and thirty-two. The main focus of interest is on delinquency, crime, and antisocial behavior. The sample size of about 400 is large enough for many statistical analyses, but small enough to permit detailed case histories of the males and their families. Information has been obtained from multiple sources, including the subjects themselves, their parents, teachers, peers, and official records. Data have been collected about a wide variety of theoretical constructs at different ages, including biological (e.g., heart rate), psychological (e.g., intelligence), family (e.g., discipline), and social (e.g., socioeconomic status) factors. The attrition rate is unusually low for such a long-term survey.

Indicators of Antisocial Tendency

Many researchers have concluded that offending, especially in the juvenile ages, is predominantly versatile rather than specialized (e.g., Farrington, Snyder, and Finnegan 1988b; for a detailed review, see Klein 1984). In other words, people who commit one type of offense have a significant tendency also to commit other types. For example, Farrington (1991b) found that forty-three out of fifty convicted violent offenders in the Cambridge Study also had convictions for nonviolent offenses. However, adult sex offenders are exceptional in that they do specialize (e.g., Stander, Farrington, Hill, and Altham 1989), and it might be expected that adult white-collar offenders would also be specialists.

Table 11.1 demonstrates the versatility of offending in the Cambridge Study by showing the relationship between burglary, measured by conviction and by self-report at different ages, and eight other types of offenses. (For more detailed comparisons of all types of offenses, see Farrington 1989.) Burglary was chosen for illustrative purposes here because it was one of the most important and frequent offenses leading to convictions. About one-seventh of the males (14.1 percent) were convicted of burglary up to age thirty-two, and just over one-fifth (21.8 percent) admitted that they had committed a burglary in at least one of the interviews up to age thirty-two.

Of the fifty-seven convicted burglars, 78.9 percent (forty-five) were also self-reported burglars, a highly significant relationship (chi-squared = 128.7, 1 d.f., p < .001; all significance tests shown in Tables 11.1 and 11.2 are of this type). The odds ratio for this relationship was 28.5, showing roughly that convicted burglars were 28.5 times as likely to be self-reported burglars as were those not convicted of burglary. (Technically, the odds of being a self-reported burglar are 28.5 times greater for convicted burglars than for those not convicted of burglary.) The fact that twelve convicted burglars were not self-reported burglars does not necessarily indicate invalid self-reports. The self-reporting periods did not cover every possible age for every male, and there is always the possibility that a few convicted burglars were innocent. (For more details about comparisons between convictions and self-reports, showing how closely they were related, see Farrington 1989.)

Table 11.1 shows that, with only one exception, people who committed burglary were significantly more likely to commit each other type of offense (whether the measure was based on convictions or self-reports). The one exception was that males convicted

TABLE 11.1
Relationships With Official and Self-reported Burglary

	% who were burglars+	
Variable (N)	Convicted (14.1)	Self-reported (21.8)
(a) Convicted:		
Burglary (57)	——	78.9 (28.5)***
Shoplifting (30)	43.3(5.7)***	44.8(3.4)**
Theft of vehicle (59)	52.5(13.5)***	59.3(8.5)***
Theft from vehicle (27)	59.3(11.9)***	66.7(9.2)***
Theft from work (15)	60.0(10.6)***	46.7(5.9)*
Assault (45)	47.7(8.2)***	55.6(3.5)***
Vandalism (20)	25.0(2.1)	50.0(4.1)**
Drug use (11)	63.6(12.0)***	54.6(4.7)*
Fraud (23)	43.5(5.5)***	60.9(6.7)***
(b) Self-reported:		
Burglary (89)	52.9(28.5)***	——
Shoplifting (197)	21.8(3.6)***	33.5(4.1)***
Theft of vehicle (95)	22.9(13.2)***	60.0(13.2)***
Theft from vehicle (88)	43.0(11.1)***	62.5(14.1)***
Theft from work (132)	22.1(2.5)**	34.1(2.7)***
Assault (286)	18.4(5.1)***	29.0(8.0)***
Vandalism (303)	17.4(4.1)**	28.4(13.6)***
Drug use (155)	26.1(4.8)***	39.4(5.2)***
Fraud (337)	16.3(4.3)*	25.5(7.9)***
(c) Other variables:		
Most troublesome 8–10 (92)	31.4(4.4)***	44.6(4.5)***
Difficult to discipline 8–10 (93)	30.2(4.0)***	40.2(3.4)***
Most dishonest 10 (88)	20.9(2.1)*	36.4(2.9)***
Gets angry 10 (77)	26.7(3.0)***	32.5(2.1)*
Frequently truant 12–14 (73)	40.0(7.0)***	42.5(3.5)***
Frequently disobedient 12–14 (52)	44.0(7.1)***	51.9(5.1)***
Frequently lies 12–14 (122)	32.2(6.7)***	42.6(5.0)***
Steals outside home 14 (60)	41.1(7.0)***	48.3(5.0)***
Bullies 14 (71)	26.1(2.6)**	35.2(2.3)**
Most hostile to police 14 (108)	26.7(3.3)***	35.2(2.6)***
Regularly smokes 14 (67)	32.8(3.9)***	43.3(3.4)***
Had sexual intercourse 14 (47)	48.9(8.2)***	55.3(5.6)***
Unstable job record 18 (92)	33.0(4.8)***	45.7(4.6)***
Member of antisocial group 18 (117)	27.6(3.7)***	42.7(4.6)***
Heavy drinker 18 (98)	32.3(4.8)***	38.8(3.1)***
Drunk driver 18 (85)	26.8(2.8)**	37.6(2.7)***
Heavy smoker 18 (104)	27.2(3.2)***	31.7(1.9)*
Heavy gambler 18 (87)	24.4(2.3)**	36.8(2.5)***
Irresponsible sex 18 (76)	32.0(3.9)***	42.1(3.4)***
Antiestablishment attitude 18 (98)	26.8(3.0)***	41.8(3.7)***
Frequently unemployed 32 (64)	31.3(3.8)***	45.3(4.0)***
Divorced/child elsewhere 32 (86)	26.7(3.1)***	38.4(2.9)***
Involved in fights 32 (140)	21.4(2.5)**	32.9(2.6)***
Heavy drinker 32 (74)	33.8(5.0)***	48.6(5.1)***
Drunk driver 32 (164)	17.7(1.7)	28.0(1.9)*
Antiestablishment attitude 32 (51)	41.2(6.2)***	51.0(4.8)***

+ Odds ratio in parentheses.   * p < .05   ** p < .01   *** p < .001

of vandalism were not significantly more likely to be convicted of burglary, but even here the odds ratio showed that convicted vandals were twice as likely to be convicted of burglary, and the other three comparisons between vandalism and burglary were statistically significant. Hence, offenders are versatile.

This versatility applies not only to offending but to all types of antisocial acts. Robins (e.g., 1986) has consistently shown how a constellation of indicators of childhood antisocial behavior predicts a constellation of indicators of adult antisocial behavior. In several longitudinal studies, the number of different childhood symptoms predicted the number of different adult symptoms, rather than there being a linkage between any specific childhood and adult symptoms (Robins and Wish 1977; Robins and Ratcliff 1978, 1980). Numerous other studies also show that childhood conduct problems predict later offending and antisocial behavior; for example, Spivack, Marcus, and Swift (1986) found that troublesome behavior in kindergarten predicted later police contacts.

Robins's research had an important influence on the classification of childhood conduct disorder and adult antisocial personality disorder in the *Diagnostic and Statistical Manual* (DSM-IIIR) of the American Psychiatric Association (1987). Childhood conduct disorder is diagnosed when a child shows a variety of symptoms such as stealing, lying, running away, truanting, burglary, vandalism, cruelty to animals or people, and starting fights. Adult antisocial personality disorder is diagnosed when an adult shows a variety of such symptoms as stealing or vandalism, fighting or domestic violence, an unstable employment history, defaulting on debts, lying, neglecting children, and frequent sexual relationships.

In the Cambridge Study, West and Farrington (1977) developed a scale of antisocial tendency at age eighteen, based on factors such as an unstable job record, heavy gambling, heavy smoking, drug use, drunk driving, sexual promiscuity, spending time hanging about on the street, antisocial group activity, violence, and antiestablishment attitudes. Their aim was to devise a scale that was not based on the types of acts (thefts and burglaries) that usually led to convictions, so that they could investigate how far the convicted males were antisocial in a variety of other respects.

Table 11.1 shows the extent to which different types of antisocial behavior at different ages from eight to thirty-two were related to burglary (measured by convictions and self-reports). It can be seen that the burglars tended to be troublesome in school, difficult to discipline, and dishonest at ages eight to ten; frequently truant, disobedient, lying, and bullying at ages twelve to fourteen; precocious in smoking and in having sexual intercourse by age fourteen; had an unstable job record and were heavy drinkers at ages eighteen and thirty-two; had irresponsible sex (without contraception) at age eighteen and tended to be divorced and/or separated from their children at age thirty-two. (For more details about these measures, see Farrington and West 1990, and the references in that paper.)

All of these types of acts could be regarded as different age-appropriate manifestations of an underlying antisocial tendency, although in some cases (e.g., unemployment and divorce) they might reflect factors outside the man's control. The only nonsignificant relationship was that drunk drivers at age thirty-two (i.e., driving after drinking ten units or more of alcohol, where one unit = one half-pint of beer, one glass of wine, one single spirits, etc.) did not tend to be convicted burglars. This may have been because drunk driving at age thirty-two did not reflect deviance to the same degree as drunk driving at age eighteen; there were twice as many drunk drivers at age thirty-two as at age eighteen (164 in comparison with 85).

Given that all these types of acts are manifestations of an underlying antisocial tendency, it is important to investigate the stability of this tendency over different ages. Farrington (1990a) measured antisocial tendency at four ages (ten, fourteen, eighteen, and thirty-two), using at least ten different indicators of the kind shown in table 11.1 at each age. The antisocial tendency scales were all significantly intercorrelated (e.g., 10 vs. 14, $r = .50$; 14 vs. 18, $r = .58$; 18 vs. 32, $r = .55$; 10 vs. 32, $r = .30$). The sizes of these correlations are surprisingly high over such long time periods, indicating considerable stability; however, they also indicate considerable change that needs to be explained.

Hence, it is plausible to assume that there is an antisocial tendency that persists from childhood to adulthood and that is expressed both in offenses and in other types of antisocial acts. Its manifestation in infancy may correspond to the construct of "difficult temperament," which has been shown to predict adult maladjustment (e.g., Thomas and Chess 1984). Therefore, research on childhood conduct disorder, adult antisocial personality and psychopathy, and substance abuse has relevance to the explanation of offending. It is also true, as shown in table 11.1, that results obtained with official records of offending are similar to results obtained with self-reports.

Correlates of Antisocial Tendency

Table 11.2 shows some of the correlates of antisocial tendency measured at different ages in the Cambridge Study. It also shows how far each factor is related to juvenile convictions (85 convicted versus 326 not convicted) and to first convictions as an adult (68 convicted versus 258 not convicted, excluding 85 convicted juveniles). The percentages of juvenile and adult offenders were almost identical (20.7 percent juvenile, 20.9 percent adult), making all the percentages directly comparable. (For more details about all these measures, see Farrington and West 1990, and the references in that paper.)

Socioeconomic Factors. Most criminological theories assume that offenders disproportionally come from lower-class social backgrounds, and aim to explain why this is so. In many criminological research projects, offenders and nonoffenders are matched on SES (socioeconomic status) or SES is controlled first in regression analyses. This reflects a widespread belief in the importance of SES, but of course it often prevents the correctness of this belief from being tested. Unfortunately, as Thornberry and Farnworth (1982) pointed out, the voluminous literature on the relationship between SES and offending is characterized by inconsistencies and contradictions, and some reviewers (e.g., Hindelang, Hirschi, and Weis 1981) have concluded that there is no relationship between SES and either self-reported or official offending.

Numerous indicators of SES were measured in the Cambridge Study, both for the man's family of origin and for the man himself as an adult, including occupational prestige, family income, housing, employment instability, and family size. Most of the measures of occupational prestige (based on the Registrar General's scale, for the family at ages eight to ten and fourteen, and for the man at age thirty-two) were not significantly related to juvenile or adult convictions. The only exception was the measure of occupational

TABLE 11.2
Relationships with Juvenile and Adult Convictions

Variable at age (N)	% Convicted +	
	Juvenile (20.7)	Adult (20.9)
(a) Socioeconomics of family		
Low family income 8 (93)	34.4(2.6)***	26.2(1.5)
Poor housing 8–10 (151)	26.5(1.7)*	34.2(3.2)***
Large family size 10 (99)	33.3(2.5)***	36.4(2.8)***
Low family income 14 (79)	25.3(1.6)	16.9(0.7)
Poor housing 14 (80)	25.0(1.4)	28.3(1.7)
Large family size 14 (85)	31.8(2.2)***	36.2(2.7)**
(b) Socioeconomics of man		
Unstable job record 18 (92)	40.2(3.7)***	38.2(3.1)***
Unskilled manual job 18 (62)	45.2(4.1)***	47.1(4.1)***
Poor housing 32 (117)	26.5(1.8)*	27.9(1.7)
Frequently unemployed 32 (64)	37.5(3.1)***	40.0(3.0)**
Low SES 32 (95)	21.1(1.1)	20.0(0.9)
(c) Family relationships		
Poor parental child-rearing 8 (96)	33.3(2.8)***	21.9(1.1)
Poor parental supervision 8 (74)	31.1(2.2)**	35.3(2.4)*
Separated from parents 10 (90)	33.3(2.4)**	33.3(2.3)*
Poor relation with parents 18 (86)	37.2(2.9)***	24.1(1.2)
Poor relation with parents 32 (78)	20.5(1.1)	22.6(1.2)
Poor relation with wife 32 (52)	36.5(3.1)**	36.4(2.7)*
Divorced/child elsewhere 32 (86)	37.2(3.4)***	37.0(2.7)**
(d) Antisocial influences		
Convicted parent 10 (104)	37.5(3.4)***	33.8(2.4)**
Delinquent sibling 10 (46)	41.3(3.2)***	29.6(1.7)
Sibling behavior problems 8 (138)	29.0(2.7)***	25.5(1.5)
Delinquent friends 14 (101)	42.6(4.8)***	29.3(1.8)
Hangs around street 18 (61)	37.7(2.7)**	39.5(2.9)**
(e) Impulsivity		
Lacks concentration/restless 8–10 (82)	32.9(2.3)**	25.5(1.4)
High daring 8–10 (121)	38.8(4.2)**	29.7(1.9)
High psychomotor impulsivity 8–10 (104)	31.7(2.3)**	26.8(1.5)
Lacks concentration/restless 12–14 (107)	42.1(4.8)***	25.8(1.4)
High daring 12–14 (53)	49.1(4.9)***	22.2(1.1)
High impulsivity 18 (105)	29.5(1.9)*	32.4(2.3)**
High impulsivity 32 (82)	29.3(2.0)*	31.0(1.9)
(f) School problems		
Low intelligence 8–10 (103)	32.0(2.3)**	31.4(2.1)*
Low attainment 11 (90)	33.3(2.6)***	36.7(2.8)**
High delinquency school 11 (77)	36.4(2.6)***	32.7(2.0)
Low intelligence 14 (118)	30.5(2.2)**	28.0(1.7)
Frequently truants 14 (73)	49.3(5.7)***	35.1(2.3)*
No exams taken by 18 (197)	34.0(5.6)***	27.7(2.0)*
(g) Physical measures		
Small 8–10 (73)	31.5(2.1)*	22.0(1.1)
Small 14 (97)	25.8(1.5)	25.0(1.4)
Small 18 (59)	32.2(2.0)*	25.0(1.3)
Tattooed 18 (35)	54.3(5.4)***	31.3(1.8)
Tattooed 32 (59)	42.4(4.0)***	41.2(3.0)**

+ Odds ratio in parentheses.   * p < .05   ** p < .01   *** p < .001

prestige of the man at age eighteen. Nearly half of those who were unskilled manual workers at that age were convicted as juveniles (45.2 percent), and nearly half were convicted as adults (47.1 percent). The odds ratio in both cases was quite high (4.1). However, unskilled manual workers at age eighteen tended to have an unstable job record with periods of unemployment at that age, so an unstable job record may be a more important causal factor, as indeed the research of Farrington et al. (1986b) suggests. Frequent unemployment at age thirty-two was also significantly related to juvenile and adult offending, but low occupational prestige was not (table 11.2).

Low family income at age eight was significantly related to juvenile but not adult offending, and low family income at age fourteen was not related to either. The family income measure at age eight took account of family size, whereas the measure at age fourteen purely reflected income. Large family size (number of children) at ages ten and fourteen was significantly related to both juvenile and adult offending. Family income and family size at ages eight to ten were closely related, and it is plausible to suggest that the more important factor was family size. The comparative unimportance of socioeconomic factors in the Cambridge Study may possibly be because the whole sample was drawn from a poor area; however, the criminological literature as a whole does not suggest that such factors have much importance in relation to offending.

Family Factors. In contrast, the importance of family factors as correlates of offending is much more securely established. The exhaustive review by Loeber and Stouthamer-Loeber (1986) showed that poor parental supervision or monitoring, erratic or harsh parental discipline, parental disharmony, parental rejection of the child, and low parental involvement with the child were all important predictors of offending. For example, the important longitudinal survey of McCord (e.g., 1979, 1990) shows the link between parental supervision, discipline, conflict, and lack of affection and later juvenile delinquency and adult crime. In addition, child physical abuse or neglect significantly predicts both juvenile and adult offending (Widom 1989). Separations or broken homes caused by divorce or disharmony predict official offending, but not those caused by death or hospitalization (Wadsworth 1979).

Table 11.2(c) shows that, in the Cambridge Study, poor parental child rearing at age eight (reflecting erratic or harsh discipline), poor parental supervision at age eight (not knowing where the boy was when he went out), and temporary or permanent separations up to age ten caused by divorce or disharmony all significantly predicted juvenile convictions. However, only supervision and separations were significantly related to adult convictions.

Offenders tend to have difficulties in their personal relationships. Men who were in conflict with their parents at age eighteen tended to be juvenile but not adult offenders. However, conflict with parents at age thirty-two was not related to offending. Both juvenile and adult offenders tended to have a poor relationship with their wife or cohabitee at age thirty-two, or had struck her, and they also tended to be divorced and/or separated from their children.

Antisocial Influences. Numerous studies show that criminal, antisocial, or alcoholic parents tend to have criminal sons (e.g., McCord 1977; Robins 1979). In the Cambridge Study, having convicted parents or delinquent siblings by age ten, and having siblings with behavior problems at age eight, significantly predicted juvenile offending. However, only convicted parents significantly predicted adult offending.

There are also many demonstrations in the literature that offenders tend to have friends who are also offenders (e.g., Hardt and Peterson 1968; Elliott, Huizinga, and Ageton 1985). Table 11.2(d) shows that, in the Cambridge Study, having delinquent friends at age fourteen was significantly related to juvenile but not adult offending. However, spending time hanging about on the street at age eighteen was significantly related to both juvenile and adult offending.

Impulsivity. Many investigators have reported a link between the constellation of personality factors variously termed "hyperactivity-impulsivity-attention deficit" or HIA (Loeber 1987) and offending. After extensively reviewing the literature on this topic, Farrington, Loeber, and Van Kammen (1990b) showed that HIA from ages eight to ten significantly predicted juvenile convictions independently of conduct problems from ages eight to ten. Hence, it might be concluded that HIA is not merely another measure of antisocial tendency. Other studies have also concluded that hyperactivity and conduct disorder are different constructs (e.g., Blouin, Conners, Seidel, and Blouin 1989). Indicators of HIA such as restlessness can be measured in infancy (e.g., at age three) and predict conduct disorder in childhood (e.g., at age eight; Richman, Stevenson, and Graham 1982). Similar constructs to HIA, such as sensation seeking, are also related to offending (e.g., White, Labouvie, and Bates 1985).

In the Cambridge Study, the boys nominated by teachers as lacking in concentration or restless, those nominated by parents, peers, or teachers as the most daring, and those who were the most impulsive on psychomotor tests all tended to be juvenile but not adult offenders. However, later self-report questionnaire measures of impulsivity (including such items as "I generally do and say things quickly without stopping to think") were related to both juvenile and adult offending.

School Problems. Numerous studies show that low intelligence and attainment are important predictors of offending (e.g., Loeber and Dishion 1983; Loeber and Stouthamer-Loeber 1987). In the Cambridge Study, low nonverbal intelligence at ages eight to ten (on the Progressive Matrices test) and low junior school attainment at age eleven (on arithmetic, English, and verbal reasoning tests) were significantly related to juvenile and adult offending. Similarly, frequent truancy from school at age fourteen and not taking any examinations by age eighteen were significantly related to both. The key explanatory factor underlying the link between intelligence or attainment and offending is probably the ability to manipulate abstract concepts.

Recent research has focused not only on intelligence but on detailed patterns of cognitive and neuropsychological deficit. For example, in a New Zealand longitudinal study, Moffitt and Silva (1988) found that self-reported offending was related to verbal, memory, and visual-motor integration deficits, independently of low SES and family adversity. The "executive functions" of the brain, located in the frontal lobes, include sustaining attention and concentration, abstract reasoning and concept formation, anticipation and planning, and the inhibition of inappropriate behavior (see, e.g., Moffitt 1990). Deficits in these executive functions may cause low intelligence and attainment.

It is clear that the prevalence of offending varies dramatically between different schools. However, what is far less clear is how much of this variation is caused by differences in school climates or practices, and how much by differences in the intake of students to the school. In the most famous project on school effects on offending, Rutter, Maughan, Mortimore, and Ouston (1979) showed that differences between schools in delinquency rates could not be entirely explained by differences between the students entering them at age eleven, and concluded that these differences must have been caused by features of school structure, organization, or functioning. In the Cambridge Study, boys who went to high delinquency rate schools at age eleven were significantly likely to become juvenile but not adult offenders (table 11.2(f)).

Community Influences. The prevalence of offending also varies a great deal between communities. The classic studies of Shaw and McKay (1969) in Chicago and other American cities showed that delinquency rates (based on where offenders lived) were highest in inner city areas characterized by physical deterioration, neighborhood disorganization, and high residential mobility. A high proportion of all offenders came from a small number of deprived areas.

As Reiss (1986) argued, high crime rate areas often have a high concentration of single-parent, female-headed households with low incomes, living in low cost, poor housing, and a high number of children and teenagers hanging around on the streets. However, distinctive features of the inner city, such as high population density and physical deterioration, may produce frustration, tension, anonymity, diffusion of responsibility, and a breakdown of community ties and neighborhood patterns of mutual support. It is important to investigate how types of individuals interact with types of areas to explain area influences on offending.

Biological Factors. Studies of twins and adopted children suggest that there is some kind of genetic influence on offending. (For reviews, see Wilson and Herrnstein 1985; Eysenck and Gudjonsson 1989). This is indicated by the greater concordance (similarity) of monozygotic (identical) than dizygotic (fraternal) twins in offending. It might be argued that identical twins behave more identically because they are treated more similarly in their social environment, not because of their greater genetic similarity. Against this, however, identical twins reared apart are as similar in many respects (e.g., intelligence, personality, attitudes) as identical twins reared together (Bouchard et al. 1990). Similarly, the offending of adopted children is more similar to that of their biological parents than to that of their adoptive parents (e.g., Mednick, Gabrielli, and Hutchings 1983; see also Cloninger, Sigvardsson, Bohman, and von Knorring 1982).

Numerous psychophysiological and biochemical factors have also been linked to offending, through the key theoretical construct of arousal. Offenders have a low level of arousal according to their low alpha (brain) waves on the EEG, or according to autonomic nervous system indicators such as heart rate, blood pressure, or skin conductance, or they show low autonomic reactivity (e.g., Venables and Raine 1987). Similarly, adult offenders showed low adrenaline (epinephrine) levels at age thirteen (Magnusson 1988); violent offenders tend to have low levels of 5HIAA, a metabolite of serotonin, in their cerebrospinal fluid (Virkkunen 1988); and aggressive children tend to have low adrenaline and high plasma testosterone levels (Olweus 1987). All these researchers focus on impulsivity as the key intervening construct, and low arousal may also mediate the relationship between hypoglycemia and offending. The causal links between low autonomic arousal, consequent sensation seeking, and offending are brought out explicitly in Mawson's (1987) theory of transient criminality, which aims to explain variations within rather than between individuals.

Heart rate was measured in the Cambridge Study at age eighteen. While a low heart rate correlated significantly with convictions for violence (Farrington 1987), it did not significantly relate to juvenile or adult convictions in general. However, other physical measures taken in this research showed that smaller boys at ages eight to ten and eighteen were significantly more likely to be convicted as juveniles (see Table 11.2(g)). This may reflect the influence of poor nutrition. In addition, being tattooed was significantly related to juvenile and adult convictions in the Cambridge Study. While the meaning of this result is not clear, tattooing may reflect risk taking, daring, and excitement seeking.

Numerous prenatal and perinatal factors also predict a child's antisocial behavior, including pregnancy and birth complications (e.g., Szatmari, Reitsma-Street, and Offord 1986), low birth weight (e.g., Breslau, Klein, and Allen 1988), and teenage parenting (e.g., Brooks-Gunn and Furstenberg 1986). Also, stressful life events are related to antisocial behavior (e.g., Novy and Donahue 1985; Werner 1989). It is not possible to cover these topics in more detail within the scope of this chapter.

Two final points should be made at the end of this section. First, the strength of relationships with juvenile offending (as indicated by the odds ratios in table 11.2) often differs from the strength of relationships with adult offending. This suggests that causes of a juvenile onset of offending are different from causes of an adult onset, just as Farrington and Hawkins (1991) found that the predictors of early onset were different from the predictors of desistance. Second, all influences on offending tend to be intercorrelated, making it very difficult to disentangle causal influences and sequences. Impulsive children, for example, tend to come from criminal families with poor supervision, tend to have school problems and delinquent peers, and tend to live in criminal areas. It is, of course, important in projects to investigate the extent to which factors such as those shown in table 11.2 are independently related to offending. Multivariate analyses in the Cambridge Study (e.g., Farrington 1990b) suggest that each group of factors (e.g., family influences or school problems) was related to offending independently of each other group.

A Theory of Offending

Table 11.3 summarizes the key elements of the latest version of my theory of offending, which must be regarded as tentative and speculative. The fundamental distinction is between influences on antisocial tendency and influences on offending (including how the individual difference factor of antisocial tendency interacts with other factors to produce offending). Influences on antisocial tendency are generally long-term, between-individual factors, whereas influences on offending are generally short-term, within-individual, or situational factors. Putting this another way, antisocial tendency corresponds to a trait while offending corresponds to a state.

Influences on Antisocial Tendency

The first important construct or group of constructs includes impulsivity, hyperactivity, sensation seeking, risk taking, and a poor ability to defer gratification. This construct is related to

TABLE 11.3
Summary of my Theory

---

(1) Influences on Antisocial Tendency (long-term, between-individual)
(a) Impulsivity, hyperactivity, sensation seeking, risk taking, poor ability to defer gratification. (Related to physiological arousal.)
(b) Poor ability to manipulate abstract concepts, low IQ, low achievement, low self-esteem. (Related to deficits in executive functions of brain, influenced by genetic factors.)
(c) Low empathy, emotionally cold, callous, egocentric, selfish. (Depends on cold family relationships.)
(d) Weak conscience, low guilt or remorse, low internal inhibitions against antisocial behavior. (Depends on social learning process and past pattern of reinforcements, e.g., by parents.)
(e) Internalized norms and attitudes favoring antisocial behavior. (Depends on exposure to models and surrounding social influences, e.g., parents, peers, schools, communities.)
(f) Long-term motivating factors, e.g., desire for material goods, status with peers, sexual satisfaction, combined with difficulty of achieving these aims legitimately.

(2) Influences on Offending (short-term, within-individual)
(a) Antisocial tendency. (Slowly changing; may lead to many outcomes other than offending.)
(b) Short-term situationally induced motivating factors, e.g., boredom, frustration, alcohol consumption, getting fired, quarreling with spouse.
(c) Life circumstances or events, e.g., unemployment, drug addiction, shortage of money.
(d) Situational opportunities for offending, victims. (Depends on routine activities.)
(e) Costs and benefits of offending versus legitimate behavior, subjective probabilities of different outcomes. (Note: The decision to offend is essentially rational or hedonistic, depending on subjectively expected utilities.)

Gottfredson and Hirschi's (1990) fundamental construct of low self-control. In general, the more impulsive a person is, the more antisocial he will be. As already indicated, impulsivity may be a behavioral consequence of the biological construct of low arousal, as measured by psychophysiological and biochemical factors.

The second important group of constructs includes a poor ability to manipulate abstract concepts, low measured intelligence, low scholastic achievement, and low self-esteem. The fundamental construct is probably a poor ability to manipulate abstract concepts, which may cause low measured intelligence and low scholastic achievement, which in turn may cause low self-esteem. This fundamental construct may depend on the executive functions of the brain, as already mentioned, and it may have an important genetic component.

I have included low empathy, an emotionally cold or callous person, egocentricity, and selfishness as a third important group of constructs, although I have not reviewed them in detail above. They are often cited as characteristics of delinquents (e.g., Ross and Ross 1988) or psychopaths (e.g., Hare 1980). Emotional coldness probably depends on the lack of a consistent warm relationship with a caretaker, as theories dating back to Bowlby's (1951) "affectionless character" suggest. Cold, harsh, rejecting parental attitudes, and temporary or permanent separations from parents, are likely to cause emotional coldness.

The fourth important group of constructs includes a weak conscience, low guilt or remorse, and generally low internal inhibitions against antisocial behavior. The construct of a conscience, favored by psychologists (e.g., Trasler 1962; Eysenck 1977), seems related to the construct of a bond to society, favored by sociologists (e.g., Hirschi 1969; Hawkins, Lishner, Catalano, and Howard 1986). Many psychological theories suggest that the development of a conscience depends on a social learning process in which the key factor is the pattern of rewards and punishments given by parents. If parents consistently and contingently reward prosocial behavior (e.g., by praise) and punish antisocial behavior (e.g., by disapproval), the child will build up inhibitions against antisocial behavior in a learning process (possibly depending again on autonomic reactivity). This theory is the basis of the type of behavioral parent training used, for example, by Patterson (1982). Poor parental supervision or monitoring, large family size (which may cause poor supervision, because of the diffusion of parental attention), and erratic parental discipline will interfere with this social learning process.

Internalized norms and attitudes favoring antisocial behavior constitute the fifth important group of constructs. Several theories (e.g., Sutherland and Cressey 1974) suggest that social influences from parents, peers, schools, and communities are important. Possibly through a modelling process, people tend to internalize the norms and attitudes held by significant others to which they are exposed in their social environment, which may include criminal parents, delinquent siblings or peers, delinquent schools, and criminal areas. These social influences change with age. Before the teenage years, children are most influenced by their parents, who generally disapprove of offending and antisocial behavior. In the teenage years, the major social influence arises from peers, who often encourage antisocial behavior. In the twenties, at least for males, conventional influences from wives or girlfriends take over again. Hence, internalized norms and attitudes favoring antisocial behavior are greatest in the teenage years.

The final group of influences on antisocial tendency are motivating factors such as the desire for material goods, status with peers, or sexual satisfaction. In themselves, these motivations do not produce antisocial tendency. However, as Cloward and Ohlin (1960) suggested, they will produce antisocial tendency in people who cannot satisfy these needs by legitimate means.

The main thing that is required in further developing this part of the theory is to specify sequential relationships, especially causal sequences. In order to do this, better longitudinal data with frequent measurement over long time periods is needed, to determine when behaviors begin, escalate, and end. For example, it may be that impulsivity and a poor ability to manipulate abstract concepts cause school failure during the teenage years, which in turn makes it difficult to achieve status legitimately, which in turn fosters antisocial tendency. Attempts to specify the theory also need to be age-related. For example, impulsivity and a poor ability to manipulate abstract concepts (together with past school failure) may cause frequent unemployment and low-paid jobs in the twenties, making it difficult to achieve material goods, status, and girlfriends legitimately, again fostering antisocial tendency.

Influences on Offending

As already indicated, I assume that offenses arise from the interaction between the individual and the environment. The individual brings with him a certain degree of antisocial tendency, but is also influenced by short-term situationally-induced motivating factors and life circumstances. Offenses require opportunities before they can occur, and whether an offense is committed in any opportunity will depend not only on the individual difference factor of antisocial tendency but also on the subjectively perceived costs, benefits, and probabilities of the different possible outcomes.

I assume that each individual in any environment has a certain degree of antisocial tendency that is relatively consistent over time. Depending on age and circumstances, this can lead to offending or to other possible outcomes (e.g., truancy or school disruptiveness in childhood; spouse abuse or child neglect in adulthood). This part of the theory focuses only on offending outcomes. Some other theories also propose an underlying construct that leads to offending and other outcomes; for example, Gottfredson and Hirschi (1990) suggest that low self-control leads not only to offending but also to road accidents, sexual promiscuity, job instability, and so on.

Short-term, situationally-induced motivating factors that are conducive to offending include boredom, frustration, alcohol consumption, getting fired from a job, or quarrelling with a wife or girlfriend. Slightly longer-lasting life circumstances or events may also be important, such as unemployment, drug addiction, and shortage of money. A number of these kinds of factors are included in the models outlined by Cornish and Clarke (1986).

While it is obvious that offenses require opportunities, it is also likely that some individuals are more likely than others to seek out and create opportunities for offending and to select suitable victims. The "routine activities" theory of Cohen and Felson (1979) attempts to explain how opportunities for crime arise and change over time. They argue that criminal opportunities vary with routine activities that provide for basic needs such as food and shelter. For example, the increasing number of working women, coupled with the increase in single-parent, female-headed households, has created increasing numbers of houses left unoccupied during the day, thus providing increasing opportunities for burglary.

The final element of my theory proposes that whether an offense is committed in any opportunity is essentially a rational, hedonistic decision. Potential offenders weigh the benefits of offending (e.g., material goods stolen, enhanced status among peers, pleasure gained by seeing someone suffer) against the costs of offending (e.g., being caught by the police and punished by the courts, disapproval from parents or spouses) in relation to the benefits and costs of alternative behaviors. What matters are subjective probabilities and utilities of outcomes. For example, Farrington and Knight (1980) carried out a number of studies which suggested that the probability of stealing depended on subjectively expected utilities (i.e., probabilities × utilities).

Several other researchers have also proposed rational choice theories of offending (e.g., Wilson and Herrnstein 1985; Cornish and Clarke 1986), and these kinds of ideas underlie deterrence research (e.g., Erickson, Gibbs and Jensen 1977; Blumstein, Cohen, and Nagin 1978). It should be noted that a rational choice theory of offending is not necessarily incompatible with the fact that most offenses are committed impulsively—on the spur of the moment—rather than with advance planning (e.g., Erez 1987). Impulsively committed offenses are those with too much weight (utility) placed on immediate as opposed to long-term outcomes.

On my theory, the onset of offending depends partly on an increase in antisocial tendency (e.g., caused by a change in social influence from parents to peers) and partly on changes in situational factors, opportunities, benefits, and costs. Similarly, desistance occurs when there is a decrease in antisocial tendency (e.g., caused by a change in social influence from peers to spouses or girlfriends) and changes in situational factors. In the Cambridge Study, Farrington (1990a) showed that there was a significant decrease in the prevalence of several kinds of antisocial behaviors between ages eighteen and thirty-two, although the males who were relatively more antisocial at age eighteen were still relatively more antisocial at age thirty-two. Hence, there was both absolute change and relative consistency in antisocial tendency from the teenage years into adulthood.

Conclusions

In explaining the development and causes of offending and antisocial behavior, it seems clear that the cluster of constructs including impulsivity, hyperactivity, sensation seeking, and risk taking is very important. Furthermore, this crucial relevance has not previously been widely recognized, at least not by criminologists, who have rarely tried to measure impulsivity. Hence, an essential priority for the future should be to mount a research program centering on the link between impulsivity and antisocial behavior at different ages from birth to adulthood.

This research program should begin with a series of cross-sectional studies of people of different ages, and should aim to establish the interrelationships among all the different indicators of impulsivity and similar constructs. The key questions are whether there is only one underlying construct and which indicators are the most valid measures of the underlying construct(s). Other constructs should also be measured, such as the ability to manipulate abstract concepts, and there should be age-appropriate measures of antisocial behavior.

The cross-sectional studies should then be followed by multiple-cohort accelerated longitudinal studies of the type recommended by Tonry, Ohlin, and Farrington (1991). They proposed that seven cohorts should be followed up from the same city, beginning in the prenatal period and at ages three, six, nine, twelve, fifteen, and eighteen. The major focus in these projects would be to establish developmental and causal sequences including measures of impulsivity, antisocial behavior, and other constructs at different ages. Biological, psychological, family, peer, school, and community factors should all be measured, and changes within individuals in some factors linked to changes within individuals in others.

Frequent data collection (e.g., once a year) would be needed to pinpoint when changes and important life events occurred, especially the onsets of different types of offenses and antisocial acts. By linking up the different cohorts, it should also be possible to identify the escalation and deescalation of antisocial behavior and the eventual desistance which happens in many cases by the twenties. It is important to study how different explanatory factors interact to influence antisocial behavior, and especially to detect protective factors that might have important implications for prevention or treatment. This research program, in my view, would lead to a great advance in knowledge about the development and causes of offending and antisocial behavior.

References

Amdur, R. L. 1989. "Testing Causal Models of Delinquency: A Methodological Critique." *Criminal Justice and Behavior* 16, 35–62.

American Psychiatric Association. 1987. *Diagnostic and Statistical Manual of Mental Disorders*, 3rd ed. revised. Washington, D.C.: Author.

Blouin, A. G., C. K. Conners, W. T. Seidel, and J. Blouin. 1989. "The

Independence of Hyperactivity from Conduct Disorder: Methodological Considerations." *Canadian Journal of Psychiatry* 34, 279–82.

Blumstein, A. and J. Cohen. 1987. "Characterizing Criminal Careers." *Science* 237, 985–91.

Blumstein, A., J. Cohen, and D. P. Farrington. 1988. "Longitudinal and Criminal Career Research: Further Clarifications." *Criminology* 26, 57–74.

Blumstein, A., J. Cohen, and D. Nagin, Eds. 1978. *Deterrence and Incapacitation: Estimating the Effects of Criminal Sanctions on Crime Rates.* Washington, D.C.: National Academy of Sciences.

Blumstein, A., J. Cohen, J. A. Roth, and C. A. Visher, Eds. 1986. *Criminal Careers and "Career Criminals."* Washington, D.C.: National Academy Press.

Bouchard, T. J., D. T. Lykken, M. McGue, N. L. Segal, and A. Tellegen. 1990. "Sources of Human Psychological Differences: The Minnesota Study of Twins Reared Apart." *Science* 250, 223–28.

Bowlby, J. 1951. *Maternal Care and Mental Health.* Geneva: World Health Organization.

Breslau, N., N. Klein, and L. Allen. 1988. "Very Low Birthweight: Behavioral Sequelae at Nine Years of Age." *Journal of the American Academy of Child and Adolescent Psychiatry* 27, 605–12.

Brooks-Gunn, J., and F. F. Furstenberg. 1986. "The Children of Adolescent Mothers: Physical, Academic, and Psychological Outcomes." *Developmental Review* 6, 224–51.

Cloninger, C. R., S. Sigvardsson, M. Bohman, and A. von Knorring. 1982. "Predisposition to Petty Criminality in Swedish Adoptees. II. Cross-Fostering Analysis of Gene-Environment Interaction." *Archives of General Psychiatry* 39, 1242–47.

Cloward, R. A. and L. E. Ohlin. 1960. *Delinquency and Opportunity.* New York: Free Press.

Cohen, A. K. 1955. *Delinquent Boys.* Glencoe, IL: Free Press.

Cohen, L. E. and M. Felson. 1979. "Social Change and Crime Trends: A Routine Activity Approach." *American Sociological Review* 44, 588–608.

Cornish, D. B., and R. V. Clarke, Eds. 1986. *The Reasoning Criminal.* New York: Springer-Verlag.

Elliott, D. S., D. Huizinga, and S. S. Ageton. 1985. *Explaining Delinquency and Drug Use.* Beverly Hills, CA: Sage.

Erez, E. 1987. "Situational or Planned Crime and the Criminal Career." In *From Boy to Man, From Delinquency to Crime,* edited by M. E. Wolfgang, T. P. Thornberry, and R. M. Figlio, 122–133. Chicago: University of Chicago Press.

Erickson, M., J. P. Gibbs, and G. F. Jensen. 1977. "The Deterrence Doctrine and the Perceived Certainty of Legal Punishment." *American Sociological Review* 42, 305–17.

Eysenck, H. J. 1977. *Crime and Personality*, 3rd ed. London: Routledge and Kegan Paul.

Eysenck, H. J. and G. H. Gudjonsson. 1989. *The Causes and Cures of Criminality*. New York: Plenum.

Farrington, D. P. 1986. "Age and Crime." In *Crime and Justice*, vol. 7, edited by M. Tonry and N. Morris, 189–250. Chicago: University of Chicago Press.

Farrington, D. P. 1987. "Implications of Biological Findings for Criminological Research." In *The Causes of Crime: New Biological Approaches*, edited by S. A. Mednick, T. E. Moffitt, and S. A. Stack, 42–64. Cambridge: Cambridge University Press.

Farrington, D. P. 1988. "Studying Changes Within Individuals: The Causes of Offending." In *Studies of Psychosocial Risk*, edited by M. Rutter, 158–83. Cambridge: Cambridge University Press.

Farrington, D. P. 1989. "Self-Reported and Official Offending from Adolescence to Adulthood." In *Cross-National Research in Self-Reported Crime and Delinquency*, edited by M. W. Klein, 399–423. Dordrecht, Netherlands: Kluwer.

Farrington, D. P. 1990a. "Age, period, cohort, and offending." In *Policy and Theory in Criminal Justice: Contributions in Honor of Leslie T. Wilkins*, edited by D. M. Gottfredson and R. V. Clarke, 51–75. Aldershot, England: Avebury.

Farrington, D. P. 1990b. "Implications of Criminal Career Research for the Prevention of Offending." *Journal of Adolescence* 13, 93–113.

Farrington, D. P. 1991a. "Antisocial Personality from Childhood to Adulthood." *The Psychologist* 4, in press.

Farrington, D. P. 1991b. "Childhood Aggression and Adult Violence: Early Precursors and Later Life Outcomes." In *The Development and Treatment of Childhood Aggression*, edited by D. J. Pepler and K. H. Rubin, 5–29. Hillsdale, NJ: Lawrence Erlbaum.

Farrington, D. P., B. Gallagher, L. Morley, R. J. St. Ledger, and D. J. West. 1986b. "Unemployment, School Leaving, and Crime." *British Journal of Criminology* 26, 335–56.

Farrington, D. P., B. Gallagher, L. Morley, R. J. St. Ledger, and D. J. West. 1988a. "Are There any Successful Men from Criminogenic Backgrounds?" *Psychiatry* 51, 116–30.

Farrington, D. P., and J. D. Hawkins. 1991. "Predicting Participation, Early Onset, and Later Persistence in Officially Recorded Offending." *Criminal Behavior and Mental Health* 1, 1–33.

Farrington, D. P. and B. J. Knight. 1980. "Four Studies of Stealing as a Risky Decision." In *New Directions in Psycholegal Research,* edited by P. D. Lipsitt and B. D. Sales, 26–50. New York: Van Nostrand Reinhold.

Farrington, D. P., R. Loeber, D. S. Elliott, J. D. Hawkins, D. B. Kandel, M. W. Klein, J. McCord, D. C. Rowe, and R. E. Tremblay. 1990a. "Advancing knowledge about the onset of delinquency and crime." In *Advances in Clinical Child Psychology,* vol. 1, edited by B. B. Lahey and A. E. Kazdin, 283–342. New York: Plenum.

Farrington, D. P., R. Loeber, and W. B. Van Kammen. 1990b. "Long-term Criminal Outcomes of Hyperactivity-Impulsivity-Attention Deficit and Conduct Problems in Childhood." In *Straight and Devious Pathways from Childhood to Adulthood,* edited by L. N. Robins and M. Rutter, 62–81. Cambridge: Cambridge University Press.

Farrington, D. P., L. E. Ohlin, and J. Q. Wilson. 1986a. *Understanding and Controlling Crime.* New York: Springer-Verlag.

Farrington, D. P., H. N. Snyder, and T. A. Finnegan. 1988b. "Specialization in Juvenile Court Careers." *Criminology* 26, 461–87.

Farrington, D. P. and D. J. West. 1990. "The Cambridge Study in Delinquent Development: A Long-Term Follow-up of 411 London Males." In *Criminality: Personality, Behavior, Life History,* edited by H. J. Kerner and G. Kaiser, 115–38. Berlin: Springer-Verlag.

Gottfredson, M. and T. Hirschi. 1987. "The Methodological Adequacy of Longitudinal Research on Crime." *Criminology* 25, 581–614.

Gottfredson, M., and T. Hirschi. 1988. "Science, Public Policy, and the Career Paradigm." *Criminology* 26, 37–55.

Gottfredson, M., and T. Hirschi. 1990. *A General Theory of Crime.* Stanford, CA: Stanford University Press.

Hardt, R. H. and S. J. Peterson. 1968. "Arrests of Self and Friends as Indicators of Delinquency Involvement." *Journal of Research in Crime and Delinquency* 5, 44–51.

Hare, R. D. 1980. "A Research Scale for the Assessment of Psychopathy in Criminal Populations." *Personality and Individual Differences* 1, 111—19.

Hawkins, J. D., D. M. Lishner, R. F. Catalano, and M. O. Howard. 1986. "Childhood Predictors of Adolescent Substance Use: Toward an Empirically Grounded Theory." *Journal of Children in Contemporary Society* 8, 11–48.

Hindelang, M. J., T. Hirschi, and J. G. Weis. 1981. *Measuring Delinquency.* Beverly Hills, CA: Sage.

Hirschi, T. 1969. *Causes of Delinquency.* Berkeley, CA: University of California Press.

Klein, M. W. 1984. "Offense Specialization and Versatility Among Juveniles." *British Journal of Criminology* 24, 185–94.

Loeber, R. 1987. "Behavioral Precursors and Accelerators of Delinquency." In *Explaining Criminal Behavior*, edited by W. Buikhuisen and S. A. Mednick, 51–67. Leiden: Brill.

Loeber, R., and T. Dishion. 1983. "Early Predictors of Male Delinquency: A Review." *Psychological Bulletin* 94, 68–99.

Loeber, R., and M. Stouthamer-Loeber, 1986. "Family factors as correlates and predictors of juvenile conduct problems and delinquency." In *Crime and Justice*, vol. 7, edited by M. Tonry and N. Morris, 29–149. Chicago: University of Chicago Press.

Loeber, R. and M. Stouthamer-Loeber. 1987. "Prediction." In *Handbook of Juvenile Delinquency*, edited by H. C. Quay, 325–82. New York: Wiley.

Magnusson, D. 1988. *Individual Development from an Interactional Perspective*. Hillsdale, NJ: Erlbaum.

Mawson, A. R. 1987. *Transient Criminality*. New York: Praeger.

McCord, J. 1977. "A Comparative Study of Two Generations of Native Americans." In *Theory in Criminology*, edited by R. F. Meier, 83–92. Beverly Hills, CA: Sage.

McCord, J. 1979. "Some Child-Rearing Antecedents of Criminal Behavior in Adult Men." *Journal of Personality and Social Psychology* 37, 1477–86.

McCord, J. 1990. "Long-Term Perspectives on Parental Absence." In *Straight and Devious Pathways from Childhood to Adulthood*, edited by L. N. Robins and M. Rutter, 116–34. Cambridge: Cambridge University Press.

Mednick, S. A., W. F. Gabrielli, and B. Hutchings. 1983. "Genetic Influences on Criminal Behavior: Evidence from an Adoption Cohort." In *Prospective Studies of Crime and Delinquency*, edited by K. T. Van Dusen and S. A. Mednick, 39–56. Boston: Kluwer-Nijhoff.

Moffitt, T. E. 1990. "The neuropsychology of juvenile delinquency: A critical review." In *Crime and Justice*, vol. 12, edited by M. Tonry and N. Morris, 99–169. Chicago: University of Chicago Press.

Moffitt, T. E., and P. A. Silva. 1988. "Neuropsychological Deficit and Self-Reported Delinquency in an Unselected Birth Cohort." *Journal of the American Academy of Child and Adolescent Psychiatry* 27, 233–40.

Novy, D. M., and S. Donahue. 1985. "The Relationship Between Adolescent Life Stress Events and Delinquent Conduct Including Conduct Indicating a Need for Supervision." *Adolescence* 20, 313–21.

Olweus, D. 1987. "Testosterone and Adrenaline: Aggressive Antisocial Behavior in Normal Adolescent Males." In *The Causes of Crime: New*

Biological Approaches, edited by S. A. Mednick, T. E. Moffitt, and S. A. Stack, 263–82. Cambridge: Cambridge University Press.

Patterson, G. R. 1982. *Coercive Family Process*. Eugene, OR: Castalia.

Reiss, A. J. 1986. "Why are Communities Important in Understanding Crime?" In *Communities and Crime*, edited by A. J. Reiss and M. Tonry, 1–33. Chicago: University of Chicago Press.

Richman, N., J. Stevenson, and P. Graham. 1982. *Preschool to School*. London: Academic Press.

Robins, L. N. 1979. "Sturdy Childhood Predictors of Adult Outcomes: Replications from Longitudinal Studies." In *Stress and Mental Disorder*, edited by J. E. Barrett, R. M. Rose, and G. L. Klerman, 219–35. New York: Raven Press.

Robins, L. N. 1986. "Changes in Conduct Disorder Over Time." In *Risk in Intellectual and Social Development*, edited by D. C. Farran and J. D. McKinney, 227–59. New York: Academic Press.

Robins, L. N., and K. S. Ratcliff. 1978. "Risk Factors in the Continuation of Childhood Antisocial Behavior into Adulthood." *International Journal of Mental Health* 7, 96–116.

Robins, L. N., and K. S. Ratcliff. 1980. "Childhood Conduct Disorders and Later Arrest." In *The Social Consequences of Psychiatric Illness*, edited by L. N. Robins, P. J. Clayton and J. K. Wing, 248–63. New York: Brunner/Mazel.

Robins, L. N., and E. Wish. 1977. "Childhood Deviance as a Developmental Process: A Study of 223 Urban Black Men from Birth to 18." *Social Forces* 56, 448–73.

Ross, R. R., and B. D. Ross. 1988. "Delinquency Prevention Through Cognitive Training." *New Education* 10, 70–75.

Rutter, M., B. Maughan, P. Mortimore, and J. Ouston. 1979. *Fifteen Thousand Hours*. London: Open Books.

Shaw, C. R., and H. D. McKay. 1969. *Juvenile Delinquency and Urban Areas* (rev. ed.). Chicago: University of Chicago Press.

Spivack, G., J. Marcus, and M. Swift. 1986. "Early Classroom Behaviors and Later Misconduct." *Developmental Psychology* 22, 124–31.

Stander, J., D. P. Farrington, G. Hill, and P. M. E. Altham. 1989. "Markov Chain Analysis and Specialization in Criminal Careers." *British Journal of Criminology* 29, 317–35.

Sutherland, E. H., and D. R. Cressey. 1974. *Criminology* (9th ed.). Philadelphia: Lippincott.

Szatmari, P., M. Reitsma-Street, and D. R. Offord. 1986. "Pregnancy and Birth Complications in Antisocial Adolescents and their Siblings." *Canadian Journal of Psychiatry* 31, 513–16.

Thomas, A., and S. Chess. 1984. "Genesis and Evolution of Behavioral

Disorders: From Infancy to Early Adult Life." *American Journal of Psychiatry* 141, 1–9.

Thornberry, T. P., and M. Farnworth. 1982. "Social Correlates of Criminal Involvement: Further Evidence on the Relationship Between Social Status and Criminal Behavior." *American Sociological Review* 47, 505–18.

Tonry, M., L. E. Ohlin, and D. P. Farrington. 1991. *Human Development and Criminal Behavior.* New York: Springer-Verlag.

Trasler, G. B. 1962. *The Explanation of Criminality.* London: Routledge and Kegan Paul.

Venables, P. H., and A. Raine. 1987. "Biological Theory." In *Applying Psychology to Imprisonment,* edited by B. J. McGurk, D. M. Thornton and M. Williams, 3–27. London: Her Majesty's Stationery Office.

Virkkunen, M. 1988. "Cerebrospinal Fluid: Monoamine Metabolites Among Habitually Violent and Impulsive Offenders." In *Biological Contributions to Crime Causation,* edited by T. E. Moffitt and S. A. Mednick, 147–57. Dordrecht, Netherlands: Nijhoff.

Wadsworth, M. 1979. *Roots of Delinquency.* London: Martin Robertson.

Werner, E. E. 1989. "High-risk Children in Young Adulthood: A Longitudinal Study from Birth to 32 Years." *American Journal of Orthopsychiatry* 59, 72–81.

West, D. J. 1969. *Present Conduct and Future Delinquency.* London: Heinemann.

West, D. J. 1982. *Delinquency: Its Roots, Careers and Prospects.* London: Heinemann.

West, D. J. and D. P. Farrington. 1973. *Who Becomes Delinquent?* London: Heinemann.

West, D. J. and D. P. Farrington. 1977. *The Delinquent Way of Life.* London: Heinemann.

White, H. R., Labouvie, E. W. and M. E. Bates. 1985. "The Relationship Between Sensation Seeking and Delinquency: A Longitudinal Analysis." *Journal of Research in Crime and Delinquency* 22, 197–211.

Widom, C. S. 1989. "The Cycle of Violence." *Science* 244, 160–66.

Wilson, J. Q. and R. J. Herrnstein. 1985. *Crime and Human Nature.* New York: Simon and Schuster.

12

Autonomic Activity/Reactivity, Behavior, and Crime in a Longitudinal Perspective

David Magnusson, Britt af Klinteberg, and Håkan Stattin

Although the role of biological factors in individual functioning was emphasized early (cf., Angell 1907), until very recently one of the main characteristics of psychological research has been its neglect of such factors. This circumstance has considerably limited the effectiveness of research, the purpose of which is to understand why individuals think, feel, act, and react as they do in real life, which is the ultimate goal of psychology as a scientific discipline (Magnusson 1988).

One of the main reasons underlying the reluctance of researchers to incorporate biological factors in their theoretical models and to integrate them in the planning and implementation of empirical research has been the reductionistic view of the role of such factors. This implies that the role of biological factors in individual functioning has been one of one-way directed causality: biology first, followed by the individual's thoughts, feelings, actions, and reactions. This view is still influential, both in medicine and psychology. However, it has been increasingly superseded, theoretically, by a competing approach according to which biological factors operate in a process of continuous reciprocal interaction of factors within the individual and factors in his/her environment (cf., Hofer 1981; Weiner 1977). Such a view forms a core element in the interactional model of individual functioning (Magnusson 1988).

According to the interactional model of individual functioning, an individual functions and develops as a totality, in a way that can be described as a *multidetermined, stochastic process.* The model implies many factors operating in a probabilistic, most often non-linear way. The functioning of an individual is characterized by a continuously ongoing, reciprocal interaction between perceptual-cognitive-emotional factors and biological factors within the individual and social and physical factors in his/her environment. This interactive process may seem complex and chaotic but is coherent and lawful. It is a scientific challenge to identify the factors involved and the mechanisms by which they operate. (For a more comprehensive presentation and discussion of this view, see Magnusson 1988, 1990). One consequence of this view is that we have to include biological factors in our models, if we wish to effectively study individual functioning in general and delinquency and criminal activity in particular.

The autonomic nervous system plays a central role in the physiological system of the individual. Of particular interest for our purposes is the way the sympathetic nervous system is alerted by perceived external demands of achievement or threat (via nerve impulses from the hypothalamus) and how it activates the medulla of the two adrenal glands that are located just above the kidneys, causing excretion of the hormone adrenaline. The excretion of adrenaline is, therefore, a sensitive measure of an individual's general level of physiological activity and of his/her reactivity to external stimulation.

The purpose of this paper is to present empirical data on the relationships between adrenaline excretion, as an indication of autonomic reaction to environmental events and conditions, on the one hand, and problem behaviors and criminal activity, on the other, and to discuss these results in a theoretical framework. The issue will be illuminated by cross-sectional data for relationships among these factors and by data obtained from longitudinal studies designed to elucidate the development process underlying adult antisocial behavior. The data originate from a longitudinal research program that was based on an interactional model of individual functioning.

Data

The total research group consisted of all boys in a mid-Swedish community of about 100,000 inhabitants who attended grade three of the compulsory school system in 1965, at an average age of ten. For our purpose it is noteworthy that more than 99 percent of the ten-year old boys in the community did attend the compulsory school. The community consists of a town with a heterogenous labor market and the surrounding rural area. Thus, a broad range of upbringing conditions were represented. Data collection, and the analyses of the psychometric properties of data and other relevant information were presented in Magnusson (1988) and Magnusson, Dunér, and Zetterblom (1975). A brief presentation of the data relevant to the purposes of this article is given here.

Behavior

All boys were rated by their teachers at the age of ten and thirteen, with respect to various aspects of manifest behavior. Different teachers performed the ratings at the two age levels, after having had the opportunity to observe their pupils during three years of schooling. The behavior patterns rated included aggressiveness, motor restlessness, and lack of ability to concentrate. For each of these behaviors the teacher rated his/her pupils on a seven-point scale with verbal descriptions of the endpoints. In the analyses presented here the sum of the two latter variables was used as an indicator of hyperactive behavior.

It should be observed that the ratings were obtained for all boys who belonged to the appropriate age group in the school system at the time of data collection.

Criminal Activity

Data on criminal activity were based on registered instances of law-breaking, and were collected from national and local sources (Stattin and Magnusson 1989). Information on offences committed before the subjects' fifteenth birthday was supplied by the local police and social authorities. Police and social authorities in all police districts in which the boys had lived up to fifteen years of age were contacted and asked to provide information on offences. Information on offences committed by the subjects after their fifteenth birthday was supplied by the National Police Board. These data cover all offences leading to public prosecution and conviction. Finally, data on arrests and temporary custody were supplied by all police districts in which the subjects had lived up to age thirty.

In summary, data on delinquency cover: (1) offences committed up to age fifteen leading to any form of proceedings taken by social authorities, i.e., the Child Welfare Committee; (2) offences leading to prosecution and conviction after the age of criminal responsibility (fifteen years of age); and (3) offences leading to arrest or temporary custody (most often due to disorderly conduct or drunkenness). Data on criminal offences were obtained for all the subjects in the research group. Therefore, there were no drop outs.

Autonomic Activity/Reactivity

As a measure of autonomic activity/reactivity, data for the excretion of adrenaline in urine were collected during two different situations. This was done for a subsample of boys when they were about thirteen years of age. Urine samples were collected under standardized conditions after a normal, nonstressful situation (viewing a film on ore-mining) and after a stressful, achievement-demanding situation (performance on an attention-demanding mental arithmetic test). The samples were analyzed according to a fluorimetric technique (von Euler and Lishajko 1961) and analytical procedures are described in detail in Johansson, Frankenhaeuser, and Magnusson (1973).

Behavior and Autonomic Activity/Reactivity—a Cross-Sectional Perspective

In general, empirical findings point to a positive correlation between good social and personal adjustment and high adrenaline excretion. This has been shown for relative achievement (Bergman and Magnusson 1979), for emotional balance, and concentration ability in schoolwork (Johansson et al. 1973), for ego strength (Roessler, Burch, and Mufford 1967) and for well-adjusted social behavior and intellectual level (Lambert, Johansson, Frankenhaeuser, and Klackenberg-Larsson 1969). In agreement with these results, a negative relationship has been observed between antisocial behavior and delinquency, on the one hand, and adrenaline excretion, on the other. In a study using the same research sample as that used in the present study, Johansson et al. (1973) reported significant negative correlations on a magnitude of $-.22$ to $-.34$ between level of adrenaline excretion and different types of conduct disturbances. In a subsequent study Magnusson, Stattin, and Dunér (1983) showed that the relationship was nonlinear. While the boys with the most extreme ratings for conduct disturbance were characterized by low adrenaline excretion, marginal differences were obtained among the rest of the boys.

Catecholamine excretion in criminals was investigated by Lidberg, Levander, Schalling, and Lidberg (1978). A group of men taken into custody and rated as highly psychopathic (indicated by measures of low socialization, high impulsiveness, and low empathy), showed a conspicuously lower increase in adrenaline and noradrenaline excretion when faced with a strong relevant stressor, that is, the situation immediately before a trial, than did men in custody who were rated as slightly psychopathic. For a subgroup of maximum security patients who were convicted for physically violent offenses, arrested men who were low in psychopathy, showed lower levels of adrenaline than for subgroups of mixed offenders and normal control subjects (Woodman, Hinton, and O'Neill 1977). Olweus (1986) has presented data that show a strong, significant, negative correlation between adrenaline level and a composite of ratings of unprovoked aggressive, destructive behavior.

Empirical studies by Boydstun and coworkers (1968), Satterfield and Dawson (1971), Satterfield, Cantwell, and Satterfield (1974), and Klove and Hole (1979) indicated a systematic relationship between physiological arousal and hyperactivity, implying low CNS arousal in hyperactive children (see also Taylor 1980). Taken together, the empirical studies in this area generally indicate lower adrenaline levels for subjects with social adjustment problems.

Aggressiveness and Hyperactivity vs. Adrenaline Excretion

Two specific aspects of antisocial behavior appear to be particularly relevant in relation to autonomic activity/reactivity, that is to say, aggressiveness and hyperactive behavior. So far, empirical results support the assumption that both aggressiveness and hyperactivity are systematically related to low autonomic activity/reactivity. Since it has been assumed that the sympathetic-adrenal medullary system that regulates excretion of the catecholamines adrenaline and noradrenaline plays a major role in mobilizing the acute adaptive resources used to manage environmental situations (Frankenhaeuser 1979), it is noteworthy that some results have revealed "paradoxical" adrenaline reactivity in some subjects; that is, lower adrenaline excretion during periods of high mental load than during control periods. This might indicate a "lack of response" to environmental demands (Johansson 1976) or a coping deficiency. Low levels of adrenaline output in puberty have accordingly been found in young delinquent adults (Magnusson 1987) as well as in hyperactive delinquents (Levander, Mattsson, Schalling, and Dalteg 1987).

According to DSM IIIR (American Psychiatric Association 1987) the criteria for clinical hyperactivity include the following: Difficulty in sustaining attention (especially in unstructured situations); excessive general hyperactivity or motor restlessness (fidgeting); and impulsive behavior (careless working). Early research considered aggressiveness to be part of this syndrome (Mendelson, Johnson, and Stewart 1971; Stewart, Pitts, Graig, and Dieruf 1966). Recently, however, hyperactivity has been found to occur both with and without aggressive components (McGee, Williams, and Silva 1984; Stewart, Cummings, Singer, and de Blois 1981; Bergman and Magnusson 1984). The importance of considering aggressiveness in the diagnosis of hyperactive children has been suggested (Langhorne and Loney 1979; Loney, Langhorne, and Paternite 1978). Motor restlessness and aggressiveness have an activity component in common and are interrelated, although aggressiveness has been found to be more situation-dependent (McGee et al. 1984). Recently, there has been an increasing interest in mild forms of aggressiveness and hyperactivity and, consequently, a tendency to regard the concepts more as dimensions or continuous traits than as diagnostic syndromes (cf., af Klinteberg, Magnusson, and Schalling 1989).

However, few studies have been conducted using representative groups of normal children. A study in the present longitudinal project was designated to elucidate the relationships between early behavioral and physiological indicators of a possible underlying vulnerability for aggressiveness and hyperactivity, and later social and/or pervasive conduct problems for a representative group of boys thirteen years of age (af Klinteberg and Magnusson, 1989).

The relationships between aggressiveness and hyperactive behavior (as defined by summarized ratings of Motor Restlessness and Concentration Difficulties), versus adrenaline excretion in a normal (An) and a stressful situation (As) (as described above) were investigated in the same subjects and found to be significantly negatively related. The relationships between aggressiveness and hyperactive behavior versus adrenaline excretion in the two situations were then further examined by studying the partial relationships, that is, the unique effects of the two aspects of antisocial behavior on adrenaline excretion. A dichotomization of the distribution of scores for Aggressiveness and Hyperactive behavior yielded four groups (see table 12.1).

The results presented in table 12.1 indicate that a combination of Aggressiveness and Hyperactive behavior is particularly related to low autonomic activity/reactivity. However, in subsequent two-way ANOVAs, in which each main effect is adjusted for the other factor and two-way interactions assessed with all main effects held constant, there were no significant effects in the normal situation. In the stressful situation, however, there was a significant main effect

TABLE 12.1
Mean Adrenaline Excretion in a Normal (An) and a Stressful (As) Situation (±
standard errors; SE) in Four Groups with Various Combinations of Aggressiveness
and Hyperactive Behavior.

Aggressiveness	Hyperactive behavior	An (SE)	As (SE)	N
Low	Low	9.90 (0.9)	12.93 (1.0)	50
Low	High	8.03 (1.9)	10.60 (2.7)	5
High	Low	8.50 (1.9)	12.71 (2.0)	11
High	High	6.45 (0.8)	7.33 (0.6)	20

of Hyperactive behavior on adrenaline excretion (p<0.03) when Aggressiveness was controlled for, but not of Aggressiveness (ns) when Hyperactive behavior was controlled. Thus, the lower adrenaline excretion levels were found in the group classified as "high" in Hyperactive behavior. These results imply that the significant, negative relationship between Aggressiveness and adrenaline excretion, reported earlier, was accounted for by the Hyperactive behavior component of the ratings of Aggressiveness.

Hyperactive Behavior Components and Adrenaline Excretion

In order to further elucidate the relationship between hyperactive behavior and adrenaline excretion, the specific relationships of each hyperactive behavior component to adrenaline excretion were studied. A dichotomization of the distributions of scores in the hyperactivity-related variables yielded another set of four groups. Boys classified as "low" on both Motor Restlessness and Concentration Difficulties formed the non-hyperactive group (cell A in figures 12.1 and 12.2) and boys classified as "high" on both these variables the hyperactive group (cell D in figs. 12.1 and 12.2). Means and standard errors of adrenaline excretion (ng/min) in the two situations for the groups A–D are presented in figures 12.1–12.2.

Three questions, related to the figures 12.1 and 12.2 were examined. Question 1: Do those who were characterized by high ratings on both Motor Restlessness and Concentration Difficulties differ from those who were classified as "low" in both respects? Planned t-tests of differences in adrenaline excretion between the hyperactive (cell D) and the non-hyperactive (cell A) groups were significant in both the normal and the stressful situations (p<0.03; and p<0.01, respectively), which could be expected from the results reported above. Question 2: Does the nonhyperactive group differ in adrenaline excretion from all other subjects? One-way analyses of variance indicated that subjects in the non-hyperactive group (cell A) had significantly higher levels of adrenaline excretion in the normal situation than did subjects with high scores in either Motor Restlessness or Concentration Difficulties, or both, (p<0.01). A similar tendency was seen in the stressful situation (p<0.06). Question 3: Does the hyperactive group differ with respect to adrenaline excretion from all the other subjects? There was no significant difference

FIGURE 12.1

Mean Adrenaline Excretion (ng/min) in a Normal (An) Situation in Four Groups of
Boys (A–D) at the Age of Thirteen, Yielded by Dichotomized Scores in Motor
Restlessness and Concentration Difficulties at the Same Age.

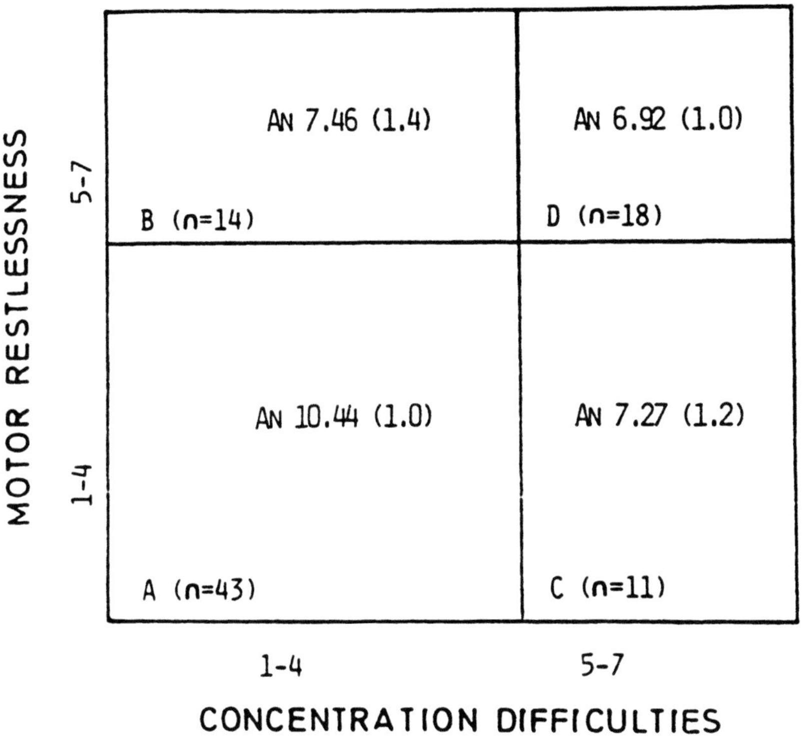

	CONCENTRATION DIFFICULTIES	
MOTOR RESTLESSNESS 5-7	AN 7.46 (1.4) B (n=14)	AN 6.92 (1.0) D (n=18)
MOTOR RESTLESSNESS 1-4	AN 10.44 (1.0) A (n=43)	AN 7.27 (1.2) C (n=11)
	1-4	5-7

in adrenaline excretion in the normal situation. In a covariance
correction for base-line adrenaline excretion (An), the adjusted
difference in adrenaline output in the stressful situation between
the hyperactive group (cell D) and all other subjects was still
significant ($p < 0.05$), with hyperactive boys having lower adrenaline
excretion (cf. figure 12.2).

To study the combination of hyperactivity and low autonomic
reactivity in individuals, patterns of autonomic activity/reactivity
and hyperactive behavior components were studied using a configural frequency analysis (CFA; Bergman and Magnusson 1984;
Krauth and Lienert 1982). As shown in table 12.2 a significant
excess of cell frequencies ("types") was found: one supporting the
hypothesis that hyperactive behavior is related to low adrenaline

FIGURE 12.2
Mean Adrenaline Excretion (ng/min) in a Stressful (As) Situation in Four Groups of
Boys at the Age of Thirteen, Yielded by Dichotomized Scores in Motor Restlessness
and Concentration Difficulties at the Same Age.

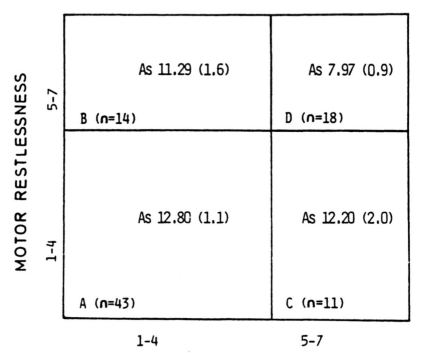

TABLE 12.2
Significant configurational types for dichotomized variable measures of adrenaline
output in a normal (An) and a stressful (As) situation, and two hyperactivity-related
variables, Motor Restlessness (MR) and Concentration Difficulties (CD), for a group
of normal boys (N = 86) at the age of 13.

Pattern				Size		z	Level of sign
An	As	MR	CD	Obtained	Expected		Adjusted level
low	low	high	high	13	2.51	6.72	<.0001
high	high	low	low	22	9.57	4.25	<.0003

Note: The adjustment level of significance was obtained by multiplying the nominal significance level by 16 (the number of all possible variable combinations in the present
design).

excretion in both a normal and a stressful situation, the other indicating a frequent combination of high adrenaline output in a normal and a stressful situation with low scores on hyperactivity-related variables such as Motor Restlessness and Concentration Difficulties. No other combination of variables yielded groups with frequencies that approached significance.

Comments

The results of strong relationships between hyperactivity and low autonomic activity/reactivity, in terms of adrenaline excretion in a cross-sectional perspective, support the hypothesis that low sympathetic-adrenal reactivity to external demands might be considered as a possible indicator of vulnerability for social and/or pervasive conduct disturbances. It is of interest that the significant correlation between Aggressiveness and adrenaline excretion in the stressful situation vanished when the effect of Hyperactive behavior was controlled for, whereas the relationship between Hyperactive behavior and adrenaline excretion was still significant when the effect of Aggressiveness was controlled. This is important in view of recent research with hyperactive children treated with stimulants. This research provides evidence of clinical improvements, operationally defined as decreased motor activity and impulsivity, and improvement on vigilance tasks (Rapoport 1984), and improved information processing (Coons, Klorman, and Borgstedt 1987). Improvements following stimulant treatment are also reported in Attention Deficit Disorder (ADD) adults who were hyperactive as children (Wender, Reimherr, and Wood 1981). Such improvements are suggested to be mediated by catecholamine release (Brown, Ebert, Mikkelsen, and Hunt 1979, 1980).

There is further support for the hypothesis that hyperactivity might be related to an underlying vulnerability related to more persistent maladjustment: Subjects in the present hyperactive behavior group were found to have higher Impulsiveness-scale scores than did the non-hyperactive group ($p < .01$) at an early adult age, that is, fourteen years later (af Klinteberg et al. 1989). The results indicated that hyperactive behavior is an important antecedent of adult impulsivity, which in turn has been shown to be connected with criminal behavior, alcohol abuse, and other disinhibitory syn-

dromes (Schalling, Edman, and Åsberg 1983; Gorenstein and Newman 1980).

Criminal Activity and Autonomic Activity/Reactivity in a Longitudinal Perspective

The studies and empirical results referred to in the preceding
sections all concerned the relationship between conduct and autonomic activity/reactivity in a cross-sectional perspective. To understand the role of biological factors in the developmental processes
underlying criminal activity, longitudinal data are needed for each
individual. This section will analyze the relationship between autonomic activity/reactivity at an early age and later criminal activity.

In an earlier study of data from the research project the differences between three groups of males, that is, those who had been
registered for 0, 1–3 (sporadic offenders) and four or more (frequent
offenders) crimes, were analyzed with respect to crime registration:
(a) not at all; (b) before the age of eighteen; and (c) from the age of
eighteen.

The results revealed an interesting pattern. An overall test of the
differences in mean adrenaline excretion among the three groups of
males with respect to registration during adolescence was not
significant. However, it was noteworthy that the small group of
males who were registered for four or more criminal offences before
the age of eighteen had considerably lower adrenaline excretion
than those who were not registered for crime and those who had
committed sporadic offences. The standard deviation for frequent
offenders was considerably lower than that for the other groups,
indicating that they form a more homogeneous group.

In adulthood, from eighteen years of age, the picture was different. The overall test of differences among the means showed a
significance at the 1 percent level for the normal situation and at
the 5 percent level for the stressful situation. At this age level, both
those registered for sporadic crimes and those registered for four
or more crimes had not only significantly but also considerably
lower mean adrenaline excretion in both situations, again with
considerably lower standard deviations. The results indicated that
these groups were more homogeneous with respect to autonomic
activity/reactivity than those not registered for crime.

Of particular interest in the pattern of relationships revealed by this study was the fact that the level of adrenaline excretion was not significantly related to sporadic offences during adolescence. It is possible that subcultural and age-bound factors behind delinquency during adolescence, being unrelated to mechanisms underlying excretion of adrenaline, operate to mask the adrenaline-delinquency association during this age period. If this is the case it might mean that those boys who conform after delinquency during adolescence constitute a somewhat different group of boys, neurophysiologically, than those who continue with later criminal activity. Taken together with the finding of lower levels of adrenaline excretion in boys with severe behavior problems than in boys without or with less behavior problems documented earlier, this would suggest that within the group of delinquent boys during adolescence, those who continued with criminal activity can be expected to show lower levels of adrenaline excretion than those who conform. One indication in this direction was the fact that all those five adolescents who had been registered for four or more criminal offences also had been registered at adulthood at least two times.

The assumption is supported by the data presented in figure 12.3. The mean adrenaline excretion at the age of thirteen in the two independent situations is shown for four groups of males: (a) those not registered for crime before the age of thirty; (b) those registered only before eighteen years of age; (c) those registered only from the age of eighteen; and (d) those registered both during adolescence and as adults.

Figure 12.3 validates the assumption that two groups of adolescent delinquents can be distinguished with respect to autonomic activity/reactivity as reflected in adrenaline excretion. Those who conform before the age of eighteen actually showed a somewhat, but not significantly, higher adrenaline excretion than those not registered for crime. The mean adrenaline excretion for those males registered for crime from adolescence through adulthood differs significantly from the mean adrenaline excretion in the group with no criminal offences. This is true for both the normal situation ($p = .004$) and the stressful situation ($p = .007$). The adulthood group also differ significantly in both situations ($p = .025$ and $p = .012$,

FIGURE 12.3

Adrenaline excretion (ng/min) in a normal and in a stressful situation, for individuals with: (a) no registered crime; (b) registered crime only before the age of eighteen; (c) registered crime only from the age of eighteen; and (d) registered crime both before and from the age of eighteen.

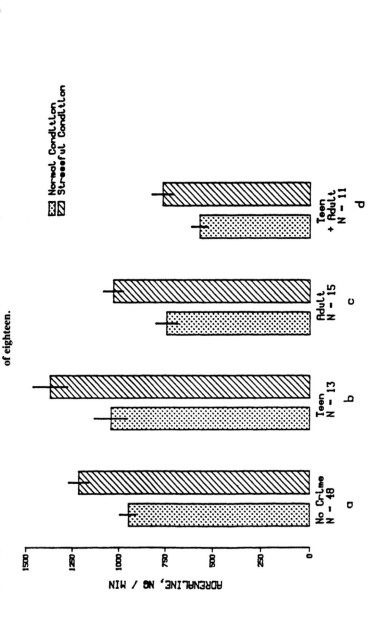

respectively) from those registered for crime only during adolescence.

Comments

These results of lower autonomic activity/reactivity in the persistent criminal group might be of interest to consider in a broader perspective of relationships between autonomic arousal, socialization, and criminal activity (for reviews, see Hare 1978; Schalling 1978; Venables 1987). While most previous studies have pointed to results of lower autonomic arousal in delinquents than in nondelinquents, some studies have not been able to support these results (cf., McCord 1990). In the present longitudinal study, it was expected that a sub-group of persistent criminals would have a history of hyperactive behavior. Subjects in this subgroup were significantly overrepresented among the persistent criminals in the present study: Ten out of the eleven persistent criminal subjects had high hyperactivity scores at age thirteen (sum score of ten or higher on ratings of Motor Restlessness and Concentration Difficulties), which is significantly more frequent than could be expected by chance ($p<.0001$). Thus, the lower adrenaline excretion in these persistent criminals compared to all the other subjects (An: $p = .05$; As: $p = .02$) is in line with expectations. It should be noted that there was no assumption that all persistent criminals have lower adrenaline excretion, here used as an indicator of autonomic arousal. From a theoretical point of view, however, it is of interest to see that the hypothesized sub-group was markedly overrepresented among the persistent criminals, a result which might have some implications for future research and for intervention programs.

Hyperactivity and Criminality

So far, the present study has demonstrated that low autonomic activity/reactivity characterizes both hyperactive children and persistent offenders. In this perspective it is important to note that a strong relationship existed between early adolescent hyperactivity and criminal behavior in the groups studied as indicated in the preceding section. This is further illustrated in table 12.3, which

TABLE 12.3

Relationship between criminality and hyperactivity (sum of teacher ratings of Motor Restlessness and Concentration Difficulties) at the age of 13 for four groups of males.

GROUP	M	SE	N
a) No criminal offences	7.08	0.16	347
b) Criminal offences during adolescence only	9.40	0.33	60
c) Criminal offences during adulthood only	8.72	0.33	74
d) Criminal offences during both adolescence and adulthood	10.78	0.36	59

Significance levels for differences:
a-b: p<.0001   b-c: ns
a-c: p<.0001   b-d: p<.005
a-d: p<.0001   c-d: p<.0001

shows the relationships between hyperactivity at the age of thirteen (sum of teacher ratings of Motor Restlessness and Concentration Difficulties used as an index of hyperactivity) and criminality in early adolescence (criminal registers through age seventeen), in adulthood (eighteen through age thirty), or persistent criminal activity for both age periods.

Table 12.3 indicates that excessive hyperactive behavior at the age of thirteen was connected with persistent criminal activity. The persistent offenders who recurred in criminal registers both in adolescence and in adulthood had significantly higher hyperactivity scores (p<.0001) at age thirteen than the nonregistered subjects, and significantly higher hyperactivity scores than the subjects who were registered exclusively in adolescence (p<.005) or exclusively in adult life (p<.0001). Furthermore, both those subjects registered only in adolescence and those exclusively registered in adulthood, had significantly higher hyperactivity scores (p<.0001 respectively) than the non-registered subjects.

The results presented in table 12.3, demonstrating a significant relation between early hyperactivity and later criminality, particularly strong for persistent criminal activity, were calculated for the total group of 540 males. For our specific purposes it is of interest to study whether this relationship holds for the sample in which the relationship between adrenaline excretion on the one hand, and hyperactivity and criminal activity on the other, was investigated and reported in the previous sections.

In figure 12.4 persistent (pervasive) hyperactivity measured as

FIGURE 12.4

Hyperactivity (summarized scores for ratings of motor restlessness and concentration difficulties at age ten and at age thirteen) for males with: (a) no registered crime; (b) registered crime only before the age of eighteen; (c) registered crime only from the age of eighteen; and (d) registered crime both before and from the age of eighteen.

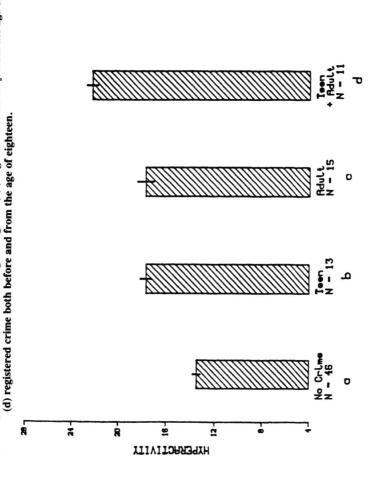

the sum of ratings of Motor Restlessness and Concentration Diffi-culties at ages eleven and thirteen, is shown for the four groups of males, distinguished above.

The results presented in figure 12.4 show a very consistent picture. Those characterized by persistent criminal activity are, already at an early age, characterized by persistent hyperactivity. The group with persistent criminal activity differs highly signifi-cantly with respect to early persistent hyperactivity both from those without any criminal records (p<.001) and those with criminal records during adolescence only (p<.001) or during adulthood (p = .009).

The reported findings are compatible with results presented ear-lier in this article. From the clinical and neuropsychological points of view, early hyperactivity is recognized as a main precursor of delinquency (Barcai and Rabkin 1974; Cantwell 1978; Robins 1966; Satterfield 1978, 1987; Schuckit, Petrich, and Chiles 1978; Weiss 1983; Weiss and Hechtman 1979). While exceptions occur (Weiss, Hechtman, Perlman, Hopkins, and Wener 1979), much empirical data, both cross-sectional and longitudinal, support the connection between hyperactivity and antisocial behavior. Hyperactivity has been found to be strongly related to conduct problems in children and adolescents (Borland and Heckman 1976; Loeber 1986), and a number of follow-up studies from the mid-1960s have found chil-dren with sustained hyperactive behavior to be at excessive risk of developing a criminal career (Nylander 1979). Weiss, Minde, Werry, Douglas, and Nemeth (1971) reported that one out of four in their sample of sixty-four children, diagnosed as sustained hyper-actives at age eight, had in the mid-teenage years a history of acting out antisocial behavior. One out of six had court referrals. Mendel-son et al. (1971) reported on eighty-three children at age thirteen, who two to five years earlier had been diagnosed as hyperactives. Almost 60 percent of the group studied had had some police contact and 18 percent had been referred to the juvenile court. About half of this sample had a history of fighting and stealing, and more than eight out of ten were found to lie frequently according to their mothers. Out of fourteen hyperkinetic children with MBD (Menkes, Rowe, and Menkes 1967), only eight were found to be self-support-ing in their early thirties. Of these eight, three had spent time in correctional institutions. Of twenty boys characterized as overactive with short attention span at age seven, seven were classified as sociopaths in their early thirties (Borland and Heckman 1976). These studies had certain limitations in that they were characteristically based on small clinical samples of subjects who were retrospectively classified as hyperactives, and the analyses were performed without adequate control groups. However, more recent studies involving better statistical controls (Farrington, Loeber, and Van Kammen 1990; Gittelman, Mannuzza, Shenker, and Bonagura 1985; Hechtman, Weiss, Perlman, and Amsel 1984; Satterfield, Hoppe, and Schell 1982; Weiss and Trokenberg Hechtman 1986), support these earlier findings.

A particularly important finding was reported by Farrington et al. (1990) using data from 411 males in the Cambridge Study in Delinquency Development. They noted that a hyperactivity-impulsivity-attention deficit measure, obtained at the age of eight and ten years, was especially predictive of future chronic offending. This agrees with the results of the present study, that persistent criminally registered subjects were rated as highest in hyperactivity at the age of thirteen.

Conclusion and Discussion

Traditional research on delinquency and criminal activity has been characterized by a search for factors in the individual and in the environment which can serve as *predictors*. High prediction has been a goal in the search for an explanation of the process leading to delinquency and adult criminality and as a basis for the introduction of effective prevention. This approach is reflected in research designs applied with the distinction between independent and dependent variables and in the statistics used for data processing. Predictive efficiency has often been expressed in results from the application of linear regression models.

The predictive approach to criminal research on delinquency and adult criminality has its background in and is connected with the search for explanatory, scientific "laws" underlying the developmental process. In the natural sciences, particularly physics, from which psychological research has obtained so many of its values, explanatory laws have played an essential role. The formulation of such laws has contributed to the high scientific status of the natural sciences. However, for those scientific disciplines whose object of interest is dynamic processes, such as psychology, biology, meteorology, and ecology, the character of the phenomena limits the possibility to formulate such laws. The Noble Laureate, Crick (1989), who started his career as a physicist and later turned to biology, has discussed this issue extensively and draws the following conclusion which is also relevant to the study of individual functioning:

> Physics is also different because its results can be expressed in powerful, deep, and often counter-intuitive general laws. There is really nothing in biology that corresponds to special and general relativity, or quantum electro-dynamics, or even such simple conservation laws as those of Newtonian mechanics; the conservation of energy, momentum and angular momentum. Biology has its "laws", such as those of Mendelian genetics, but they are often only rather broad generalizations, with significant exceptions to them . . . what is found in biology is mechanisms, mechanisms built with chemical components and that are often modified by other, later, mechanisms added to the earlier ones. (Crick 1989, 138)

This view, which has been strongly fostered by the formulation of chaos theory (Gleick 1987), has the important implication that dynamic processes are lawful but not necessarily predictable. In this perspective, the goal of research on individual functioning is to identify the factors involved in a certain process and the mechanisms by which the factors operate (Magnusson in press). The aim of this report is to contribute to this understanding. Some possible underlying mechanisms are discussed.

By using data from a representative sample of males, the results presented here strongly support the basic assumption that individual functioning cannot be understood without reference to biological aspects of individual functioning. Knowledge about what biological factors are operating and about the mechanisms by which they do so in the total functioning of individuals will contribute much to our understanding of why individuals think, feel, act, and react as they do in real life (cf., Cairns 1979). To generalize, the results demonstrate a strong, significant relationship between autonomic activity/reactivity, in terms of adrenaline excretion, in two independent situations, and hyperactivity in a cross-situational perspective. They also indicate a strong significant relationship between persistent criminal activity and early adrenaline excretion, while there is no systematic relationship between autonomic activity/reactivity in these terms and criminal activity restricted to adolescence. Pervasive hyperactivity and persistent criminality are closely linked to each other.

In an individual, autonomic responsivity in terms of adrenaline excretion might be hypothetically explained as depending primarily on four interrelated subfunctions: (1) perceptual-cognitive processes, that is, the individuals' specific interpretation of situational information; (2) the hypothalamus response to this interpretation by giving impulses to adrenal-medullary activity; (3) the tendency of the medulla of the adrenal glands to respond to stimulating impulses with adrenaline excretion; and (4) inhibiting activity from the parasympathetic nervous system (see Figure 12.5).

The level of an individual's capability to adapt his/her level of arousal to the needs of a specific situation might be one of the more important aspects of individual functioning expressed in hyperactivity and criminal activity. It is noteworthy that individual differences in sensitivity to environmental demands have been observed at the receptor level and have been related to coping behavior in

FIGURE 12.5.
Physiological Responsivity in Terms of Adrenaline Excretion According to Four Interrelated Subfunctions.

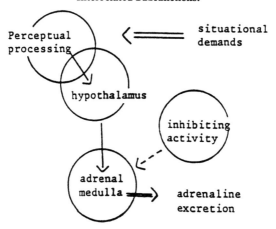

animal research (Weiss, Glazer, Pohorecky, Bailey, and Schneider 1979) and to depression in humans (Depue and Monroe 1979). Accordingly, "attention" has been suggested as more appropriate for investigation than is general arousal level (Douglas and Peters 1979; cf., also Wender et al. 1981). An association between the two is, however, conceivable and some support for this suggestion is given by the findings of low adrenaline excretion being related to "underachievement" (Bergman and Magnusson 1979) and to poor performance on mental tests (Magnusson 1988).

The present finding of low activity/reactivity of the sympathetic-adrenal system in terms of adrenaline excretion in boys with high ratings in hyperactivity-related behaviors is supported by an arousal theory (Vanderwolf and Robinson 1981). This theory claims that adrenergic input from the reticular activity system to neocortex and hippocampus is important for motor activity. Low autonomic activity/reactivity might, in line with earlier suggestions (Franken-haeuser 1979), indicate a loss of resources for handling stressful situational demands, resulting in difficulties for the child to respond adequately. It is thus logical to consider low adrenaline output a vulnerability factor for hyperactive behavior in childhood. It might also be regarded as a biochemical mediating factor between coping deficiency and more broadly defined conduct disturbances and criminal activity.

Trait-Bound vs. Situation-Bound Criminal Activity

The results presented here demonstrate a significant relationship between the interrelated hyperactivity and persistent criminal activity, on the one hand, and autonomic activity/reactivity in terms of adrenaline excretion, on the other. At the same time the results show a lack of a systematic relationship between aggressiveness and temporary criminal activity, on the one hand, and adrenaline excretion, on the other. These results taken together support a distinction between traitbound antisocial behavior, linked to persistent biological dispositions, and situation-influenced antisocial behavior, without such a link and more closely linked to situational and environmental conditions of various kinds.

There is then a possible, suggested distinction between two groups of adolescents showing antisocial behavior in terms of registered crimes, one with a persistent disposition of low autonomic activity/reactivity and hyperactivity and the other without this disposition but probably susceptible to environmental factors. This implied distinction has important implications both for further theoretical and empirical research into the processes underlying antisocial behavior and for discussions about appropriate preventive actions. The fact that the distinction has not been made in earlier research may explain the incoherent results in studies on the relationship between delinquency and autonomic arousal (cf., McCord 1990).

Trait-Bound Antisocial Behavior and Low Autonomic Reactivity

From the discussion above we conclude that the results presented here contribute to identifying low autonomic activity/reactivity as an operating factor underlying hyperactive behavior and persistent criminal activity.

There are at least four possible interpretations of our finding of a lower level of adrenaline excretion among hyperactive boys than among nonhyperactive boys. These interpretations also apply to our finding of a lower level of adrenaline excretion among persistent criminal males than among males without reported criminal activity, and males with criminal activity only during adolescence or only during adulthood.

First, those with a disposition for hyperactive behavior and persistent criminal activity may have been born with a "malfunction" (not necessarily genetic, cf. Offord, Sullivan, Allen, and Abrams 1979; Raine and Mednick 1989) in the way the individual system of psychological and physiological factors function (as previously discussed and described in figure 12.5). The malfunction may be located at one or several points in the total system.

Second, the low level of reactivity in terms of adrenaline excretion may be learned, for example, as a result of early experiences in an inconsistent social environment. As interpreted here, adrenaline excretion occurs as a result of the individual's interpretation of something as threatening or demanding in the environment. If reward and punishment are distributed randomly, during the infant socialization process, when biological systems are being established, the physiological system, which regulates adrenaline production, will not learn when and how to react adequately. As a result the system might become passified. Thus, a consistent set of conduct rules, maintained by distinct, appropriate reactions from the environment is a prerequisite for the physiological system to learn when and how to react to external threats and demands.

This explanation is supported by data from a large follow-up study of a sample of Swedish criminals and a control group. Data from the social environment showed that the most important characteristic that differentiated the family background of criminals from that of controls was the lack of consistency in family rules for upbringing (Olofsson 1973).

Third, the lower adrenaline excretion in males with a disposition for hyperactivity and for delinquency may be the result of a combination of an innate physiological vulnerability and lack of consistency in the social environment during early years. Thus, a child born with physiological vulnerability may need a more consistent social environment than a child with low vulnerability, who may be able to develop adequately even under severe social conditions.

Genetic, physiological, and biochemical factors have been proposed to be causal agents of criminal behavior in the same sense as family and environmental factors (Mednick and Finello 1983; Cadoret, Troughton, Bagford, and Woodworth 1990). In this context, it is of interest that persistent offenders as a group have been found to have more central nervous system dysfunctions than control groups of non-offenders. It has also been suggested that unrecognized cognitive dysfunctions interfere with the development of the socialization process (Buikhuisen 1982; see also Douglas 1984), inhibit social adaptation, and promote delinquency in juveniles (Buikhuisen 1987).

A fourth interpretation is possible, namely that the contemporaneous appearance of hyperactivity and persistent crimes across age levels, on the one hand, and low adrenaline excretion, on the other, does not necessarily imply that they are related to each other. Too often and too easily, wrong conclusions are drawn from contemporaneous events, reflected, for example, in significant correlations.

All four interpretations of the role of low autonomic activity/ reactivity in the development of antisocial behavior are made in the frame of reference of the interactional model of individual functioning. The model indicates a multidetermined, stochastic process in which biological factors are involved in a constant, reciprocal interaction with other factors in the individual and the environment.

Methodological Implications

The interactional frame of reference for the research presented here has important theoretical, methodological, and research strategical implications for the study of individual functioning, both in a current and in a developmental perspective (Magnusson 1988, 1990). The results presented clearly demonstrate two important methodological consequences of an interactional framework.

First, it is possible to understand and explain how an individual functions and develops as a whole only by following the same individual over time, for example, by longitudinal research.

Second, the study of one specific aspect of the total interactive process, criminal activity for example, as a nomothetical variable in linear regression analysis, as is carried out in much research on the developmental background of adult criminality, without considering the specific patterning of other relevant, operating factors has limited value. This conclusion emphasizes the need to complement variable-directed analyses on the developmental background of adult criminal activity with a person approach, in which development is studied in terms of patterns of relevant variables (Bergman, Eklund, and Magnusson, in press; Magnusson et al. 1983; Magnusson and Bergman 1984, 1990).

References

Angell, J. R. 1907. "The Province of Functional Psychology." *Psychological Review* 14, 61–91.

American Psychiatric Association. 1987. *Diagnostic and Statistical Manual of Mental Disorders* (3rd ed., revised). Washington, D.C.: APA.

Barcai, A., and L. Rabkin. 1974. "A Precursor of Delinquency: The Hyperkinetic Disorder of Childhood." *Psychiatric Quarterly* 48, 387–99.

Bergman, L. R., and D. Magnusson. 1979. "Overachievement and Catecholamine Excretion in an Achievement-Demanding Situation." *Psychosomatic Medicine* 41, 181–88.

Bergman, L. R., and D. Magnusson. 1984. "Patterns of Adjustment Problems at Age 13." *Reports from the Department of Psychology, University of Stockholm, No. 620.*

Bergman, L. R., G. Eklund, and D. Magnusson. (in press). "Studying Individual Development: Problems and Methods." In *Problems and Methods in Longitudinal Research: Stability and Change,* edited by D. Magnusson, L. R. Bergman, G. Rudinger, and B. Törestad. Cambridge: Cambridge University Press.

Borland, B. L., and H. K. Heckman. 1976. "Hyperactive Boys and their Brothers: A 25 Year Follow-Up Study." *Archives of General Psychiatry* 33, 669–75.

Boydstun, J. A., P. T. Ackerman, D. A. Stevens, S. D. Clemens, J. E. Peters, and R. A. Dykerman. 1968. "Physiologic and Motor Conditioning and Generalization in Children with Minimal Brain Dysfunction." *Conditional Reflex* 3, 81–104.

Brown, G., M. Ebert, E. Mikkelsen, and R. Hunt. 1979. "Clinical Pharmacology of D-Amphetamine in Hyperactive Children." In *Pharmacokinetics of Psychoactive Drugs,* edited by L. A. Gottschalk, 137–53. New York: Spectrum.

Brown, G., M. Ebert, E. Mikkelsen, and R. Hunt. 1980. "Behavior and Motor Activity Response in Hyperactive Children and Plasma Amphetamine Levels Following a Sustained Release Preparation." *Journal of American Academy of Child Psychiatry* 19, 225–39.

Buikhuisen, W. 1982. "Aggressive Behavior and Cognitive Disorders." *International Journal of Law and Psychiatry* 5, 205–17.

Buikhuisen, W. 1987. "Cerebral Dysfunctions and Juvenile Crime." In *The Causes at Crime. New Biological Approaches,* edited by S. A. Mednick, T. E. Moffitt, and S. A. Stack, 168–84. Cambridge: Cambridge University Press.

Cadoret, R. J., E. Troughton, J. Bagford, and G. Woodworth. 1990. "Genetic and Environmental Factors in Adoptee Antisocial Personality." *European Archives of Psychiatry and Neurology Sciences* 239, 231–40.

Cairns, R. B. 1979. *Social Development: The Origins and Plasticity of Interchanges.* San Francisco: Freeman.

Cantwell, D. P. 1978. "Hyperactivity and Antisocial Behavior." *Journal of American Academy of Child Psychiatry* 17, 252–62.

Coons, H. W., R. Klorman, and A. Borgstedt. 1987. "Effects of Methylphenidate on Adolescents with a Childhood History of Attention Deficit Disorder: II. Information Processing." *Journal of American Academy of Child Psychiatry* 26, 368–74.

Crick, F. 1989. *What Mad Pursuit.* New York: Basic Books.

Depue, R., and S. Monroe. 1979. "The Unipolar-Bipolar Distinction in the Depressive Disorders: Implications for Stress-Onset Interactions." In *The Psychobiology of Depressive Disorders: Implications for the Effects of Stress*, edited by R. A. Depue, 123–53. New York: Academic Press.

Douglas, V. 1984. "Attentional and Cognitive Problems." In *Developmental Neuropsychiatry*, edited by M. Rutter, 280–329. New York: Churchill Livingstone.

Douglas, V. I., and K. G. Peters. 1979. "Toward a Clearer Definition of the Attentional Deficit of Hyperactive Children." In *Attention and the Development of Cognitive Skills*, edited by G. A. Hale and M. Lewis, 173–247. New York: Plenum.

Euler von, U. S., and F. Lishajko. 1961. "Improved Technique for the Fluorimetric Estimation of Catecholamines. *Acta Physiologica Scandinavica* 51, 348–55.

Farrington, D. P., R. Loeber, and W. B. Van Kammen. 1990. "Long-term Criminal Outcomes of Hyperactivity-Impulsivity-Attention Deficit and Conduct Problems in Childhood." In *Straight and Devious Pathways from Childhood to Adulthood*, edited by L. N. Robins and M. Rutter, 62–81. Cambridge: Cambridge University Press.

Frankenhaeuser, M. 1979. "Psychoneuroendocrine Approaches to the Study of Emotion as Related to Stress and Coping." In *Nebraska Symposium on Motivation, 1978*, edited by H. E. Howe, and R. A. Dienstbier, 123–61. Lincoln, NE: University of Nebraska Press.

Gittelman, R., S. Mannuzza, R. Shenker, and N. Bonagura. 1985. "Hyperactive Boys Almost Grown Up: I. Psychiatric Status." *Archives of General Psychiatry* 42, 937–47.

Gleick, J. 1987. *Chaos: Making a New Science*. New York: Penguin Books.

Gorenstein, E. E., and J. P. Newman. 1980. "Disinhibitory Psychopathology: A New Perspective and a Model for Research." *Psychological Review* 87, 301–15.

Hare, R. D. 1978. "Electrodermal and Cardiovascular Correlates of Psychopathy." In *Psychopathic Behaviour: Approaches to Research*, edited by R. D. Hare and D. Schalling, 107–43. Chichester: Wiley.

Hechtman, L., G. Weiss, T. Perlman, and R. Amsel. 1984. "Hyperactives as Young Adults: Initial Predictors of Adult Outcome." *Journal of the American Academy of Child Psychiatry* 23, 250–60.

Hofer, M. A. 1981. *The Roots of Human Behavior. An Introduction to the Psychobiology of Early Development*. San Francisco: Freeman.

Johansson, G. 1976. "Subjective Wellbeing and Temporal Patterns of Sympathetic-Adrenal Medullary Activity." *Biological Psychology* 4, 157–72.

Johansson, G., M. Frankenhaeuser, and D. Magnusson. 1973. "Catecholamine Output in School Children as Related to Performance and Adjustment." *Scandinavian Journal of Psychology* 14, 20–28.

Klinteberg af, B., and D. Magnusson. 1989. "Aggressiveness and Hyperactive Behaviour as Related to Adrenaline Excretion." *European Journal of Personality* 3, 81–93.

Klinteberg af, B., D. Magnusson, and D. Schalling. 1989. "Hyperactive Behavior in Childhood and Adult Impulsivity: A Longitudinal Study of Male Subjects." *Personality and Individual Differences* 10, 43–50.

Klove, H., and K. Hole, 1979. "The Hyperkinetic Syndrome: Criteria for Diagnosis." In *Hyperactivity in Children, Etiology, Measurement, and Treatment Implications,* edited by R. L. Trites, 121–36. Baltimore: University Park Press.

Krauth, J., and G. A. Lienert. 1982. "Fundamentals and Modifications of Configural Frequency Analysis (CFA)." *Interdisciplinaria* 3, 1–14.

Lambert, W. W., G. Johansson, M. Frankenhaeuser, and I. Klackenberg-Larsson. 1969. "Catecholamine Excretion in Young Children and their Parents as Related to Behavior." *Scandinavian Journal of Psychology* 10, 306–18.

Langhorne, J. E., and J. Loney. 1979. "A Four-Fold Model for Sub-Grouping the Hyperkinetic/MBD Syndrome." *Child Psychiatry and Human Development* 9, 153–59.

Levander, S. E., Å. Mattsson, D. Schalling, and A. Dalteg. 1987. "Psychoendocrine Patterns Within a Group of Male Juvenile Delinquents as Related to Early Psychosocial Stress, Diagnostic Classification and Follow-up Data." In *Psychopathology: An Interactional Perspective,* edited by D. Magnusson and A. Öhman, 235–52. New York: Academic Press.

Lidberg, L., S. E. Levander, D. Schalling, and Y. Lidberg. 1978. "Urinary Catecholamines, Stress, and Psychopathy: A Study of Arrested Men Awaiting Trial." *Psychosomatic Medicine* 40, 116–125.

Loeber, R. 1986. "Behavioral Precursors and Accelerators of Delinquency." Paper presented at the Conference Explaining Crime, June 1986, University of Leiden, Holland.

Loney, J., J. E. Langhorne, and C. E. Paternite. 1978. "An Empirical Basis for Subgrouping the Hyperkinetic/Minimal Brain Dysfunction Syndrome." *Journal of Abnormal Psychology* 87, 431–41.

Magnusson, D. 1987. "Adult Delinquency and Early Conduct and Physiology." In *Psychopathology: An Interactional Perspective,* edited by D. Magnusson and A. Öhman, 221–34. New York: Academic Press.

Magnusson, D. 1988. *Individual Development from an Interactional Perspective*. Hillsdale, NJ: Erlbaum.

Magnusson, D. 1990. "Personality Development from an Interactional Perspective." In *Handbook of Personality: Theory and Research*, edited by L. Pervin, 193–222. New York: Guilford Press.

Magnusson, D. (in press). "Back to the Phenomena." *Zeitschrift für Psychologie*.

Magnusson, D., and L. R. Bergman. 1984. "On the Study of the Development of Adjustment Problems." In *Human Action and Personality: Essays in Honor of Martti Takala*, edited by L. Pulkkinen and P. Lyytinen, 163–71. Jyväskylä, Finland: University of Jyväskylä.

Magnusson, D., and L. R. Bergman. 1990. "A Pattern Approach to the Study of Pathways from Childhood to Adulthood." In *Straight and Devious Pathways from Childhood to Adulthood*, edited by L. N. Robins and M. Rutter, 101–15. Cambridge: Cambridge University Press.

Magnusson, D., A. Dunér, and G. Zetterblom. 1975. *Adjustment: A Longitudinal Study*. Stockholm: Almqvist & Wiksell.

Magnusson, D., H. Stattin, and A. Dunér. 1983. "Aggression and Criminality in a Longitudinal Perspective." In *Prospective Studies of Crime and Delinquency*, edited by K. T. van Dusen and S. A. Mednick, 277–301. Boston: Kluwer-Nijhoff.

McCord, J. 1990. "Problem Behaviors." In *At the Threshold: The Developing Adolescent*, edited by S. S. Feldman and G. R. Elliott, 414–30; 602–14. Cambridge, MA: Harvard University Press.

McGee, R., S. Williams, and P. A. Silva. 1984. "Behavioral and Developmental Characteristics of Aggressive, Hyperactive, and Aggressive-Hyperactive Boys." *Journal of the American Academy of Child Psychiatry* 23, 270–79.

Mednick, S., and K. M. Finello. 1983. "Biological Factors and Crime: Implications for Forensic Psychiatry." *International Journal of Law and Psychiatry* 6, 1–15.

Mendelson, W., N. Johnson, and M. Stewart. 1971. "Hyperactive Children as Teenagers: A Follow-Up Study." *The Journal of Nervous and Mental Disease* 153, 272–79.

Menkes, M., J. Rowe, and J. Menkes. 1967. "A Twenty-Five Year Follow-Up Study on the Hyperkinetic Child with Minimal Brain Dysfunction." *Pediatrics* 39, 393–99.

Nylander, I. 1979. "A 20-Year Prospective Follow-Up Study of 2.164 Cases at the Child Guidance Clinics in Stockholm." *Acta Paediatrica Scandinavica*, Suppl. 276, 1–45.

Offord, D. R., K. Sullivan, N. Allen, and N. Abrams. 1979. "Delinquency and Hyperactivity." *The Journal of Nervous and Mental Disease* 167, 734–41.

Olofsson, B. 1973. *Unga lagöverträdare III. Hem, uppfostran, skola och kamratmiljö i belysning av intervju- och uppföljningsdata.* (Young delinquents III. Home, upbringing, education and peer relations as reflected in interview- and follow-up data). Stockholm: Statens Offentliga Utredningar.

Olweus, D. 1986. "Aggression and Hormones. Behavior Relationship with Testosterone and Adrenaline." In *The Development of Antisocial and Prosocial Behavior: Research, Theories and Issues,* edited by D. Olweus, J. Block, and M. Radke-Yarrow, 51–72. New York: Academic Press.

Raine, A., and S. A. Mednick. 1989. "Biosocial Longitudinal Research in Antisocial Behavior." *Revue of Epidemiology* 37, 515–24.

Rapoport, J. 1984. "The Use of Drugs: Trends in Research." In *Developmental Neuropsychiatry,* edited by M. Rutter, 385–403. London: Churchill Livingstone.

Robins, L. N. 1966. *Deviant Children Grown Up: A Sociological and Psychiatric Study of Sociopathic Personality.* Baltimore: Williams & Wilkins.

Roessler, R., N. R. Burch, and R. B. Mufford, Jr. 1967. "Personality Correlates of Catecholamine Excretion Under Stress." *Journal of Psychosomatic Research* 11, 181–85.

Satterfield, J. H. 1978. "The Hyperactive Child Syndrome: A Precursor to Adult Psychopathy?" In *Psychopathic Behavior: Approaches to Research,* edited by R. D. Hare and D. Schalling, 329–46. New York: Wiley.

Satterfield, J. H. 1987. "Childhood Diagnostic and Neurophysiological Predictors of Teenage Arrest Rates: An 8-Years Prospective Study." In *The Causes of Crime: New Biological Approaches,* edited by S. A. Mednick, T. E. Moffitt, and S. A. Stack, 147–67. Cambridge: Cambridge University Press.

Satterfield, J. H., D. P. Cantwell, and B. T. Satterfield. 1974. "Pathophysiology of the Hyperactive Child Syndrome." *Archives of General Psychiatry* 31, 839–44.

Satterfield, J. H., and M. E. Dawson. 1971. "Electrodermal Correlates of Hyperactivity in Children." *Psychophysiology* 8, 191–98.

Satterfield, J. H., C. M. Hoppe, and A. M. Schell. 1982. "A Prospective Study of Delinquency in 110 Adolescent Boys with Attention Deficit Disorder and 88 Normal Adolescent Boys." *American Journal of Psychiatry* 139, 795–98.

Schalling, D. 1978. "Psychopathy-Related Personality Variables and the Psychophysiology of Socialization." In *Psychopathic Behaviour: Approaches to Research,* edited by R. D. Hare and D. Schalling, 85–106. Chichester: Wiley.

Schalling, D., G. Edman, and M. Åsberg. 1983. "Impulsive Cognitive Style and Inability to Tolerate Boredom: Psychobiological Studies of Temperamental Vulnerability." In *Biological Bases of Sensation Seeking, Impulsivity and Anxiety,* edited by M. Zuckerman, 129–51. Hillsdale, NJ: Erlbaum.

Schuckit, M. A., J. Petrich, and J. Chiles. 1978. "Hyperactivity: Diagnostic Confusion." *Journal of Nervous and Mental Disease* 166, 79–87.

Stattin, H., and D. Magnusson. 1989. "The Role of Early Aggressive Behavior for the Frequency, Seriousness, and Types of Later Crime." *Journal of Consulting and Clinical Psychology* 57, 710–18.

Stewart, M. A., C. Cummings, S. Singer, and C. S. de Blois. 1981. "The Overlap Between Hyperactive and Unsocialized Aggressive Children." *Journal of Child Psychology and Psychiatry* 22, 35–46.

Stewart, M., F. Pitts, A. Graig, and W. Dieruf. 1966. "The Hyperactive Child Syndrome." *American Journal of Orthopsychiatry* 36, 861–67.

Taylor, E. 1980. "Psychophysiology of Childhood Disorders." In *Handbook of Biological Psychiatry,* part 2, edited by H. M. van Praag, M. H. Lader, O. J. Rafaelson, and E. J. Sachar, 393–419. New York: Marcel Dekker.

Vanderwolf, C. H., and T. E. Robinson. 1981. "Reticulo-Cortical Activity and Behavior: A Critique of the Arousal Theory and a New Synthesis." *The Behavioral and Brain Sciences* 4, 459–514.

Venables, P. H. 1987. "Autonomic Nervous System Factors in Criminal Behavior." In *The Causes of Crime: New Biological Approaches,* edited by S. A. Mednick, T. E. Moffitt, and S. A. Stack, 110–36. Cambridge: Cambridge University Press.

Wender, P. H., F. W. Reimherr, and D. R. Wood. 1981. "Attention Deficit Disorder (Minimal Brain Dysfunction) in Adults: A Replication Study of Diagnosis and Drug Treatment." *Archives of General Psychiatry* 38, 449–56.

Weiner, H. 1977. *Psychobiology and Human Disease.* New York: Elsevier.

Weiss, G. 1983. "Long-term Outcome: Findings, Concepts and Practical Implications." In *Developmental Neuropsychiatry,* edited by M. Rutter. New York: Guilford Press.

Weiss, G., H. Glazer, L. Pohorecky, W. Bailey, and L. Schneider. 1979. "Coping Behavior and Stress-Induced Behavioral Depression: Studies of the Role of Brain Catecholamines." In *The Psychobiology of Depressive Disorders: Implications for the Effects of Stress,* edited by R. A. Depue, 125–60. New York: Academic Press.

Weiss, G., and L. Hechtman. 1979. "The Hyperactive Child Syndrome." *Science* 205, 1348–54.

Weiss, G., L. Hechtman, T. Perlman, J. Hopkins, and A. Wener. 1979.

"Hyperactives as Young Adults: A Controlled, Prospective Ten Year Follow-Up of 75 Children." *Archives of General Psychiatry* 6, 675–81.

Weiss, G., K. Minde, J. Werry, V. Douglas, and E. Nemeth. 1971. "Studies on the Hyperactive Child. VIII: Five Year Follow-Up." *Archives of General Psychiatry* 24, 409–14.

Weiss, G., and L. T. Trokenberg Hechtman. 1986. *Hyperactive Children Grown Up. Empirical Findings and Theoretical Considerations.* New York: Guilford Press.

Woodman, D., J. Hinton, and M. O'Neill. 1977. "Relationship Between Violence and Catecholamines." *Perceptual and Motor Skills* 45, 702.

Contributors

JUDITH S. BROOK is professor of psychiatry and director of research at the New York Medical College and adjunct associate professor at Mount Sinai Medical Center. Her research interests cover developmental epidemiology and drug use. She is a member of the Epidemiology and Research Committee of the National Institute of Drug Abuse and has been recipient of the Research Scientist Development Award (Level II) and consulting editor of the *Journal of Genetic Psychology*.

BEVERLY D. CAIRNS is co-director of the Social Development Laboratory and research associate in the Department of Psychology at the University of North Carolina at Chapel Hill. She was trained in education and psychology at Pasadena College and Stanford University. She has been co-director (with Robert Cairns) of the CLS longitudinal project since its inception in 1980.

ROBERT B. CAIRNS is a professor in the Department of Psychology at the University of North Carolina at Chapel Hill and director of the Carolina Consortium on Human Development. He completed the Ph.D. in psychology at Stanford University (1960). In collaboration with Beverley D. Cairns, he initiated the CLS longitudinal project eleven years ago. He is a member of the Core Scientific Group of the Program on Human Development and Criminal Behavior, Harvard School of Public Health.

PATRICIA COHEN is co-director of the Psychiatric Epidemiology Training Program, Columbia University Department of Epidemiology and Psychiatry and on the faculty of the Department of Psychi-

319

atry, Columbia University College of Physicians and Surgeons. Her research about the etiology of drug use, models of parenting and temperament, and psychopathology in children has been funded by the National Institute of Mental Health and the National Institute of Drug Abuse.

ELLEN S. COHN is associate professor of psychology at the University of New Hampshire. Her research interests include legal socialization, legal reasoning, and attributions about wife abuse and date rape. She recently co-authored a book, *Legal Socialization. A Study of Norms and Rules,* with Susan O. White. Her research has been supported by grants from the National Science Foundation Law and Social Science Program.

LEONARD D. ERON is Emeritus Professor of Psychology at the University of Illinois at Chicago, past president of the Midwest Psychological Association and of the International Society for Research on Aggression. His research has focused on the development of aggression in children and on effects of media on behavior. He was editor of the *Journal of Abnormal Psychology* from 1973 to 1980 and received the American Psychological Association Award for Distinguished Professional Contributions to Knowledge, in 1980. He is a member of the National Research Council Panel on Understanding and Control of Violence and chairman of the American Psychological Association Commission on Violence and Youth.

DAVID P. FARRINGTON is Reader in Psychological Criminology at Cambridge University, England. Winner of the Sellin-Glueck Award from the American Society of Criminology, his main research interest is in the longitudinal study of crime and delinquency. He has published profusely in that arena. He is president of the British Society of Criminology and vice chair of the U.S. National Academy of Sciences Panel on Understanding and Control of Violence.

DANIEL GLASER is Emeritus Professor of Sociology and senior research associate at the University of Southern California. His research interests have been aimed at affecting public policy through communicating about criminological theory and research. Past president of the American Society of Criminology, he has chaired the criminology sections of the American Sociological Association and the Society for the Study of Social Problems. He is one of only two people to have been recipient of both the American Society of Criminology Sutherland Award and Volmer Award.

L. ROWELL HUESMANN is professor of psychology at the University of Illinois at Chicago. His main research interests pertain to cognitive psychology and the relation of television to aggression, with studies in Poland, Finland, Israel, and Australia as well as the United States. He is executive secretary of the International Society for Research on Aggression and a fellow of the American Psychological Association.

ROY KING is an associate professor in the Department of Psychiatry and Behavioral Sciences at Stanford University. He holds a doctorate in mathematics and trained as a psychiatrist. Research investigations include theoretical models of psychopathology, particularly those relevant to the biological substrata of the personality disorders.

BRITT AF KLINTEBERG is an assistant professor in the Department of Psychology, University of Stockholm. Her research interest is in the development of neuropsychology.

GUENTHER KNOBLICH is a third-year medical student at Stanford University School of Medicine. He is concurrently a research associate funded through a grant supported by the National Institute of Drug Abuse. His research interests include the neuropharmacology and psychophysiology of substance abuse and criminal behavior.

ROBIN L. LASHLEY is an assistant professor in the Department of Psychology, Kent State University. She is interested in opponent process theory and studies of human development.

DAVID MAGNUSSEN is Olof Eneroth Professor of Psychology at the University of Stockholm. His research interests encompass methodological questions and substantive issues pertaining to the development of individuals in social settings. He has received the Medal of Science in Sweden and an honorary doctorate from the University of Jyväskylä in Finland. He was vice president of the Academia

Europaea in 1989, and is currently vice president of the Swedish Royal Academy of Sciences.

JOAN MCCORD is professor of criminal justice at Temple University. Her research has included studies of the etiology and prevention of various forms of deviant behavior. Past president of the American Society of Criminology, and former chair of the Crime, Law, and Deviance Section of the American Sociological Association, she is vice chair of the National Research Council's Committee on Law and Justice.

ROBERT A. ROSELLINI is professor and chair of psychology at the State University of New York at Albany. His research interests involve learning and conditioning theories.

ROBERT J. SAMPSON is professor of sociology at the University of Chicago. His research interests include the study of crime and deviance from a life-course perspective, community social organization, and informal social control. He is a member of the Core Scientific Group of the Program on Human Development and Criminal Behavior, Harvard School of Public Health.

HÅKAN STATTIN is associate professor in the Department of Psychology, University of Stockholm. His research interests include personality development, social psychology, and antisocial behavior.

RICHARD E. TREMBLAY is professeur agrégé at the Ecole de Psycho-Education of the University of Montreal. He is director of the Research Unit on Children's Psychosocial Maladjustment and conducts research on the development of aggressive and antisocial behavior. He is recipient of the Prix Beccaria from the Society of Criminology of Quebec.

SUSAN O. WHITE is professor of political science at the University of New Hampshire. Her research interests include law enforcement, compliance, legal socialization, and legal reasoning. Her most recent publication is *Legal Socialization. A Study of Norms and Rules,* which she co-authored with Ellen S. Cohn.

Subject Index

Abuse, 75–76, 85, 86, 117

Addiction, 47–48, 55–59

Adolescence, 25–27, 30, 34, 36, 39

Age, 24, 25, 26, 201

Aggression, 5–15, 116–126, 137–152, 167–169, 171–180, 197–199, 203, 206–207, 212–215, 217–222, 234, 246, 291–298, 308

Alcohol, 15, 30, 33, 38, 88, 207–208

Altruism, 117–126

Animal behavior, 5–12, 15, 47, 141–142, 158

Anomie, 35–38, 40

Anxiety, 4, 9–11, 14, 146, 148, 197, 200–201, 203, 204, 208

Arousal, 2–5, 13–15, 32–33, 50, 59, 273

Behaviorism, 97

Biological factors, 1–15, 33, 38–39, 141–143, 146, 203–206, 208, 222, 272–273, 287–288, 290–302, 306–311

Birth weight, low, 72–74, 76, 85

British Crime Survey, 68–69

Classification systems, 194–206, 308–309

Community, 63–88, 238, 240–244, 245, 272

Conditioning, 49, 55–58, 97

Conduct disorder, 2–3, 13, 14, 121–123, 208, 265, 270–271

Conscience, 276

Control, 68, 78, 80, 82, 85

Crime patterns, 24–34, 263–265, 301–304

Crime rates, 25–27, 34, 63, 65, 68, 71, 80, 85

Crime, organized, 29, 30–31

Crime, professional, 30–31, 36

Crime, white collar, 31–32

Culture, 70–71, 81, 86, 88

Delinquent subcultures, 34–35, 70–71, 88–89

Deterrence, 41–42

Developmental change, 71–76, 105, 108, 138–143, 170–175, 184, 198–200, 206, 246, 254, 255, 258–259, 265–267, 276–277, 279, 287–288, 298–302, 309–311

Deviance, general, 264–267

Drugs, illicit, 4, 7, 13, 30, 33, 38, 42, 48, 49, 50, 52–57, 60, 74, 86, 231–247

Egoism, 116, 123–126, 276

Ethnographic research, 70–71, 82–85

Extroversion, 200–203

Family socialization, 77–79, 81–85, 117–118, 126, 149, 232–234, 238–239, 240–244, 246, 268–270, 274, 276, 309–310

Family structure, 75, 80–81, 238, 240–243, 245, 270

Gangs, 67, 69, 70, 85

Gender, 159–161, 168–169, 170, 172–179, 184, 233, 241

323

Harm violence, 204–208, 209–211, 217–221
Health care, 71–76
Hyperactivity, 197, 199–200, 203, 270, 274, 291, 292–298, 301–305, 308–310

Impulsivity, 4, 9–13, 14, 15, 120, 199, 201–205, 217, 270–271, 273–275, 279–280, 297–298
Insanity defense, 33, 39

Just desert, 42–43

Kwakiutl Indians, 120

Labeling, 40–42
Laws, 27–30, 32, 37

Mobility, residential, 65, 69, 70, 75, 85
Mortality, infant, 72–74, 76
Motives, 47–60, 103–104, 115–126, 278–279

Networks, 66–67, 69, 73–76, 78–79, 82–84, 86, 88, 150, 164
Neurochemical factors, 3–4, 9–15, 132, 204–206
Neuroticism, 200–201

Peers, 27, 35, 39, 67, 69, 76, 79, 80, 81, 86, 99–100, 106–107, 148, 149–150, 167–171, 234–235, 239, 240–245, 270, 276–277
Poverty, 70, 72–73, 75, 79, 83, 85, 87
Prediction, crime, 197–200, 305–306
Pregnancy, teenage, 73–74
Prevention, crime, 33–43, 126, 141, 152, 247
Prevention, drug abuse, 247
Prosocial behavior, 117–119, 122–126, 143, 150, 197, 200, 201, 204, 219
Psychopathy, 1–5, 11, 14, 197, 202, 203, 206, 291
Psychoticism, 200–203

Punishment, 5, 13, 124, 125, 126, 202, 241, 246, 276

Race, 81, 82–83, 87–88, 137–138
Reasoning, legal, 100–104, 108–111
Recidivism, 40–41, 42, 59–60
Reward, 202–205, 206–208, 217–221
Role-taking, 104–108

School failure, 26–27, 118, 169, 184, 235, 268, 271, 275
Self concept, 179–180, 275
Sensation (novelty) seeking, 2, 4, 14, 48–49, 55, 57, 58–59, 204–208, 209–211, 212, 214, 217–221, 273–275
Social capital, 63–64, 76–79, 81–86, 88
Socioeconomic factors, 267–269
Suicide, 12, 13
Supervision, 67, 69, 77–78, 79–80, 81, 82, 85, 86

Theory, attribution, 123
Theory, biosocial, 203–208, 212–214, 217–222
Theory, cognitive developmental, 95–111
Theory, control, 34, 36, 37, 38, 39, 40
Theory, differential association, 34, 36–37, 39–41, 97
Theory, differential expectation, 36, 38
Theory, legal development, 95, 105
Theory, opponent process, 47–60
Theory, psychoanalytic, 39–40
Theory, reactance, 124
Theory, script, 145–151
Theory, social control, 233–235
Theory, social disorganization, 63–88
Theory, social learning, 95–111

Vice, 27–30, 31, 33, 36
Victimization, 69, 81
Violence, 9–13, 32–33, 68–69, 70, 73, 76, 81, 87, 88, 88–89fn, 122–123, 171–174, 270, 273, 291

Weapons, 173

Names Index

Aaronson, R., 142, 154
Abadinsky, H., 30, 43
Abbott, W., 44
Abelson, R. P., 145, 152
Abrams, N., 309, 315
Achenbach, T. M., 196, 223, 237, 247
Ackerman, P. T., 312
Ackerson, L., 195, 223
Adams, D., 199, 223
Adams, G. R., 188
Adams, K., 92
Adelson, J., 131
Aderman, D., 118, 126, 127
Adler, F., vii
Ageton, S. S., 270, 281
Agron, H., 9, 16
Akers, R. L., 97, 111, 112
Albert, D. J., 6, 16
Allan, E. A., 46
Allen, L., 273, 281
Allen, N., 309, 315
Allport, G. W., 184, 186
Altham, P. M. E., 263, 285
Altman, K., 18
Amdur, R. L., 260, 280
Amsel, R., 305, 313
Anderson, E., 70, 80, 88, 89
Angell, J. R., 287, 311
Ansel, M., 132
Arato, M., 16
Arms, R. L., 117, 130
Arps, K., 128
Åsberg, M. L., 9, 16, 19, 20, 298, 317
Axelrad, S., 195, 226

Bachman, J. G., 231, 235, 247, 249
Baert, A. E., 130
Bagford, J., 310, 312
Bailey, W., 308, 317
Baldwin, J. M., 171, 186
Ball, R. A., 43
Ballenger, J. C., 4, 9, 13, 16, 17
Baltes, P. B., 191
Bandura, A., 111, 112, 115, 116, 117, 127, 143, 144, 152, 157, 187
Banki, B. M., 15, 16
Banki, C. M., 9, 16
Banks, W. C., 135
Barcai, A., 304, 311
Barkley, R. A., 199, 203, 223
Baron, R. M., 112
Barrett, D. E., 173, 187
Barrett, J. E., 285, 286
Barrett, R. J., 10, 20
Bartko, J., 14, 20
Bates, M. E., 271, 286
Batson, C. D., 125, 127
Batson, J. G., 127
Battjes, R. J., 250
Baumann, D. J., 124, 127
Beaman, A., 128
Beck, L. W., 131
Beeman, E. A., 5, 16
Behar, D., 20
Behar, L., 196, 209, 223
Benedict, R., 120, 127
Bentler, P. M., 233, 244, 249, 250
Beresford, T. P., 17
Berger, M., 127, 129
Bergeron, G., 172, 190

Bergman, L. R., 117, 132, 180, 183, 190, 206, 227, 290, 292, 295, 308, 311–312, 315
Berkowitz, L., 117, 118, 123, 126, 127, 129, 132, 133, 134, 143, 144, 153
Bernstein, I. S., 7, 19
Bertilsson, L., 19, 20
Bigelow, B. J., 169, 187
Billy, J. O. G., 170, 191
Bjorkqvist, K., 172, 190
Blane, H. T., 251
Blalock, H. M., 102, 112, 113
Blanchard, C., 188
Blanchard, R. J., 188
Blasi, A., 100–101, 113
Blau, P. M., 120, 127
Blishen, B. R. 209, 223
Block, J., 128, 129, 131, 132, 133, 188, 190, 191, 228, 249, 316
Blouin, A. G., 270, 280
Blouin, J., 270, 280
Blow, F. C., 17
Blumstein, A., 25, 43, 91, 133, 197, 200, 223, 233, 247, 254, 255, 279, 281
Blurton Jones, N., 196, 224
Blyth, D. A., 166, 191
Boas, F., 120, 127
Bohman, M., 207, 224, 273, 281
Bolger, N., 187
Bonagura, N., 305, 313
Booth, A., 7, 16
Borgstedt, A., 297, 312
Borland, B. L., 304, 305, 312
Bott, E., 66, 89
Bouchard, T. J., 141, 153, 272, 281
Bowlby, J., 276, 281
Boydstun, J. A., 291, 312
Brackbill, R. M., 61
Braithwaite, J., 37, 38, 43
Brandt, J. R., 127
Brehm, J. W., 124, 128
Brehm, S. S., 124, 128
Breslau, N., 273, 281
Brice, P. 172, 188
Bridger, W. H., 20
Bridges, K. M. B., 195, 224
Brim, O. G., Jr., 191
Bronfenbrenner, U., 72, 74, 76, 89

Bronson, F. H., 5, 8, 16, 19
Brook, D. W., 233, 235, 244, 247, 248
Brook, J. S., ix, 231, 233, 234, 235, 237, 238–239, 240, 241, 244, 246, 247–248
Brooks-Gunn, J., 273, 281
Brower, K. J., 7, 17
Brower, S., 92
Brown, G. L., 9, 13, 16, 17
Brown, G. M., 297, 312
Brush, F. R., 61
Bryan, J. H., 117, 128
Bryjak, G. J., 116, 130
Buikhuisen, W., 198, 224, 284, 310, 312
Burch, N. R., 291, 316
Bursik, R. J., Jr., 64, 65, 66, 85, 89
Byrne, J., 64, 65, 85, 89

Cadoret, R. J., 310, 312
Cairns, B. D., viii, 120, 128, 162, 166, 168, 169, 179, 180, 184, 186, 187–188
Cairns, C. B., 171, 187
Cairns, R. B., viii, 118, 120, 128, 158, 159, 162, 164, 165, 166, 167, 168–169, 173, 175, 179, 180, 183, 184, 186, 187–188, 189, 190, 191, 195, 199, 224, 306, 312
Cambell, A., 168, 188
Cantwell, D. P., 198, 224, 291, 304, 312, 316
Carroll, J. S., 116, 128
Carroll, W. K., 209, 223
Carter, R. M., 45
Caspi, A., 187
Castellan, N. J., Jr., 165, 188
Catalano, R. F., 276, 283
Cepeda, C., 19
Cernkovich, S. A., 189
Chafetz, M. E., 251
Chaiken, J. M., 30, 44
Chaiken, M. R., 30, 44
Chambliss, W. J., 32, 44
Chandler, M. J., 126, 128
Chapman, A. J., 188
Charlebois, P., 121, 134, 229
Chess, S., 266, 285
Chiles, J., 304, 317
Christ, M. A. G., 227, 229

Christopher, F. S., 129
Church, R., 90
Cialdini, R. B., 124, 127, 128
Clark, J. P., 37, 45
Clark, R. D., III, 124, 128
Clarke, R. B., 36, 44
Clarke, R. V., 116, 128, 278, 279, 281, 282
Clayton, P. J., 156, 285
Clayton, R. R., 231, 248
Cleckley, H., 197, 206, 224
Clemens, S. D., 312
Clinard, M. B., 45
Cloninger, C. R., 141, 153, 203–206, 207, 208, 210, 212, 214, 215, 217, 219–221, 222, 224, 273, 281
Cloward, R. A., 254, 277, 281
Coccaro, E. F., 9, 17
Coe, C. L., 8, 17
Cohen, A. K., 115, 128, 254, 281
Cohen, J., 43, 91, 133, 237, 240, 248, 254, 255, 279, 281
Cohen, L. J., 137, 153
Cohen, L. E., 278, 281
Cohen, P., ix, 235, 237, 238, 240, 241, 247, 248, 249
Cohn, E. S., viii, 95–96, 97, 98, 100, 111, 113
Coie, J. D., 168, 188
Coleman, J. S., 63, 77, 78, 79, 80, 89
Conners, C. K., 196, 224, 270, 280
Coombs, R., 233, 249
Coons, H. W., 297, 312, 317
Coover, G. D., 3, 17
Corbit, J. D., 47, 62
Cornish, D. B., 116, 128, 278, 279, 281
Cornish, D. V., 36, 44
Costello, A., 237, 248
Couchoud, E. A., 125, 126, 128
Craig, R. L., 47, 61
Cressey, D. R., 34, 46, 115, 134, 255, 276, 285
Crick, F., 306, 312
Crouter, A., 75, 90
Crutcher, R., 194, 195, 224
Cummings, C., 292, 317
Cummings, E. M., 128, 130, 132, 134, 191
Curtis, K., 18

Dabbs, J. M., 14, 15, 17, 124, 131
Dalteg, A., 292, 314
Dalton, K., 142, 153
Darley, J. M., 124, 131
Darwin, C., 194, 224
Davis, N., 226
Dawe, H. C., 195, 224
Dawson, M. E., 291, 316
Day, J. M., 249
de Blois, C. S., 292, 317
Deakin, J. F. W., 10, 17
DeJong, J., 14, 20
Denham, S. A., 125, 126, 128
Dennis, A., 206, 226
Denno, D., 142, 155
Depue, R., 308, 313, 317
Desjardins, C., 5, 16
Desmarais-Gervais, L., 121, 134, 229
Devaud, L. L., 190
Dienstbier, R. A., 313
Dieuf, W., 292, 317
Dishion, T., 138, 154, 235, 249, 271, 284
Ditton, J., 37, 44
Dix, T., 123, 130
Dodge, K. A., 126, 128, 144, 153, 168, 188
Doering, C. H., 6, 18
Doherty, W. J., 233, 250
Dohrenwend, B. S., 131
Dollard, J., 116, 118, 129
Donahue, S., 273, 284
Donnerstein, E., 118, 129
Doob, L. W., 129
Dornbusch, S. M., 38, 44
Douglas, V., 304, 310, 313, 318
Douglas, V. I., 308, 313
Downey, G., 187
Dreger, R. M., 195, 196, 224
Dudzinski, D., 90
Dulcan, M. K., 237, 248
Dumas, J. E., 246, 250
Duncan, D. D., 102, 113
Dunér, A., 138, 154, 289, 291, 315
Durkheim, E., 36, 44
Duval, S., 126, 129
Duval, V. H., 126, 129
Duveen, G., 209, 230
Dyck, J. L., 127

Dykerman, R. A., 312
Dyson, E. M., 6, 16

Earls, F., 92, 230
Earp, J. A., 173, 191
Ebbesen, E. B., 128
Ebert, M., 297, 312
Eckenrode, J., 248
Edelbrock, C. S., 196, 223, 237, 247, 248
Edman, G., 297, 317
Edwards, D. A., 5, 17
Eich, E., 126, 129
Eichelman, B., 11, 18
Eisenberg, N., 117, 118, 129, 134
Eklund, G., 311, 312
Elias, M., 7, 17
Ellingboe, J., 15, 21
Elliott, D. S., 25, 45, 167, 185, 188, 194, 225, 231, 248, 270, 281, 283
Elliott, G. R., 315
Emery, G. N., 125, 133
Ensminger, M. E., 116, 121, 129, 131, 138, 153
Epstein, S. M., 47, 48, 61
Erez, E., 116, 129, 279, 281
Erickson, M. L., 116, 129, 279, 282
Eron, L. D., viii, 117, 123, 126, 129, 131, 138, 144, 154, 159, 172, 173, 185, 186, 188, 189, 197, 198, 200, 225, 226, 227
Estrich, S. B., 45
Euler von, U. S., 290, 313
Eve, R., 137, 154
Everitt, B. J., 10, 20
Eysenck, H. J., 4, 141, 156, 200–201, 203, 225, 272, 276, 282
Eysenck, S. B. G., 201, 225

Fabes, R. A., 118, 129
Farnworth, M., 267, 286
Farran, D. C., 285
Farrington, D. P., ix, 26, 43, 44, 76, 91, 92, 116, 117, 129, 130, 137, 138, 153, 154, 180, 185, 188, 194, 197, 199, 200, 203, 223, 225, 233, 234, 235, 244, 247, 249, 250, 253, 254, 256–259, 261, 263, 265–266, 267,

269, 270, 273, 274, 278, 279, 280, 281, 282–283, 285, 286, 305, 313
Fawzy, I., 233, 249
Feldman, S. S., 315
Fell, D., 132
Felson, M., 44, 278, 281
Ferguson, L. L., 169, 187
Ferguson, T. J., 172, 173, 189
Ferracuti, F., 89, 93
Feshbach, N. D., 169, 174, 189
Feshbach, S., 118, 130
Festinger, L., 126, 130
Figlio, R. M., 129, 281
File, S. E., 10, 17
Finello, K. M., 132, 310, 315
Fingerhut, L. A., 171, 189
Fink, B., 132
Finnegan, T. A., 263, 283
Fischer, C., 19
Fischer, P., 172, 188
Fishbein, D. H., 13, 17
Fleeting, M., 137, 154
Flinchum, T. R., 162, 180, 186, 187
Foot, H. C., 188
Fowles, D. C., 204, 210, 223, 225
Fox, S. W., 153
Frankenhaeuser, M., 290, 291, 292, 308, 313, 314
Fréchette, M., 212, 226
Freleigh, M. J., 44
Freud, S., 116, 130
Frick, P. J., 227, 229
Friedrich, L. K., 117, 130
Friedrich-Cofer, L., 166, 189
Fuelling, C., 17
Fulker, D. W., 141, 156
Fultz, J., 128, 129
Furstenberg, F., 77, 82–84, 88, 89, 273, 281

Gabrielli, W. F., 141, 155, 198, 228, 273, 284
Gadlow, K. D., 227
Gagnon, C., 121, 134, 229
Gallagher, B., 44, 282
Gandelman, R., 5, 18
Gangestad, S., 199, 225
Garbarino, J., 75, 76, 89, 91
Garcia, M., 237, 248

Gariépy, J-L., 158, 164, 168, 169, 187, 188, 190
Gariépy, J., 128
Gauthier, R., 196, 229
Gaziri, L. C. J., 15, 18
Gerber, B., 233, 249
Gest, S. D., 128, 168, 188
Gibbons, F. X., 126, 130
Gibbs, J. P., 116, 129, 279, 282
Giller, H., 26, 45
Gilligan, C., 111, 113
Giordano, P. C., 168, 189
Gittelman, R., 305, 313
Glaser, D., vii, 26, 34, 36, 43, 44, 45, 46, 116, 130
Glazer, H., 308, 317
Gleick, J., 306, 313
Glickman, S., 195, 226
Glueck, E. T., 34, 35, 44, 77, 90
Glueck, S., 34, 35, 44, 77, 90
Goldstein, J. H., 117, 130
Goodwin, F. K., 4, 13, 14, 16, 17, 18, 20
Gordon, A. S., 233, 234, 235, 237, 247, 248
Gordon, G. G., 7, 15, 18
Gordon, T. P., 19
Gore, S., 248
Gorenstein, E. E., 199, 203, 225, 298, 313
Goslin, D. A., 113
Gottesman, A., 141, 153
Gottfredson, D. C., 26, 44
Gottfredson, D. M., 282
Gottfredson, G. D., 26, 44
Gottfredson, M. R., 25, 31, 44, 45, 77, 80, 90, 116, 130, 137, 154, 255, 275, 278, 283
Gottfredson, S., 92
Gottschalk, L. A., 312
Gouldner, A. W., 120, 130
Goyer, P. F., 17
Graham, P., 197, 225, 271, 285
Graig, A., 292, 317
Grasmick, H. G., 116, 130
Gray, J. A., 10, 18, 201–202, 203–205, 207–208, 210, 217, 222, 223, 225–226
Green, A. R., 10, 20
Green, J. A., 165, 188

Green, S., 229
Greenberg, G., 187
Greenberg, S., 88, 90
Griffitt, C., 127
Groves, W. B., 66, 68–69, 78–81, 85, 91
Grusec, J. E., 123, 130
Gudjonsson, G. H., 200–201, 225, 272, 282
Gulian, D., 15, 18
Gullota, T. P., 188
Gundry, G., 117, 130
Gunn, J., 154

Hagedorn, J., 137, 153
Hale, G. A., 313
Hall, J., 28, 44
Hall, W. M., 189
Halls, W. D., 44
Hamlin, J. E., 95, 103, 104, 113
Hamon, M., 10, 20
Haney, C., 135
Hanson, B. A., 227
Hardt, R. H., 270, 283
Hare, R. D., 202, 206, 226, 229, 276, 283, 301, 313, 316
Harer, M. D., 46
Harris, W. R., 19
Hart, E. L., 227
Hart, H. H., 195, 226
Harter, S., 166, 189
Hartung, F. E., 95, 103, 113
Hartup, W. W., 169, 189
Harvey, J. A., 9, 18
Harway, M., 132
Hastie, R., 109, 113
Hatfield, E., 124, 130
Hawkins, D., 137, 153
Hawkins, J. D., 225, 231, 235, 249, 255, 274, 276, 282, 283
Hechtman, L. T., 197, 203, 230, 304, 305, 313, 317
Heckman, H. K., 304, 305, 312
Heer, D. M., 26, 44
Hegstrand, L. R., 11, 18
Heider, F., 124, 131
Heimer, K., 59, 61
Heine, K., 137, 154
Herrnstein, R. J., 233, 234, 235, 245, 246, 251, 272, 279, 286

Hersov, L. A., 127, 129
Hetherington, M., 189, 190
Hewitt, L. E., 195, 226
Heymer, A., 195, 226
Hill, G., 263, 285
Hinde, R. A., 120, 124, 131, 195, 206, 226
Hindelang, M. J., 35, 44, 137, 153, 267, 283
Hinton, J., 291, 318
Hirschi, T., 25, 26, 31, 34, 35, 44, 45, 77, 80, 90, 116, 130, 131, 137, 153–154, 234, 244, 249, 255, 267, 275, 276, 278, 283
Hochschild, A., 33, 45
Hodge, R. W., 44
Hofer, M. A., 287, 313
Hoffman, H. S., 47, 61
Hoffman, M. L., 124, 125, 131
Hole, K., 291, 314
Hollinger, R. C., 37, 45
Holt, R., 125, 126, 128
Homans, G. C., 120, 131
Hood, K. E., 158, 159, 188, 189
Hopkins, J., 304, 317
Hoppe, C. M., 305, 316
Hopper, C. H., 14, 15, 17
Horn, J. M., 141, 154
Horowitz, R., 70, 90
Houlihan, D., 128
Howard, M. O., 276, 283
Howard, R. C., 2, 18
Howe, H. E., 313
Huba, G. J., 244, 249
Huesmann, L. R., viii, 117, 123, 126, 129, 131, 138, 140, 144–146, 150, 152, 154, 159, 172, 173, 185, 188, 189, 197, 198, 200, 225, 226, 227
Huff, C. R., 43
Huizinga, D., 167, 188, 231, 248, 270, 281
Hull, C. L., 97, 113
Hunt, R., 297, 312
Hutchings, B., 141, 155, 273, 284
Huxley, L., 194, 226
Hyde, J. R. G., 10, 17

Ianni, F. A. J., 30, 45
Iannotti, R., 128, 130, 132, 134, 191

Isen, A. M., 118, 131
Iversen, S. D., 10, 20

Jacklin, C. N., 6, 18
Jackson, L. D., 142, 154
Jacob, T., 250
Jaffe, D., 135
Jaffe, J. H., 13, 17
Janowitz, M., 66, 90
Jarjoura, G. R., 81, 92
Jenkins, R. L., 195, 226
Jenkins, S., 235, 249
Jensen, G. J., 137, 154
Jensen, G. F., 116, 129, 279, 282
Jessor, R., 169, 170, 189, 231, 249
Jessor, S. L., 169, 170, 189, 231, 249
Johansson, G., 290, 291, 292, 313–314
Johnson, E. H., 249
Johnson, J., 238, 240, 248, 249
Johnson, J., 90
Johnson, N., 292, 315
Johnston, L. D., 231, 235, 247, 249
Jones, C. L., 250
Jones, F., 142, 155
Jones, J., 18
Jurkovic, G. J., 14, 15, 17

Kagan, J., 139–140, 154
Kaiser, G., 189, 283
Kalas, R., 237, 248
Kandel, D. B., 169, 170, 189, 225, 235, 249, 283
Kanner, L., 195, 226
Kant, I., 123, 131
Kantak, K. M., 11, 18
Kaplan, H. B., 231, 249
Kasarda, J., 66, 90
Kasen, S., 238, 249
Katz, D. L., 7, 19
Katz, R. J., 11, 18
Kaufman, E., 247
Kaufmann, P., 247
Kazdin, A. E., 225, 283
Kellman, S. G., 121, 129, 131, 138, 153
Kelling, G., 88, 93
Kemper, T. D., 33, 45
Kenny, D. A., 112
Kenrick, D. T., 124, 127
Kerner, H. J., 189, 283

Kessen, W., 180, 187, 189
Kindermann, T., 164, 188
King, R. A., 117, 118, 134
King, R. J., vii, 4, 7, 18
Kintsch, W., 148, 152, 154
Kittok, R., 16
Klackenberg-Larsson, I., 291, 314
Klaris, S. H., 237, 248
Klein, M. W., 225, 263, 282, 284
Klein, N., 273, 281
Klein, W. J., 17
Kleinman, J. C., 171, 189
Klerman, G. L., 285
Kling, A. S., 17
Kling, J. K., 197, 229
Klinteberg af, B. ix, 121, 131, 293, 297, 314
Klockars, C. B., 30, 45
Klorman, R., 297, 312
Klove, H., 291, 314
Klugel, J., 137, 153
Knight, B. J., 278, 283
Knoblich, G., vii
Kogan, L., 235, 249
Kohlberg, L., 98, 102–103, 104, 105, 108, 111, 113, 114
Kohn, M., 196, 226
Kolvin, I., 137, 154
Kolvin, P. A., 137, 154
Konecni, J., 128
Kornhauser, R., 65, 66, 67, 69, 70, 71, 85, 91
Kraepelin, E., 195, 198, 226
Kramer, J., 197, 203, 227
Krauth, J., 295, 314
Kurcz, M., 16

Labouvie, E. W., 271, 286
Lader, M. H., 317
Ladosky, W., 15, 18
Lagerspetz, K., 142, 154
Lagerspetz, K., 189
Lagerspetz, K. M. J., 142, 154, 172, 185, 190
Lahey, B. B., 225, 227, 229, 283
Lambert, W. W., 291, 314
Land, K., 137, 153
Lander, B., 44
Landy, F. J., 47, 61
Langhorne, J. E., 292, 314

Lann, I. S., 194, 224, 229
Lash, T., 72, 90
Lashley, R. L., viii, 47, 61
Latané, B., 124, 131
Laub, J., 77, 90
Laufer, W. S., vii, 249
Lauritsen, J., 65, 80, 85–87, 91
Lawry, J. A., 61
Leach, C. S., 133
LeBlanc, M., 180, 190, 212, 226
Ledingham, J. E., 172, 190
Lefkowitz, M. M., 116, 123, 131, 138, 154, 185, 189, 196, 198, 225, 226, 227
Leiderman, P. H., 44
Leighton, B., 66, 90
Lemert, E. M., 30, 40–41, 45
Lepenies, W., 227
Levander, S. E., 18, 291, 292, 314
Levin, P. F., 118, 131
Levine, F. J., 98, 105, 113, 114
Levine, S., 8, 17
Levy, P., 124, 132
Lewis, D. O., 142, 154
Lewis, M., 313
Lewis, M. H., 158, 190
Lewis, S., 240, 248
Leyens, J. P., 127
Lickona, T., 113
Lidberg, L., 3, 18, 291, 314
Lidberg, Y., 18, 291, 314
Lieber, C. S., 15, 18
Liebert, D. E., 228
Liebow, E., 71, 90
Lienert, G. A., 295, 314
Lilly, J. R., 43
Linder, B., 61
Linnoila, M., 9, 12, 14, 18, 20
Lipsitt, P. D., 283
Lishajko, F., 290, 313
Lishner, D. W., 235, 249, 276, 283
Liska, A. E., 35, 45
Loeber, R., 77, 90, 117, 132, 138, 154, 172, 180, 190, 194, 197, 199, 203, 215, 225, 227, 229, 235, 249, 269, 270, 271, 283, 284, 304, 305, 313, 314
Loehlin, J. C., 141, 154
London, P., 117, 118, 128, 132
Loney, J., 197, 199, 203, 227, 292, 314
Long, J., 137, 155

Lopatka, C., 126, 129
Loppa, K., 227
Löw, H., 19, 142, 155
Lozovsky, D., 13, 17
Lukoff, I. F., 231, 248
Lundgren, D., 132
Lykken, D. T., 281
Lyman, S. M., 109, 113
Lyytinen, P., 190, 315

Macaulay, J., 132
Maccoby, E. E., 6, 18, 67, 90, 118,
  132
Macedo, C. A., 19
Mackintosh, N. J., 56, 61
MacLeod, N. K., 10, 17
Magnusson, D., ix, 117, 121, 131, 132,
  138, 154, 166, 169, 170, 180, 183,
  185, 186, 190, 206, 227, 273, 284,
  287–289, 290, 291, 292, 293, 295,
  306, 308, 311–312, 314–315, 317
Maher, B. A., 61
Maier, S. F., 47, 61
Mailman, R. B., 190
Major, L. F., 13, 16, 17
Mannuzza, S., 305, 313
Marcus, J., 265, 285
Marcus, R. F., 118, 132
Marks, V., 15, 19
Maser, J. D., 62
Masten, A., 196, 227
Masters, R. D. 195, 227
Matsueda, R. L., 59, 61, 137, 154
Mattsson, A., 19, 142, 155, 292, 314
Matza, D., 95, 103, 104, 114, 115, 134
Maughan, B., 238, 250, 272, 285
Maurer, D. W., 30, 45
Mawson, A. R., 273, 284
May-Plumlee, T., 129
Mazur, A., 7, 16, 19
McBurnett, K., 208, 227, 229
McCord, J., 77, 90, 116, 117, 118,
  121, 126, 132, 137, 143, 154–155,
  185, 190, 197, 200, 225, 227, 233,
  234, 244, 250, 269, 270, 283, 284,
  301, 309, 315
McCord, W., 197, 227, 234, 250
McEvoy, L., 121, 133
McEwen, B. S., 15, 18
McGee, R., 292, 315

McGee, W. C., 197, 199, 203, 227
McGillis, D., 45
McGrath, J. E., 132
McGrew, W. C., 195, 227
McGue, M., 281
McGurk, B. J., 286
McKay, H. D., 34, 35, 45, 63, 65, 67,
  68, 70, 85, 91, 272, 285
McKee, G. J., Jr., 43, 45
McKinley, M., 125, 126, 128
McKinney, J. D., 285
McKissack, I. J., 26, 45
McMaster, M. R., 127
McMullen, M. F., 8, 19
Mead, G. H., 104, 113
Mednick, S. A., 38, 45, 129, 130, 132,
  141, 153, 155, 198, 224, 228, 229,
  273, 282, 284, 285, 286, 309, 310,
  312, 315, 316, 317
Meier, R. F., 92, 132, 284
Mellstrom, B., 20
Menard, S., 25, 45, 167, 188
Mendelson, W., 304, 315
Mendoza, S. P., 8, 17
Menkes, J., 304, 315
Menkes, M., 304, 315
Mermelstein, R., 172, 188
Merton, R. K., 35, 36, 45
Messner, S., 137, 155
Miczek, K. A. 15, 21
Miethe, T., 137, 155
Mikkelsen, E., 297, 312
Milgram, S., 119, 132–133
Milich, R., 197, 199, 203, 227
Miller, F. J. W., 137, 154
Miller, N. E., 129
Millman, N., 11, 21
Minde, K., 304, 318
Mischel, H. N., 111, 113
Mischel, W., 111, 113
Moen, P., 89
Moffitt, T. E., 45, 138, 153, 155, 199,
  203, 224, 228, 229, 230, 271, 282,
  284, 285, 286, 312, 316–17
Moitra, S., 197, 200, 223, 233, 247
Molnar, G., 9, 16
Monroe, S., 308, 313
Montemayor, R., 188
Moore, B. S., 118, 132
Moore, C., 209, 223

Moore, M. H., 30, 45
Moore, R., 72, 92
Moorehouse, M., 187
Moos, R. H., 238, 250
Moreau, P., 195, 228
Morison, P., 227
Morley, L., 44, 282
Morris, N., 43, 44, 45, 90, 132, 153, 190, 224, 228, 247, 282, 284
Mortimore, P., 238, 250, 272, 285
Mowrer, O. H., 129
Moy, E., 142, 154
Moyer, K. E., 6–7, 19, 142, 155
Mufford, R. B., Jr., 291, 316
Murison, R., 17
Murphy, L. B., 195, 228
Mussen, P. H., 117, 118, 129, 155, 187, 189, 190, 224

Nachson, I., 142, 155
Nagin, D., 116, 133, 279, 281
Neale, J. M., 228
Neale, M. C., 141, 156
Neckerman, H. J., 128, 162, 168, 169, 180, 184, 186, 187, 188
Needle, R. H., 233, 250
Neely, R., 126, 129
Nelli, H. S., 30, 45
Nemeth, E., 304, 318
Nemhauser, J., 171, 187
Newcomb, M. D., 233, 250
Newman, J. P., 199, 202, 203, 225, 228, 298, 313
Nias, D. K. B., 141, 156
Nicewander, 229
Nieman, J., 171, 187
Nikkilä, E. A., 15, 19
Noel, J. M., 169, 191
Nomura, C., 235, 248
Novy, D. M., 273, 284
Nuttila, A., 18
Nylander, I., 304, 315

O'Hagan, S. E. J., 197, 229
O'Keefe, S. J. D., 15, 19
O'Malley, M. O., 249
O'Malley, P. M., 231, 235, 247
O'Neill, M., 291, 318
Offord, D. R., 273, 285, 309, 315

Ohlin, L. E., 76, 92, 254, 255, 277, 280, 281, 283, 286
Ohman, A., 314
Olds, D., 74, 91
Olofsson, B., 310, 315
Olweus, D., 6, 19, 123, 128, 129, 131, 132, 133, 138, 140, 142, 155, 185, 188, 190, 191, 198, 228, 249, 273, 284, 291, 316
Oreland, L., 12, 19
Osgood, D. W., 198, 229
Osofsky, J., 74, 91
Ouston, J., 238, 250, 272, 285
Overmier, J. B., 47, 61
Owen, K., 8, 19
Owen, S., 226

Paine, R. L., 61
Papp, Z., 16
Parke, R. D., 89, 127, 140, 155, 167, 190
Paternite, C. E., 292, 314
Patterson, G. R., 77, 91, 165, 190, 198, 228, 234, 246, 250, 276, 285
Pavlov, I. P., 49, 55–57, 58, 61
Pawelczynska, A., 119, 133
Pekarik, E. G., 196, 228
Pelligrini, D., 227
Peltonen, T., 172, 190
Pennington, N., 109, 113
Penrod, S. D., 109, 113
Pepler, D. J., 130, 153, 229, 282
Perlman, T., 304, 305, 313, 317
Pervin, L., 315
Peters, J. E., 312
Peters, K. G., 308, 313
Peters, P. J., 8, 19
Peterson, D. R., 196, 228
Peterson, S. J., 270, 283
Petrich, J., 304, 317
Petrovic, D. M., 6, 16
Piaget, J., 98, 105, 113
Piliavin, J. A., 124, 130
Pitkanen, L., 222, 228
Pitts, F., 292, 317
Plato, ix, 119, 133
Ploog, D., 227
Pohorecky, L., 208, 317
Pohorecky, L. A., 15, 18
Pollack, L., 20

Pontius, A. A., 142, 155
Pope, H. G., 7, 19
Post, R. M., 4, 16
Powell, A., 200, 229
Powell, A. L., 127
Preyer, W., 195, 228
Price, J., 118, 130
Prinz, R. J., 194, 228
Provost, M. A., 229
Pryzbeck, T. R., 233, 250
Pugh, M. D., 189
Pulkkinen, L., 117, 120, 133, 185, 186, 190, 222, 228, 315
Pyle, C., 125, 134

Quay, H. C., 50, 61, 196, 227, 228, 284

Rabkin, L., 304, 311
Rachman, S., 126, 129
Radke-Yarrow, M., 117, 118, 125, 128, 129, 131, 132, 133, 134, 165, 188, 190, 191, 228, 249, 316
Rafaelson, O. J., 317
Raine, A., 2, 3, 19, 142, 155, 273, 286, 309, 316
Rainwater, L., 70, 91
Rapaport, P., 61
Rapoport, J., 297, 316
Ratcliff, K. S., 138, 156, 265, 285
Rawls, J., 110, 113
Reider, J., 137, 155
Reimherr, F. W., 297, 317
Reinisch, J. M., 5, 18
Reiss, A. J., Jr., 65, 67, 80, 91, 92, 137, 155, 272, 285
Reitsma-Street, M., 273, 285
Restifo, N., 142, 154
Rheingold, H., 125, 133
Richman, N., 271, 285
Ricks, D. F., 131
Rimon, R., 18
Risch, S. C., 227
Ritter, P. L., 44
Roberts, D. F., 44
Robins, L. N., 121, 133, 138, 156, 159, 190, 191, 225, 227, 230, 231, 233, 248, 250, 265, 270, 283–285, 304, 313, 315, 316
Robinson, T. E., 308, 317

Rodgers, J. L., 170, 191
Roessler, R., 291, 316
Rogeness, G. A., 3, 19
Rohe, W., 90
Rose, R. M., 7, 19, 285
Rosellini, R. A., viii, 47, 61
Rosenhan, D. L., 117, 118, 124, 133
Ross, B. D., 276, 285
Ross, D., 117, 127
Ross, R. R., 276, 285
Ross, S. A., 117, 127
Roth, J. A., 91, 255, 281
Routh, D., 227
Rowe, D. C., 92, 141, 156, 198, 225, 229, 283
Rowe, J., 304, 315
Royce, J. R., 200, 229
Rubin, B. R., 129, 138, 153
Rubin, E., 18
Rubin, K. H., 130, 153, 229, 282
Rubin, Z., 135
Rudinger, G., 312
Rule, B. G., 172, 173, 189
Rushton, J. P., 117, 133, 141, 156
Russo, M. F., 229
Rutter, M., 26, 45, 132, 133, 190, 194, 197, 224, 225, 227, 229, 238, 248, 250, 272, 282, 283, 284, 285, 313, 315, 316, 317
Rydin, E., 9, 19

Sachar, E. J., 317
Sadowski, L. S., 173, 191
Sales, B. D., 283
Sampson, R. J., viii, 63, 64, 65, 66, 67, 68–69, 77, 78, 79, 80, 81, 85–87, 88, 89, 90, 91, 92
Sandnabba, K., 142, 154
Sapolsky, R. M., 8, 19
Satterfield, B. T., 291, 316
Satterfield, J. H., 197, 229, 291, 304, 305, 316
Schaeffer, G. J., 10, 20
Schaller, M., 128
Schalling, D., 9, 18, 19, 121, 131, 142, 155, 197, 202, 206, 226, 229, 291, 292, 293, 298, 301, 313, 314, 316–317
Scharff, W. H., 117, 118, 134
Scheinin, M., 18

Schell, A. M., 305, 316
Schenker, R., 305, 313
Scheuer, J. W., 18
Schlosberg, J. A., 9, 18
Schlottman, R. S., 117, 118, 134
Schneider, L., 308, 317
Schneider, W., 145, 152, 156
Schuckit, M. A., 304, 317
Schwartz, J., 68, 92
Schwartzman, A., 172, 190
Scott, M. B., 109, 113
Sears, R. R., 129
Sebastian, J., 127
Segal, N. L., 281
Seidel, W. T., 270, 280
Seigel, P. S., 47, 61
Seligman, M. E. P., 62
Serra, S., 142, 154
Shaw, C. R., 34, 35, 45, 63, 65, 67,
   68, 70, 85, 91, 272, 285
Shelley, G., 16
Sherman, D., 75, 90
Shorey, P., 133
Short, J. F., 64, 67, 69, 91, 92
Shover, N., 43, 46
Shriffrin, R., 145, 152, 156
Sigal, H., 90
Sigvardsson, S., 207, 224, 273, 281
Silva, P. A., 197, 199, 203, 227, 230,
   271, 284, 292, 315
Simcha-Fagan, O., 68, 92
Simmons, R. C., 166, 191
Simon, M. B., 121, 131
Simos, A., 142, 154
Simpson, G., 44
Singer, S., 292, 317
Sjobring, H., 203, 229
Sjoquist, F., 20
Sjostrand, L., 19
Skinner, B. F., 97, 114
Skogan, W., 67, 88, 92
Skolnick, J. H., 27, 46
Slaby, R. G., 140, 155, 167, 190
Slotnick, B. M., 8, 19
Smith, D. R., 81, 92
Smith, E. R., 8, 17
Smith, J., 235, 249
Smith, J. R., 188
Snarey, J., 111, 114

Snyder, H. N., 263, 283
Snyder, J. J., 246, 250
Snyder, M., 199, 225
Solomon, R. L., 47, 48, 50–54, 61, 62
Somberg, D. R., 126, 128
Sones, G., 169, 174, 189
Soubrié, P., 10–11, 20
Southerland, S. B., 190
Southren, A. L., 15, 18
Spaulding, J. A., 44
Spelman, W., 45
Sperling, P. I., 195, 226
Spielberger, C. D., 197, 229
Spivack, G., 138, 156, 265, 285
St. Ledger, R. J., 44, 282
Stack, S. A., 45, 153, 155, 224, 229,
   282, 285, 312, 316, 317
Stafford, M., 137, 155
Stander, J., 263, 285
Stangler, R. L., 11, 21
Starr, M. D., 47, 62
Stattin, H., ix, 289, 291, 315, 317
Staub, E., 117, 118, 119, 125, 134
Steffensmeier, D. J., 26, 30, 46
Stein, A. H., 117, 130
Steklis, H. D., 17
Stevens, D. A., 312
Stevenson, J., 271, 285
Stewart, M. A., 292, 315, 317
Stinchcombe, A. L., 26, 46
Stocking, S., 91
Stoff, D. M., 13, 20
Stott, D. H., 196, 229
Stouthamer-Loeber, M., 77, 90, 118,
   132, 197, 227, 229, 269, 271, 284
Strachey, J., 130
Strayer, F. F., 169, 191, 196, 229
Streifel, C., 46
Stringfield, S., 196, 209, 223
Strodtbeck, F., 69, 92
Struening, E., 72, 73, 92
Su, S., 233, 250
Sullivan, K., 309, 315
Sullivan, M., 69, 80, 87, 92
Sully, J., 195, 229
Sutherland, E. H., 30, 32, 34, 46, 115,
   134, 255, 276, 285
Suttles, G., 70, 92
Swift, M., 265, 285

Sykes, G. M., 95, 103, 104, 114, 115, 134
Szatmari, P., 273, 285

Taine, H., 194, 229
Tanioka, I., 26, 46
Tanner, J. M., 166, 191
Tapp, J. L., 98, 105, 113, 114
Tardiff, K., 137, 155
Taskinen, M. R., 15, 19
Taylor, E., 291, 317
Taylor, R., 67–68, 79–80, 92
Tellegen, A., 281
Tharp, G., 16
Thiébot, M. H., 10, 20
Thomas, A., 266, 285
Thorén, P., 9, 13, 16, 19, 20
Thornberry, T. P., 129, 267, 281, 286
Thornton, D. M., 286
Thrasher, F., 67, 69–70, 92
Tobach, E., 187
Tonry, M., 43, 44, 45, 76, 90, 91, 92, 132, 137, 153, 155, 190, 224, 228, 247, 280, 282, 284–286
Torestad, B., 312
Träskman, L., 9, 16, 19, 20
Trasler, G. B., 276, 286
Tremblay, R. E., viii, ix, 92, 121, 134, 197, 199, 209, 225, 229, 283
Trites, R. L., 314
Trokenberg Hechtman, L. T., 305, 318
Troughton, E., 310, 312
Tsaltas, E., 226
Tuchfeld, B. S., 231, 248
Tuma, A. H., 194, 224, 229
Tybring, G., 19
Tye, N. C., 10, 20

Udry, J. R., 170, 191
Underwood, B., 118, 133
Ursin, H., 17

Valsiner, J., 187
Valzelli, L., 11, 20
van Dusen, K. T., 129, 132, 153, 155, 284, 315
van Kammen, W. B., 197, 203, 225, 270, 283, 305, 313
van Praag, H. M., 317

Vanderwolf, C. H. 308, 317
Velez, C. N., 237, 248
Venables, P. H., 2, 3, 19, 273, 286, 301, 317
Vetiello, B., 20
Virkkunen, M., 4, 14, 18, 20, 273, 286
Visher, C. A., 91, 255, 281
vom Saal, F. S., 5, 18
von Knorring, A., 273, 281
Von Kranach, M., 227
Vorhees, C. V., 10, 20

Wadsworth, M., 269, 286
Wagner, E., 125, 134
Wahler, R. G., 246, 250
Waldbillig, R. J., 11, 20
Walder, L. O., 123, 131, 138, 154, 198, 225, 226, 227
Walker, J. L., 208, 229
Wallace, D., 63, 72–74, 76, 92
Wallace, R., 63, 72–74, 76, 92
Walsh, M. E., 30, 46
Walsh, M. L., 6, 16
Walster, G. W., 124, 130
Walters, R. H., 116, 127, 157, 187
Watson, J. B., 222, 230
Weiner, H., 287, 317
Weiner, N. A., 153
Weintraub, S., 228
Weir, K., 209, 230
Weis, J. G., 231, 249, 267, 283
Weiss, G., 197, 203, 230, 304, 305, 308, 313, 317–318
Wender, P. H., 297, 304, 308, 317
Wener, A., 304, 317
Werner, E. E., 273–274, 286
Werry, J., 304, 318
Werry, J. S., 228
West, D. J., 44, 117, 130, 180, 185, 188, 234, 250, 261, 265–266, 267, 282, 283, 286
West, S., 127
Wheatley, K. L., 61
White, G. M., 117, 133, 134
White, H. R., 271, 286
White, J. L., 199, 230
White, S. O., viii, 95–96, 97, 98, 100, 111, 113
Whiteman, M., 231, 233, 234, 235, 237, 247–248

Whiting, B. B., 118, 134
Whiting, J. W. M., 118, 134
Wiberg, A., 19
Wicklund, R. A., 126, 130, 134
Widom, C. S., 76, 93, 117, 134, 269, 286
Wilkens, J. L., 117, 118, 134
Wilkins, L. T., 45
Wilkinson, L., 240, 251
Willerman, L., 141, 154
Williams, J., 90
Williams, M., 2, 3, 19, 286
Williams, S., 197, 199, 203, 227, 292, 315
Wilson, D. W., 118, 129
Wilson, J. Q., 88, 90, 93, 233, 234, 235, 245, 246, 251, 255, 272, 279, 283, 286
Wilson, W. J., 83, 87, 93
Wing, J. K., 156, 285
Winslow, J. T., 15, 21
Wish, E., 231, 250, 265, 285
Wispé, L., 130, 133

Wolfgang, M. E., vii, 89, 93, 129, 153, 281
Wolraich, M., 227
Wong, R., 6, 16
Wood, D. R., 297, 317
Wood, J., 16
Woodman, D., 291, 318
Woodworth, G., 310, 312
Word, L. E., 124, 128

Yen, C. Y., 11, 21
Younger, A., 172, 190
Youniss, J., 169, 191
Yunger, L. M., 9, 18

Zahn-Waxler, C. 117, 118, 125, 128, 130, 132, 134, 165, 191
Zarcone, V. P., 18
Zetterblom, G., 138, 154, 289, 315
Zillmann, D., 118, 135
Zimbardo, P. G., 119, 135
Zucker, R. A., 233, 251
Zuckerman, M., 202, 226, 230, 317

Advances in Criminological Theory

Volume 1, edited by William S. Laufer
and Freda Adler. 1988.

Volume 2, edited by William S. Laufer
and Freda Adler. 1990.

Volume 3, Facts, Frameworks, and Forecasts,
edited by Joan McCord. 1992.